B9353

THE BIBLE DOCTRINE OF MAN

THE BIBLE DOCTRINE
OF MAN

By

C. RYDER SMITH, B.A., D.D.

Formerly Professor of Theology in the
University of London

'What is man, that Thou art mindful of him?'
(PSALM 8⁴; HEBREWS 2⁶)

LONDON : THE EPWORTH PRESS

PUBLISHED BY

THE EPWORTH PRESS
(FRANK H. CUMBERS)
25-35 CITY ROAD, LONDON, E.C.1

New York . Toronto
Melbourne . Capetown

*

SET IN MONOTYPE BASKERVILLE AND PRINTED IN
GREAT BRITAIN BY THE CAMELOT PRESS LTD.
LONDON AND SOUTHAMPTON

TO THE MEMORY OF

GEORGE GILLANDERS FINDLAY

TEACHER AND FRIEND

CONTENTS

Part One

THE OLD TESTAMENT

Part Two

FROM HEBREW INTO GREEK

Part Three

THE NEW TESTAMENT

INTRODUCTION

IN THE latter part of last century and the earlier part of this students of Biblical Theology tended to concentrate upon the doctrine of each writer or class of writers within the Bible. At that time this was both desirable and valuable. It readily led, however, to an emphasis on the differences within the Bible rather than upon the unity of Bible teaching. More recently it has been recognized that Biblical Theology is an organic unity, beginning, however imperfectly, in the Old Testament, and reaching its completion in the New. Again, within the latter it is being more and more recognized that the doctrine of the Apostles, however much it may seem to differ from that of Jesus, is the proper outcome of that teaching as interpreted in the light of our Lord's Life, Death, and Resurrection. There is, therefore, need today to resume the treatment of Biblical Theology as a whole. This is to revert to an older method, but the results vary from those of our fathers because consideration has to be given to the work of the recent generations on the dates of documents, the gradual development of Biblical doctrine, and so on. I have made some earlier endeavours, as far as I have been able, to deal with two parts of the vast subject—though in an illogical order. Some thirty years ago I wrote three books that sought to deal with the *social* doctrine of the Bible, beginning with this because there seemed special need then that it should be treated. A few years ago there followed a volume, *The Bible Doctrine of Salvation*, because it seemed to me that most books on 'The Work of Christ', while they deal fully with the history of this doctrine since the Apostolic Age, have not given adequate attention to the teaching of the Bible itself. With this subject there are involved three other doctrines that are usually grouped together—Man, Sin, and Grace. Indeed, here as elsewhere, the separation of topics, while useful and even necessary for the purposes of study, is quite artificial. It is obvious, again, that the doctrine of Man should end with an examination of the Bible teaching about his lot in the Hereafter. As, however, I studied this group of subjects, it became clear that the material was so large that it would be advisable to devote a volume to each of the four subjects. This book is the first of these volumes. It is hoped that the issue of the others will not be very long delayed. The present book, it is also hoped, is fairly complete in itself, but I have not hesitated to refer the reader fairly often to the others, and in particular to those on Sin and Grace. As I have already attempted to deal with social doctrine, man is here considered, so far as may be, as an individual, though this, of course, implies another artificial division, for man, being 'personal', is thereby an 'individual' and 'societary' being at one and the same time. Where necessary, I have referred to my earlier works on the doctrines of society. Of course, two other doctrines are also involved in this study—the doctrines of God and of Nature, especially the former. I have kept references to these as few as possible.

The difficulty of the separation of subjects is peculiarly acute in the chapters that deal with 'What a man ought to be'. In these chapters it is argued that a man ought to be 'righteous' and 'holy' and 'wise' because God is. Ought he not also to be loving because 'God is love'? But the term 'love' denotes a societary concept rather than an individual one, and the subject of man's likeness to God under it has been examined in *The Bible Doctrine of Society*.[1] Again, the doctrine of the 'love of God' is discussed at length in the coming volume on *The Bible Doctrine of Grace*. I have therefore been driven to a compromise. The doctrine of love, of course, is implied in the doctrine of the Fatherhood of God and the Sonship of true men. This doctrine is examined in the present volume, 'love' being left to the two just named. One reason for this is the noteworthy fact that, while the phrases 'the righteous', 'the holy', and 'the wise' are used throughout the Bible for certain kinds of men, there is no parallel phrase 'the loving'. The truth here is that, just as the doctrine of righteousness came to include the concept of 'mercy', so the doctrine of 'holiness', when it worked itself out, included the doctrine of 'love'. For instance, the Second Great Commandment, 'Thou shalt love thy neighbour as thyself', first occurs as the climax of a passage whose subject is, 'Ye shall be holy, for I, the LORD your God, am holy' (Lev 19¹⁻¹⁸), and the 'love' of Paul's famous encomium (1 Co 13) is the greatest of the three universal marks of the Christian, or, in the Apostle's phrase, of the 'saint' or 'holy one'.

In discussing any Biblical doctrine there is, of course, a certain

[1] The writer would not now attempt to describe the distinctive kind of Christian love under the term 'meekness'.

difficulty. Since all its books were written for 'practical purposes', no doctrine is fully exhibited in any one passage. Even when such a writer as Paul or the author of the Epistle to the Hebrews deals at some length with a particular subject, he does not attempt to cover the whole of it. The complete doctrine, therefore, has to be collected from a number of passages, and what they imply has to be considered as well as what they say. This is especially true of the doctrine of Man. Again, this doctrine naturally falls under three questions—What was man when God made him? What is he now? What is he to become? In the Bible that last takes the form, 'What ought he to be?', and it is here that the emphasis falls. The Bible says comparatively little of the first, and it is here taken with the second. This explains the arrangement of the book. Especially in the New Testament, however, the two subjects cannot be kept entirely apart.

Two methods of treatment attracted me. One was to take certain great *subjects* and to trace their development one by one in the Bible. The other was to take the Bible in its two parts, the Old Testament and the New, and to deal with *all* subjects under each. On the whole the latter seemed preferable. Any reader who wishes to trace a particular doctrine by itself will be able to do so with the help of the second index. Within each Testament an attempt has been made to trace the historical development. Under the Old Testament the principal divisions are made at the rise of the great Prophets and the Exile. In the New Testament the natural division is between the teaching of Christ in the Synoptic Gospels, the teaching of the Epistles, and that of the Gospel and Epistles ascribed to 'John'. Under the Old Testament the documents are dated in accordance with the findings of the majority of modern scholars. In the New all the Epistles ascribed to Paul are taken together, since it is agreed that even the disputed books were written by 'Pauline men'. Similarly, the Epistles of 'John' are taken with the Fourth Gospel. The Apocalypse, however, is treated as a separate source. Modern writers' discussions of the many topics are not named. To discuss them would have much more than doubled the size of the book, and there is, perhaps, an advantage in going back to the original sources and considering them, as far as possible, *de novo*. This means, of course, that often there is silent agreement with others—or silent disagreement. For statements that refer to subjects outside the Bible I have usually quoted from Hastings' *Dictionary of the Bible* (*HDB*) and his *Encyclopædia of Religion and Ethics* (*ERE*), since these are generally accessible. The letters BDB refer to Brown, Driver and Briggs' *Hebrew and English Lexicon*.

Almost all the material falls under certain *terms*, considered in relation to their context. The passages where they are used are often numerous, and many texts need to be correlated. Very occasionally a passage needs to be named where a *term* itself does not occur but its *idea* is implied. In nearly all instances I have put the number of a term's occurrences in italic figures when it is first named. This seems better than to use such terms as 'frequent' or 'rare'. With the larger numbers, in particular, the figures may not be quite exact, if only because there are 'variant readings' in the documents, but they are, I think, sufficiently accurate for the present purpose. Hebrew and Greek terms have been transliterated, not only to help the printer, but because there may be readers who are not acquainted with these languages. For their sakes it may be mentioned that the signs ' and ' stand for two Hebrew gutturals which are often omitted in pronouncing words, and that in the transliteration of Hebrew words, *ch* is to be pronounced as in 'loch', and in Greek words as in 'chaos'. Where it seems necessary, the length of vowels is marked once. Except in *psyche*, which is now almost an English word, I have used *u* for the Greek *hupsilon*. There is no need to defend the large space given to the Septuagint (LXX), for it is agreed that the use of a term there always, or nearly always, has much to do with its meaning in the New Testament. Even when New Testament writers give a term a distinctively Christian meaning, as they often do, they generally adapt and modify the sense of the word in LXX. Many today claim that there is a 'Septuagint Greek', which varies from the common Greek of the time as displayed in the *papyri*, etc. This question is here left to the experts. Whether the use of a term in LXX is the same as that of the Greek-man-in-the-street or not, it is almost always the forerunner of the New Testament use. Indeed, it is agreed that LXX was 'the Bible of the earliest Christians', even though some New Testament writers do not always quote that version. Such exceptions only 'prove the rule'. LXX, of course, contains books that are not in the Hebrew Bible. The lists of these are not uniform in the manuscripts. I have almost entirely confined myself to the books gathered in the 'Apocrypha' of the English Bible, for these sufficiently serve the present purpose. The use of some terms in the

Greek of the Apocrypha shows a significant change from the use in rendering the Hebrew books. Where this is so, the discussion has largely concentrated on the Apocrypha. As Second (or Fourth) Esdras has only survived in a Latin version, it is generally hazardous to use it to illuminate the meaning of the Greek terms found in the New Testament, and it is very rarely quoted.

In the Septuagint, as elsewhere, I have followed the names of the books as they appear in the English versions, except that I have used 'Sirach' uniformly for 'Ecclesiasticus' and 'Koheleth' occasionally for 'Ecclesiastes'. Usually references from 'Sirach' precede those from 'Wisdom', as the use of a term in the latter sometimes shows a development from that of the former. In references I have followed the numbering of chapters and verses in the English versions. Quotations are from the Revised Version except where a translation more nearly literal is preferred. Where the *tetragrammaton* JHVH appears in the Hebrew Old Testament I have often followed the Revised Version and used the term 'LORD' in small capitals. Sometimes I have added the letters J, E, D, and P to references to the Pentateuch to show to what period a text belongs.

Finally, I owe very great thanks to my friends the Rev. Professor F. Bertram Clogg and the Rev. George W. Anderson, M.A., for their ready help. The latter has read the typescript of the first two Parts of the book and the former of the third Part, and both have made very valuable suggestions and comments. I am indebted too to the Rev. Frederic A. Tomlinson for making a fair copy of a very crabbed typescript, and to Mr. R. W. Young, of the Epworth Press, for compiling the long index of texts. Some of my findings—for instance, on the doctrine that man is 'made in the image of God'—bear upon current discussions, but I have left readers to make their own applications.

C. RYDER SMITH

March 1949

ABBREVIATIONS

for the names of

BOOKS OF THE BIBLE

Old Testament

Gn—Genesis
Ex—Exodus
Lv—Leviticus
Nu—Numbers
Dt—Deuteronomy
Jos—Joshua
Jg—Judges
Ru—Ruth
1 S, 2 S—1 and 2 Samuel
1 K, 2 K—1 and 2 Kings
1 Ch, 2 Ch—1 and 2 Chronicles
Ezr—Ezra
Neh—Nehemiah
Est—Esther
Job
Ps—Psalms
Pr—Proverbs
Ec—Ecclesiastes

Ca—Canticles
Is—Isaiah
Jer—Jeremiah
La—Lamentations
Ezk—Ezekiel
Dn—Daniel
Hos—Hosea
Jl—Joel
Am—Amos
Ob—Obadiah
Jon—Jonah
Mic—Micah
Nah—Nahum
Hab—Habakkuk
Zeph—Zephaniah
Hag—Haggai
Zec—Zechariah
Mal—Malachi

Apocrypha

1 Es, 2 Es—1 and 2 Esdras
Ad. Est—Additions to Esther
Wis—Wisdom
Sir—Sirach or Ecclesiasticus
Bar—Baruch
Three—Song of the Three Holy
 Children

To—Tobit
Jth—Judith
Sus—Susanna
Bel—Bel and the Dragon
Pr. Man—Prayer of Manasses
1 Mac, 2 Mac—1 and 2
 Maccabees

New Testament

Mt—Matthew
Mk—Mark
Lk—Luke
Jn—John
Ac—Acts of the Apostles
Ro—Romans
1 Co, 2 Co—1 and 2 Corinthians
Gal—Galatians
Eph—Ephesians
Ph—Philippians
Col—Colossians

1 Th, 2 Th—1 and 2
 Thessalonians
1 Ti, 2 Ti—1 and 2 Timothy
Tit—Titus
Philem—Philemon
He—Hebrews
Ja—James
1 P, 2 P—1 and 2 Peter
1 Jn, 2 Jn, 3 Jn—1, 2, and 3 John
Jude
Rev—Revelation of John

PART ONE—THE OLD TESTAMENT

CHAPTER ONE

WHAT A MAN IS

WHAT is a man? Through the many centuries covered by the Old Testament the Hebrew answer to this question does not vary much. For the most part, therefore, it is not necessary in this chapter to distinguish documents by their age, for any document may be quoted to illustrate most of the ideas. The few exceptions will be noted where they occur.

'Things are what they seem.' This has always been the silent postulate of human experience. It is true that men long ago learnt to make exceptions and to admit that there are times when 'things are not what they seem', but none the less even today, when a man sees something that he has never seen before, he assumes that it is what it looks like until he has reason to think otherwise. For instance, many people still think that a whale is a fish and that a bat is a bird. For the most part the Hebrew just assumed that things *are* what they seem.

This means, in the first place, that modern men need to clear their minds of certain modern ideas. Three of these may be named. First, we think it is 'obvious' that man is a being made of two disparate elements called 'body' and 'soul'. For the latter term we have a number of synonyms—such as 'mind' and 'spirit' and 'personality'. In reality, this dichotomy is not 'obvious', in the literal sense of the word. On the contrary, it is an inference from a prolonged historical examination of the implications of the relevant phenomena which began with the Greeks. The 'obvious' thing is that a man is a single being. As we shall find later, so far as the Hebrew had his own dichotomy in his account of man, it was not the same as the Greek (or rather Aristotelian) and modern dichotomy. Indeed, some recent psychologists seem to teach that the Hebrew was right in emphasizing the unity of man, however disparate soul and body may be. It will be found below that he thought of man as a being with *many* parts, but they were parts of *a whole* and never anything more. As our language in this realm has been moulded by Greek thought, it is sometimes impossible to translate Hebrew terms exactly, as we shall see. It is hard to banish Greek dichotomy from the mind, for it is a postulate of modern thought, but here it has to be done.

BBM

Next, we need to remember that the Hebrew did not know even the alphabet of modern *physiology*. He did not know that when, for instance, a finger touches anything, something or other passes along a nerve to the brain, where a miracle turns it into what we call a 'sensation'. The word 'brain' does not occur in the English Bible. The Hebrew knew nothing of the nervous system. Again, he knew nothing of the muscular system. He had a word, indeed, for certain muscles or tissues connected with muscles. He knew that there are tendons or 'sinews'—but he thought of these as things which do no more than tie bones together, for on examining a corpse this is what they *seem* to be (cf. Ezk 37⁸). For the Hebrew it was not through the muscular system that the hand, for instance, grasps an axe, but, as will appear, through a pervasive 'life'. It was the same with the foot, the eye, the ear, and so on. Once again, while the Hebrew, of course, knew that there is such a thing as blood, and while he knew that it is almost everywhere in the body, he knew nothing of an arterial system that centres in the heart. Similarly, he knew little or nothing of the respiratory system. The word 'lung' does not occur in the Old Testament. When we breathe, the breath *seems* to permeate the whole trunk— and the Hebrew thought that it did.

Thirdly, we need to be on guard against too exact a distinction between thought, feeling or emotion, and will. In times not long past psychologists tended to treat the intellectual, emotional, and voluntative aspects of experience almost as though they existed separately, but today they rather say that, while one or other of the three may be more prominent than the other two in any given experience, all three are always there. Hebrew has no nouns for 'feeling' and 'will'. It has a noun for 'knowledge', but this word does not confine itself to the cognitive or intellectual. The Hebrew was far too practical in his outlook for that. Sometimes, and perhaps always, the nearest English word for the term rendered 'to know' is 'to experience'. To choose a clear example, the phrase 'to know one's wife' could hardly have been used of the sexual act by a people who were thinking of the merely intellectual. It is true that an 'ox *knoweth* his master's crib', but is this pure cognition? Under several Hebrew terms, as will appear below, it is not possible to draw any sharp distinction between the intellectual, the emotional, and the volitional aspects of experience.

So far the question 'What does a thing *seem* like?' has usually meant 'What does it *look* like?', but, of course, there are cases where it means: 'What does it sound or smell or taste or feel like (to the touch)?' The appeal may be to any of the senses. But these give us evidence about a man's 'outside'. The Hebrew might and did come to know a man's 'inside' in the same way, for, of course, men were sometimes torn or cut in pieces. But, so long as a man was alive, appeal could not here be made to the five senses. The question now took another form, 'What does it *feel* like?', the term 'feel' here referring not to touch but to pleasure and pain. These occur inside a man, and often seem to belong to one or other of the organs in the lower parts of the body. The Hebrew was not as reticent about these as we are—partly, perhaps, just because he located many of his emotions there, and not merely physical pleasure and pain. When a Psalmist wrote 'My reins (kidneys) instruct me in the night season' (Ps 16[7]), he meant that God taught him through the *thoughts* that he ascribed to his 'reins' along with the physical *feeling*. Quite literally he thought that things are what they seem, and that in this particular experience a particular organ itself felt and thought and knew. We readily forget that we are never aware of the brain. Even when the head aches, it seems to be the skull that does so (cf. the case of sunstroke in 2 K 4[19]). For the Hebrew it is nearer the truth to say that a man is one *living* being with many parts that are themselves conscious and active, than to say, with a great preacher, that 'man *is* a soul and *has* a body'. It was 'life' that unified a man.

When the Hebrew looked at the world, he divided it, as others did, into the animate and inanimate, the living and the life-less, though he did not do this quite accurately. In the Old Testament the term 'life' (*chayyim*) occurs about a hundred and fifty times. God, men, and animals all 'live'. There is only one passage where *chay may* be used of plants (Ps 58[9]). In the story of Creation the word first emerges when animals are mentioned (Gn 1[20, 24]), not when plants are made (1[11]). On the other hand, water might be called 'living' when it seemed to move of itself, like animals (e.g. 26[19]). In the earlier account of the making of man he is quite clearly classed with animals (2[7, 19f.]), but he is also the chief and master of animals for he gives them names and in the Bible to give a name is to assert authority (e.g. 2 K 23[34]). The early story means that God made man to be master in the animal world. He is classed with animals because they have bodies much like his, they move about as he does, and when their bodies are divided, it is found that their internal organs are much like his—but he stands at their head. The words rendered 'a living soul' which describe man in Gn 2[7] are also used of animals (e.g. 1[20, 24]). As will be seen below, 'soul' does not give the right idea. Perhaps the nearest English for the whole phrase would be 'a living thing' or 'being'.

What is this living being made of? The Hebrew, like others, noticed, that when a man dies, the breath leaves his body and the flesh gradually turns into dust. He concluded that man is breath and dust, though, as will appear presently, he found that 'blood' complicated the matter. In the earlier account of the creation of man (Gn 2) God makes a kind of large doll out of 'the dust of the ground' (as, in the case of the animals, 'out of the ground'). Then He blows up the doll's nostrils and man 'becomes a living being'. On the other hand when living beings die they 'return to their dust' (Ps 104[29]).

The passage in Genesis introduces the phrase 'the breath (neshāmāh—23) of life'. Neshamah is used six times of God (first in Is 30[33]), and occasionally of 'every breathing thing' (e.g. Dt 20[16]), but most frequently of man (e.g. 1 K 17[17]). As the text in Genesis implies, it is something from outside that God gives to man. Man is not neshamah, but has it. Except possibly in one passage (Pr 20[27]), no psychical function—neither feeling nor thinking nor willing—is ascribed to it. It is altogether what we call 'a physical phenomenon'. It is, therefore, not important in the study of the Biblical concept of man on his 'higher side'.

It is very different with another Hebrew term, nĕphĕsh (756). It has often been claimed that the original meaning of this term is 'breath', but, according to BDB, 'there is no sufficient evidence for this in Biblical Hebrew', and we can only leave the question open. The difficulty of translating the term appears from the fact that the Authorized Version uses forty-two different renderings! By far the commonest, however, are 'life' (117) and 'soul' (428). The editors of BDB catalogue nine meanings—'soul', 'living being', 'life', 'self', 'person', 'desire', 'appetite', 'emotion', 'passion'—and divide their article under ten main divisions, with many more sub-divisions! English has no one word for nephesh because we have no wholly corresponding ideas. In some passages there is nothing for it but to render the term by 'soul', yet few people think that animals have souls and nephesh is used of animals. For instance, as we have seen, the phrase 'nephesh of life' is used of animals as well as men (Gn 2⁷, ¹⁹). To render the phrase so as to include both we have to use some such phrase as 'living creature'. In the first of the texts just named, God, having fashioned a doll of 'dust' or earth, 'breathes into its nostrils the *neshamah* of life' and man becomes 'a *nephesh* of life'—that is, *he comes alive.*

The term *nephesh* has three chief uses. First, it means 'life' as opposed to 'death'. There are examples in the following quotations—'All the men are dead that sought thy life' (Ex 4¹⁹ J), 'Life shall go for life' (Dt 19²¹), 'If thou save not thy life tonight' (1 S 19¹¹), 'All that a man hath will he give for his life' (Job 2⁴), '(Greed of gain) taketh away the life of the owners thereof' (Pr 1¹⁹), and in the phrase 'seek thy life', which is especially frequent in Jeremiah (e.g. 4³⁰).

Secondly, *nephesh* is often used where we should say 'a man', and its plural where we say 'people'. We have a like use of the words 'souls'—for instance, in the text 'All the souls (*nephashim*) that came with Jacob into Egypt . . . were three-score and ten' (Gn 46²⁷ P). This is chiefly a late use. Again, in a like use, the phrase 'my *nephesh*' is often a synonym for 'I' or 'me'. There are many examples in the Book of Psalms—e.g. 'Return, O Lord, deliver my *nephesh*' (6⁴), 'Thou wilt not leave my *nephesh* to Sheol' (16¹⁰), 'Our *nephesh* hath waited for the LORD' (33²⁰), 'My *nephesh* is among lions' (57⁴). It is here that the very few passages fall in which *nephesh* is used of God—as in 'My chosen in whom my *nephesh* delighteth' (Is 42¹; cf. Is 1¹⁴; Jer 5⁹, Zec 11⁸). By an easy transition *nephesh* may stand for our reflexive pronouns. For instance, in Nu 30³ᶠᶠ· 'her *nephesh*' is rendered alternatively 'her soul' and 'herself', and to 'wrong one's *nephesh*' (Pr 8³⁶) is to 'wrong oneself'. The use of the term to mean 'a man' went so far that, from the Exile onward, the phrase 'a dead *nephesh*' occurs (e.g. Nu 6⁶ P), the English versions translating *nephesh* by 'body'! We ourselves can speak of 'dead souls', as in the title of a famous Russian novel. Finally, by the topsyturvydom that sometimes attends the history of words, *nephesh* is even used without 'dead' to mean a 'dead man' (e.g. Lv 19²⁸). Perhaps the nearest we come to this use is in such a phrase as '*a man* is buried there'.

Thirdly, it is the *nephesh* that experiences everything whether it belongs to the realm of feeling or knowing or willing. It is true that the emphasis is on feeling, but this is probably because feeling is the most obvious element of the three in everyday experience. BDB has 'the seat of emotions and passions' under this use of *nephesh* and hesitates to admit *any* intellectual or voluntative element. But surely, while in such a text as 'What things my *nephesh* refused to touch, these are as my loathsome meat (Job 6[7]), feeling is uppermost, knowledge and will are also implied. A few further texts may be quoted to show the wide range of experiences ascribed to the *nephesh*—'Thou mayest eat flesh with all the desire of thy *nephesh*' (Dt 12[20]), 'My *nephesh* shall not abhor you' (Lv 26[11]), 'Fellows bitter of *nephesh*' (Jg 18[25]), 'And his *nephesh* clave unto Dinah' (Gn 34[3]), 'Bless the LORD, O my *nephesh*' (Ps 103[1]).

It will be seen that the three uses overlap. It needs to be emphasized that *nephesh* is only used of God under the meaning 'I myself' and then very rarely. It is not an *element* within His nature, as it is with men and animals.

Such a sentence as '(God) breathed into his nostrils the *neshamah* of life and man became a living *nephesh*' (Gn 2[7]) shows that the Hebrew closely connected *neshamah* and *nephesh*, 'breath' and 'life'. He had noticed, of course, that when the breath leaves the body, the man, or animal, dies, and he came near saying 'The breath *is* the life'.[1] But, of course, he also noticed that when a man's (or animal's) *blood* is 'shed', he dies (e.g. Gn 9[6]), and he said outright 'the blood *is* the *nephesh*' (Dt 12[23]), 'the *nephesh* of all flesh is the blood thereof' (Lv 17[14]), and 'the *nephesh* of all flesh is in the blood' (Lv 17[11]). We do not know how he connected the ideas that 'life' is both breath and blood, but it has been surmised that he noticed that when blood is spilt, reek rises from it, and that he supposed that the breath permeates the blood, and that therefore, as the blood is everywhere in the body, so is the breath. In every kind of sacrifice the blood was given to God because it was thought to be *alive*. In the Temple there must have been an almost continuous reek from the blood when, on some great

[1] Perhaps the claim, made by some Semitic philologists, that *nephesh* sometimes means 'neck' or 'throat' should be noticed. They base the claim on the meaning of the parallel root in rather remote Semitic languages, adding that in certain texts it suits best the Hebrew context. But it is doubtful whether this can be made good. For instance, in Is 5[14] the idea may be 'Sheol hath enlarged its gulp', as a wine-bibber does (Hab 2[5]). Similarly, in texts that refer to a drowning man (Jon 2[5-7], Ps 69[1], 124[4 f.]) the idea may be 'choke'. In these texts, as elsewhere, LXX has *psyche*. It never renders *nephesh* by *trachelos* ('neck') or *larungx* ('throat'). In Pr 23[7] the Hebrew is probably corrupt and LXX rightly renders the accompanying verb by 'gulp' (*katapinein*). It is not likely that a man sunk, like Jonah, to the 'reeds' of the sea-bottom would say 'The waters compassed me even to the neck', and in the context the *nephesh* faints, which hardly suits 'neck'. Gulping and choking, of course, have much to do with 'the breath of life' that became in man 'the *nephesh* of life'. In any case this use is secondary and here it is the chief uses that are in question.

feast day, it was poured out at the altar. But, while the Hebrew concept of the living blood is important for the Christian doctrine of the Atonement[2] it is not so important for the development of the Bible doctrine of man. It is clear, however, that the *neshamah* was closely connected with the *nephesh* and the *nephesh* with the blood. There does not seem to be any text where any of these three terms denotes anything ethical. The use of *nephesh* in such texts as Nu 21⁴ E and Ps 35⁹ comes nearest.

A third term *rūǎch* (*378*) describes, like *nephesh* and *neshamah*, a universal element in human nature. Of its seventeen renderings in AV by far the commonest are 'spirit' (*232*), 'wind' (*91*), and 'breath' (*29*). Here the Hebrew term itself will generally be used. Like *nephesh, ruach* is connected with *neshamah*. A man is a being 'in whose nostrils is the *neshamah* of the *ruach* of life' (Gn 7²² J; cf. Job 27³, Is 42⁵, etc.). But, while *nephesh* denotes something that permeates the body with the breath of life, *ruach* is the word for the breath that comes and goes in breathing. Its primary meaning does not refer to the body at all. This is 'wind', usually a 'strong wind', and sometimes 'tempest'—though it can be used of the evening breeze (Gn 3¹ J). It *moved*, and for the ancient mind, where anything moves, someone is *doing* something. In the wind this is God or a god, for men cannot make the winds blow. For the Hebrew it was 'the LORD' who 'brought' or 'turned' a strong wind or 'blew' with it (Ex 10¹³, ¹⁹, 14²¹, 15¹⁰; Nu 15¹⁰). When 'the *Ruach* of the LORD' swept away Elijah (1 K 18¹²) or 'lifted up' Ezekiel with 'the sound of a great rushing' (Ez 3¹²), the *ruach* would be a great wind. The Hebrew had the winds of the desert at his doors. For him in storms the LORD rode 'upon the wings of the wind' and, at least sometimes, the wind itself was 'the *neshamah* of the *Ruach* of (God's) nostrils' (2 S 22¹¹, ¹⁶; cf. Ex 15⁸, 2 K 19⁷). When a strong wind arose, God was in action. The dominant idea is power, or will mightily at work. In the phrase 'the Spirit of the LORD', God's *power* is the dominant idea. Unhappily in the word 'spirit', at any rate as used today, this is not so. Even when, after the Exile, the idea of wind fell into the background, the idea of power remained. It is still dominant, for instance, when Trito-Isaiah says 'the *Ruach* of the LORD' gave 'rest' to His people *in the wilderness* (Is 63¹⁴). *There* it needs strong men to guard 'cattle' as they gently wend their way to a spring in the 'valley'. Are not marauders out for booty?

[2] See the writer's *The Bible Doctrine of Salvation, sub voce* in the index.

It is no part of the present subject to trace the whole doctrine of the *Ruach of God* in the Old Testament, but a contrast with *nephesh* may here be noted. As already shown, there are a very few texts which speak of God's *nephesh* under a secondary use of the word, but there is no parallel under this term to the phrase 'the *Ruach* of the LORD' or 'of God'. This phrase occurs about forty times and it is implied many times more. It is one of the master phrases of the Old Testament. It concerns the present subject only where the *Ruach* of God acts upon *man*. Before this is discussed, however, the use of *ruach* to denote an element in man himself will be considered.

Where *ruach* occurs in the documents from Genesis to Second Kings (omitting the late Priestly document), the idea of *vigour*, or strength to act, is dominant. For instance, when a spent man has eaten, 'his *ruach* comes again to him' (1 S 30¹²; cf. Jg 15¹⁹). Similarly, aged Jacob's *ruach* 'revives' when he sees Joseph's 'wagons' (Gn 45²⁷). When men are terrified 'there is no *ruach* in them any more' (Jos 5¹; cf. 2¹¹), but a man of courage has 'another *ruach*' than theirs (Nu 14 ²⁴). Or again, when the Queen of Sheba sees Solomon's splendours, 'there is no more *ruach* in her' (1 K 10⁵). The *ruach* of angry men 'abates' when a diplomatist speaks softly to them (Jg 8³), and when 'the sons of the prophets' see that Elisha can cleave Jordan, they say 'The *ruach* of Elijah doth rest upon Elisha' (2 K 2¹⁴ᶠ·). Three passages seem at first exceptional, but they all speak of a *baffled ruach* (Gn 41⁸; 1 S 1¹⁵; 1 K 21⁵). The vigour of a man's *ruach* ebbs and flows. When an unsophisticated man (or a child) is angry he '*breathes* hard'; when he is frightened, he 'hardly dares to *breathe*'. In these documents the original idea that *ruach*, a 'wind', is 'power at work' has been applied to man.

In the Prophets before Ezekiel there are few texts about man's *ruach*, but the few are significant. In the phrase 'the *ruach* of Egypt' Isaiah uses the word of a *people* (19³), a use fairly common later of the people of Israel. When the same prophet says that the war-horses of Egypt are 'flesh and not *ruach*' (31³), he means that they are weak and not strong, 'flesh' denoting weakness (cf. Gn 6³ J). He implies too that animals have no *ruach*. The latter term is only once used of a 'beast' in the Old Testament (Ec 3²¹), and there Koheleth seems to be sneering at the word. With very few exceptions *nephesh* denotes an element in men *and animals*, but *ruach* in men *and God*. Hosea twice speaks of 'a *ruach* of whoredom'

(4¹², 5⁴), and, while this may refer to an evil *ruach* or 'spirit' and not to man's own *ruach*, it does connect *ruach* with sin (cf. Is 19¹⁴). But it is with Ezekiel that the use of the term begins to be frequent. *Ruach* is one of his characteristic words. He speaks both of 'the heat' and 'faintness' of a man's *ruach* (3¹⁴, 21⁷), and of 'foolish prophets that follow their own *ruach*' (13³). But his significant contribution to the subject is his doctrine of 'the *new ruach*'. At the end of the chapter where God expounds the *individualism* of His judgement, He cries: 'O house of Israel . . . make you a new heart and a new *ruach*' (18³⁰ᶠ·). In two passages there is a higher note—'*I will put* a new *ruach* within you*' (11¹⁹, 36²⁶). In the second passage this leads to a higher ideal still, '*I will put my ruach* within you' (36²⁷). This phrase recurs twice (37¹⁴, 39²⁹). Its discussion falls later. The idea that man's *ruach* is either ethically good or ethically bad is here implied, for a new *ruach* is needed because the old one is bad. In the later part of Isaiah, while God gives *ruach* to every man (42⁵), the ethical aspect appears under the phrases 'a grieved', 'contrite', 'humble', and 'heavy' *ruach* (54⁶, 57¹⁵ᶠ·, 61³, 66²; cf. 65¹⁴). In other Prophets the mention of man's *ruach* is rare. God can 'stir up' the *ruach* of kings (Jer 51¹¹, Hag 1¹⁴). Malachi, writing of divorce, says: 'Take heed to your *ruach*' (2¹⁵ᶠ·). In the Prophets the reference to 'wind' sometimes falls into the background. For them, *ruach* in man is that in him that shows itself in action. In Apocalyptic passages there is always a reference of some kind to the relation of man's *ruach* to God (Is 26⁹, 28⁶, 29¹⁰, ²⁴; Dn 2¹, ³; Zec 12¹).

In the Psalms God 'cuts off the *ruach* of princes' (76¹²), and in the Wilderness the *ruach* of rebellious Israel was not 'stedfast with God' (78⁸). In the other relevant texts Psalmists speak of *their own ruach*, and *always* relate it to God. 'Into thy hand I commend my *ruach*' (31⁵) is a typical text. The godly wait upon God in persecution because without Him their *ruach* 'faints' and 'fails' (142³, 143⁴, ⁷). The LORD 'saveth such as be of a contrite *ruach*' (34¹⁸), for they long for a *ruach* in which there is 'no guile' (32²). The climax comes in the Psalm of *Ruach* (51). In this the *relation* between God's *Ruach* and man's is *the* theme. In most of these Psalms there is an ethical background. Ezekiel had done his work.

In Job too, where *ruach* occurs, there is always a reference to God, but Job's *ruach* is always a *ruach* of expostulation. Is not his *ruach* 'drinking up' the poison of God's 'arrows' (6⁴)? His *ruach* is 'anguished' and 'impatient' because God's 'care' has only 'preserved' his *ruach* to his misery (7^{11}, 21^4, 10^{12}; cf. 32^{18}). On the other hand, Eliphaz accuses Job of a rebellious *ruach*, and Zophar rebukes him 'in haste' out of his own superior *ruach* (15^{13}, 20^3). So far an ethical reference may be discerned. But there are also passages which imply that every man's *ruach* is a gift of God and may *in this sense* even be called 'God's *Ruach*' (27^3; cf. 32^8). It is God's *Ruach* that 'makes' man by giving him 'life' (33^4), and when a man dies God 'gathers unto himself' the man's *ruach* (34^{14}). This use of the phrase 'the *Ruach* of God' is clearly distinguishable from the use of the same phrase to denote God's gift of His *Ruach*, not to *every* man, but to particular men, such as prophets. One use relates to creation, the other to inspiration. In creation it is as though God took a part of His perennial fund of air and gave it to man, withdrawing it at death, when man's *ruach* returns to God's fund (Ec 12^7). It is here that the phrase 'My *Ruach* shall not always abide in man' (Gn 6^3 LXX) falls. God's gift of *ruach* to man is only to last for '120 years' and there are to be no more Methuselahs.

In the Book of Proverbs four passages speak of a 'broken *ruach*' as a disaster ($15^{4, 13}$, 17^{22}, 18^{14}). A man with a 'broken *ruach*' is a *weak* man. Other texts put a 'haughty' or 'hasty' *ruach* over against a 'lowly' or 'cool' *ruach* (14^{29}, $16^{18f.}$, 17^{27}, 29^{23}; cf. Ec $7^{8f.}$, 10^4). A 'lowly *ruach*' is meek, not weak. A man of a 'faithful *ruach*' keeps quiet about a neighbour's faults (11^{13}). A man who 'rules his *ruach*' is both strong and worthy (16^{32}, 25^{28}). In brief, as is a man's *ruach*, so is the man; and as is a man's *ruach*, so are his acts. Finally, there is a text that expresses the wise man's constant postulate—'The LORD weigheth the *ruchoth* of men' (16^2). Some passages in Ecclesiastes have already been named, but his characteristic phrase is 'vexation of *ruach*' ($1^{14, 17}$, $2^{11, 17, 26}$, $4^{4, 6, 16}$, 6^9). In the Priestly documents the word is rare. One passage speaks of the '*ruach* of jealousy' (Nu $5^{14, 30}$). Joshua has the *ruach* that a leader needs (Nu 27^{18}; Dt 34^9). God is 'the God of the *ruchoth* of all flesh' and therefore He can 'consume them in a moment' (Nu $16^{21f.}$; cf. 27^{16}; Gn 6^{17}, 7^{15}). Another text is almost a definition of the Hebrew concept of a man's *ruach*—'Every one whom his *ruach* made willing' (Ex 35^{21} P). This, however, does not mean that *ruach* is to be equated with what is now called 'will', for 'will' is abstract and *ruach* is concrete. It is not a quality but 'something'. Again, just as with *nephesh* and, as will appear below, with *lēb*, *ruach* may refer to feeling and thought as well as will. Indeed, especially in the Psalms and Job, two of the three words often appear in parallelism, as reference to the texts named above will show. It is true that *ruach* refers chiefly to will, but so does *leb* ('heart'), as is shown later. Possibly *ruach* lays more emphasis on the will *as leading to action*, especially ethical action. But its real *differentia* lies in the use of the phrase 'the *Ruach* of the LORD' to denote His action upon man in a way to which there is no parallel under 'the *nephesh* of God' or 'the *leb* of God'. It will be seen that in all the later literature some passages have an ethical reference and some have not. Every man has a *ruach*, and in every man it may be good or bad. There is here another contrast with *nephesh*.

The doctrine of 'the *Ruach* of the LORD' is only pertinent here so far as it is related to men. The first thing to note about it is that the Spirit of God is always active. In the Old Testament, and indeed throughout the Bible, what it *is* has to be deduced from what it *does*. The discussion includes almost all the passages where the *Ruach* of the LORD or of God is mentioned, for, while there are a few texts—notably in the story of Creation (Gn 1² P)—where it acts upon nature, in the great majority it is its action upon men that is in question. One or two conclusions may be anticipated. The *Ruach* of God always acts from *outside* a man. It is true that it may enter into him, as will appear below, but it does this from without. Strictly speaking, immanence is 'from everlasting to everlasting', and in this sense there is no doctrine of immanence anywhere in the Bible. From this it follows that the *Ruach* of God is never *identified* with the *ruach* of man. It will be found that until Ezekiel nothing is said of the relation between the two. In the earlier books it is upon the man himself that the *Ruach* of God is said to act, and not upon his *ruach*. In the discussion below the chronological treatment of the documents is abandoned at one point. Ezekiel is considered *after* all the later Prophets and the Apocalyptists. This is because his teaching, which is of capital importance, does not show itself clearly in them but in the Psalms and Wisdom Literature.

In the historical books of the period before the Exile the phrase is used chiefly of the action of the *Ruach* of God upon 'judges' (e.g. Jg 6³⁴, 11²⁹, 13²⁵) and 'prophets' (e.g. Nu 11²⁵ᶠ· JE; 1 S 10⁶, 19²⁰; 1 K 22²⁴). In the case of the latter it is clear that people could tell that prophets had the LORD's *Ruach* by looking at them (e.g. Nu 11²⁵ᶠ· JE). Probably this was because, like some hypnotic patients, they snorted under the prophetic *afflatus*. This would be so too with such a 'judge' as Samson. Similarly the LORD's *Ruach* shows itself in Saul's 'anger' when he hears the news of Jabesh Gilead (1 S 11⁶). It may be doubted, however, whether the *afflatus* was manifest when Joseph interpreted Pharaoh's dreams and advised him about them (Gn 41³⁸ E). The *Ruach* of the LORD might 'carry Elijah away' from one place to another (1 K 18¹²; 2 K 2¹⁶). This shows that it was a power outside a man, though it entered into prophets. Nothing is said of the relation of 'the *Ruach* of the LORD' to the man's own *ruach*, but it looks as if it strengthened the *ruach* of a warrior, and overwhelmed the *ruach* of a prophet (cf. Nu 24²⁻⁴, ¹⁵ᶠ·). It is noteworthy that the Deuteronomists, who don't use the phrase themselves, left it in the early stories in Judges when they gave them a 'Deuteronomic framework'. These passages, taken together, show that for the early Hebrew the *Ruach* of God was more than an influence though less than a 'person'. This is so throughout the Old Testament. *Ruach*, even when used of God, does not lose the sense of 'wind'. This, like water, is 'a living thing' that *acts*. Like water, it can be 'poured' (Is 32¹⁵; Ez 39²⁹; Jl 2²⁸; Zec 12¹⁰).

In the pre-Exilic Prophets the phrase 'the *Ruach* of the LORD' only occurs once or perhaps twice (Mic 3⁸; Is 11²). It is suggested by some experts that this is because the *false* prophets had the *afflatus* and appealed to this fact to prove that they *were* 'prophets' (cf. Mic 2⁷). When the people saw ecstasy they would say '*Ruach!*' On the other hand, other experts hold that wherever such phrases as *ne'um Jahweh* (rendered 'Thus saith the LORD') or 'the hand of the LORD was upon me' occur, they imply ecstasy and *afflatus*, and these phrases are found in the pre-Exilic books (e.g. Hos 2¹³; Am 2¹¹; Is 1²⁴; Jer 1⁸; Mic 4⁶; cf. Am 7¹²ᶠᶠ·). On this showing every oracle, from first to last, was spoken in ecstasy. But, if a Prophet had ecstasy and *afflatus*, had he not the LORD's *Ruach*, whether this is mentioned or not? If so, it appears to follow that a true oracle now included three things—the *afflatus* (and the *Ruach*), a *message*, and a *true* message. For the present subject the important word is 'message'. It seems likely that, sometimes at least, the ordinary prophet had the *afflatus* without any intelligible message (cf. 1 S 10¹⁰ᶠᶠ·), but it is certain that every great Prophet had a message and that from Elijah onward this message was, at least in part, ethical (cf. 1 K 21¹⁷ᶠᶠ·). With Amos this ethical element became and remained dominant.

If the first class of experts named above is right, it follows that the concept of an ethical message as the mark of a Prophet arose *apart from* any doctrine of the *Ruach* of the LORD. If the second account is correct, it follows that, while the true Prophet had the *Ruach* of God, this is no more than implied, the emphasis being on his message. Under all the instances so far, the *Ruach* of God comes upon special men for special purposes—i.e. it is an individual gift.

After Ezekiel, whose teaching is taken later, the phrase 'the *Ruach* of the LORD' occurs rather more often in the Prophets and Apocalyptists than in the Prophets before him. The texts fall into three classes. In some the *Ruach* of God is given to individuals— to Prophets (Is 48¹⁶, 61¹; Zec 7¹²), to the Servant of the LORD (Is 42¹), and, under the phrase 'the *ruach* of the holy gods', to Daniel (Dn 4⁸ᶠ·, ¹⁸, etc.). Next there are texts where the reference is general (Is 40¹³; Zec 4⁶; cf. Mal 2¹⁵). Third, there are passages where the *Ruach* of God has been or is to be given to a *community*. God put His 'holy *Ruach*' 'in the midst of' the Israelites to guard and guide them in the Wilderness (Is 64¹⁰ᶠ·, ¹⁴; Hag 2⁵; cf. Ps 106³³). This does not imply a universal ecstasy. Apparently too God spoke to Moses in a higher way than He did to prophets (Nu 12⁵⁻⁸ E). In other passages the *Ruach* of God is to be given to the *righteous* Israel of the future (Is 32¹⁵, 44³, 59²¹; cf. Zec 12¹⁰). Here it is not clear whether the *ruach* is the cause or only the accompaniment of righteousness, but ecstasy is very much in the background, if not absent. It is emphasized, however, in Joel's Apocalyptic account of the phenomena that are to prelude 'the great and terrible day of the LORD' (2²⁸⁻³¹). At last 'all the LORD's people' are to be prophets through the universal gift of His *Ruach* (cf. Nu 12²⁹ JE). It is under this third class of uses— i.e. in the repeated promise of this universal gift—that the *differentia* of the post-Exilic Prophets and the Apocalyptists lies. The idea that a man is not what he ought to be unless he has the *Ruach* of God, is implicit.

In Ezekiel the term *ruach* occurs forty-two times and he might be called 'the Prophet of the Spirit'. In his first vision 'the four living creatures' of the theophany carry the throne hither and thither with the speed of lightning because they are alive with *ruach* (1¹²ᶠ·, ²⁰ᶠ·). Elsewhere Ezekiel illustrates the first and third uses just named. He himself is an *individual* into whom 'the *Ruach* enters' (2², 3²⁴), upon whom it 'falls' (11⁵), and, most frequently, whom it 'lifts up' and carries away ($3^{12, 14}$, 8^3, $11^{1, 24}$, 37^1, 43^5). If, as is likely, the Prophet was cataleptic, his body would seem lifeless during trance, and he would tell his congregation afterwards where he had been, what he had seen, and what he had heard. This is why the three verbs named occur in the past tense. There is here a variant on the customary *afflatus*. But it is in the two passages where Ezekiel speaks of God's gift of His *Ruach* to the exiled *community* that he is significant, for in them the *ruach* of man and the *Ruach* of God are named for the first time *in the same passage*. In one of the two (36^{24-8}) God promises to 'cleanse' Israel, to give her 'a new heart' and 'a new *ruach*' and so cause her 'to walk in (his) statutes' and 'keep (his) judgements'. Here Ezekiel, perhaps intentionally, interprets what Jeremiah, who never uses the term *ruach* in this way, had expressed in other words in his account of the new Covenant—'I will put my law in their inward parts, and in their heart will I write it' (31^{33}). Jeremiah adds 'And (so) I will be their God, and they shall be my people', and Ezekiel has practically the same phrase (e.g. Ezk 36^{28}). The latter, however, is the first Prophet to say 'I will put *my ruach* within you' (36^{27}). This is not to be identified with the '*new ruach*', for the latter is *man's ruach*. To identify them would be to find in this passage a doctrine of immanence that is alien to all Old Testament thought and especially to Ezekiel's, for he is a chief exponent of the transcendence of God (e.g. in Chap. 1). In Chapter 36 man's *ruach* and God's are *both* found in a man. It is implied that it is through the *Ruach* of God that man's own 'new *ruach*' will keep God's 'judgements and do them', another phrase that repeats Jeremiah. It will be seen that, while the promise is to the community, Ezekiel implies that God will give His *Ruach* to the individual members of it.

The second passage is the Oracle of the Dry Bones (37^{1-14}). In it *ruach* occurs in three ways. At the beginning it is 'in the *Ruach* of the LORD' that Ezekiel is carried into a desert valley where the bones of the men of lost caravans scatter the sand. An earthquake shakes them into skeletons. Then 'sinews' tie them together, 'flesh and skin' cover them, and the skeletons have become corpses—but 'there is no *ruach* in them'. This is not the *Ruach* of the LORD but the *ruach* of man. Next: 'Thus saith the Lord GOD, come from the four *ruchoth*, O *ruach*, and blow upon these slain that they may live.' And at the word, an 'exceeding great army' leaps alive to its feet. Here the *ruach* is the same as the *ruach* given to every man at his creation. The dispirited exiles have been saying that they are 'a dead race' whose very 'bones are dried'. They did not mean, of course, that the *ruach* with which every man is born had left them and that they were *literally* dead. Ezekiel, however, accepting their parable, declares that God, the Creator, can and will give life to the 'dead', and, applying the parable, passes to a *third* sense of *ruach*, the *ruach* of redemption—'I will put *my ruach* in you, and ye shall live'. One might say that by the Spirit of God Israel is to be 'born again'. The immediate promise is 'I will place you in your own land', but in Ezekiel Israel returns home because she is now a holy and righteous people (e.g. 37²¹⁻⁸)—that is, a people on whom the LORD has 'poured his *Ruach*' (39²⁹). In Chapters 36 and 37 Ezekiel's doctrine of the Spirit reaches a significant climax. The LORD now no longer merely gives His *Ruach* to special men at special times for special purposes. 'I the LORD do sanctify Israel' (37²⁸) and *every* holy and righteous Israelite is *always* to be a 'man of the Spirit'. *Ruach* still denotes power, and the *Ruach* of God is still strong far beyond the compass of men—but now it has power 'to turn a bad man into a good man'. Here the community and its individual members go together. The *Ruach* of the LORD belongs to 'one and all'.

The Wise Man says the same thing in his own way when he declares that Wisdom offers 'to pour out (her) *ruach* unto' *any one* who will 'turn at (her) reproof' (Pr 1²³). There are three relevant passages in the Psalms. In one a man who longs to be righteous finds it at first terrifying but ultimately comforting that he cannot escape the *Ruach* of God (139⁷). This, of course, is not the *ruach* of creation, but of redemption (139²³ᶠ·). Another Psalmist cries to '*my own*' God, 'Let thy good *ruach* lead me' (143¹⁰). The relation of the LORD's *Ruach* to moral character is clear in both these Psalms. But it is in the fifty-first Psalm that the doctrine reaches its climax. Here, as in the two passages in Ezekiel, man's *ruach* and God's are both mentioned. The Psalmist, a man of 'a broken *ruach*' and 'a broken and a contrite heart' (51¹⁷), prays that God will 'create in (him) a clean heart' and 'renew a stedfast *ruach* within (him)', and cries, 'Take not *thy* holy *ruach* from me' (v.11 f.). Then there is a verse where *ruach* may mean *either* God's *Ruach* or *man's* (v. 12). LXX has 'Stablish me with a guiding spirit (*hēgemonikos*)', but RVm reads 'Uphold me with a willing spirit'. In this Psalm God's spirit and man's spirit go together in the righteous. Though it does not use the word, it teaches that man, if he is to be what he ought to be, needs the fellowship of God. The last word of the Psalter is the same as the last word of Ezekiel. The way is ready for the Pauline verse, 'The Spirit himself beareth witness with our spirit, that we are children of God' (Ro 8[16]).

Turning now from terms that denote something that pervades the whole body to its various parts, we may begin with the outward and visible organs, or rather with the most important of them— the hand and foot, the eye and ear, the mouth and lips and tongue. If we rid our minds of the modern ideas of the nervous and muscular systems, we find that these organs *seem themselves* to feel and act—and the Hebrew thought that this is what they do. There are examples for the hand and arm in 'Thine hand shall find out all thine enemies' (Ps 21[8]—Job 26[13]; Ps 45[4]; Is 31[7]) and 'Put on thy strength, O arm of the LORD' (Is 51[9]); for the foot in 'Let not the foot of pride come against me' (Ps 36[11]; cf. 26[12]); for the eye in 'His eyes are privily set against the righteous' (Pr 23[6]; cf. Ec 1[8]; Is 17[7]); for the ear in 'Doth not the ear try words?' (Job 12[11]; cf. Ps 130[2]; Is 32[3]); for the mouth and lips in 'My vows, which my lips have uttered, And my mouth hath spoken' (Ps 66[14]; cf. Job 15[6]); and for the tongue in 'My tongue shall talk of thy righteousness' (Ps 35[28]; cf. Job 33[2]; Is 59[3]). On reference to a concordance it will be found that a very large number of texts are patient of the interpretation now suggested, though they may not demand it. Probably, in view of the habit of early peoples to think that 'things are what they seem', this interpretation is the right one. Yet it is a mistake to speak of hand and eye and mouth and so on as 'autonomous'. There has never been a people that has not had *some* idea of the unity of what we call 'personality', or it could not have used personal pronouns. It is quite another thing to suppose that this 'personality' is altogether psychical[3]—i.e. Greek dichotomy must not be imposed on the idea. From a series of other texts—for instance, 'Stretch out thine hand' (e.g. Ex 9[22]), 'Refrain thy foot' (Pr 1[15]), 'Lift up thine eyes' (e.g. Gn 13[4]), 'I will set mine eyes' (Am 9[4]), 'Incline thine ear' (e.g. Ps 45[10]), 'I will keep my mouth' (e.g. Ps 39[1]), 'Keep thy tongue from evil and thy lips from speaking

---

[3] The term 'psychical' is preferred to 'spiritual' because in the Bible the latter word is needed as the adjective corresponding to 'spirit'.

guile' (Ps 34¹³)—it is clear that the Hebrew had *some* idea of the unity of the body. The two sets of passages may be reconciled if it is supposed that there was something that permeated the whole body, and that to say 'Mine eye saw' and 'I saw with mine eyes' (e.g. Is 6¹⁰) were two ways of saying the same thing. This connects with the idea that the '*nephesh* of life' pervades the body. A man's eye sees, thought the Hebrew, because *nephesh* is in it. An approximation to the concept still survives in poetry—e.g. in the phrase 'Mine eyes have seen the glory of the coming of the Lord'. There is even a hymn that begins with the line 'Give heed, my *heart*, lift up thine *eyes*'! For the Hebrew the organs of the body were not autonomous and independent, but under control. It is true that he did not conceive them as the physical organs of a psychical 'self', but he did conceive them as the living organs of a single living being. While he believed that there are many seats of action, the actions are all the actions of one man. It is not easy to find a modern phrase that sums up the Hebrew concept—or rather concepts, for the Hebrew sometimes ascribed a given activity to the whole man and sometimes to one part of him, even within a single verse. Dr. Wheeler Robinson suggested, the phrase 'diffused consciousness', but what the Hebrew noticed, at least primarily, was not consciousness but activity. The fact seems to be that the Hebrew ascribed an experience *both* to the whole *and* to the part that was active while the other parts were not. For instance, Isaiah says both 'I saw the LORD' and 'Mine eyes have seen the King' (6¹, ⁵)—i.e. *he* saw, but his *eyes* did the seeing. Similarly, when a Psalmist writes '(The LORD) hath delivered me from all trouble, and mine eye hath seen my desire upon mine enemies' (54⁷), it is the *whole* man who has been saved, the proof lying in the activity of the *eye*. From observation the Hebrew, like other men, ascribed a certain kind of activity to a certain organ. The differentiation, however, was not logically exact. Speech, for instance, could of course be ascribed both to the tongue and the lips, and Jeremiah could cry 'My *bowels*, my bowels! I am pained at the walls of my *heart*' (4¹⁹). If this be borne in mind, perhaps the phrase 'differentiated vitalism' is as good as any, for it denotes both the unity of a man's 'life' and the locating of a particular instance of life in the organ that is active in the corresponding experience.

Special mention should be made of a particular phrase which occurs five times in the Old Testament, 'an evil eye' (Dt 15⁹, 28⁵⁴, ⁵⁶; Pr 23⁶, 28²²), particularly as among some other peoples

CBM

a man with 'an evil eye' was thought to have it willy-nilly and to harm those at whom he looked whether he wished it or not.[4] This seems not to have been so in Israel, or at any rate among its teachers, for all the passages where the phrase occurs, except one, imply that a man only has 'an evil eye' if he *chooses* to have it, and in the remaining passage this notion is possible. The omission of the 'head' (*rō'sh*) in the list of the external organs is noteworthy. Today we habitually think of the head as controlling the body, as phrases like 'he kept his head' show, but this is because *we* know that a man controls his body through the nerves which run up into his brain. The Hebrews knew nothing of the brain and the nervous system. It is true that they often called 'the head-man' of a community its 'head' (e.g. Dt 1[15]; Hos 1[11]; Is 7[8]) as other peoples have done (cf. 'chief' and 'captain'), but this only meant that he was 'on top' (cf. Gn 8[5], 11[4]). A man was head of a community as a stone might be 'head of a corner' (Ps 118[22]; cf. 18[43], 24[7], 110[6], etc.).

Of the *inward* organs of the body the most important is the *lēb* or *lēbāb*. When either of these synonyms is used of man, it is regularly rendered by 'heart'. BDB, however, says that the original meaning is doubtful and gives the renderings 'inner man, mind, will, heart'. It puts first the rare use of the two words about *things*, with the meaning 'inner, middle, or central part', as in the phrase 'in the *midst* of the sea' (e.g. Ex 15[8]). But while the *Lexicon* gives no examples of the use of the words to describe the literal 'heart' of a man, there are a few clear instances of this. For instance, the phrase 'the heart and reins' (Ps 7[9]; cf. 26[2]; Jer 11[20], 20[12]) describes two of the internal organs; 'bones', 'heart' and 'bowels' are put together in one verse (Ps 22[14]); the phrase 'Thine heart shall tremble and be enlarged' (Is 60[5]) seems to refer to what we sometimes call 'palpitations'—and these are felt in the heart. Both the 'heart' and the *nephesh* are said to 'pant' (Ps 38[10], 42[1]). There is a very clear example of the reference to the physical heart in Ezekiel's phrase 'I will take away the stony heart out of your flesh and I will give you an *heart of flesh*' (36[26]). On the other hand there are hardly any passages where the meaning 'inner man'—that is, the whole of the inside of the body— appears to be quite clear. Among the clearest is the phrase 'My *leb* and my flesh' (Ps 84[2]), which seems to mean 'the whole man, within and without'. Similarly the wider meaning suits better

[4] See Article 'Evil Eye', *ERE*, V. 608–15.

the text 'I will fetch a morsel of bread, and comfort ye your heart' (Gn 18⁵), and the common phrase 'with all the heart and with all the *nephesh*' seems to mean 'with thy whole self'. But even in these passages it is by no means certain that the whole 'inner man' is meant, and the general opinion (as against the apparent implication of BDB), that the fundamental sense is 'the (physical) heart', all others being derivative, may easily be right, even if it is admitted that the etymology of the term is obscure. The number of texts where 'inner man' and 'heart' would both give the required sense is large. The phrase 'I said in my heart' is an example.

Lebab and *leb*, like *nephesh*, are used of any mental experience, whether thought, feeling, or will. Yet, just as the Hebrew tended to use *nephesh* when feeling is uppermost, so he tended to use *lebab* and *leb* when thought (and will, in a certain sense, as will presently appear) is uppermost. Then these words almost mean 'mind'. The use where the *whole* experience—thought, feeling, and will—is meant appears, for instance, in the phrase 'with all thy heart' and in Shulammith's beautiful phrase 'I was asleep but my heart waked' (Ca 5²). There are examples where feeling is uppermost in such texts as 'Comfort ye, comfort ye my people. . . . Speak ye to the heart of Jerusalem' (Is 40¹f.), 'He will be glad in his heart' (Ex 4¹⁴), 'My heart is sore pained within me' (Ps 55⁴), 'My heart is like wax; it is melted in the midst of my bowels' (Ps 22¹⁴). But, as already suggested, the use of 'heart' as equivalent to 'mind'—a use that is foreign to English, where 'heart' is still thought of as the seat of feeling in spite of modern physiology— is far commoner. There are examples in such texts as the following—'Hear now this, ye foolish people and without heart' (Jer 5²¹), 'Make the heart of this people fat . . . lest they understand with their heart' (Is 6¹⁰), 'The wise in heart will receive commandments' (Pr 10⁸), and the phrase 'I said in my heart'—that is, 'I made up my mind'. The reason why 'heart' should be counted the seat of thought is not clear, unless in such passages 'inner life' is the real sense, for, of course, when we think, we have no direct evidence that consciousness is located either in the heart or the brain or any other particular part of the body.⁵

---

⁵ The only place in the Old Testament where thought seems to be located in the brain is in the phrase 'the visions of the head' which occurs in the Aramaic part of Daniel (e.g. 2²⁸), but this describes what a man sees with his eyes shut—for instance in a dream—and probably implies that the man was supposed to see these visions by looking backward into his head. If so, the phrase means that the eye sees, not that the brain thinks.

We have already noticed that acts are often referred to the organs that perform them, as though the hand, the eye, and so on, were themselves able to will. But all men have the experience of 'turning things over in their mind' and coming to a resolve that does not at once express itself in act. This resolve we refer to 'the will'. *Lebab* and *leb* are often used about this in Hebrew and they may be said in this way to be 'the seat of the will'. While the phrase 'I said in my heart', for instance, may mean 'I made up my mind that so-and-so is the fact', it may also mean 'I made up my mind to *do* so-and-so.' These two senses of the phrase show that thought and will were not clearly distinguished. There is an example of the first sense in the phrase 'He saith in his heart, I shall not be moved' (Ps 10[6]), of the second in 'They said in their heart, Let us make havoc of them' (Ps 74[8]), and of both together in 'Esau said in his heart, The days of mourning for my father are at hand; then will I slay my brother Jacob' (Gn 27[41]). There are other examples of the use of 'heart' to denote thought *plus* will in the phrases 'His heart shall work iniquity' (Is 32[6]), 'An heart that deviseth wicked devices' (Pr 6[18]), and 'A man's heart deviseth his way' (16[9]).

While these two Hebrew terms are not the only words used to describe character, they predominate when the question 'What sort of a man is he?' arises. While *leb* occurs of courage in the phrase 'His heart is as the heart of the lion' (2 S 17[10]), and of conscience in 'And David's heart smote him' (1 S 24[6]), under this question *lebab* is the usual term. It occurs, for instance, to describe good men in the phrases 'uprightness of heart', 'integrity of heart', 'pure in heart', and 'perfect heart' (e.g. Dt 9[5]; 1 K 9[4]; Ps 24[4]; 1 K 8[61]). Similarly such concepts as 'hardness of heart', 'loftiness of heart', 'frowardness of heart' (e.g. Dt 15[7], 8[14]; Ps 24[4], 101[4]), are applied to the whole character of evil men. The terms *lebab* and *leb* occur in the Old Testament over eight hundred and fifty times, but enough has been said to give an idea of their wide range of meaning.

It is in the lower parts of the trunk of the body that we feel a number of our more intense emotions of pleasure and, still more, of pain. To these, therefore, the Hebrew often referred these emotions. He noticed that when animals (or men) were cut into pieces, the chief organs fall into two groups. In the accounts of the sacrificial system the three organs that form the first group are mentioned together—'The caul of the liver, the reins (or kidneys), and their fat' (e.g. Lv 8¹⁶). When a sacrifice was divided between God and the people (or, later, between God, the priests, and the people) in the so-called 'peace-offerings' these three were given to God (e.g. Lv 3). This may have been because, taken together, they were thought of, with the blood, as the seat of life, or as especially tasty morsels, or for both reasons. Emotion is only ascribed to the liver in one passage, as the Hebrew text now stands (La 2¹¹), and there it is associated with the eye and bowels to describe sorrow. In Hebrew, however, the consonants of *kābēd* (liver) are the same as those of *kābōd* (honour), and, as in ancient times the vowels were not written, it is at least possible that where *kbd* is used in parallel to other parts of the body the rendering should be 'liver' and not 'honour'. For instance *kbd* is used along with *nephesh* (Gn 49⁶; Ps 7⁵) and with *leb* (Ps 16⁹, 108¹). *Kbd* might also be taken to mean 'liver' in Ps 30¹². If this is so, it seems to follow that the liver was reckoned an organ of joy as well as of sorrow. It may be doubted whether *kabod* ever occurs with the meaning 'the seat of honour in the inner man' (BDB). The term *kelayoth*, reins or kidneys, is used of men thirteen times. Here the typical phrase is 'Thou triest my reins' or 'my reins and my heart' (e.g. Ps 7⁹; Jer 11²⁰). Probably there is always a direct or indirect reference to God's searching of what *we* call the conscience. Sometimes when a man felt intensely that he had fallen 'under the hand of God' it showed itself in physical feeling. This was usually a painful feeling (e.g. Ps 73²¹), but it might be a glad one (Pr 23¹⁶).

As to the fat, it seems that all fat, and not only one piece, was given to God in sacrifice with the blood (Lv 3¹⁶ᶠ·; Is 1¹¹). There are several terms for it in Hebrew, the chief being *cheleb*, *shemen*, and *deshen*. The 'fat' are the prosperous (e.g. 2 S 1²²; Neh 9²²; Ps 92¹⁴). 'He that putteth his trust in the LORD shall be fat' (Pr 28²⁵), says the Wise Man, yet the prosperous are often the sinful, as in 'Jeshurun waxed fat and kicked' (Dt 32¹⁵; cf. Ps 17¹⁰; Ez 32¹⁶). To 'make the heart of this people fat' is to 'harden' it through prosperity (Is 6¹⁰; cf. Neh 9²⁹). Perhaps the association of psychical ideas with fat seems as curious an example of the Hebrew way of thought as any, though we have it in the colloquial phrase 'fat-head'.

The second group of words for organs in the lower part of the body consists of 'bowels' (*me'im*), 'belly' (*bĕtĕn*), and the plural of 'womb' (*rachamim*). The first of these is sometimes used of the whole of the internal organs, for the 'heart' might be said to be 'in the midst of the bowels' (Ps 22¹⁴), and a child could be said to come forth from his father's or mother's 'bowels' (Gn 15⁴; Ps 71⁶). Apparently the term was also used sometimes for the 'intestine' only (Nu 5²²). When it denotes emotion it is not clear whether it is used in the wider or narrower physical sense, but the emotion in question is 'pity' or the love that issues in pity. It is in the distress of pity for his doomed people that Jeremiah cries 'My bowels, my bowels' (Jer 4 ¹⁹), and it is pity for Moab that drives Isaiah to cry 'My bowels sound like an harp' (Is 16¹¹). Deutero-Isaiah speaks of 'the yearning of (the LORD's) bowels and compassions (*rachamim*)' (Is 63¹⁵). *Beten*, 'belly', is not often used of emotion, but Proverbs has the text 'It is a pleasant thing if thou keep (the words of the wise) in thy belly' (22¹¹), and no doubt an idea of emotion accompanies a literal trembling in the text 'I heard and my belly trembled' (Hab 3¹⁶). The third word, *rachamim* ('mercies'), is the plural of the word for 'womb', but it can be used for the 'mercies' or 'compassion' of men as well as of women. The word *beten* is sometimes used for a woman's womb, as a synonym for *rechem* (e.g. Ps 139¹³), and the latter was perhaps thought of as a part of the belly. *Rachamim* may therefore have been used of the mercy that was felt in a man or a woman's *beten*. Otherwise it must be supposed that here the Hebrew, while he used a term derived from a physical organ, forgot the origin of the term in the 'psychical' meaning. It will be found below that he sometimes did something like this when he ascribed emotions to God. Some examples of the use of *rachamim* for 'mercies' are— 'He corrupted his compassions' (Am 1¹¹), '(The Medes) shall have no *rachamim* on the fruit of the *rechem*' (Is 13¹⁸), 'The mercies of the wicked are cruel' (Pr 12¹⁰). It is used most often of the LORD's mercy (e.g. 2 S 24¹⁴; Dt 13¹⁷; Hos 3¹⁹; Jer 13¹⁴; Is 63¹⁵; Ps 51¹), but to explore this use belongs to the book on Grace.

For the *whole* 'body' the precise Hebrew term (*gevīyyāh*) is rare. It occurs in three passages of a man's living body (Gn 47¹⁸; Neh 9³⁷; Dn 10⁶; cf. Ez 1¹¹, ²³) and three of a man's dead body (e.g. 1 S 31¹⁰, ¹²). In practice, when the Hebrew meant 'body', he said 'flesh' (*basar*). As we have seen, he thought that a man was made of breath and dust; he seems also to have thought that on his creation the dust turned into flesh and came alive (Gn 2⁷, ²¹). 'All flesh' can be used either for 'all men' or 'all living creatures' (e.g. Gn 6¹²ᶠ·, ¹⁷). In Hebrew 'near of flesh'

stands for 'near of kin' (Lv 18⁶; cf. Gn 2²³ᶠ·). While the word can
be used over against particular parts of the body to include all
the *rest* of it—for instance, over against *nephesh* (Ps 63¹), or *leb*
(Ps 84²), or bones and tendons (Ez 37⁷ᶠ·)—it is also used, especially in late documents, for a man's body as a whole (e.g. Lv 14⁹).
At least sometimes it denotes man in his feebleness as over against
God (Jer 17⁵; cf. Ps 78³⁹; Is 31³), not least in the phrase 'all
flesh'. Though it has to be translated 'flesh', it does not denote
the merely physical. Like the heart, it can 'cry out unto the living
God' (Ps 84²); though the dust, out of which it is made and to
which it returns, cannot praise God (Ps 30⁹), the 'flesh' can long
for Him (Ps 63¹); when 'a heart of stone' is turned into a 'heart of
flesh' it becomes a heart that obeys (Ez 11¹⁹ᶠ·); the 'flesh' may
trust in God (Ps 16⁸ᶠ·); when Jeremiah says 'No flesh hath peace'
(12¹²) he does not refer merely to ease of body but also to peace
of mind; no merely physical interpretation is possible for the
several texts where 'all flesh' stands for 'all men'—for instance,
'all flesh' can see and bless and know and worship (Is 40⁵; Ps
145²¹; Is 49²⁶, 66²³). In the Hebrew concept of a living man
there is *nothing* that is merely physical.⁶ While it is through his
'bone and flesh' that Job (2⁵) undergoes the long and ultimate test
of his 'perfection', there is nowhere the suggestion that the 'flesh'
is ethically evil. It may be weak, but it is not sinful. Did not
God make it? On a review of the whole Hebrew account of the
unit called 'a man' it may perhaps be said that *neshamah, nephesh*,
and *ruach* stand on one side and everything else on the other—
but this is not Greek dichotomy.

It is assumed throughout the Old Testament that, within
certain limits, men (and animals) can do as they like. This
doctrine of *liberty* goes with another—belief in the sovereignty of
God. While it does not belong to the immediate subject to discuss
the underlying philosophical question 'How can both these things
be?', something needs to be said about it. The Hebrew was not
of a philosophical and speculative turn of mind, and his ideas are

---

⁶ Israel, of course, had no monopoly of the psychical use of physical terms. For
instance, in James Morier's *Hajji Baba of Ispahan* there are a number of Persian parallels
—e.g. in Chapter 24 a girl says to her lover 'My *liver* is become water and my soul is
withered up'; in Chapter 35 a trembling officer tells the chief executioner that he
knows he is 'of invincible courage' and 'of *bowels* immovable'; and in Chapter 44 one
friend on meeting another cries 'My *eyes* are refreshed by the sight of you' (cf. the
English phrase 'a sight for sore eyes'). Of course 'heart' is similarly used in many
languages.

best understood by a comparison with the *practice* of life. He had
large experience of kingship, and he knew how a strong king,
such as Solomon or Nebuchadnezzar, was the master of his realm
even though there were insubordinate elements in it, such as
Moab and Phoenicia. Under the most powerful kings, again,
there would be many individuals who were rebels at heart and
who often did things that contradicted the king's will (e.g. 1 K
11²⁶ᶠᶠ·). These phenomena occur also between masters and slaves.
The Hebrew term for 'free' (*chŏphshi*—*17*) is always the correlative
of 'slave' (e.g. Ex 21²; Job 3¹⁹; Jer 34⁹). The Hebrew thought of
God and His subjects in a similar way. While from the beginning
to the end of the Old Testament, there is no suggestion that the
LORD could not do anything that He wanted to do, either individuals (like Saul) or nations (like Israel) might be disobedient
or rebellious. The best English word is the old one, 'over-rule'.
On the basis of his experience of kingship and of a master's lordship over bondmen the Hebrew believed both in the sovereignty
of God and the freedom of man. For him God was King and Lord.
Philosophically the human mind is unable to harmonize omnipotence and freedom. Can man by searching find out God? At
the same time, an omnipotence that can prevail even though some
of its creatures are free, however inscrutable this may be, is a
higher kind of omnipotence than that which just controls a
creation of puppets. The Hebrew belief has always, of course,
been the belief of the multitudes of non-philosophical theists.
It is true that there are a very few Old Testament texts that seem
to require that man is not free, but this is because their writers are
concentrating on the doctrine of divine sovereignty and it is
doubtful whether it is right to take them absolutely. Three may be
mentioned because they recur in the New Testament. There is
Jeremiah's parable of the Potter and the Clay (18¹⁻¹⁷). Here the
Prophet's chief purpose is to show that God can re-make a disobedient people even as a potter can re-make a 'marred' vessel.
If the parable be taken beyond this, one would need to deduce,
not only that man has no freedom, but that God, like the potter,
at first did His work badly and made a 'marred' vessel without
meaning to do so! There is no doubt that Jeremiah believed that
Israel's misuse of freedom had led to its 'marring'. Then there is
the passage in Isaiah 'Make the heart of this people fat, and make
their ears heavy, and shut their eyes . . .' (6¹⁰). This describes
the law of habit—the law that a good man grows better and a bad

man worse through his right or wrong choice—and this is a law that God *has imposed* on men. Under it God's sovereignty at last prevails over a man's initial freedom—but it is the man who decides whether it shall prevail in weal or woe. The third passage, where God is said to 'harden Pharaoh's heart' (Ex 4²¹, etc.), is an example of this law, for Pharaoh had begun to wrong Israel *before* the phrase occurs. While it is true that the Hebrew spoke of God's *direct* action and not of the operation of a *law*, for a serious theist the law is *God's* law. But in any case there is no doubt that, apart from a very few passages, the Hebrew combined belief in the Divine sovereignty with belief in a limited human freedom. Man, of course, cannot do *anything* he likes—for instance, control the rain—but there is a realm within which he can and does choose. He can help or hurt his neighbour; he can choose one bit of ground to dig rather than another; and so on. It is a Hebrew postulate that man has some freedom of will.[7]

All other nations, of course, apart from speculative thinkers, share this postulate. This is why ordinary men rarely use such a verb as 'to will' apart from some account of the thing willed. Few people examine and name their postulates. In practice, too, a man always wills *something*, and to sever the connexion between the will and the thing willed is a process of mental abstraction. The Hebrew was not inclined to abstract thought, and there does not appear to be any Hebrew verb that means 'to will' without any reference to what is willed. The three that come nearest to this are *bāchār* (*166*), *'ābāh* (*54*), and *nādāb* (*72* with cognates). The first means 'to choose' and in reality it is *assumed* that the person who chooses is free, the stress being on what is chosen. In an overwhelming number of texts the word denotes God's choice, but there are examples of man's choice in Gn 13¹¹; Dt 30¹⁹; Job 7¹⁵; Ps 119³⁰; Pr 1¹⁹; Is 7¹⁵. *'abah* denotes 'to consent' rather than 'to will', and always refers to a *response* to a command or suggestion. It is remarkable that almost always the word for 'not' goes with it (e.g. Gn 24⁵; Dt 1²⁶; 1 S 26²³). It occurs of man's refusal to say 'Yes' to God in such texts as Dt 1²⁶; Ps 81¹¹; Pr 1²⁵; Is 30¹⁵. Almost the only example of the use of the verb without a negative is in the tell-tale phrase 'If ye be willing and obedient' (Is 1¹⁹). While there is a word under which the

_____
[7] The author discusses this more fully in his forthcoming book *The Bible Doctrine of Grace.*

Hebrews said 'Yes' to God—the word 'Amen' (*30*)—the pre-
valence of 'No' is significant. Man is free to sin. For the third
word, *nadab*, 'to be liberal' gives the right idea, for, except
perhaps in Dt 23²⁴, it always refers to a free *gift*. God's liberality
in the dew, the rain, and so on, is mentioned twice (Hos 14⁴ᶠᶠ·;
Ps 68⁹). Otherwise the term and its cognates always denote a
man's free gift, usually (and probably always) to God. The most
frequent term is a cognate, which denotes free gifts, as distinct
from 'dues', in ritual (e.g. Am 4⁵; Ez 46⁴²; Ex 35²⁷ p; Ps 119¹⁰⁸).
The verb itself is used of the willing service of true men in fighting
for the LORD and His people (e.g. Jg 5², ⁹; 2 Ch 17¹⁶; Ps 110³),
in making gifts for the building of the Temple (e.g. 1 Ch 29⁵),
or in consenting to live in ruined Jerusalem (Neh 11²). A noun
that has to be rendered 'nobles', but whose best illustrations
would be such men as Boaz, Barzillai, and the eleven 'Judges',
has similar implications (e.g. 1 S 2⁸; Is 13², 32⁵, ⁸; Ps 47⁹; Pr
19⁶). In Ps 51¹²ᶠᶠ· it denotes a 'spirit that is ready to give a
testimony which is better than ritual sacrifice.' The word for
'to refuse', *mā'ēn* (*46*)—e.g. Gn 37²⁵; 2 S 2²³; Ps 77²; Jer 9⁶—
comes nearest of all to denoting 'will' and nothing else. Perhaps
nations, like children, begin to say 'I won't' earlier than 'I will'!
Such other words as *chāphētz* ('to delight in'), *rātzāh* ('to be pleased
with'), and *chāmad* ('to desire') might be mentioned as approxi-
mating to the concept 'to will', but under them it is clear that
the Hebrew, assuming that man is free, describes feelings that
accompany freedom. There is no *noun* in Hebrew for 'will'
simpliciter, for this is an abstract idea.

In relation to nature man's freedom shows itself in the doctrine
of his 'dominion'. The *term* occurs in the Priestly document in
Genesis (1²⁶, 9²), but the idea is anticipated in the older account
of the creation of man (2⁷ J). There animals, like men, are made
'out of the ground' (2¹⁹) and in their nostrils, as in his, there is
'the *neshamah* of the spirit of life' (7²²), but while man is here
grouped with animals, he *controls* them, for to give a name to
another was a sign of control (2¹⁹ ᶠ·; cf. 41⁴⁵, etc.). The *term*
'dominion' recurs in a Psalm that also links creation and man
(Ps 8⁶). The Hebrew word is derived from the verb *rādāh*, whose
original meaning was 'tread down'. While man, of course, cannot
control everything in nature, there was nothing theoretical about
the idea. Man was bidden to 'subdue' the earth and to exercise
'dominion' over animals and birds (Gn 1²⁸)—that is, God gave

him a *right* to till the soil, to kill dangerous animals, domesticate others, drink their milk or clothe himself with their wool, eat their flesh (9^3), and so on. In the passage just named it is added that the 'fear' and 'dread' of man are to lie upon animals, birds, and fishes (9^2). This, of course, just expounds 'dominion'. In other words when God gave man 'dominion over the works of (his) hands', and 'put all things under his feet', the reference, as the context shows, is to 'all sheep and oxen, Yea, and the beasts of the field; The fowl of the air, and the fish of the sea, Whatsoever passeth through the paths of the sea' (Ps 8^{6-8}). Man's 'dominion', that is, is a delegated control. Limits, indeed, are put to it in very practical ways—man, for instance, is not to 'eat of the blood' (Dt 12^{16}; Gn 9^4) or of 'unclean beasts' (Lv 9). Men, of course, have always *assumed* that they have this kind of 'dominion' whenever they have taken upon themselves to eat a berry or cut down a tree or kill a sheep or quarry stone or smelt iron—for without it they cannot live. Today when they ask themselves by what *right* they do such things, some of them reply that its basis lies in the 'worth of human personality' and that under this a 'person', being 'an end in himself', has a right to use other things as 'means'. The Hebrew asked himself the same question millenniums ago and *his* answer was 'Man's dominion is by the appointment of God'. Modern science is continally enlarging the scope of this dominion. It has two postulates—that anything that can be discovered in 'nature' is good, at least in the sense 'worth knowing', and that man has the right to use *all such discoveries* for his own ends. What is the ground of these postulates? The Hebrew said that they are grounded in the will of God.

This leads to the text 'And God said, Let us make man in our image (*tzĕlĕm*), after our likeness, (*dēmūth*)' (Gn $1^{26f.}$; cf. 5^1, 9^6 P), for this is the ground on which God gives man 'dominion' over His other creatures. What then is meant by the Hebrew terms *tzelem* and *demuth*? They have often been interpreted to mean 'spiritual and moral likeness' or 'personality'. In support of this the text 'Behold, the man is become as one of us, to know good and evil' (Gn 3^{22} J) might be quoted, were it not that this comes from an earlier document and describes man, not as he was at his creation, but as he became after the first sin. Probably here the phrase 'good and evil', while it may include moral distinctions, is not to be confined to them. Again, this interpretation does not suit either the original meaning of *tzelem* and *demuth* or the context of their use in other passages. *Tzelem* means literally 'something cut out', and denotes 'form'. In Genesis it seems to be used of angels as well as God in the phrase 'Let *us* make man'. Perhaps God, angels, and man, as over against animals, were supposed to share an erect gait, but *tzelem* means more than this. It is probable that the Hebrew thought of 'form' or 'shape' as separable from 'body' in a way that is not common now, though many people seem to think that a 'ghost' has 'form' without 'body'. So too the term 'spectre', as its etymology implies, means something that can be seen, but it is conceived apparently as 'form' without 'substance'. 'Fire' has a *tzelem* (Ezk 8²), as have images and pictures (e.g. 1 S 6⁵; Ezk 23¹⁴). The best renderings of the word is perhaps 'outline' or 'shape'. *Demuth* means much the same. It denotes something that can be *seen*, however dimly. In Is 13⁴ it describes the vague outline of a distant mass of men. It is common in Ezekiel who speaks of 'the appearance (*mar'ĕh*) of the *demuth* of the glory of the LORD' and says that this *demuth* was 'like the appearance (look) of a man' (Ezk 1²⁶, ²⁸). Here, as in Genesis, God and man are put together under the term *demuth*, and here there is no doubt that the term describes something that could be seen (cf. 2 K 16¹⁰; Dn 10¹⁶). This means that the Hebrews did not believe that 'God is spirit'—and nothing else. He had 'form'. It is true that there is a passage in Deuteronomy (4¹²) that, introducing a new term, declares that at Mount Sinai the Children of Israel '*saw* no form (*temūnāh*)' (cf. Job 4¹⁶), but this need not imply that there *was* no 'form' to see, for a *temunah* is ascribed to God (Ps 17¹⁵), and Moses, Isaiah, and Ezekiel are all said to have 'seen' the LORD (Ex 33²³; Is 6¹; Ezk 1²⁶, ²⁸). If, as is likely, God speaks to the heavenly host in the words 'Let us make man in our image, after our likeness', it follows that under all these three terms the Hebrews thought of God, angels (cf. Ezk 1⁵, ¹⁰), and men as having the same kind of 'form'.

CHAPTER TWO

WHAT A MAN OUGHT TO BE

AFTER 'What is the truth about God?' the paramount questions in the Bible are: 'What ought a man to be?' and 'How can he be it?' In the answer to the first of these questions there are two elements, which need to be considered separately. One of them did not change: under the other there was development.

The permanent idea may be stated in this way—A man is what he ought to be when he does what the LORD commands him to do. The idea has a first illustration in the three Patriarchs, for their stories, like the early legends of other peoples, depict the early ideal of the people who told the stories. Abraham is not a soldier, like Achilles the Greek, or Hermann the German; he is not a statesman, like Alfred the Englishman; he is not a patriot, like Washington. He is a servant of the LORD. His story begins with two things: a command, 'Get thee out of thy country, and from thy kindred, and from thy father's house, unto a land that I will show thee', and a response, 'So Abraham went, as the Lord had spoken unto him' (Gn 12^{1,4}). It is a mistake to think that the three Patriarchs were typical nomads. It is true that nomads wander, but they wander from one well-known oasis to another in a routine that their fathers have followed for many generations. Abraham, on the other hand, 'went out, not knowing whither he went' (He 11^8). He was an adventurer—but not an adventurer like Ulysses or William the Conqueror; he did not follow his 'star' like Napoleon—he obeyed his God. It is not, of course, meant that religion played no part in the stories of other heroes, but that religion is not the master key to their stories. For the Hebrews Abraham, Isaac and Jacob were ideal men because they obeyed God. This is the key to the Old Testament.

From Moses to David the Israelite heroes were either Prophets or soldiers. Of the Prophets, Moses himself came to be the type (Dt 18^{11})—and the dominant idea in his story is 'And God said unto Moses', do so-and-so, and he did it. For the soldiers the word to Joshua is representative—'As captain of the host of the LORD am I now come' (Jos 5^{14}). When the editors of the Books of Kings told the story of the Monarchy they did not tell the whole story.

but selected from their sources—and they selected under the question, 'Did this king and that and that do that which is right in the sight of the LORD or not?', referring their readers for almost everything else to such authorities as 'The books of the chronicles of the kings' (which, of course, are not the books now called 'Chronicles'). In the Exile and the centuries that followed it the few heroes and heroines—such as Ezekiel and Nehemiah and Ezra and Daniel and Esther—with all their differences, are true to the same type. They obeyed God. In this period, however, the 'common man' comes into his own[1] and the question 'What is the right kind of *man*?' takes the place of 'What is the right kind of *hero*?' The answer to the new form of the question is unmistakable. The right kind of man is the man who 'walks in the way of the LORD'. The one problem that vexed the mind of the Jew grew out of this idea, for it ran: 'There are men who walk in Jehovah's way—and suffer!' Even the pessimistic inconsistencies of Ecclesiastes pre-suppose this problem. Throughout the story of Israel from Abraham to this day, there has been a constant element in the answer to the question, 'What is the right kind of man?', and there is no mistaking what this is—a true man is 'God's man' even as Achates was 'Aeneas' man'. While the idea, of course, is found elsewhere, particularly among so-called primitive peoples, among the peoples that have 'made a difference' in the history of mankind it is Israel alone (along with Christianity and Islam, which are here its debtors) that has declared from first to last that the faithful servant of God and none other is what a man ought to be. A true man is a man who does the will of God.

But what *is* the will of God? This leads to the second element in answer to the question, 'What ought a man to be?' and it is here that there was change and development. In the early stories the characteristic instances relate to *specific acts*. God tells Abraham to go to an unknown land—and Abraham goes. God tells Moses to challenge Pharaoh—and Moses challenges him. God tells Joshua to lead Israel over Jordan—and Joshua does so. God sends Elijah to arraign Ahab—and Elijah does so. The heroes of Israel perhaps all come within this category.

The concept that God tells particular men to do particular things, however, probably never stood alone. From the first early peoples had each its distinctive way of life, and many or all

[1] See *The Bible Doctrine of Society*, Ch. 4.

of them believed that these ways were prescribed by their gods. Some things were 'done' and 'not done' that differentiated one people from another, however much they may have been alike in others. Even when these distinctive things were attributed to custom, the custom would be attributed in turn to the will of the god. In a passage where mere custom seems at first to rule early Hebrew conduct, the reference to the Exodus suggests that the LORD prescribed it (Jg 19^{30}; cf. 20^{18}). There was a way of life for every Hebrew as well as particular commands to early leaders. This way of life expressed itself in part in the early codes of law. The laws of Israel were the laws of God. There is no need here to describe the way in which early law developed in Israel, finding two later expressions in the Deuteronomic code of the seventh century B.C. and the Priestly Code after the Exile. The important point here is that the idea that the law of Israel was the Law of the LORD was perennial. One of the marks of Israel is that, alone among the peoples that 'count' in the story of civilization, it has maintained this concept to this day. Again, it has often been pointed out that the Hebrew law-codes, including the Dacalogue, contain ritual commands as well as moral ones. Alongside commands such as 'Thou shalt do no murder' there lie such commands as 'Thou shalt not offer the blood of my sacrifice with leavened bread' (Ex 20^{13}, 34^{25}). *We* call the first moral and find a reason for it; the second *we* call 'ritual' and 'arbitrary' (though the early Hebrew probably thought that he could see a reason for it). The point to notice here is that it is not the way of law, in any nation, to give reasons, whether there are any or not. Again, in all codes of law there are commands that are 'arbitrary'. There is, for instance, no logical reason why the 'rule of the road' should run as it does in England. It is 'arbitrary' to decide which side of the road motorists shall follow. Similarly, it was 'arbitrary' that the law of Israel should prescribe liberty to enslaved Hebrews every seven years, rather than every six or every eight (Ex 21^2). This example shows that the 'arbitrary' element in Israelite law was not confined to ritual. The *differentia* of Israel at this point is not that its law contained both moral and arbitrary elements, for all codes do this, but that it attributed *every* law, whether moral or arbitrary, *to the will of God*. No one claims that the 'rule of the road' is a Divine law. It is not peculiar to Israel, again, that the law should include 'ritual'—i.e. rules for worship. In the time of the early Christian persecutions 'Sacrifice to Caesar' was a 'ritual' rule, and so was the rule in Stuart England that every man must attend his parish church at the three great Festivals. No doubt ritual plays a very large part in the Priestly code, but the distinctive point, none the less, is that for Israel the whole Law, detail by detail, expressed, not the will of man, but of God. The LORD prescribed a distinctive way of life.

Midway in the development of Hebrew law there came the great Prophets. One of their marks, of course, is that they declared that to follow right ritual—or, as the writer thinks, *only* to follow right ritual—was useless. But there is more than this. It is true that their teaching influenced the development of law, particularly in Deuteronomy—but there is more still. The Prophets, indignant with the way in which people treated one another, proclaimed that there is a moral law that covers the whole of life. It is often said that they preached an 'ethical monotheism', but it is the second word that should be emphasized. The Prophets did not preach a universal system of ethics which could be justified *per se*, but ethical principles that were laid down by God. Their distinctive phrase is not 'This is good in itself', but 'Thus saith the LORD'. They taught that *He* demands a 'righteousness' that could not be reduced to a series of rules. They applied this concept to many kinds of acts that are not named in Deuteronomy. Here it is necessary to do justice to the Rabbis. Scholars have shown that they did recognize that there was a righteousness that transcended their law-codes. Indeed, their inclusion of the Prophets in the canon would, by itself, be enough to show this. The pertinent point here falls under what may be called 'the variety of standards'. To use a modern term, while it was believed that it was a man's duty to seek to reach the Prophetic standard of life, it was also taken for granted that this was an 'ideal' that was beyond the scope of all men, or, at any rate, of most men. But the Pharisees, in particualr, maintained that there was none the less a standard, the standard set by the Law, that men could reach and that God required that they should reach. The ordinary Jew found even this impossible, or all but so (Ac 15¹⁰; Jn 7⁴⁹). Yet there would be a still lower standard, however ill defined, that 'respectable' Jews—say, the Sons of Zebedee—would reach. Here, too, it is important to note what was distinctive in Israel. In every people a variety of standards of conduct obtains at one and the same time. In England, for instance, the law of the land prescribes a minimum standard for all citizens; 'respectable' people have a higher code, however ill defined, for they do and leave undone many things that the law of the land does not touch; the standard for Christians is, or ought to be, higher still; and above all there is a standard often called 'ideal', which, it is assumed, every man ought to aim at but none can reach. The distinction of the Jew was not that he had a variety of standards—still less that he was a 'hypocrite' for having several—but that he related them *all* to the will of God. To take the two that concern Biblical doctrine most, the Jew believed that the Law of the LORD, and not 'the law of the land', prescribed the minimum for all Jews— and that there was also a higher standard, embodied most explicitly in the canon of the Prophets, that a man should seek, however unsuccessfully, to reach, which *God* had prescribed. The Hebrew knew nothing either of *secular* law-codes or of an ethic that is authoritative *in its own right*. In the account given of *what* God wills there was unique progress, but from first to last the answer to the question 'What ought a man to be?' is 'He ought to be what God wills him to be'. For the present subject the highest of the standards named, first elucidated by the Prophets, is the one in question.

This means that throughout the Old Testament the concept of man's 'independence'—apart from the false independence of the sinner—does not occur, and that the idea of the ineluctable dependence of the creature on the Creator is always taken for granted as we take the 'solid earth' for granted in all our life. Yet there is something more. Abraham, for instance, was 'a man of the covenant'. The idea of covenant is another of the concepts that are postulates everywhere in the Old Testament—a true Israelite was what he ought to be just in proportion as he kept Israel's covenant with God. Here, again, a summary statement must suffice. Fundamentally every Patriarch was just a man in covenant with Jehovah. Then, from Sinai onward, Israel was the '*people* of the covenant'. When Jeremiah, in his greatest oracle, foretold a 'new covenant' (Jer 31³¹ᶠᶠ·), he did not say that its contents would be new but that every Hebrew would 'know the LORD' for himself and willingly obey Him always and everywhere. To understand the word 'covenant' the best modern starting-point is perhaps the word 'fellowship'. In all human intercourse there is some degree of fellowship, though this is often assumed rather than asserted—from the small area of agreement when buyer and seller exchange goods for their mutual benefit (which

DBM

is not the same idea as 'bargain') to the life-wide agreement of home. In particular the idea of fellowship is integral to all societies. The members of a cricket club, for instance, agree to practise fellowship within a game, and the citizens of a country to practise a political and social and economic fellowship. Today we speak often of a common 'way of life'. The Hebrew used a similar metaphor when he spoke of a man's life as his 'walk'. One of his accounts of the right kind of man is 'he walked in the way of the LORD' or 'walked in His statutes', or 'walked before Him', or even 'walked with God' (e.g. Gn 6⁹, 24⁴⁰; Ezk 11¹²; Ps 119³; cf. Dt 23¹⁴; Lv 26¹²). The connexion with covenant is explicitly made in the story of Abraham. God said unto him: 'I am God Almighty; walk before me, and be thou perfect. And I will make my covenant between me and thee' (Gn 17¹ᶠ·). Two cannot 'walk together except they be agreed' (Am 3³). Abraham could rightly be called 'the friend of God' (Is 41⁸) because friendship is a fine form of fellowship. It is of course true that all real religion involves some degree of fellowship between the divine and the human, or at least the search for it. For Israel God was not only the Creator but the Comrade. He is said to 'dwell' or 'walk' in the midst of His people (Ex 29⁴⁵; Dt 23¹⁴; Lv 26¹²). 'I am with you, saith the LORD' is the conviction of Hebrew after Hebrew, from Abraham to Daniel. Of course it is God who takes a man for His friend, if the man is willing, and not *vice versa*. 'Ye have not chosen me, but I have chosen you' is yet another pervasive concept. God commands, and the right kind of man obeys— 'What doth the LORD require of thee but to do justice, to love mercy, and humbly to walk with thy God?' (Mic 6⁸).

Here a certain psychological truth is pertinent. There can be no fellowship between two persons who are altogether alike—nor between two who are altogether un-like. Indeed, both concepts are artificial, for every man is in some ways like every other and in some unlike all others. It is from this human analogy that we may best begin to understand the fellowship of God with man. Between them there is the difference between the infinite and the finite—in power, wisdom, holiness, love, and so on—and therefore there is between them a gulf beside which the difference between the sun and a grain of sand is small. The sentence, 'Ye shall be holy, for I the LORD your God am holy' (Lv 19²), is very far from meaning 'Ye shall be *as holy as* the LORD your God'. On the other hand, God is not 'wholly other', in the sense of 'wholly different',

or man could not know Him at all. There are likenesses between
man and God, even as there are likenesses between the sun and
a sand-grain. There is an example in the text: 'With the merciful
thou wilt show thyself merciful; With the perfect man thou wilt
show thyself perfect; With the pure thou wilt show thyself
pure' (Ps 18$^{25f.}$). It is the likeness between God and man that is
here relevant. The first and cardinal point of likeness clearly
emerges in the Written Prophets. Prophet after Prophet teaches
that righteousness is what God demands in man. The Deuteronomist sums it all in the cry: 'Righteousness, righteousness
shalt thou follow' (Dt 16^{20}). Yet once again, this does not mean
that righteousness has value *per se,* as when idealist philosophers
say that 'the good, the true, and the beautiful' are 'of ultimate
value'. The Hebrew knew nothing of abstract ideas which exist
somehow in their own right. For him all perfection is personalized
in God. Jeremiah's phrase 'The Lord is our righteousness' (Jer
23^6) gives the point of view. Jehovah intends and commands
and expects men to be righteous *because He Himself is righteous.*
In other words, man is called at this point to be like God—and,
in his degree, may be like Him. Indeed, just in so far as a man is
'righteous'—and the Old Testament knows of those who are—he *is*
like God. 'The LORD', 'covenant', and 'righteousness', taken
together, are the three words that dominate the final teaching of
the Old Testament. It is under 'righteousness' and not under
tzelem and *demuth* that the Old Testament doctrine of man's
likeness to God really appears. The modern definition under
which 'the image of God' in man is described as 'moral and
spiritual likeness' does not root in the First Chapter of Genesis
but in the teaching of the Prophets.

The term 'righteousness' has so far been used, as it sometimes
is in the Old Testament, as an inclusive term. In particular, as
will presently appear, it describes the whole of man's right way
of behaviour to other men. None the less, certain other terms need
discussion in this chapter even though they might be included
under 'righteousness' in its widest sense. It is not pretended
that any terms, however carefully chosen, exhaust the doctrine
of man's likeness to God—but only that they sufficiently illustrate it. In other words, the method of this book, to proceed
chiefly by the examination of the meaning and use of terms,
applies here.

The term for 'righteous' is *tzaddīq.* It and its cognates occur more than five hundred times, and in some four hundred they are rendered by 'righteous', or 'righteousness', or 'be righteous'. The alternatives arc 'just', 'justice', and, under one form of the verb, 'justify'. All the relevant terms—'righteous', 'righteousness', and even 'justify' (Ps 51⁴)—are used both of God and man. A text in the Psalms, 'For the LORD is righteous; He loveth righteous deeds' (11⁷), expresses the constant idea. Its scope is as wide as life. The chief elements in the concept are 'justice', 'mercy', 'truth', and 'peaceableness'. These are all social, not individual, concepts and the writer has explored them, with the involved doctrine that man ought to be like God, in his earlier work, *The Bible Doctrine of Society*. A few of the passages that describe righteousness more or less fully, may be named—Is 11¹⁻⁹; Jer 7¹⁻⁷; Ezk 18⁵⁻⁹; Ps 15, 72¹⁻⁷; Job 29¹¹⁻¹⁷; Lv 19¹⁻¹⁸ (except v. 5-8). It may be mentioned that the root *tzdq* is sometimes used in the narrower sense of 'justice' as well as in the wider one of 'righteousness'. The concept of 'mercy' is examined in *The Bible Doctrine of Grace*. 'Truth' does not mean mere accuracy of fact, as in our phrase 'scientific truth', nor mere truthfulness in speech, but a reliability, a firmness, a staunchness, that permeates the whole of life. Though the phrase does not happen to occur, 'Ye shall be righteous, for I, the LORD your God am righteous' summarizes the Old Testament teaching under this term.

One of the commonest synonyms for *tzaddiq* is a word (*yāshar*, *114*) whose root idea is 'straight' and which is well rendered by 'right' or 'upright'. Unfortunately the corresponding verb has eight renderings. This term too may be used either of God (e.g. Dt 32⁴; Ps 25⁸) or man (e.g. Ps 36¹⁰). The characteristic Hebrew attitude to uprightness appears in the frequent Deuteronomic phrase: 'To do that which is right in the eyes of the LORD' (e.g. Dt 6¹⁸). Another frequent synonym is 'good' (*tōb*—*615*). This word has as wide a use as its English counterpart, everything being good 'after its kind' from a blade of grass to a man, but everything is good because God made it so (Gn 1, *passim*), and when a man is good 'after his kind' he is ethically so, like God (e.g. Ps 25⁸), though Gn 1 does not say this. 'He hath shown thee, O man, what is good' is the prelude to a great verse in Micah (6⁸). One might take all the moral or societary terms of the Old Testament in just the same way. Under every one of them God and man are somehow linked. This is, of course, just a leading instance of the truth that whenever religion is alive, and not otiose, the doctrine of man roots in the doctrine of God. In however small a way man is to be righteous and upright and good after the manner of God. Under these terms a man is what he ought to be when he is like God.

There is an *explicit* illustration of this in a text that dates at earliest from the Exile—'Ye shall be *holy*, for I the LORD your God am *holy*' (Lv 19²). Ever since Otto wrote his book on *The Idea of the Holy* there has been discussion about the meaning of the word 'holiness'. It is necessary to say something summarily of the results of the discussion, as the writer understands them, before any account of the meaning of the term 'holy' as applied to the right kind of man can be given. This summary statement falls into two parts—the meaning of 'holiness' in religion generally and especially in primitive religion, and its meaning in the Old Testament. It is mainly with the first that the discussions of the last generation have dealt.

Many students of the subject now agree that primitive man distinguished three different kinds among the beings that he 'encountered' in his normal life. He encountered other *men*; he encountered *things*; he encountered *something or someone* who could not be classed either with men or things. Many add that the 'something or someone' was less un-like a man than a thing. Yet perhaps the nearest approximation in current experience to the primitive idea is the sense of the 'eerie'. Otto's term is 'numinous', and three others of his terms are pertinent. The first is *mysterium*; there was the sense of the unknown. With this there went the sense of helplessness and therefore of fear. The *mysterium* was a *mysterium tremendum*. Yet all the time the 'eerie' fascinated as well, if only as a snake fascinates a bird. The *mysterium* was *fascinosum* as well as *tremendum*. Here lies the paradox of the 'holy'. It may be put in other terms. A god is separate from man, though he acts upon him; man does not want to be *altogether* separate from God though he fears too close a link. This is why the idea of separation used to be dominant in attempts to explain the term 'holy'. There is no idea of *ethical* separation in the primitive concept. Under it 'holiness' is 'awe'.

There is no need here to enter into the discussion of Otto's account of 'holiness', for this has chiefly related to the *origin* of the idea and there was no doubt that it was well developed long before the Hebrews appear in history. In the Old Testament, the word for 'holy' (*qādōsh*) and its cognates are very common (605).

They have some twenty renderings in the Authorized Version, but the commonest are 'holy' (with 'holiness'), and 'sanctify' (with 'saints', though this is not frequent). Since there was an older opinion that the root meaning of the terms was 'separate', it is important to remember that the concepts '*tremendum*' and '*fascinosum*' easily lead to the paradox 'separate' and yet 'not separate'. For instance, both the Tabernacle and the Temple were 'holy' and therefore 'separate', but they were 'separate' *within* Israel. In both cases this was because they contained the Ark, which only priests or Levites must touch (cf. 2 S 6⁶ᶠ·)—yet which was also the *palladium* of the Hebrew people. The history of the term 'holy' in the Old Testament contrasts with that of 'righteous'. The former was taken over from the ancient world and did not develop much; the latter, no doubt, had some antecedents, however little differentiation, but, as has been seen, in Israel, chiefly under the preaching of the Prophets, it developed in a unique way. If *qadosh* has any *differentia*, it would be in the fact that throughout the Old Testament the dominant idea is not so much that men are drawn, spite their fear, to a holy god as that the Holy God comes to certain men. This is already clear in the story of Abraham. In one account of the way in which the LORD made covenant with him the 'feel' of God's holiness in the primitive sense is very clear even though the word 'holy' does not occur (Gn 15). At its beginning *God comes to* Abraham in a vision, and His first word is 'Fear not'. Later Abraham under God's command undertakes such ritual arrangements for the making of a covenant as men used when one of them made covenant with another—he lays the divided parts of sacrifices in two rows so that the parties to the covenant may pass between them, taking oath. Then 'when the sun was going down, a deep sleep fell upon Abram; and, lo, an horror of great darkness fell upon him. . . . And it came to pass that, when the sun went down and it was dark, behold a smoking furnace and a flaming torch that passed between these pieces'. The sense of the *mysterium tremendum* permeates the story—yet this is only the background of the 'covenant'. The dominant idea is not separation but fellowship—'In that day the LORD made a covenant with Abraham' (v. 18). God and Abraham go together.

The same perspective holds throughout the Old Testament. For instance in the story of the Exodus the people are forbidden to come near to the holy mountain, not because they are sinful but because it is numinous—yet Moses has led them to the Mount of

God and the chief point of the whole story is that Jehovah is *their* god, who links himself with them through Moses. The Ark too was always numinous, yet 'all Israel shouted with a great shout' of welcome when it was brought 'into the camp' (1 S 4⁵). With the Tabernacle and Temple we pass to the term 'holy' itself. In both there was a 'holy place' and a 'holy of holies'. In post-exilic times, if not before, all except priests were excluded from the first, and everyone except the High Priest from the second. Yet the dominant concept was not this separateness but another— that Jehovah dwelt in the midst of His people. Perhaps the most impressive Old Testament example of the numinous is the story of Isaiah's Call, where the cry 'Holy, holy, holy is the LORD of Hosts' rings through the Temple and even the Seraphim veil their faces—yet, with this as background, the LORD speaks to Isaiah. In the Old Testament the LORD is everywhere 'the Holy One *of Israel*', even though the phrase does not occur until Hosea (11¹²). No one can look at the sun, yet no one can see unless it gives him light—and the light *comes* to the eye. In the Old Testament the Holy One *comes* to Israel and 'dwells' in her midst. Even in Ezekiel, where God leaves the Temple for a while, He returns to it (43⁴). In the Temple God was both isolated and in the midst.

As already implied, the primary concept is that *the LORD* is 'holy'. Before the texts where this is affirmed are considered, it will be convenient to say something briefly about the holiness of *things*. About three out of four of the texts where *qadosh* and its cognates are used refer to their holiness. This, however, happens because the Priestly documents spend themselves upon the details of ritual. The significance of this will appear later. Meanwhile the fundamental idea may be noted. It is that since the LORD is holy a derivative holiness passes from Him to everything that He chooses to use in His worship. While men provide these things, He hallows them. In early thought, at least, holiness was a kind of Divine emanation that hallowed all it touched. The word is used, for instance, over fifty times in the book of Leviticus to describe the Tabernacle (and so the Temple)—frequently in the phrase 'the holy place', but also, for instance, of 'holy convocations' to be held in the Tabernacle and of the 'holy day'. The last clause in the command, 'Remember the rest day to keep it holy', shows that the Sabbath was to be a day of leisure in order that Israel might fulfil the ritual of worship. This brings out clearly the fact that the preponderating idea, when the term is used of *things* and occasions that are 'holy', is a ritualistic one. This use would also occur in the worship of other gods, and here the *differentia* of Israel is not under 'holy' but under 'the LORD'. At the Deuteronomic reform the idea, which had probably long been growing, that the Temple was *par excellence*, 'the holy place', reached its climax in the claim that it was the *one* place where God had 'put his name' (2 K 23$^{8ff.}$; Dt 12^5). Thereafter the unique holiness of the Temple was a maxim in Israel. God manifested His holiness primarily in the 'holy of holies'. From thence it spread to the 'holy place', then on to the whole Temple and all its *cultus*, and, at least ideally, to the 'city' and even the 'land' beyond (e.g. Neh 11$^{1, 18}$; Ps. 2^6; Is 48^2; Zec 2^{12}). It is plain that there would be less and less of the numinous as the distance from the 'holy of holies' lengthened. The city, for instance, was separate unto the LORD rather than awesome. While separation was a derivative idea, in practice it bulked large. In the realm of things, of course, holiness belongs wholly to ritual, and ethics cannot be in question. The 'sacrifices' do not seem ever to be called 'holy', perhaps because they were given *by* man *to* God.

Throughout the Old Testament the holiness of *God* is a postulate, and, as with most of the postulates of life, it is only mentioned when there is need. Postulates would not be postulates if they could not be taken for granted. Occasionally this postulate shows itself indirectly, as in the phrase 'The place whereon thou standest is holy ground' (Ex 3^5 E; Jos 5^{15}). Perhaps the earliest passage where the perennial holiness of the LORD is *mentioned* is in the story of the Ark on its way back from the Philistines. This whole story illustrates the *terrors* of the numinous—when these fall upon Bethshemesh, its men say, 'Who is able to stand before the LORD, this holy God?' (1 S 6^{20}). The phrase '(The LORD) is a holy god' has another early example (Jos 24^{19}), but the phrase 'the holy LORD' never occurs, for some adjectives can be taken for granted. The concept emerges once in Amos (4^2) and once in Jeremiah (23^9), but Isaiah is the first of the three great Prophets of Holiness. Even in Kings the phrase 'the Holy One of Israel' occurs on his lips (2 K 19^{22}), and it is found fourteen times in Is 1–33. The primary passage is in the story of the Prophet's Call (Ch. 6). Here the threefold peal of the word 'holy' provokes Isaiah's sense of his own 'iniquity' and 'sin'. Now for the first time there appears quite clearly the idea that God's holiness *demands right-eousness* in His worshippers. This is the *differentia* of Israel. In the sequel Isaiah learns that the mass of Israel will persist in its sin but that there is a 'holy seed' or godly Remnant which *ex hypothesi* is righteous. The same ideas occur in Is 1. The people have 'despised the Holy One of Israel', even while they 'trample (his) courts', for their 'hands' are filthy with sin, yet there is 'a very small remnant'. Wherever the phrase 'Holy One of Israel' occurs in this Prophet there is in the context either a condemnation of sin (e.g. 5²⁴, 10¹⁷, 30¹¹ᶠ.) or, more often, a promise of the blessedness of righteousness (e.g. 5¹⁶, 10²⁰, 17⁷, 29¹⁹). It is not necessary here to ask whether any Prophet wholly repudiated ritual, but it is not easy to believe that Isaiah, who led Judah in the defiance of Sennacherib when he threatened the city and Temple of 'the Holy One of Israel' (2K19²²), and whose own Call came upon him in the Temple, repudiated its worship. It is more likely that he and the 'holy seed' frequented its courts. None the less Isaiah's message is 'God the Holy One is hallowed in righteousness' (5¹⁶). He does not say outright that the 'holiness of God', which was numinous indeed for him (4¹⁻⁴), included God's righteousness but this is implied.

While the phrase 'The Holy One of Israel' occurs occasionally in other Prophets (Jer 1²⁹, 51⁵; Ezk 39⁷; Hab 1¹², 3³), its second great exponent is Deutero-Isaiah. He uses the phrase thirteen times (and Trito-Isaiah twice—60⁹, ¹⁴). The dominant idea here is that 'the Holy One' will 'redeem' or 'save' those who had been faithful to Him in Babylon (41¹⁴, 43³, ¹⁴, 47⁴, 48¹⁷, 49⁷, 54⁷). It is not so much stated as assumed that they had been faithful. But, apart from the keeping of the Sabbath, they could not be faithful *to ritual* in Babylon for their one shrine was far away. The implication is that they had been faithful because they had been righteous, as Trito-Isaiah practically declares (57¹⁵⁻²¹), adding that they are to return to their beloved Temple (60⁹, ¹⁴). The passages where appeal is made to God in his 'holy habitation' in 'heaven' may be added here (Dt 26¹⁵; Is 63¹⁵; Ps 20⁶; cf. 2 Ch 30²⁷). Under this phrase the numinous blazes out again. In the context of one of these passages there falls one of the two passages where the phrase 'holy spirit' occurs (Is 63¹⁰ᶠ.). In it God's 'holy spirit' is the power of the great Shepherd to save even in the Wilderness. Israel, however, had later 'grieved' the holy Spirit—that is, once more holiness, which demands righteousness, is set over against sin (cf. Is 48¹⁶⁻¹⁸).

With the significant phrase 'the Holy One' there go two others. The first of these is 'My (or Thy) holy Name'. Probably this phrase always refers to the Name 'Jahweh' (cf. Ex 6³, ⁷). It seems to be agreed now that, at any rate for Israel, the fundamental meaning of this name is 'the Active One', the 'Name' being the revelation of God in what He *does*. 'Holy Name', therefore, denotes that what He does shows that He is holy. The phrase is found in Amos (2⁷), but it is first frequent in Ezekiel, the third Prophet of Holiness, who uses it nine times. He has, for instance, a passage where he denounces the 'profanity' (*chll*) of the contemporary *cultus* of the Temple (20²⁷⁻⁴⁴), the 'profane' being in every god's *cultus* the contrary of 'the holy'. One phrase, 'Ye profane my holy Name' (v. 39), summarizes the oracle. The context dwells on ritual, but it would be easy to draw false deductions from this. In Jerusalem in Ezekiel's day people were apostates both in ritual and ethics, and inextricably so. The Prophet condemns their life as one loathsome whole. But his account of the righteous man is mainly ethical (18⁵⁻⁹), and in a passage where the LORD declares that He will 'hallow (his) great Name' for its own sake, the 'hallowing' is to be by the cleansing of Israel from all her 'iniquities' 'through the Spirit' (36²²ᶠ·, ²⁵⁻⁷, ³³). For Ezekiel ethics and ritual are indissoluble, as they should be. As much of his book insists, there cannot be a new and true Temple until there is a righteous people. Of the two instances of 'holy name' in Leviticus one is a compendium of the doctrine of holiness (22³²); the other occurs in a passage that denounces the sacrifice of boys to Molech (20³) and illustrates the blending of ritual and ethics. The phrase is found eight times in Psalms. In some the ethical idea predominates as the use of 'righteous' in the context shows (33¹, ²¹, 103¹, ⁶, 145¹⁷, ²¹); others celebrate the LORD's past deliverances of Israel and pray for another deliverance (105¹⁻³, 106⁴⁷; 1 Ch 16¹⁰, ³⁵); one psalm unites the two ideas (111³, ⁹). Every Psalmist would believe that the holy LORD is righteous.

The third significant phrase is the Levitical command: 'Ye shall be holy, for I the LORD thy God am holy.' This occurs characteristically both in passages about the ritual of food (Lv 11⁴⁴ᶠ·, 20²⁶), in a passage that describes the ethics of daily life and ends with the command, 'Thou shalt love thy neighbour as thyself' (19²⁻¹⁸, where verses 5–8 are a later intrusion), and in a passage that requires both certain ritual practices and a

certain ethical distinction in a priest (21¹⁻⁸; cf. Mal 1¹¹). A
Psalm whose refrain is 'Holy is he', celebrates 'righteousness in
Jacob' (99⁴; cf. 22³, ³¹). The idea is present, though the full
phrase is not used, in Psalms of God's might (30⁴, 47¹, 60⁶, 89³⁵,
108⁷; 1 S 2²). Behind them all there is a concept that is expressed
in one—'Be glad in the LORD, ye righteous' (Ps 97¹²).

It will have been noticed that this examination of the doctrine
of the Holiness of God issues in that of the holiness of man. Here
the primary use is of the *people* Israel, and not of individual men.
One particular people is to be holy because the LORD has chosen
her to be His. This idea underlies every text where the Law,
both in early and late codes, mentions the holiness of *Israel*
(Ex 19⁶ E, 22³¹ E; Lv 11⁴⁴ᶠ·, 19², 20⁷; Nu 15⁴⁰, 16³; Dt 7⁶, 14², ²¹,
26¹⁹, 28⁹). One text enunciates the constant idea—'Ye shall be
holy unto me, for I the LORD thy God am holy, and have *separated*
you from the peoples that ye should be mine' (Lv 20²⁶).

While the term *qadosh* occurs in one passage in Genesis, as will
appear below, the earliest text that relates Israel to God is in
Exodus: 'Ye shall be unto me a kingdom of priests and a *holy
nation*' (Ex 19⁶ E). Here separateness, and not awesomeness, is
the notion, for there was nothing numinous about Israel. She is
separate because God has chosen her to do His will as declared in
His 'covenant' and 'words'. Primarily her distinction, which
began in the Wilderness, is not that she dwells in a separate land
but that she follows, or ought to follow, a separate and distinctive
way of life, which God lays down for her. The text quoted occurs
in the story of the awesome theophany of Sinai, and the whole
passage (19⁵⁻²⁵) illustrates the paradox that only God is holy and
yet that, as God is manifesting Himself to Israel, she must be holy
too. But, while He is numinous and therefore separate *per se*, she
is derivatively separate and separate *unto Him*.

This passage has for its prelude, 'If ye will obey my voice', and
Deuteronomy expands the phrase (26¹⁶⁻¹⁹). These passages
imply, not only that Israel's holiness is contingent upon her
obedience to the Law, but also that she is only too likely not to
obey. This concept lies behind *all* the passages quoted. Since
disobedience is sin, to fail to keep any command, whether ritual
or ethical, is sinful. As already seen, in all the law-codes, ritual
commands and ethical go inextricably together, describing a given
way-of-life taken as a whole. It must not be forgotten that,
particularly in Deuteronomy, but also in Leviticus, there is an

ethical element—undifferentiated, indeed, but present. There can be little doubt that from Israel's nomadic days onward, there were always faithful Israelites, who followed a way of life that was distinctive among 'the nations' and was not only different in ritual observance but higher in moral level. But it is also, of course, certain that a great part of Israel quickly deviated from this distinctive way-of-life, both in ritual and behaviour. Jeremiah expresses this by saying that in the Desert Israel had been 'Holiness unto the LORD', but never afterwards (2³; cf. Is 63¹⁸). In one of the two other texts where he uses the term, God's 'holy words' are set over against sin in the true ethical sense (23⁹⁻¹⁴), and in the other he foretells that Jerusalem shall one day be 'a habitation of *righteousness*, a mountain of *holiness*' (31²³). This means, not so much that righteousness and holiness are synonyms, as that righteousness is an ingredient, and the dominant ingredient, in the holiness of the people of the LORD. This idea had been anticipated by Isaiah. For him the future Israel was to grow out of a present little 'holy seed' (6¹³; cf. Ezr 9²), a righteous remnant that shall be 'left in Zion' and for whom the LORD will renew the ritual of His 'glory' (4³⁻⁶). In other words, only the righteous can be 'holy'. This idea recurs in later passages in the present Book of Isaiah. It is the 'clean' in the ethical sense of the word that are alone to take 'the way of holiness' to Zion (35⁸), yet they are to 'come to Zion'—that is, to the place of right ritual (cf. 62¹¹ᶠ·). In Apocalyptic—one of whose postulates is that Israel is now righteous—a 'holy people' (Dn 12⁷) is to rule the nations and the 'bells of the horses' and the 'pots of the LORD's house' are to be 'holy' (Zec 14 ²⁰ᶠ·). While the doctrine of the 'holiness' of Israel described at first a distinctive way-of-life in which ritual and ethics were blent indistinguishably, at the last it denoted a way-of-life where the two were still blent but in which ethics were the essential and paramount element.

But the terms 'holy' and 'hallow' (or 'sanctify') are often closely related to a certain class of men, the *priests* (and with them the Levites). In an early story they are mentioned as those who usually 'come near unto the LORD' (Ex 19²²), and from first to last priests go with 'sanctuaries', that is, they are ministers of the *cultus*. At first they do not all belong to given families (e.g. Jg 17⁵; 2 Sam 8¹⁸), but there was probably an early tendency this way (e.g. Jg 18³⁰; 1 S 1³), and ultimately only sons of Aaron, 'the holy one of the LORD' (Ps 106¹⁶), were priests, even though they were not *born* priests but had to be 'hallowed' (Lv 8). Sooner or later, again, the rule ran 'no priest, no sacrifice'. They were the agents of the *cultus* who drew nearer to God than any other men. The whole Temple was planned according to this idea. The priests mediated holiness. In early days there was therefore something numinous about a priest (1 S 22^{17}) and it is possible that the idea was permanent. None the less, here too it is likely that separation came to be the dominant idea. There are perhaps some faint signs that a priest and his family must reach a certain ethical standard (Lv 10^9, 21$^{6-9}$), but this is not the primary concept. The priest was a holy man because he was agent of the holy *cultus*. It is no accident that the three great priests who appear at crises in the story of Israel—Jehoiada, Hilkiah, and Jeshua—are all vindicators of the right worship of the LORD in the Temple. Similarly, in the passages where it is asserted that priests (and Levites) are holy, the context relates them to the *cultus* (Ex 28^{36}; Lv 21^6; Nu 16$^{5,\ 7}$; 2 Ch 35^3; Ezr 8^{28}). But this is not all. First, there was a point in Canaanitish worship where *cultus* and ethics coalesced and where pre-Exilic Israel was prone to follow the Canaanites. There were sacred harlots and sacred Sodomites, the name for such a one being 'a holy woman' or 'a holy man'! The woman appears in the story of Judah among the Canaanites (Gn 38$^{21f.}$). Hosea uses the term and denounces the practice (4^{14}) as though it were of course un-Hebrew (cf. 1 K 14^{24}, 15^2, etc.). Deuteronomy prohibits it (23^{18}; cf. Job 36^{14}), and Deuteronomy was the law as declared *through priests*. This leads to a wider issue. It is fairly well agreed now that the earliest law-codes were collected at holy places such as Shechem and Hebron and that priests were their exponents. Deuteronomy, in turn, was the *Temple* code, as was the Levitical law. The priests were not mere sacrificers but teachers of the law, and (apart from Ex 34 $^{10-26}$) in all the codes, though in varying degrees, there are many ethical commands as well as ritual ones. The two were entangled in the laws because they were undifferentiated in life, but the priests did teach ethics. The Decalogue was sooner or later paramount in *their* teaching and six of the Ten Words are ethical. The passage (Lv 19$^{2-18}$) that begins with the text, 'Ye shall be holy, for I the LORD your God am holy' culminates in the command: 'Thou shalt love thy neighbour as thyself.' Indeed, since verses 5–8 are an intrusion from a later source, the whole passage shows how the principles of the Six Words were being

applied in daily life. There was an ethical element in the concept
of the Holiness of God and therefore in the priests' message.

There were other specially 'holy' men besides priests. Warriors
were hallowed before going to battle (e.g. Jer 6[4]; Joel 3[9]), and
Nazirites were 'holy' (Nu 6[5, 8]). But there was another kind of
'holy' man, whom God chose to be holy—not, as with priests,
because they belonged to a certain family—but individually.
These were the 'prophets'. In one passage this is asserted (2 K
4[9]), but the phrase 'holy prophet' no more occurs than 'holy
LORD' or 'holy priest', for it is taken for granted that a 'prophet'
is 'holy'. Prophets appear early and late in connexion with holy
places (1 S 10[5, 13]; Mal 1[7]), and there are few in the long list of
whom this is not in some way true. Probably the earliest token
of their 'holiness' was a numinous ecstasy. This kind of evidence
attended at least some of the great Prophets. Such phenomena
were put down to 'the spirit of the LORD' (e.g. 1 S 10[6]), which,
again, was of *course* 'holy', for it was the '*ruach* of *the LORD*'. This
explains why the phrase 'holy spirit' is so rare in the Old Testament. There was no need for the adjective. The Ark, similarly,
is only once *called* 'holy' (2 Ch 35[3]). The pivotal change made by
certain of the great Prophets in the analysis of 'holiness' has
already been described. It was not, however, that they were the
first to draw a line between ethics and ritual in the Hebrew
way-of-life. The people practised the differentiation without
defining it when they kept holi-day at shrines but neglected such
things as the last Six Commandments (e.g. Is 1). Ritual was
pleasant, but ethics were irksome! It was in answer to this challenge that the Prophets asserted that 'righteousness' is paramount
with God. It was, however, under this word, rather than under
'holiness', that they waged their war. It is probable that they
preferred it because in the minds of their hearers the *term* 'holiness'
inevitably suggested ritual.

After the Exile this was certainly so. This appears in various
ways. As already noted, *qadosh* and its cognates are used very
predominantly of the holiness of *things*, and it is chiefly in the
post-Exilic documents that the terms occur in this way. Next, of
holy *men*, the priest survived the prophet and the High Priest
became the representative and to some degree the ruler of Israel.
The holy Temple was the *palladium* of Israel once more and to it
the faithful came not only from Palestine, but, as time went on,
from every part of the Dispersion. Whenever they gathered either

for feast or fast, it was the priests, headed by the High Priest, in whom everything centred. No priest, no sacrifice! No priest, no one in the Holy Place! No High Priest, none ever in the Holy of Holies! The priest, therefore, was *ipso facto* ritually 'holy'. But there was no guarantee that he would be righteous. Malachi bears witness that one of the reasons why the Palestinian Jews neglected the worship of the Temple was that the priests neither taught nor practised the Law and had ceased to 'turn men away from iniquity' (Mal 2¹⁻⁹). While there is evidence that there were good priests (Ps 132⁹, ¹⁶), there was no guarantee that priests would be righteous.

As in earlier times, so after the Exile, *qadosh* is rarely used to describe *men*, but under the implication that priests are 'holy' the idea would be wholly, or almost wholly, ritual, as probably it had always been with most of the people. Now, however, as Malachi shows, there were laymen who stood out as those who 'feared the LORD' (3¹⁶). To judge by the tenor of his whole book, they would keep the *whole* law and would be distinguished both by the high ethical standard of their lives and by the constancy of their sincere worship in the Temple (e.g. 1¹⁴, 3¹⁸). There is a distinctive name for this class of men, but it is not 'the saints' or 'holy ones'.² For them the recurrent and distinctive word here is *chāsīd* (usually rendered 'saint'). A *chasid* was a man who responded aright to the favour or grace of God (*chĕsĕd*). To discuss this term belongs to another book, but the plural, *chasidim*, is used fifteen times in the Psalms to describe the class now in question (and also in 1 S 2⁹; Pr 2⁸). In some cases the context shows that they were righteous (e.g. Ps 31²³, 37²⁸), but in others it shows too that these righteous men rejoiced in the Temple ritual (e.g. 50⁵, 79², 149¹, ⁵, ⁹). The immediate point is that the distinctive name for them is not *qadosh*. The evidence shows that between the Exile and the Maccabean outbreak the term 'holy'— except when it is used of God, whose 'holiness' was at once numinous, righteous, and separate—normally denoted ritual separateness. It was in this sense that men and things were holy. In other words the Temple dominated the term. It is true that two Psalms in particular (15, 24¹⁻⁶) show that there were those who believed that only the righteous were fit 'to stand' in God's 'holy place' and 'dwell' in His 'holy hill', and that a third, at

---

² This phrase is used of the angels (Ps 89⁵, ⁷; Job 5¹; Zec 14⁵; Dn 8¹³), but only twice of men (Ps 16³, 34⁹).

least as it stands in the final Psalter, teaches uniquely that only by the power of God's 'holy spirit' could any man be fitted to offer 'the sacrifices of righteousness' (51[11, 19]), but even here the term *qadosh* is not applied to *men*.[3] In spite of the teaching of three great Prophets, the concepts of holiness and righteousness did not *inevitably* imply each other in normal Jewish thought about man. But in the long run it is the Prophets who count.

The idea of 'purity' goes with that of 'holiness'. It describes it in its negative aspect, for 'impurity' or 'uncleanness' is abhorrent to the 'holy'. Of the nine Hebrew roots rendered by 'clean' or 'pure' the two most frequent are *thr* (*200*) and *brr* (*30*). The first is common in a ritual sense (e.g. in the phrase 'pure gold' in Ex 25[11], etc.), but rare in a moral one. Yet this word too may be used both of God and man—e.g. 'Thou art of purer eyes than to behold evil' (Hab 1[13]); 'The words of the LORD are pure words' (Ps. 12[6]); 'Shall a man be more pure (or, pure before) his maker?' (Job 4[16]); 'The pure speak pleasant words' (Pr 15[26]). Words from the second root, *brr*, which is not so frequent with a ritual meaning, occur in: 'With the pure thou wilt show thyself pure' (Ps 18[26]); 'The commandment of the LORD is pure' (Ps 19[8]); 'He that hath innocent hands and a pure heart' (Ps 24[4]); 'A pure lip' (Zeph 3[9]). God is pure and man ought to be.

In the later Old Testament literature there is another noun which is used both of God and the right kind of man—'wisdom' (*chŏkmāh*). Here it is best to begin with the use of this word and of its adjective 'wise' (*chākām*) to describe men and women. Their uses are very wide. For instance, one or other of them is used of a woman who 'knew her way about' in a story of a besieged city (2 S 20[22]; cf. Ec 9[13]), of a king who could 'see round a corner' (1 K 2[6]), of the '*nous*' of a man who 'built a house' (i.e. established the prosperity of a family—Pr 24[3]), of the skill of a spinner of goats' hair or of a craftsman in many crafts (Ex 35[26, 35]), of a true leader (Dt 34[9]), and of the right kind of statesman and king (Gn 41[39]; 1 K 3[12]). Nearly all the sayings collected in the Book of Proverbs are maxims of the peasant proprietors who were always the backbone of Israel, and describe the art of living

---

[3] In its Aramaic form (*13*) it occurs in two chapters of Daniel—in the fourth of 'the holy gods' and the angels (e.g. v. 8 and 13), and in the seventh of 'the holy ones of the Most High' (v. 18–27). It would be possible to take the last to be angels who fight for Israel (cf. Ps 12[1]; Dt 33[2f]), but it is more likely that here the Maccabean martyrs are called 'holy ones'. These 'saints' died for the *whole* ethico-ritual Law (e.g. 1 Mac 1[57]). But this use of the term for individual *men* is the exception that proves the rule.

aright in a village. For instance, the 'wise' man knows how to hold his tongue (17$^{17f.}$), how to be busy (26^{16})—and how to use the rod to his child (29^{15})! Indeed, even where the terms 'wise' and 'wisdom' do not themselves occur, this practical kind of 'wisdom' is still the subject of Hebrew proverbs, as of the proverbs of all other nations. At the end of the book there is a full-length portrait of a 'woman of worth' (31$^{10ff.}$). The term 'wisdom' is used of her speech, but the whole description tells of the thrift and foresight and sagacity of a woman who knows how to manage a home and a homestead.

Yet amid all this variety there is unity in two ways. All the different kinds of people described as 'wise' are *doing* something. In other words, 'wisdom' is the art of life. It refers to practice, not to mere theory. It describes the character of a man who not only *knows* how to deal with 'practical affairs', but *does* deal with them in the right way. This, of course, is just an illustration of the truth that the Hebrew, unlike the Greek, was not interested in philosophy, but in action. For him, thought was nothing but the servant of practice, and his interest lay in life and so in history, not in metaphysics. More important, in the second place the Hebrew connected 'wisdom'—the art of the practice of the whole of life—with *religion*. The typical and distinctive Hebrew proverb is: 'The fear of the Lord is the beginning of wisdom' (Pr 1^7). There are many illustrations of this. For instance, the whole book of Job might be quoted, for Job's three 'comforters' set themselves up to be 'wise men' (e.g. 12^2) and their one theme is that Job *cannot* have lived the right kind of life—that is, however much he protests he cannot have been righteous in the sight of God (cf. 1^1). Indeed, amid all the contention all the disputants have one postulate in common—'Behold, the fear of the Lord, that is wisdom; And to depart from evil is understanding' (28^{28}). The same idea occurs in the Books of Psalms and Proverbs,—e.g. 'The mouth of the righteous talketh of wisdom, And his tongue speaketh justice' (Ps 37^{30}); 'Behold thou desirest truth in the inward parts; And in the hidden parts thou shalt make me to know wisdom' (Ps 51^6); 'So teach us to number our days, That we may get us an heart of wisdom' (Ps 90^{12}); 'The mouth of the righteous bringeth forth wisdom' (Pr 31^{30}); 'The fruit of the righteous is a tree of life; And he that is wise winneth souls' (i.e. 'has many children'—Pr 11^{30}). There are not a few passages in the Book of Proverbs where the terms 'wise' and 'righteous',

EBM

'wisdom and righteousness', are found in the same context. Indeed, the temper of the whole book is epitomized in the personalized appeal of 'wisdom' to men to 'choose the fear of the LORD' (Pr 1²⁰, ²⁹). It is true, of course, that among the proverbs of Israel, as of all other nations, there are some that teach a prudential selfishness—or what some call 'an enlightened self-interest'— but this only means that the Book of Proverbs is not in the New Testament, but the Old. Neither the 'law and the prophets' nor any other book in it is perfect. On the other hand, all this means that for the Hebrew life was not divided into 'sacred' and 'secular' parts. Such nineteenth-century sayings as 'I don't mix religion and business' and 'Economics have nothing to do with ethics' are altogether alien to the temper of the Old Testament. For instance, a Hebrew would have agreed with the old-fashioned people who 'ask a blessing' before such a 'secular' business as eating and drinking, or with the 'business man' who once said to the writer: 'God has called me to be a tanner.' Especially after the Exile, the Hebrew defined a true *man* as a 'wise' man.

In the Old Testament the adjective 'wise' (*chakam*) is only used twice to describe God (Is 31²; Job 9⁴), but, especially after the Exile, the noun 'wisdom' (*chokmah*) frequently describes His character. There are examples in such texts as 'He hath established the world by wisdom' (Jer 10¹²); 'O Lord how manifold are Thy works! In wisdom hast thou made them all: The earth is full of thy riches' (Ps 104²⁴); and 'Blessed be the name of God for ever and ever: for wisdom and might are his' (Dn 2²⁰). A climax is reached in the '*Wisdom* Literature'. For instance, there is a passage in Job which, after describing the strange ways in which a miner pries into the hidden places of the earth, asks 'But where shall wisdom be found?'—and replies that 'man knoweth not' either its place or its price, for only God 'understandeth the way thereof', and it is He who 'saith unto man, Behold, the fear of the LORD, that is wisdom, And to depart from evil is understanding' (Job 28). It will be seen that here, as in the first two of the previous texts, an appeal is made to God's ways *in nature* in order to describe what 'wisdom' is. The sudden reference to 'evil' in the last verse may surprise a modern reader, for he thinks that nature has nothing to do with ethics. The same apparent *non sequitur* recurs when at last 'the LORD answered Job out of the whirlwind' (Job 38¹). Through four magnificent chapters God challenges the man who has arraigned Him from his dung-hill, with the wonders of His creation. In other words, just as the Hebrew made no distinction between the ethical and the non-ethical when he spoke of *man's* wisdom, so he made no distinction when he spoke of *God's*. For him, as for all theists, the word and idea expressed by the term 'secular' cannot be applied to anything that *God* does—nor to anything that the right kind of man does. It is not true, as some have said, that the Book of Job gives no help with the problem, 'Why do the righteous suffer?' Here for the first time the Jew gave the answer: 'There are many things in creation that I cannot understand—yet when I look at God's universe, I see past contradiction that He is wise. So too, when I look at Job on his dung-hill, there is something that I cannot understand, yet here too the God of creation *must* be wise (and wisdom includes righteousness).'

The Hebrew account of 'wisdom' culminates in the eighth chapter of Proverbs. This is one of the passages where 'wisdom' is said to be 'personalized'. Perhaps, instead of using this modern word, it is better to take this use as an extension of the idea under which various parts of the body—as the hand, or the eye, or the heart—appear as acting for themselves. Not only 'wisdom' but also such qualities as 'goodness', 'mercy', and 'truth', sometimes seem themselves to be alive (e.g. Ps 23[6], 85[10]). The closest parallel is with 'word' (e.g. Ps 107[20], 147[15]). In any case in the passage in question 'wisdom' 'cries' unto men wherever they gather (Pr 8[1-4]). She offers them herself. Four reasons are given. First, there is a series of verses where the righteousness and value of wisdom are blent (v. 5–21); then, at the close of the chapter, men are told that with wisdom lies the secret of life and death (v. 32–6); third, between these two passages there is a description of creation (v. 22–31)—'Seek me', cries 'wisdom', 'for I am worth more than rubies. Do not I teach the way of righteousness and therefore of life? See! I am God's artificer and artist in the universe!' (Here too there is no *non sequitur* for the Jew); fourth, underlying the whole passage there is the idea that, as God does nothing that is not wise, so neither should a man—that is, under the concept of 'wisdom', as under others, man is called to be like God. In his own small way he is to 'do things' as God does them —and this by the gift of God. 'Unto you, O man, I call; And my voice is to the sons of men' (v. 4).

In the previous chapter it was noted that every man has some 'dominion over the works of (God's) hands'. How will the right kind of man *use* this control? The story of creation in Genesis suggests the answer, for in it man's likeness to God is the ground of man's delegated 'dominion'. It is for man to control animals and plants as God's delegate. The doctrine of 'wisdom' bears the same witness. It is by a 'wisdom' that is like God's that a wise man will 'drive his team afield' to plough his land (Pr 20[4]); by it he will buy and sell (11[26]); by it he will know how to deal with a 'ruler' and will flee from drunkenness (23[1, 29ff.]), and so on. The fact that the ethics of the Book of Proverbs sometimes fall below the New Testament level does not invalidate the truth that the whole *motif* of this book, as we have it, is that a 'wisdom' which in its small way is like God's, ought to guide a man in little things as in great, in 'secular' things as in 'sacred'. 'Wisdom' is nothing less than the guide of the whole of life. A certain doctrine of man's freedom is implicit here. The Hebrew had his own account of 'liberty, equality, and fraternity'. For him all Hebrews were 'brothers', for they were all in covenant with the LORD (e.g. Dt 15[1-18])—all men were equal in the sense that all were made 'in the image of God'—and all men had a limited freedom, for all did what they would in some degree with the 'works of (God's) hands'. All three concepts rooted in religion.

It will now be clear that the Old Testament doctrine that the true kind of man is like God does not depend upon a verse or two in the first chapter of Genesis (v. 26 ff.), however that may be interpreted. It has a far broader basis. A man is called to be righteous, holy, and wise, after the fashion in which God is righteous, holy, and wise. It is true, of course, that he can only be like him as a drop of water is like the ocean—yet there is a true likeness.

There is another pertinent term, 'glory'. While this word too is used both of God and man, the relation between the two uses is not quite the same as with righteousness, holiness, and wisdom. In the English Old Testament at least nine Hebrew words are rendered 'glory' or 'glorify', but here only one, *kābōd*, is considered. The literal meaning of the word is 'weight'. English uses a metaphor like the Hebrew one in the phrase 'a man of weight' (cf. Latin *gravis*). Another English phrase 'a man of worth' expresses the same idea, not in the degenerate sense by which we say that a man is 'worth a million' of money, but in the sense that he has 'value' for others. Here the idea of 'reputation' is not absent, but only of a reputation that corresponds to character.

A man's 'glory' expresses what a man *seems* like if and when it expresses what he *is* like. Job, for instance, speaks of the reputation which had rightly been his in the days of his prosperity but of which God had 'stripped' him (Job 29²⁰, 19⁹; cf. Ps 30¹¹ᶠᶠ·). 'Glory' denotes the manifestation or expression of character in life. Joseph's 'glory in Egypt' was not mere power, but a power based on his reliability and wisdom, and these in turn on 'the spirit of God' in him (Gn 45¹³, 41³⁸ᶠ·). When used of man, *kabod* is the outward manifestation and accompaniment of true character.

The word is used more often of God than of man. Here it has three main uses and it is only in the third that its use about men is at all parallel. First, 'the glory of the LORD' is a phrase that occurs throughout the Old Testament to describe the physical splendour of God (e.g. Ex 33¹⁸ ᴊ; Dt 5²⁴; 1 K 8¹¹; Is 6³; Ps 19¹; Ex 24¹⁶ ᴘ). It was numinous and expounds what holiness originally meant. There is a great example in the Book of Ezekiel, where the term only occurs once of man's 'glory' (31¹⁸), but eighteen times of the LORD's. Under the meaning 'physical splendour' the 'glory' of man, of course, is not like the 'glory' of God. Under the second main use the word is used of the 'mighty acts' of the LORD—not least of His deliverances of Israel from Egypt and Babylon (e.g. 1 Ch 16²⁴; Is 40⁵). This use, too, is of course confined to God. The third use is perhaps only an instance of the second. It appears in the story of Isaiah's Vision (Is 6³), where the phrase 'The fullness of the whole earth is his glory' relates 'glory' to the universe of God's *creation*. This idea recurs in later writings—for instance, in the 'Psalm of the Seven Thunders' (29) and, notably, in the 'Psalm of Creation' (104³¹). Here the phrase 'Let the LORD rejoice in his works' echoes an earlier verse, 'O LORD how manifold are Thy works. In wisdom hast Thou made them all: The earth is full of Thy property' (v. 24). The Hebrew knew that a thing is most of all anyone's property when he has made it. There is no like way to 'acquire' it (*qinyān*). In other words, God's wealth in the universe is an element in His 'glory' (v. 31). His 'glory' is the outward expression of His character.

There are passages where a *man's* wealth is said to be his 'glory' (e.g. Gn 31¹; Ps 49¹⁶ᶠ·). With these there may be taken the use of the phrase 'mighty man of worth' to describe such a man as Boaz (Ru 2¹), for 'worth' is probably the best rendering of the

Hebrew word (*chayil*). It is by no means to be confined to 'valour' in its military sense. Indeed, the English word 'valour', like 'value', is derived from a Latin root that denotes both 'health' and 'worth'. As already seen, the last chapter of Proverbs describes 'the woman of worth'. A true man's wealth manifested his 'glory'. In a Hebrew village—and in the peace of the Persian period, with which we are now chiefly concerned, the typical Hebrew was a villager—a family throve by the right use of its 'inheritance', counted as the gift of God, and its wealth was the proper outcome of its use of its land. It was here that a man exercised control over 'the works of (God's) hands', and so was 'crowned with *glory and honour*' (Ps 85ff.). A true man's diminutive 'glory' was manifested in his possessions and their enjoyment, even as God's 'glory' shone out in His magnificent enjoyment of His universe (e.g. Pr 830f.). Similarly, they that love Jerusalem are one day to 'rejoice' because they with her are to inherit the wealth and 'glory of the nations' (Is 6610ff.). To a true man 'the LORD will give grace and glory' (Ps 8411, cf. 42). On the other hand, when He smites a land with suffering and poverty He 'changes (its) glory into shame' (Hos 47; cf. Hab 216). A true man's 'glory', even when it means welfare and wealth, comes from God. It is the tiny human counterpart of God's own 'riches'.

Yet prosperity, let alone money, is not *per se* a man's 'glory'. Wicked men may think it so, but God will undeceive them (Is 103; cf. Ps 4916ff.). 'Glory will dwell in the land' only when 'mercy and truth are met together' and 'righteousness and peace have kissed each other' (Ps 859ff.). It is the 'saints' who are to 'exult in glory' (Ps 1495), the 'wise' are to 'inherit' it (Pr 335), it is for '(God's) glory' that He has 'created' man (Is 437), when the wrongs of the wicked rich are done away, 'the earth shall be filled with the knowledge of the glory of God' (Hab 214), and so on. It is at this ethical point, as might have been expected, that the idea of the 'glory' of God is distinctively Hebrew. For the Prophets the 'glory of God', as need hardly be said, is not primarily a fiery smoke but an overwhelming righteousness (e.g. Jer 1316; Mal 22). The ninety-sixth Psalm is just a triumphant exposition of this one idea, and with Ezekiel, the 'glory of the LORD' which had forsaken the wicked city where it used to dwell could only return to Jerusalem when she had been cleansed from her iniquity (Ezk 1, 9, 10, 431-9). It is here that the 'glory' of God and man come nearest to being identified. The climax is reached when the LORD Himself is called 'the glory' both of Israel and of a true Israelite (Mic 1¹⁵; Jer 2¹¹; Ps 3³, 106²⁰). Possessions, whether God's or man's, are only the furnishings of righteousness. The twenty-first Psalm is just a description of the glad 'glory' of a man, this time a king, who 'trusteth in the LORD'. In the Old Testament the meaning of the term 'glory' varies with the context, yet it has a characteristic use. When the word is used of a man, this involves God, the man himself, and his neighbours. When God gives a man the ample opportunities of wealth—when the man uses them aright—and when his neighbours recognize his worth—this was his 'glory'. The term 'horn' is a symbolic synonym for it, especially as over against enemies. Psalm 112, for instance, describing the man 'that feareth the LORD' declares that 'his horn shall be exalted in glory' (v. 1, 9). Again, the phrase 'the light of Thy countenance' describes the 'glory of the LORD' when the latter is thought of as displaying the favour of God, and the term 'light', occurring alone, often unites the ideas of God's splendour and His 'truth' or 'righteousness'—i.e. His character—just as 'glory' does. Any concordance will show that, as with 'glory', the meaning of 'light' hovers, in Hebrew fashion, between the literal and the symbolical. Under both uses the idea that light *guides* is probably always present. The two terms occur together, for instance, in the text: 'Arise, shine; for thy light is come, and the glory of the LORD is risen upon thee' (Is 60¹⁻³; cf. 9¹ᶠ·). 'Light' is sometimes used of man as well as of God, though less often—for instance, in the text: 'The path of the righteous is as the light of dawn, That shineth more and more unto the perfect day' (Pr 4¹⁸). So in Deutero-Isaiah the Servant is 'called in righteousness . . . for a light to the Gentiles' (Is 42⁶). Sometimes the term is closely connected with joy—as in 'Light is sown for the righteous, And gladness for the upright in heart' (Ps 97¹¹; cf. 30¹²). Yet there is no pride in the gladness of man's glory, for it is not his own achievement but God's gift. For instance, the 'light' and 'brightness' of the Zion that is to spring from the 'glory of the LORD' that is 'seen upon' her (Is 60¹⁻³; cf. 58⁸, 60¹⁹ᶠ·), and the glory of a true man, described, as we have seen, in Psalm 112, both derive from the 'light' of God (v. 4; cf. Nu 6²⁴⁻⁷). To use a later phrase, for the Hebrew there was some tinge of *spiritual* splendour in the character of a true man, but it was 'not his own'. On the other hand, under the word 'light' it is once again implied that he is not without *some* resemblance to God.

The mention of 'joy' shows that the representative Hebrew believed that God would see to it that the right kind of man was a happy man. His word for 'happy', however, is properly rendered 'blessed', for its root idea is that the happy man is the man who 'goes straight forward' (*'āshar*) *in the ways of God*. The first Psalm describes him, as its first words show, but it only epitomizes the declarations of the Prophets and Deuteronomists. There were, of course, many exceptions to the rule that in 'whatsoever' such a man 'doeth he shall prosper' (Ps 1³, RVm), and this led to the one problem that deeply troubled the Hebrew mind, 'Why does any righteous man suffer?'—which produced a whole literature. To pursue this problem would be out of place here, but no adequate answer was found. Yet the belief that prosperity normally goes with righteousness was never abandoned, problem or no problem. Indeed, there was much evidence on the other side. The majority of Hebrews were always villagers, and in village life, provided there were peace, it was true that hardworking, frugal, righteous families would prosper, and that lazy, spendthrift, and vicious families would suffer and die out. This brings us back to the concept of the 'wise' man as the Hebrew understood 'wisdom'. It also brings us again to the Hebrew doctrine of wealth. Neither in the Old Testament nor in any other literature is there any praise for the man who merely seeks or merely possesses riches. On the other hand the Hebrew believed that by the blessing of God, Abraham, the typical Hebrew, was a rich man, and that God gave man 'dominion' that man might enjoy the wealth of the earth. This is man's 'glory' (Ps 8⁵ᶠ·). Here the word 'wealth' is used in its true sense— i.e. 'weal', and 'goods' are the tools and furnishings of a happy life. Without them a man could not be *all* that a true man ought to be. Even when the term 'glory' is used of things it describes them as the furnishings of men's 'glory' (e.g. Is 60¹³; Est 5¹¹).

It is plain from the several terms just examined that under the concept of righteousness, with its many constitutents, *all* men are not like God, but only the right kind of man. It is clear too that it is here that the idea of what is now called 'moral and spiritual likeness' appears. Under this idea, according to the Old Testament, *only good* men are like God. Again, it is clear that under the doctrine of righteousness a doctrine of freedom is presupposed. A man can be righteous or sinful, holy or profane, pure or impure, even wise or foolish in the Hebrew sense, as he chooses. At this point the distinction between men and animals appears. In the Old Testament, animals, within limits, are free—but they don't make *moral* choice. As we have seen, the Hebrews did not use the phrase 'the image of God' to denote the way in which good men, and good men only, are like God. It was in the doctrine of right-eousness that the concept 'spiritual and moral likeness', later denoted by this phrase, has its root. A good man is like God because he is good. His small freedom, even, is like God's, for he uses it as God uses His. For the ample use of this small freedom he needs possessions. When he uses them as God uses the universe, he has a 'glory' which is in a minute way like God's 'glory' in His ways with His creation. To use the modern word, the good man, and only the good man, is a 'person' in the Old Testament; in his infinitesimal fashion he is like the one perfect person, God. As will appear later, in the Apocrypha this appears in the doctrine that a good man is a 'son' or 'child' of God. There are some partial anticipations of this concept in the Old Testament, but these are best taken with the books where the phrase is clearly used.

There is no doubt that to complete the *final* Jewish account of the right kind of man another idea must be added—he will be a man who keeps the whole of the Law of the LORD, *ritual* as well as ethical. It was not for nothing that the priesthood dominated Israel more and more in the three centuries after the Return, or that they then codified Hebrew ritual in its final form. Ritual teaches that it is for man to worship and for God to bless, and this is a very great doctrine. Yet it is but part of a greater—that man is altogether dependent upon God and that it is man's funda-mental duty, therefore, to obey God in the whole of life and not only when he is on his knees. As has been shown, this doctrine is fundamental, for instance, in the Hebrew accounts of righteous-ness and holiness and wisdom. For the rest, whatever the history of the Hebrew *cultus* really was, *in the documents* it is based on the LORD's *unexplained* fiat. The only exception is in the phrase, 'For the life of all flesh is the blood thereof' (Lv 17¹⁴, etc.), which *explains* why blood is not to be eaten but given to God. Elsewhere God just prescribes ritual, giving no reason for it—and it was not for the Jew to 'reason why'. Ritual is not rooted in God's char-acter, but is arbitrary. Some attempt has been made under the word 'holy' to show how effective the ritual was, at its best, but 'effective' is not the same as 'essential', or Paul laboured in vain.

Yet, to do justice to the Priests, it was during the period of their sway in Israel that the Prophets and the Psalms, with their condemnations of mere ritual, were included in the Canon.

Yet the Jews, even though they put the Book of Jonah into the Canon, did not draw another conclusion that the doctrine of the Prophets demanded. It is clear that there is no intrinsic reason why a Gentile, as much as a Jew, should not seek to practise righteousness and wisdom and holiness as defined above, nor any reason why he should not exercise 'dominion' as faithfully as a Jew, nor any why he should not share in a man's proper 'glory'. In other words, the Old Testament answer to the question 'What ought a man to be?' is just as intrinsically universal as his answer to the question 'What is a man?' The Rabbis, in effect, agreed so far—but they added: 'The right kind of man must also observe a specific ritual, beginning with circumcision.' To use a homely metaphor, they wanted to keep the chicken for ever in the shell. It was, of course, impossible for every Gentile—or for *every* Jew— to keep the *whole* of the ritual law. A man who lived in Babylon could not, for instance, travel 'three times a year' to Jerusalem to keep the great Feasts. This is a well-worn theme and, apart from passing references, the particularism of Judaism will not be discussed under the New Testament.

Upon the answer to the question 'What *ought* a man to be?' another ensues: 'Were there any such men?' The 'righteous', of course, were men who on the whole 'pleased God', but this need not mean that they never sinned, as the stories of Moses and David show. A further question, therefore, emerges: 'Were there any men who were *altogether* what a man ought to be?' This leads to the two Hebrew terms rendered 'perfect'.

It is at least doubtful whether one of the terms means 'perfect'. Its root is *shlm* (*425*), which has about twenty different renderings, the most numerous being 'peace' (*200*), 'peace-offering' (*85*), and 'pay' or 'repay' (*28*). Here, however, we have only to do with the use of the root in a moral sense, and this, apart perhaps from one passage (Is 42[19]), is confined to the adjective *shālēm* (*20*). This, again, is found only in Kings and Chronicles (with Is 38[3]), and the characteristic phrase is '(This king's) heart was perfect (or, not perfect) with the LORD his God' (e.g. 1 K 15[3, 14]), the norm of kings being David (e.g. 1 K 11[4]). In the eyes of the Deuteronomists and Priestly writers, whose phrase this is, *the* question about a king was: 'Did he *worship* the LORD and the

LORD only, following the right kind of *cultus*?' It is certain that neither school of writers thought David morally perfect, for both tell the story of Uriah at length. It is true that the original meaning of the Hebrew root seems to be 'to be complete' or 'sound'—that is, 'perfect'—but this only shows how the meaning of a word may deviate from its original sense. Our word 'loyal' gives the idea. Some few kings were 'loyal', like David—and in particular, loyal to the *law* (1 K 8⁶¹)—but this need not denote perfection.

The other root is *tmm* (*130*). Its original meaning is 'to be complete'—sometimes, therefore, 'to be finished', even in the sense 'to be consumed'. It is used of animals 'without blemish' or 'spot', but its moral use is relatively rare (*20*). Here the adjective is translated by 'perfect' and the noun by 'integrity'. The use is almost confined to the Books of Job, Psalms, and Proverbs. In these there are references to a *class* of 'perfect' men. Before turning to these, two notes may be made. First, there are a few passages that refer to a real or possible 'perfection' *in a limited sphere*—e.g. in the 'dealings' of the Men of Shechem with Gideon (Jg 9¹⁶, ¹⁹) and in the realm of monolatry (Dt 18¹³). Similarly, in the Song of Songs 'Solomon' declares, as is the way of lovers, that his sweetheart is 'perfect' (5², 6⁹). Secondly, there are passages that refer to certain '*men of old time*' as 'perfect' in the whole of life. In Ezekiel there is a hint that even before the Exile tradition had distinguished three of these—Noah, Daniel, and Job (14¹⁴, ²⁰).⁴ Of the three, two are called 'perfect' in the Old Testament (Gn 6⁹; Job 1²). There is little doubt that the Jew would add Abraham (Gn 17¹). Even though it is unlikely that a post-Exilic writer would have called a *contemporary* 'perfect' if he got drunk like Noah (e.g. Pr 23²³ᶠᶠ.) or if he lied as Abraham did to Pharaoh (e.g. Pr 12¹⁷ᶠᶠ.), and even though Job did not *persist* in his 'perfection' (Job 42⁶), it seems plain that the Jews, like many other peoples, believed that 'once upon a time' there *were* some 'perfect' men.

The use of the term in the poetical books to describe a *class* of *contemporaries* is more important (e.g. Ps 37³⁷, 64⁴; Pr 2²¹, 11⁵; Job 8²⁰, 9²²). In what sense were they thought 'perfect'? Here we should recall the Hebrew belief that the good man was a man who did what God commanded, and add to this that in the latest Old Testament period the idea that 'the law' was a complete

---

⁴ This implies that the writers of two later Books, Job and Daniel, took for their heroes the names of famous men of the distant past.

guide to God's commandments was probably all but universal
among the Jews. If, then, a man 'kept the whole law' he might
be called 'perfect'. Sometimes the word is parallel to 'righteous'
and 'wise' and 'upright' and 'saint' (e.g. Pr 2⁶⁻⁹). In reading the
thirty-seventh Psalm one can hardly help taking 'the meek', 'the
righteous', 'the upright', and 'the perfect' to be four descriptions
of the same class of people (e.g. v. 11, 16 f., 18, 37). In another
Psalm (19⁷⁻¹⁴) the connexion with 'the law' is quite clear. The
writer begins with a panegyric of 'the law of the LORD', declaring
it 'perfect' in his first breath, and ending with the implication
that he himself keeps it. Next he asks for forgiveness for his
'unwitting sins',[5] and then for deliverance from the 'dominion' of
'presumptuous men' (cf. Ps 1¹). If these two prayers are answered,
he goes on: 'Then shall I be perfect; And I shall be clear from
great transgression.' Probably the last phrase means that for this
man *any* breach of the law would be a 'great transgression'.
Probably, again, the word 'meditation' in the next verse means
'meditation upon the law' (cf. Ps 1²). Already there were men,
on this showing, who 'as touching the righteousness of the law'
were 'blameless', and who might be called 'perfect'. There is
another illustration in the connexion of the word with 'way' and
'walk'. There are examples in a Psalm in which a ruler prays for
'perfection' (Ps 101). He declares that he will 'give heed unto the
perfect way', 'will walk within his house in the *integrity* of his heart',
and will choose as his ministers 'the faithful' who 'walk in a
perfect way' (cf. Ps 15²; Pr 2²¹). This use of 'walk' and 'way'
suggests 'law'. For instance, the first verse of the great Alphabet
of the Law (Ps 119) is: 'Blessed are they that are perfect of way,
Who walk in the law of the LORD'. Indeed, in this Psalm, 'way'
is just one of the many synonyms for 'law'. Similarly, it is in
Deuteronomy, a book of law, that the words occur, 'Thou shalt
be perfect with the LORD thy God' (18¹³). The ruling idea is that
the man who keeps the whole law is a perfect man. In this book,
indeed, 'To keep all the commandments' of the Law is practically
a definition of 'perfection' (e.g. 11⁸, ²², 19⁹, 27¹). The phrase
occurs almost as an account of what Christ called 'the first commandment' (6², ⁵). When the same book says expressly, 'This
commandment (i.e. the whole law) is not too hard for thee'

---

[5] The term rendered 'errors' is either a variant of the rare word for 'unwitting sin'
in Leviticus, or a mistake for it. The parallel word 'hidden' seems here to mean 'hidden from myself' (cf. Job 3²³).

(30^{11-14}), the implication is that it can be wholly kept. For completeness' sake it may be added that in the four Old Testament passages where the adjective refers to the 'perfection' *of God*, it describes His 'work' (Dt 32^4), His 'way' (Ps 18^{30}), and His 'law' (Ps 19^7).

The connexion with 'law' also appears in the use of another root, *nqh* (*95*), and its cognates. The adjective is usually translated 'innocent', but the idea is not that of the English word in such a phrase as 'an innocent child', but belongs to the law-court and its verdict 'innocent'. The verb, for instance, is sometimes rendered 'unpunished' (e.g. Jer 49^{12}; Pr 11^{21}), and the commonest use of the adjective is in the phrase 'innocent blood' (e.g. Jer 7^6; Dt $19^{10, 13}$; Ps 106^{38}), the reference being to the decisions of judges. The 'innocent' man was a man who kept the Law. There are some rare beginnings of a deeper insight (e.g. in Ps 51), but there is no doubt about the dominant doctrine of 'perfection' in Judaism. If a man kept every one of the many commandments of the Law, he was counted a 'perfect' man.

While the Hebrew was no philosopher or metaphysician, it is none the less true that if his faith be examined, it *implies* a subconscious philosophy, like all integrated human life. The Hebrew was a theist, and therefore an idealist. He was also a realist, in the sense that he believed that God and persons and things all have objective existence. Among idealists there is common agreement that at least three 'ultimates' may be distinguished—goodness, truth, and beauty. All of these are said to have ultimate 'worth' *per se*, and many have treated them as separable and equal. This is not so with the Hebrew. While for him everything of ultimate value is real in God, the fundamental value is righteousness. Everything else, even within the realm of God's character (i.e. the realm of the ultimate), is secondary to it. While the Hebrew's faith required that there is such a thing as ultimate *truth*, this was but part and parcel of righteousness as it exists in God. Again, there is evidence that he had an *æsthetic* sense—for instance, in the account of the Tabernacle and in the 'nature psalms'—but aesthetics too are subordinate to ethics. The great description of 'wisdom' at the end of the eighth chapter of Proverbs displays God's delight in creating a beautiful world and even uses the metaphor of 'play' (which is said to be fundamental in aesthetics), but this description is just a prelude to Wisdom's *ethical* appeal to men. Yet even the word 'ethics' is misleading.

God *is* 'goodness' *alive*—and so, in his small way, should a man be.

Finally, it is clear that the typical Hebrew believed that a man *can* do the *whole* will of God if he *wants* to do it. It is true that there are a few very notable passages (Jer 31$^{31ff.}$; Ezk 36$^{25ff.}$; Ps 51) where this idea is implicitly contradicted.[6] It is true, again, that one Psalmist (Ps 14^1) says outright, 'There is none that doeth good', but here he refers to the enemies of the 'poor righteous man', and even if his declaration that the LORD cannot find a single 'son of man' who has not 'gone aside' be taken universally, this does not require that no man *can* be altogether righteous. It seems clear that the *representative* Hebrew did not believe that, as he faced God's demands, he must needs say 'I can't! I can't!' because of his own incapacitating sinfulness. Like 'the man in the street' in all epochs, he thought that he could do right if he liked.

[6] These are examined in a later volume.

PART TWO

FROM HEBREW INTO GREEK

CHAPTER THREE

WHAT A MAN IS

As THE chief purpose of this book is to explore the teaching of the
New Testament, and as it is agreed that the Greek translation of
the Old Testament (LXX) was 'the Bible of the early Christians'
(even though the New Testament writers do not always follow it),
it is necessary to examine LXX renderings of Hebrew terms and
their implications. As LXX was begun in the third century B.C.,
it gives abundant evidence of the ideas of the Hellenistic Jews
from that date until New Testament times. During this period
the Old Testament Canon took final shape. The Palestinian Jews,
who from the time of the Maccabees onward, did their best to
resist Hellenization, only accepted books written in Hebrew (or
Aramaic). The Egyptian Jews, however—for whom LXX was
primarily meant—included the books that we call 'the
Apocrypha'. While some of these were written in Hebrew, they
seem all to have been current in Greek, and it was in Greek that
they passed into the Christian Bible. The one exception is Second
Esdras, which is extant in Latin. While its evidence on two of the
subjects now being examined is important, these don't belong to
this volume. It will be convenient to use the phrase 'Old Testament' for the books of the Hebrew Canon, 'Apocrypha' for those
added in the Greek Canon, and 'LXX' for the two taken together.
Usually the Greek translations of terms in the Hebrew Canon
are taken first, and then the use of these Greek renderings in the
Apocrypha.

As already noted, today the common doctrine of man resolves
him into two disparate elements called 'soul' and 'body'. This is
sometimes called 'Greek dichotomy', but it is a mistake to suppose
that the theory was universal or even general among Greek-
speaking peoples at any time. At the period now in question the
favourite philosophies were Stoicism and Epicureanism (cf. Ac
17[18]), which, in very different ways, both tried to be monist.
There was also a strong syncretist tendency, as Cicero's writings
show. This appeared in Philo's borrowings from Greek philosophers. He was by no means an Aristotelian, and it is in Aristotle
that modern dichotomism has its historical roots. As Philo wrote

FBM

in the first Christian century, a brief account of his teaching may serve both to illustrate the mental background of New Testament times, and to show how different this was from the background of today.[1]

For Philo *all living* beings consist of 'soul' (*psyche*) and 'matter' (*hyle*), but the latter has only the one quality of 'existence' (*'ousia*) or even the potentiality of existence, and therefore is not to be identified with 'body'. Again, Philo holds that in *man* the *psyche* is twofold. There is, on the one hand, a part that men share with animals, a mixture of blood and air, which is both material and mortal. On the other hand there is a part peculiar to man which Philo calls *nous* (mind). For him, man consists of matter (animal), life, and *nous*. On the whole, Philo, when he speaks of man, identifies *nous* with *sophia* (wisdom), with *logos* (reason), and with *pneuma* (spirit). *Logos*, in man as in God, has two sides—it is the organ of thought (*endiathetos*) and the organ of communication (*prophoricos*). The English translation 'word' is therefore inadequate. Philo finds *nous* and its synonyms allegorically in the Urim and Thummin! Of *pneuma* he says that it is not air (which is what *pneuma* literally means) but a certain 'stamp and character of divine power'—that is, it is the 'image of God' in man. Here he appeals not only to Genesis 1[26] but also to Gn 2[7], introducing the term *pneuma* where the Hebrew has *neshamah* and *nephesh* but not *ruach*. Philo calls *pneuma* 'a fragment or ray (*apaugasma*—cf. Wis 7[26], He 1[3]) of the Blessed Being'. It is clear that, while Philo connects man with animals under the lower part of the *psyche*, he connects him with God under the higher. It is this alone that survives death. Philo has some not very clear teaching that after death the *nous* or *pneuma* of a good man and a bad man fare differently, but what he emphasizes is that 'to see God' is 'life eternal' (*zoe aionios*)—and to lose His fellowship is the real punishment of sin. His doctrine has no place for a physical resurrection. When it is added that for Philo *hyle* does not exist *per se* but is only a potentiality, it will be seen that he is neither a clear-cut dichotomist nor a clear-cut trichotomist. To the question 'How many ultimate parts has man?' he gives no plain answer, but he does believe that they are only parts of a whole. It will be found later that it is the same with LXX, which, broadly speaking, belongs to the period between the

---

[1] Philo's teaching is conveniently gathered under his name in *HDB* (Extra Volume) and under 'Alexandrian Theology' in *ERE*.

Hebrew books and Philo. At this period Aristotelianism, from which medieval and modern dichotomy is derived, was the least influential of the great Greek philosophies. Something further is said on the subject at the end of the chapter.

For the LXX translations of the Hebrew terms under the question 'What is man?' it is best to begin with the passage: 'And the LORD God formed man out of the dust of the ground, and blew into his nostrils the breath (*neshamah*) of life (*chayyim*), and man became a living (*chayyah*) soul (*nephesh*)' (Gn 2⁷ J). Here LXX has: 'And God moulded man, dust from the earth, and blew (*emphuein*) into his face a breath (*pnoe*) of life (*zoe*) and man became a living soul (*psyche*).' Alongside this there may be placed an ironical passage in the Book of Wisdom. It contrasts a heathen potter's moulding of a lifeless idol with God's making of the potter himself, and it paraphrases the text in Genesis in this way—'For (when he was made) he (man) did not know him who moulded him, who breathed into him an active (or energizing) *psyche*, and blew into him a living (*zōtikon*) spirit (*pneuma*), but they (men) reckoned that our life (*zoe*) is a plaything and our way-of-life (*bios*) a gainful festival (Wis 15¹¹ᶠ·). Earlier the passage refers to the potter's 'debt of the soul (*psyche*)' and to his *bios* (v. 8, 10). It will be noticed that there is nothing in the passage in Genesis to correspond either with *pneuma*, *zotikon*, or *bios*, though *pnoe* is of the same root as *pneuma*.

The first term to note here is *zoe*. This is the regular term for *chay* and *chayyim* (life) in the Greek Old Testament, the corresponding verb being used for 'live'. This use continues in the Apocrypha—for instance, *zoe* occurs in the frequent phrase, 'all the days of my life' (e.g. To 1³). In the Wisdom books Sirach says 'Before man is *zoe* and death' and calls on God as 'Father and Master of my *zoe*' (Sir 15¹⁷, 23¹, ⁴), and the author of the book of Wisdom says 'Thou (O Lord) hast authority over *zoe* and death' (Wis 16¹³). Sirach, again, sets *zoe* alongside *psyche*—for instance, a man who 'sinneth against his own *psyche*' is a man who 'dishonoureth his own *zoe*' (Sir 10²⁹; cf. 32²⁷, 34¹⁷). In Judith the phrase '*pneuma* of *zoe*' can be used to mean a 'person' (Jth 10¹³). But in the passage about the creation of man in Wisdom a second term for 'life', *bios*, occurs. This is not found in the LXX in the translation of pre-Exilic books, but it occurs twice in Proverbs and eleven times in Job to render 'days'—e.g. in the phrases 'length of days' and 'my days are vanity' (Pr 3²; Job 7¹). It is perhaps accidental that in every passage in Job there is either a direct or ironical reference to man's frailty ($7^{1, \, 6, \, 16}$, 8^9, 9^{25}, $10^{5, \, 20}$, 12^{12}, $14^{5, \, 6, \, 14}$, 15^{20}, 21^{13}). There are texts where *zoe* and *bios* seem to be mere alternatives (e.g. Pr 3^2, Wis 7^6, 8^7, 14^{24}), including two where a verb formed from *bios* occurs with *zoe* (Sir $40^{28f.}$, Wis 12^{23}). Where there is any distinction, *bios*, as in ordinary Greek, refers rather to a man's outward 'manner of life' than to its inward source. There is one passage where the distinction is clear (Sir 40^{29}), and others where it may be present (e.g. Sir 29^{22}, 28^{19}, Wis $2^{1, \, 4f., \, 15}$, 5^4, 10^8). *Bios* is only once used to render *chay* (Pr 4^{10}) and never for *chayyim*. While *bios* may be 'pure' (2 Mac 7^{40}), this term's meaning does not develop as that of *zoe* does. Of this development there had been some Hebrew anticipation. Both the Hebrew term and *zoe* could be used of animals (e.g. Gn 6^{17} P), but, when used of men, there are early passages that suggest that there are different *kinds* of *zoe*—for instance, it may be 'bitter' (Ex 1^{14} J) or 'lovely' and 'pleasant' (2 S 1^{23}). While these adjectives are not ethical, Proverbs and Psalms take a step in that direction. 'Wisdom' declares, 'Whoso findeth me findeth *life*', and there are proverbs that speak of the 'true way of *life*' (Pr 8^{35}, 10^{17}, 6^{23}). Again, there is the text, 'He that followeth after righteousness and mercy Findeth *life*, righteousness, and honour' (Pr 21^{21}). In the Psalms there are such phrases as: 'Thou wilt show me the path of *life*', 'The LORD is the strength of my *life*', and 'With thee is the fountain of *life*' (Ps 16^{11}, 27^1, 36^9). In all these texts it is possible to expound 'life' as meaning no more than 'long life', but their context at least opens the way to the idea that true 'life' is righteous. The writers of Sirach and Wisdom go farther. The latter speaks of the 'error of your life', 'folly of life', and 'corruption of life' (Wis 1^{12}, 12^{23}, 14^{12}), and Sirach says, 'A faithful friend is a medicine of life', and 'He that loveth wisdom loveth life' (6^{16}, 4^{12}). He even speaks of a *bios* that cannot be counted as *zoe* (40^{29}). Of course the Hebrews had long applied ethical ideas to the *concept* of life. Here the question is of the connotation of particular *terms*. There is a dual use of *zoe*, as of 'life' in English. We say that 'where there is life there is hope', and we could use the phrase of an animal as well as a man. A similar use was permanent both with *chayyim* and *zoe*. But in English, when we speak of *men*, we also speak of 'a good' and a 'bad life'—that is, we use 'life' with an ethical connotation. This use begins for the Jews in Psalms and Proverbs and develops in

the Apocrypha. There two ideas are working themselves clear—
that a man's 'life' is intrinsically either good or bad, and that a
bad 'life' is not true 'life' at all. The phrase *zoe aiōnios*, however,
does not occur in these books and in Dn 12² it does not clearly
reach the qualitative sense found in Philo. It will be seen that
here the question 'What is a man?' runs up into the question
'What ought a man to be?' In one sense all men 'live', but in
another the only true 'life' is the good 'life'. For the Jew this is
the 'life' of the man who 'waits upon the Lord'. 'The righteous',
says God, 'shall *live* by (*ek*) my faithfulness' (Hab 2⁴ LXX).

In another phrase in Gn 2⁷, 'breathed into his nostrils the
neshamah of life', LXX renders *neshamah* by *pnoē*, and this is its
regular translation in the Old Testament. When *pnoe* is used of
man, the meaning is always (physical) 'breath', unless it be in
the phrase 'The lamp (LXX 'light') of the LORD is the *breath* of
man' (Pr 20²⁷ LXX). The term *pnoe* only occurs four times in
the Apocrypha and its renderings are 'breath' (Sir 33²⁰, Wis 2²)
and '(last) gasp' (2 Mac 3³¹, 7⁹). This term is not important for
the doctrine of man, though it may be noted that it can be used
about God as a synonym for *pneuma* (Job 32⁸, 33⁴).

In the next phrase in Gn 2⁷, 'man became a *nephesh* of life',
LXX has 'man became a living *psyche*', and the Wisdom paraphrase (15¹¹ᶠ·) has 'He breathed into him an active (in-working)
psyche'. The two texts are typical, for in LXX *psyche* is almost
always used for *nephesh*. It follows that *psyche*, like *nephesh*, has
three chief meanings—it may mean 'life'; it may stand for a personal or reflexive pronoun or mean 'a man'; it may stand for the
element in human nature that experiences. As with *nephesh*,
the three uses overlap. In the Old Testament texts cited in
Chapter One *psyche* is the regular rendering for *nephesh*. Some
examples of the three uses from the Apocrypha may be given.

Under the first, 'life', there are passages where *psyche* is used to
include animals—e.g. in 'every living thing' (Jth 11⁷), and 'the
psyche of every living thing' (Sir 16³⁰). It occurs much more
frequently, as one would expect, of men—e.g. 'He gave up the
psyche in the bed' (To 14¹¹), 'fainting' (literally, 'letting out their
psychai') (Jth 7²⁷), '(thy surety) hath given his *psyche* for thee'
(Sir 29¹⁵). When men 'put to sea' they entrust their *psychai* to a
little piece of wood' (Wis 14⁴ᶠ·), the faithful 'give their *psychai* for
the covenant of (their) fathers' (1 Mac 2⁵⁰). While *psyche* can be
used in parallel with *zoe* (Sir 10²⁹), usually it is *zoe* individualized.

In rendering 'life is precious' the Greek word would be *zoe*, but in 'a life for a life' it would be *psyche*.

Secondly, there is the use of *psyche* for the personal and reflexive pronouns—e.g. 'I kept *myself* from eating' (To 1¹¹), 'our *souls* shall live' (Jth 7²⁷), 'who in his *soul* is like thine own *soul*' (Sir 37¹²). Along with this use there come the passages where *psyche*, like *nephesh*, means 'a man'—e.g. 'a hungry *soul*' (Sir 4²), 'neither hath every *soul* pleasure in everything' (Sir 37²⁸), 'murderers of their own helpless *babes*' (Wis 12⁶)', 'to the number of a thousand *souls* of men (1 Mac 2⁵⁰). In Wis 8¹⁹ᶠ. 'I' is the soul as over against the body. The few Old Testament passages which speak of God's *psyche* belong to this use, but they have no parallel in the Apocrypha. This is noteworthy. 'Wisdom', however, may 'praise her own *soul*' (Sir 24¹). *Psyche* is never used, as *nephesh* is, to mean a corpse.

Thirdly, *psyche* is used, like *nephesh*, as the subject of all experience in the widest sense of the word—as the subject that lives and feels and thinks and wills—e.g. 'our *souls* shall live' (Jth 7²⁷), 'his *soul* was moved and he desired her exceedingly' (Jth 12¹⁶), 'the counsel of thy *soul*' (Sir 6²), 'a wife after thy *mind*' (Sir 7²⁶), 'his *wits* are with him' (Sir 31²⁰), 'let your *soul* receive instruction' (Sir 51²⁶), 'perplexed in *mind*' (1 Mac 3³¹). Here the emphasis on feeling in particular, found under *nephesh*, has disappeared.

It may be added that in Second Maccabees an adverb from *psyche* (*psychicōs*) is used twice and is rendered 'heartily' (4³⁷, 14²⁴), while in a book outside the English Apocrypha the adjective *psychicŏs* occurs—'Of desires some belong-to-the-*psyche* (*psychicos*) and some to-the-body (*somatikos*)' (4 Mac 1³²). Something will be said later of the use of 'body' along with *psyche*, but it may be noted here that by the end of the period 'body and soul' seems to have been a current phrase for 'the whole man' (2 Mac 7³⁷, 14³⁸, 15³⁰). It is under the first term rather than the second that this differs from the Hebrew combination 'dust and life', for *psyche* means 'soul' considered as 'life' and its connexion with 'breath' had not altogether lapsed—that is, the concept was not wholly immaterial. There is one text that is sometimes quoted on the other side—'The souls (lives) of the righteous are in the hand of God' (Wis 3¹)—but this does not *require* that the *psyche* is immaterial, and elsewhere the writer of Wisdom both connects *psyche* with 'breath' (15¹¹) and uses phrases about it that imply *physical* life (12^6, 14^5, 16^9). The text will be considered at length in *The Bible Doctrine of the Hereafter*.

In addition to these three uses there is a fourth in the Apocrypha. Under this, *psyche* occurs with *moral* predicates. The moral difference between 'souls', as has been seen, is *implied* in such Old Testament texts as 'Bless the LORD, O my soul' and 'the soul that sinneth, it shall die'. This implication is commoner in the Apocrypha—e.g. in 'wicked injustice drieth up his soul' (Sir 14^9), 'a whisperer defileth his own soul' (Sir 21^{28}); 'there is one that is wise to his own soul' (Sir 37^{22}); 'uprightness of soul' (Wis 9^3); '(wisdom) entered into the soul of a servant of the LORD' (Wis 10^{16}); 'defiling of souls' (Wis 14^{26}). What is more important, there are also texts in which moral adjectives *explicitly* describe *psyche*—e.g. 'a wicked soul' and 'a hot *mind*' in Sirach (6^4, 23^{16}); 'blameless souls', 'holy souls', 'a good soul', 'a distrustful soul', 'undisciplined souls', 'a sick soul' in Wisdom (2^{22}, 7^{27}, 8^{19}, 10^{17}, $17^{1, 8}$); 'abominable souls', 'a willing soul' in Maccabees (1 Mac 1^{48}; 2 Mac 1^3).[2] These passages, on analysis, involve the idea of 'conscience', which is discussed later. Sirach has especially clear examples—'Blessed is he whose soul doth not condemn him', 'There is one that slippeth and not from the soul', 'In every work trust thine own soul' (Sir 14^2, 19^{16}, 32^{23}). In the Apocrypha there are two notable novelties under *psyche*— it is no longer used of God; when it is used of man, it sometimes has a clearly moral nature.

It was noted above that in the Wisdom paraphrase of Gn 2^7 the phrase *pneuma zotikon* has no Hebrew original (Wis 15^{11}). Here the unique word *zotikon* need not detain us. It means 'belonging to (the realm of) life'.[3] The important point is the introduction of the word *pneuma* (*52*).

Pneuma, like *ruach*, originally meant 'wind', though not necessarily a violent wind. It occurs with this meaning in the Apocrypha —e.g. Sirach speaks of 'winds that are created for vengeance' (39^{28}; cf. 43^{17}), and Wisdom of a 'light wind', 'a mighty blast', 'a single breath', and 'a breath of thy power' ($5^{11, 23}$, 11^{20}; cf. 13^2, 17^{18}). It is likely that with these writers the idea that it is God who makes the wind blow is always present.

Next, *pneuma*, again like *ruach*, is used of the 'spirit' *of God*.

---

[2] The passage in Wis $8^{19\,f.}$ may mean either that the writer accepted the Platonic doctrine of the pre-existence of 'souls', or that, when a man is created, God gives him a certain kind of 'soul'.

[3] Cf. Moulton & Howard, *Grammar of New Testament Greek*, II. 378 f.

Here the idea that all *living* things are created by the Divine
spirit (Ps 104³⁰) is extended to the whole creation, inanimate as
well as animate (Jth 16¹⁴). This *pneuma*, filling the world, 'holds
all things together' and 'incorruptibly' pervades 'all things'
(Wis 1⁷, 12²). The writer of Wisdom describes it at length in a
famous passage (7²²ᶠ·). Here there are some adjectives that
clearly belong to the realm of thought and ethics, others that
describe something like the 'ether' of the physics of yesterday, and
some that might be taken with either of these classes. Two, at
least, belong to the physical realm—'tenuous'⁴ and 'freely
moving'. This means that *pneuma* is not conceived as wholly
immaterial (cf. 'vapour', as used of Wisdom itself in v. 25). On
the other hand, the phrases 'quick of understanding', 'holy',
'loving what is good', 'beneficent', 'loving toward men', 'free
from care', and 'all-surveying' describe mental and ethical
qualities. This passage will be further considered later. While
its account of *pneuma* may be compared to the Stoic concept
of a pervasive 'fire', the writer of Wisdom nowhere suggests
that all things are *made of pneuma* as the Stoics asserted that all things
are forms of the one fire. The idea is not that the Spirit of God
is immanent in the universe (and shut up in it), but that, coming
from God outside, it pervades the whole and holds it together.

But there is another and different use of *pneuma* in the
Apocrypha, as in the Old Testament. *Every man* has a *pneuma* of
his own. For instance, God is said to 'stir up' a man's *pneuma*
(1 Es 2², ⁸), a man's *pneuma* may be 'taken from' him (To 3⁶), his
pneuma may be 'distressed' (Wis 5³), it 'goes forth' at death
(Wis 16¹⁴), it may 'revive' (1 Mac 13⁷), God is 'Lord of the life
(*zoe*) and *pneuma*' of a man (2 Mac 14⁴⁶), He may 'change' a
man's *pneuma* (Ad. Est 15⁸). This use of *pneuma* has no antecedents
in Greek philosophy nor is it found in Philo.⁵ The origin of the
concept is wholly Hebrew.

The question now arises—'What is the relation between a man's
psyche and his *pneuma*?' It has been seen above that at the end of
the Old Testament period there are a few passages where *ruach*
is used as a synonym for *nephesh*. This is also true of the Greek

---

⁴ This seems to be the meaning of *leptos*, rather than 'subtil' (cf. Wis 2³), for the
word is never used in LXX of anything immaterial. Wisdom uses it elsewhere of
'foam' (5¹⁴), and it occurs also of '*lean* kine' and '*lean* ears' (Gn 4¹), of '*thin* hair'
(Lv 13³⁰), of '*light* chaff' (Dn 2³⁵), of '*mere* darkness' (Jer 51³⁴), of a '*gentle* breeze'
(1 K 19¹²), and of the '*fine*' powder of incense (Lv 16¹²).
⁵ See *HDB* IV. 167.

terms *pneuma* and *psyche*. Three phenomena appear to show this. First, there are passages where the two words occur in the same text, apparently as synonyms (Sir 9⁹; Three ⁶⁴). Secondly, *pneuma*, like *psyche*, is sometimes used as the equivalent of personal or reflexive pronouns. There are examples among the texts quoted in the last paragraph—for instance, to 'stir up' the *pneuma* of a man is to stir up the man himself, and there is a passage where 'one *pneuma*' is used to mean 'one man' (Jth 10¹³). Thirdly, there are places where *pneuma*, again like *psyche*, is said to be good— for instance, Sirach ascribes 'an excellent (literally, 'great') *pneuma*' to Isaiah (Sir 48¹²; cf. 34¹³), there is mention of a contrite heart and a humble *pneuma* (Three 16), Daniel's 'spirit' is said to be 'holy' (Sus 45), the 'spirits' of good men are called 'pure' (Wis 7²³).

Are *psyche* and *pneuma* then merely alternatives or is there, as with most pairs of synonyms, some way in which the two differ? Here the two parallel phrases in the Wisdom paraphrase may be recalled—'blew into him an active *psyche*' and 'inbreathed a living *pneuma*' (Wis 15¹¹). Why does this writer, who is not prone to parallelism, *add* the second phrase to the Hebrew? It seems to be interpretative of the first, the meaning being 'in *man psyche* is *pneuma*'. This leads to a decisive fact. A man, like an *animal*, has a *psyche*; a man, like *God*, has a *pneuma*. Just as *psyche* is never used of God in the Apocrypha, so *pneuma* is never used of an animal. In other words, at this point man is like God. He is more like God than an idol is because he has 'borrowed' his *pneuma* from God (Wis 15¹⁶). This subject recurs in the next chapter.

Yet the spirit *of* man is not the same as the Spirit of God *in* man. In the good man the *relation* between the two is very intimate. There is a passage (Wis 1⁵⁻⁷) where it is possible that, as in Psalm 51, *pneuma* occurs both of man and God. Again, in the principal text in Wisdom, the 'spirit of Wisdom' is said to 'penetrate through all the spirits' of 'wise' men (7²²ᶠ·). Yet the last phrase itself precludes the idea that they are one and the same. This is a Stoic idea, and the Stoic, however inconsistently, tended to pantheism, and sometimes seems to have reached it. The writer of Wisdom, while he teaches both that the spirit of God permeates 'all things' (except sin) and that it penetrates the spirits of good men, is yet no pantheist.

Six other points may be mentioned. First, the term *pneuma* is never used to describe a dead man, as in our phrase 'disembodied spirits'. Second, the adjective 'spiritual' (*pneumatikos*) does not occur in LXX. Third, there are super-human beings who may be called 'spirits'. God, who is 'the Sovereign of spirits', makes three of them 'manifest' to frighten and scourge Heliodorus (2 Mac 3$^{24-6}$), and in Tobit there is mention of 'a demon or an evil spirit' (able to smell—8^3) that has 'troubled' Raguel's daughter Sarah (To 6^7; cf. 3$^{8,\ 17}$). Fourth, the question arises: 'Had the writer of Wisdom, the philosopher of the Apocrypha, reached the concept of a wholly immaterial *pneuma*, or had he, like many others in many periods, only approximated to it under the notion that the *pneuma* is a kind of very tenuous air?' On the one hand, there is not only the use of the physical words 'tenuous' and 'inbreathed', but the free use of *pneuma* for 'wind' (5$^{11,\ 23}$, 7^{20}, 11^{20}, 13^2, 17^{18}), and a passage where *pneuma* may be rendered either by 'spirit' or 'wind' (7^{20}; cf. Sir 38^{23}). On the other hand, in one passage the writer implies that the wicked are mistaken in supposing that at death a man's *pneuma* is 'dispersed as thin air' (2^3). Here, however, the writer may only be protesting against a current opinion (v. 1) that man's 'breath' is *altogether* like other 'smoke', his reason *altogether* like other 'sparks', and his *pneuma altogether* like other 'air'. On the whole it seems unlikely that the writer had fully and clearly reached the concept that in *man* there is something wholly immaterial, whatever he may have thought about *God* at this point. Fifth, the phrase 'holy spirit' occurs twice of God's 'spirit' (Wis 7^{22}, 9^{17}), and once of a man's (Sus 45). Sixth, while God and man both have *pneuma*, it does not follow that man's *pneuma* is morally good *per se*. While a man's *pneuma* is never called bad, this is probably an accident, for there is a passage in Wisdom which in effect distinguishes men whose 'spirits' are 'quick of understanding, pure, very tenuous' from those whose 'spirits' are not (7^{23}; cf. Sir 34^{13}). In itself the word *pneuma* is morally neutral or it could not be used both of God and Asmodaeus! It approximates to what *we* call 'personality'.

When we turn to the external and visible *organs* of the body— the hand and foot, the eye and ear, the mouth and lips and tongue—the examples in the Apocrypha only repeat the use of the Old Testament. While there are passages where the organ itself is said to act—e.g. the 'hand' in Sir 35^{10}, 42^{12}; Wis 10^{20}, 11^{17}; the 'foot' in Sir 6^{36}, 51^{15}; 1 Mac 10^{72}; the 'eye' in Jth 2^{11}; Est 13^{15}; Sir 17^{13}, 23^{19}; the 'ear' in Sir 16^5; the 'mouth' in Wis 1^{11}; the 'lips' in Jth 9^{10}; Sir 1^{24}, 21^{25}; and the 'tongue' in Sir 5^{13}, 22^{27}, 28^{14}, 37^{18}; Wis 10^{21}—few will claim that in the Hellenistic period such texts are to be taken to mean that the various organs acted autonomously. Similarly, the use of the phrases 'an evil eye' (Sir 8⁸⁻¹⁰, 31¹³), 'an impudent eye' (Sir 26¹¹), and 'an envious eye' (To 4⁷, ¹⁶) repeats the Old Testament use. Here, however, the contrasting phrase 'a good eye' is found (Sir 35⁸, ¹⁰). As in the Old Testament, the implication of the context in these passages is that a man himself decides whether his 'eye' shall be 'evil' or 'good'. There are, of course, many passages where the organs are presented as under a man's control (e.g. 1 Es 8⁷³; Sir 4⁵, 6²³, ³⁰, 50²⁰; Wis 1¹¹; 2 Es 14³⁸). One passage, 'I have seen *with* mine eyes and *mine ear* hath heard' (Sir 16⁵), combines the instrumental use with the seemingly autonomous. As to 'head' (*kephalē*) LXX adds nothing to the Hebrew. It is never mentioned as controlling the body or as a seat of experience. Sirach has figurative uses (e.g. 11¹, 13⁷, 17²³, 25¹⁵, 44²³), but not the figure of 'control'. In the Apocrypha *kephale* does not occur for the 'head man' of a community.

Of the *internal* parts of the body far and away the most important term is 'heart'—so much so that, as will appear below, the others may be considered under it. The two Hebrew terms *leb* and *lebab* are rendered in more than thirty ways in LXX, but only a few are relevant here. In an overwhelming majority of cases the Greek rendering is *kardia*, which is rarely used for any other terms. It occurs about 150 times in the Apocrypha, of which eighty-seven occur in Sirach but only six in Wisdom. It is used, like *leb* and *lebab*, to describe the seat of the *will*. There is a good example in a passage in Sirach where the ploughman, the artificer, the smith, and the potter are each said to 'set' or 'apply' his 'heart' to his task (38²⁴⁻³⁰). Again, there are passages where the word is used in an ethical sense. For instance, the following phrases describe the 'heart' of good men—'a heart full of godliness' (1 Es 1²³), 'a good heart' (Jth 8²⁸ᶠ·, Sir 26⁴), 'set thy heart aright' (Sir 2²), 'whose hearts went not a whoring' (Sir 46¹¹), 'singleness of heart' (Wis 1¹), 'holy and humble of heart' (Three 65). Other phrases describe bad men—for instance, '(wine) maketh every heart (to seem) rich' (1 Es 3²¹), 'his own wicked heart' (Bar 1²², 2⁸), 'a double heart', a 'heart full of deceit', 'a stubborn heart', 'the heart of a proud man', (Sir 1²⁸, ³⁰, 3²⁶ᶠ·, 11³⁰). Here, too, fall the two phrases 'scorn not in thine heart' (To 4¹³) and 'cleanse thy heart from all manner of sin' (Sir 38¹⁰). A man may 'harden his neck and his heart' (1 Es 1⁴⁸).

The 'heart' is also the seat of *thought*. The Old Testament phrase 'said in his heart' occurs (Jth 13⁴, 1 Mac 6¹¹). A man 'thinks' in his 'heart' and 'lays a word up in his heart' (Jth 8¹⁴, 11¹⁰), he 'takes counsel in his heart' and 'considereth in his heart' (Sir 12¹⁶, 14²¹), he may be 'light-*minded*' (Sir 19⁴), he may submit to the 'discipline of wisdom over his heart', 'have wisdom in his heart to judge', or 'pour wisdom out of his heart' (Sir 23², 45²⁶, 50²⁷; cf. 17¹⁶, 21¹⁷, 25⁷). For the Jew 'wisdom' was more than thought but it included thought.

Kardia is also used as seat of emotion and feeling, but before this is illustrated another phenomenon may be noted. As we have seen, the Hebrew ascribed various feelings to various internal organs. In the Apocrypha, however, the use of other organs than the 'heart' as the seat of feelings dwindles. There are two terms, *kabed* and *cheleb* whose LXX equivalents (*epar* and *stear*) are never used as seats of experience in the Apocrypha. Two other Hebrew terms, *me'im* and *rechem* ('bowels' and 'womb'), are both rendered in the Old Testament by *koilia* (the stomach and intestines) or *gastēr* (stomach). In the Apocrypha these last terms are never used as the seat of emotion except in Sirach. In that book there is a passage where a 'fool's belly' is compared to a woman's womb (Sir 19¹⁰⁻¹²). The other texts run: 'Let not chambering and the appetite of the belly overtake thee' (23⁶), 'a froward belly' (36²⁰), 'in his belly a fire shall be kindled' (40³⁰), and 'my belly was troubled to seek (wisdom)' (51²¹). Another word, *nephros* (for *kelayoth*, reins), only once occurs in the Apocrypha to describe emotion (Wis 1⁶) and there it is parallel to *kardia*. The Hebrew term for 'belly' (*beten*) is usually rendered by *gaster* and *koilia*, but *kardia* occurs once (Pr 22¹¹) and *splangchna* once (Pr 26²). In the Apocrypha the first two of these words are not used except of the merely physical organs. *Splangchna*, a Greek term that denotes all the *viscera* (including the heart), is only used five times in the Apocrypha to denote emotion, the usual English rendering being 'heart' (Bar 2⁷; Sir 30⁷, 33⁵, Wis 10⁵; 2 Mac 9⁵ᶠ·). If the passages in the list are added together, there are, in the Apocrypha, only twelve instances of the use of other organs beside the heart to locate emotion, and eight of these are in Sirach. The regular word in the Apocryphal books for the seat of *feeling*, as of thought and will, is *kardia*. Here are some examples: 'If thou hopest in thine heart' (Jth 6⁹), 'Be not afraid in thine heart' (Jth 10¹⁶), 'Holofernes' heart was ravished'

(Jth 12¹⁶), 'The fear of the Lord shall delight the heart' (Sir 1¹²), 'The desires of thine heart' (Sir 5²), 'He that maketh merry in his heart' (Sir 19⁵), 'He that pricketh the heart maketh it to show feeling' (Sir 22¹⁹), 'A wounded heart' (Sir 25²³), 'For two things my heart is grieved' (Sir 26²⁸), 'There is no gladness above the joy of the heart' (Sir 30¹⁶), 'Sorrow of heart' and 'Against the heart' (Sir 28¹⁸ᶠ·), 'His heart is ashes' (Wis 15¹⁰). There is here a contrast with the Old Testament, where the use of *leb* or *lebab* to denote feelings is relatively rare.

It follows from all this that *kardia*, like *psyche* (and *pneuma*), was used to denote approximately what we call 'personality'. It is not remarkable, therefore, that there are a number of passages where the term stands for the personal and reflexive pronouns. Indeed, some passages already quoted illustrate this. There are other examples—for instance: 'They that fear the Lord will prepare their hearts and humble their souls' (Sir 2¹⁷), 'Love thine own soul, and comfort thy heart' (Sir 30²³), 'Give not thy heart unto (soothsayers)' (Sir 34⁶), 'He will apply his heart' (Sir 39⁵), 'Her heart trusteth in the Lord' (Sus 35), 'My heart faileth for care' (1 Mac 3¹⁷), 'His heart was lifted up' (2 Mac 5²¹). It is almost the same thing to say that *kardia* sometimes stands for 'the whole man' or 'the self'—as in 'Prepare thy soul for temptation, Set thy heart aright' (Sir 2¹ᶠ·), 'To a heart that is provoked' (Sir 4³), 'He shall establish thine heart' (Sir 6³⁷), 'Gold . . . that turned aside the hearts of kings' (Sir 8²), 'His heart is departed from him that made him' (10¹²), 'A cheerful countenance is a token of a heart that is in prosperity' (Sir 13²⁶), 'Of three things my heart was afraid' (Sir 26⁵), 'Wine proves hearts in the quarrelling of the proud' (Sir 31²⁶), 'To turn the heart of the father unto the son' (Sir 48¹⁰), '(God) is a true overseer of (a man's) heart' (Wis 1⁶), 'With my whole heart' (Wis 8²¹; cf. Sir 7²⁷). In some of the passages quoted here and earlier *kardia* and *psyche* are used as synonyms. There are also references to a 'change of heart' in penitence (e.g. Bar 2³⁰ᶠ·; Sir 21⁶, 37¹⁷). It is clear that, among the internal organs, the writers of the Apocrypha tended to concentrate experience in the heart.⁶

---

⁶ Another Greek term which *originally* denoted an internal organ, *phren* (midriff), is used occasionally (*10*), and usually to render *leb* (*7*). All the latter passages are in Proverbs, and all occur in the phrase *endeia phrenon* ('want of mind') to render a Hebrew phrase meaning 'want of heart' (e.g. Pr 6³², 18²). This illustrates the use of 'heart' as the seat of thought and action, but the original physical reference in *phren* had probably long lapsed in Greek. A series of words derived from the same root—*phronesis*, etc. (*81*)—is discussed below along with *sophia* ('wisdom').

There is another significant change in the use of terms for the whole 'body'. Here, as we have seen, the Hebrew term, *geviyyah*, only occurs in six passages—three of them referring to a living body and three to a corpse. In the Greek translations of the Old Testament itself there is already a certain change. Here the Greek term for 'body'—*sōma*, occurs some fifty times. It is used in all the six passages where *geviyyah* occurs, but it is also used to render *basar* (flesh) twenty-one times, *nebelah* (corpse) nine times, 'back' five times (e.g. Neh 9²⁶), 'skin' once (Job 19²⁶), and *nephesh* once (Gn 36⁶). Altogether *soma* renders twelve Hebrew terms, but it is commonest for *basar*, 'flesh'. With this evidence from the Old Testament in mind, one expects that in the Apocrypha *soma* will occur much oftener than *geviyyah* in Hebrew. It is found about forty times. The habitual use of the term in LXX shows that the Greek-speaking Jews had learnt from the Greeks to take it for granted that the body is a *whole*, whatever their fathers had done. On turning to particular Apocryphal passages, we find that some of them only repeat Hebrew use. *Soma* occurs, for instance, like *geviyyah*, both of a living body (e.g. Jth 10³; Est 14²; Sir 30¹⁴⁻¹⁶; Wis 18²²; 2 Mac 3¹⁷) and of a 'corpse' (e.g. To 1¹⁸; Jth 18⁹; Sir 38¹⁶; Wis 2³; 2 Mac 9²⁹). There are also passages that show, quite in the Hebrew way, that it was thought a disaster if a body were left unburied (e.g. To 1¹⁸; Bar 6²²; Sir 44¹⁴; 1 Mac 11⁴; 2 Mac 12²⁹). *Soma* could also be used for a 'person' (2 Mac 8¹¹, 12²⁶).

So far it is the increased frequency of the word for 'body' that is novel. But another notable point arises in texts where 'body' and 'soul' (*psyche*) are put together as though the two formed the whole of a man. Here there are three passages in the Book of Wisdom—'Wisdom will not enter into a *soul* that deviseth evil, Nor dwell in a *body* that is held in pledge by sin' (1⁴), 'Now I was a child of parts, and a good *soul* fell to my lot; Nay rather, being good, I came into a *body* undefiled' (8¹⁹ᶠ·), 'For a destructible *body* weigheth down the *soul*' (9¹⁵). In the first Christian century the writer of Second Maccabees uses the phrase 'body and soul' as though it were a customary description of the whole man (7³⁷, 14³⁸, 15³⁰; cf. 6³⁰). It may be added that while the adjective 'bodily' (*somatikos*) does not occur in our Apocrypha, it is found twice in Fourth Maccabees (1³², 3¹), and that in the first of these passages the idea 'soul and body' is also present in the phrase, 'Of desires some are *psychicae* and some *somatikae*'. Here there is an approach to what is currently called 'Greek dichotomy', but the concept that man is composed of two elements, the 'physical and psychical', or 'material and immaterial', is not fully reached, for, on the one hand, 'body' does not include the 'breath', as the use of *soma* for 'corpse' shows, and, on the other hand, *psyche* never wholly loses its connexion with 'breath' as we have seen. The distinction is not between the immaterial and the material parts of man but between that which *gives* 'life' (including both physical and psychical 'life') and that which *receives* it.

The English phrase 'a corruptible body', used in Wisdom 9[15], seems to suggest that the body is evil *per se*, but the Greek word (*phthartos*) means 'destructible' rather than 'corruptible'. The writer says elsewhere that when he was born he 'came into an *undefiled* body' (Wis 8[20]; cf. Sir 30[14-16]). Again, he was a loyal Jew —as, for instance, his passionate account of the Exodus and the conquest of Canaan shows—and no Jew, with the first chapter of Genesis in his hands, could believe that God the Creator made anything sinful (cf. Wis 9[9]; Sir 24[8]). It is probable, again, that the writer believed that Adam's body was originally indestructible and that the death of the body, its destructibility, arose from his sin (cf. 1[13], 2[23]). Would an indestructible body have 'weighed down the soul'? In Wisdom 9[15], as the context shows (e.g. v. 5), the writer is thinking of the *limitations* that a '*destructible* body' lays upon the 'soul'. This is borne out by the parallel phrase— 'the tabernacle with its earthy form (weigheth down) the mind with its many purposes'. The writer means that when the soul is rid of the limitations of a '*destructible* body' it will soar. Yet the limitations even of *this* body are not sinful *per se*. A passage where Paul all but quotes a phrase from the second part of the verse (2 Cor 5[1-4]), sustains this interpretation. Though it is after the Fall that men are 'easily destructible creatures (*euphtharta*)' (19[21]), even then a 'creature' may be 'destructible' without being morally evil.

As we have seen, in the Greek Old Testament, *soma* is used to render *basar* (flesh) about twenty times, but the literal Greek rendering of *basar* is *sarx* and this is used over a hundred and thirty times. In the Apocrypha *sarx* is not very common (*32*). It is used of the merely physical (e.g. Jth 16[17]; Sir 19[12]; Wis 7[2]; 1 Mac 7[17]), yet it may denote 'a person' (e.g. Jth 10[13]; Sir 33[20]). The commonest example of the latter use is in the phrase 'all flesh' to denote 'mankind' (e.g. Jth 2[3]; Sir 1[10], 18[13]) or even 'all men and animals' (Sir 13[16], 17[4], 40[8]). Here men are called 'flesh' to draw attention to their frailty—as also, for instance, in 'All flesh waxeth old as a garment' and in the comparison of 'the generations of flesh and blood' with the leaves of a tree (Sir 14$^{17f.}$; cf. 41^3). Similarly 'an evil man' is satirized because he 'will think on (weak) flesh and blood' instead of on 'turning again to the Most High' (Sir 17$^{25-32}$; cf. 28^5). The same idea is present in the one use of the adjective *sarkinos* ('made of flesh') in the Apocrypha (Est 14^{10}). Two passages in Ezekiel, where this adjective is used in LXX, show clearly that it has no sinful connotation (Ezk 11^{19}, 36^{26}). Sirach says that 'The body of the flesh' is the instrument of the 'hot mind' of a 'fornicator' (23$^{16-18}$), but this describes the *misuse* of the 'flesh', not the 'flesh' itself. The adjective *sarkikos* is not found in LXX. It will be noticed that a very few of the quotations suggest that it is *through* the flesh that men sin. For instance it was through his 'bones and fleshes' that Job (2^5 LXX) was *tempted* to 'renounce God'. The 'flesh' is not sinful *per se*, but weak against temptation.

In describing the answer given to the question 'What is a man?' in the period between the Testaments it is necessary to consider a Greek term which does not so much translate any Hebrew term as interpret a number of terms and phrases. This is the Greek term for 'mind' (*nous*), so prominent in Philo, with its many derivatives. For this word Hebrew has no true equivalent. It is a word proper to a race whose bent, unlike that of the Hebrews, was to thought rather than action. There had been a time when the Greeks had been great in both, but in the period of the Hellenistic despotisms, being debarred their old independent political life, they turned to the realm of thought rather than action. There were, of course, exceptions to this rule, but this is the rule. The most important term here is not *nous* itself but *dianoia* ('understanding'—literally 'through-thinking'), with its derivatives *dianoeisthai* (to pass through one's mind', 'consider') and *dianoēma* ('a thought'). It will, however, be convenient first to consider the use of *nous* and its many other derivatives. Since, as we have seen, the 'heart' (*leb*) was counted the seat of thought by the Hebrews, it is not surprising that *nous* and its derivatives are sometimes used to render *leb*. It is here that *nous* comes nearest to being a translation rather than an interpretation, yet there is no evidence that the Greeks themselves commonly thought of the heart as the seat of the mind, though there may have been Hellenized Jews who thought so.

Nous itself only occurs fourteen times in the Greek rendering of our Old Testament books, and only in six of these as translating *leb* or *lebab* (e.g. Ex 7²³; Is 10⁷). It is used also for 'ear' three times (e.g. Job 33¹⁶), and for *ruach* once (Is 40¹³). With *nous* there go *noein* (think) and at least nineteen other Greek words of the same root.⁷

As already shown for *nous* itself, these terms render other Hebrew words besides *leb* or *lebab*. For instance, *noein* renders seven Hebrew terms, *dianoeisthai* nine, and *dianoia* six. Among the Hebrew terms three may be noted. The first is *mezimmah* ('device' or 'purpose') and its verb—e.g. in 'as I purposed to do evil unto you' (Zec 8¹⁴), 'to give . . . to a young man knowledge and (right) purpose (Pr 1⁴). Next there is *chashab* ('plan'), as in 'So far is my planning from your understanding' (Is 55⁹), and 'To plan any plan' (2 Ch 2¹⁴). The third term is *bīn* ('discern'), as in 'David discerned that the child was dead' (2 S 12¹⁹), and 'To discern the words of understanding (Pr 1²). It is clear from these phrases, as it is indeed from the whole range of the uses of the terms, that *nous* and its derivatives are not used, as the Greeks sometimes used them, of speculative thought, but of practical 'sense', as this word (and indeed the word '*nous*' itself) is used in colloquial English. This, of course, is what might have been expected of Hebrew thought. Of passages where words of this group are used for *leb or lebab* there are examples in 'Pharaoh did not set his mind even to this' (Ex 7²³ J), 'He will set free his mind to destroy' (Is 10⁷), 'Every man considereth in his mind attentively with a view to evil (deeds) every day' (Gn 6⁵ J)', 'And (God) considered (for 'grieved him at his heart' in the Hebrew) and said' (Gn 6⁶f. J), 'They took counsel like-mindedly together' (Ps 83⁵).

In the Apocrypha, while there are a few examples of the use of words of this large group in a morally neutral way, the ethico-religious use is dominant. This subject belongs rightly to the next chapter, for it concerns what a man *ought* to be rather than *is*, but it will be convenient to conclude the examination of the words here. *Nous* itself only occurs seven times and, except in one text (Jth 8¹⁴), it always has a reference to moral choice.

⁷ The list is as follows, the first number in brackets showing the number of times the term occurs in the Old Testament, and the second in the Apocrypha, *noein* (*27, 8*), *anoētos*, (*4, 2*), *anoia* (*5, 6*), *dianoeisthai* (*31, 22*), *dianoia* (*45, 14*), *dianoēma* (*6, 7*) *dianoēsis* (*1, 0*) *ennoein* (*4, 3*), *ennoēma* (*0, 1*), *ennoia* (*10, 2*), *eunoia* (*2, 11*), *eunoein* (*1, 1*), *homonoia* (*2, 3*), *noeros* (*0, 1*), *noēmon*, (*7, 2*), *noēma* (*0, 2*), *noētos* (*1, 0*), *nouthesia* (*0, 1*), *nouthetein* (*9, 3*), *nouthetēma* (*0, 1*), *nouthetēsis* (*2, 0*). *Metanoein* (*18, 3*), which renders *nacham*, 'to be sorry', and its noun *metanoia* (*1, 4*), 'repentance', lie outside the present subject.

GBM

There are instances in 'All the multitude gave (their) mind unto the Law' (1 Es 9⁴¹; cf. 2⁹), 'The giddy whirl of desire perverteth an innocent mind' (Wis 1⁴, ¹²; cf. 9¹⁵), 'They perverted their own mind' (Sus 9), 'Keeping in mind the help which of old they had oft-times received from heaven' (2 Mac 15⁸). Curiously enough *nous* does not occur in Sirach. To turn to rarer words, in the two passages where *anoetos* occurs it refers to the morally 'sense-less' (Sir 21¹⁹, 42⁸; cf. Pr 17²⁸). *Anoia* is once used of animals (Wis 15¹⁸), but in its five other examples it denotes the 'senselessness' (rather than 'madness') of the sinful (Wis 19³; 2 Mac 4⁶, ⁴⁰, 14⁵, 15³³; cf. Pr 14³, 22⁵). The verb *ennoein*, 'consider', is used twice of God (Jth 9⁵; Bar 2¹⁶) and twice of the way in which a good man 'considers' (Sir 14²¹; 1 Mac 2⁶¹; cf. Job 1⁵—where '*evil* consideration' is in question). Under *ennoia* a good man is a 'reproof' of bad men's 'intentions' (Wis 2¹⁴) for these are 'wicked' (Sus 28; cf. Pr 1⁴, 5²). On the other hand 'He that keepeth the law becometh master of the intent (*ennoema*) thereof' (Sir 21¹¹). *Eunoia* is best rendered 'good will'. It occurs eight times in the Books of the Maccabees (e.g. 1 Mac 11³³; 2 Mac 9²¹), and twice elsewhere (Sir, Prologue, 13, Est 13³; cf. 2²³ LXX). Among the eight instances of *noein* ('think') in the Apocrypha we find 'The peoples, seeing and thinking not' (Wis 4¹⁴; cf. v. 17), and 'Think first and then rebuke' (Sir 11⁷; cf. Pr 1²), though this word may be used without any moral implication (e.g. 2 Mac 14³⁰). *Noeros* only occurs twice, to describe 'wisdom' (Wis 7²²ᶠ·). *Noema* also occurs twice—once of the 'thoughts' of the wicked (Bar 2⁸), and once, as an alternative reading for *ennoema*, of those of the righteous (Sir 21¹¹). *Noemon* is found twice, to describe 'a man of understanding' in both cases (Sir 19²⁹, 21⁷; cf. Pr 17²). *Homonoia* ('concord' or 'like-mindedness') occurs three times—once of the wicked (Wis 10⁵; cf. Ps 83⁵) and twice of the good (Sir 25¹; Wis 18⁹; cf. Ps 55¹⁴). It is clear that under the great majority of passages the reference is to the mind's knowledge of the morally good and evil.

Turning now to *dianoia*, the important word in this group, with its derivatives, we find that in *the Old Testament* the noun occurs forty-five times and that in thirty-eight of these it renders *leb* or *lebab*. Its best English renderings are 'mind' and 'understanding', though it also occurs in a wider sense (e.g. Gn 45²⁶ E; Jos 5¹ D; Is 35⁴). Where it translates *leb* it is often used in the rendering of the expression 'Said in (his) *heart*' and similar phrases (e.g.

Gn 17¹⁷ P, 24¹⁵ J; Dt 7¹⁷; Job 1⁵; Is 14¹³; Lv 19¹⁷ H). It is also
found in such phrases as 'astonishment of understanding' (Dt
28²⁸), 'discourage ye the mind' (Nu 32⁷ JE), 'he spake unto the
mind of the damsel' (Gn 34³ J), 'as water showeth face to face,
so the mind showeth man to man' (Pr 27¹⁹). The Satan has
dianoia (Job 9⁴), as has God (Job 1⁸). The word is also used of
practical and artistic skill, as a gift of God (e.g. Ex 35²²ᶠᶠ· P).
This leads to the passages where there is an underlying concept
of moral choice—for instance, 'The framing of the mind of man
is evil' (Gn 8²¹ J), 'Spy not out after your own mind' (Nu 15³⁹ P),
'I cannot go beyond the word of the LORD my God to do a small
or great thing in my mind' (Nu 22¹⁸ JE), 'Lay it to thy mind
that the LORD he is God' (Dt 4³⁹; cf. Is 57¹¹), 'Thou shalt love
the LORD thy God with all thy mind' (Dt 6⁵), 'A man . . . whose
mind turneth away from the LORD' (Dt 29¹⁸), 'Yea, truth is
lacking; and they changed the mind from perceiving' (Is 59¹⁵),
'I will verily give my laws unto their mind and upon their hearts
will I write them' (Jer 31³³), 'Wisdom shall enter into thy mind'
(Pr 2¹⁰), 'To know (the) law belongs to a good understanding'
(Pr 13¹⁵; cf. 9¹⁰, where *dianoia* renders *bīnah*). The connexion of
ethics with religion here is, of course, typically Hebrew.

The verb *dianoeisthai* occurs thirty times in the Old Testament
(e.g. Ex 31⁴; Zec 8¹⁴ᶠ·; thirteen times in Daniel to render *bīn*,
'discern'—e.g. 8⁵⁻²³—but only in four passages for phrases with
leb—Gn 6⁵ᶠ·, 8²¹; Jer 7³¹, 19⁵). The noun *dianoema* is found six
times in the Old Testament (e.g. Ezk 14³ᶠ·; Is 55⁹; Pr 15²⁴), but
never for *leb*.

In the Apocrypha, *dianoia* (*14*) can be used in a practical sense
without any moral implication (1 Mac 10⁷², 11⁴⁹, and perhaps
2 Mac 3¹⁶), but it occurs once of God (Jth 8¹⁴) and ten times of
man in an ethical sense. There are instances in 'Seeing and
understanding not, Neither laying this to heart' (Wis 4¹⁵), 'Evil
surmising (*hyponoia*) caused their *understanding* to slip' (Sir 3²⁴; cf.
22¹⁷, 29¹⁷), 'Antiochus was lifted up in *mind*' (2 Mac 5¹⁷; cf. 2²).
The verb *dianoeisthai* is confined to Judith (*2*) and Sirach (*20*). In
five passages it is perhaps used in an a-moral way (Jth 9⁹; Sir
3²², 16²⁰, 31¹⁵, 39¹²), but it may be used of God (Jth 9⁵; Sir 42¹⁸),
and its characteristic use in Sirach (though not in the Greek Old
Testament) is ethical—for example, 'The heart of the prudent
will *understand* a parable' (3²⁹), 'Counsel, and tongue, and eyes,
Ears, and heart, gave he them to *understand* withal' (17⁶ᶠ·), 'Him

that applieth his *psyche*, and practiseth *understanding* in the law of the Most High' (39[1]), 'They shall not *understand* the covenant of judgement' (38[33]). There are other examples in Sir 6[37], 14[21], 16[20, 23], 21[17], 27[12], 39[7, 32], 51[12]. The noun *dianoema*, confined to Sirach in the Apocrypha, occurs seven times. It is used of 'Wisdom' (Sir 23[2, 29]) and it always has a moral connotation—as in 'A fearful heart in the *thought* of a fool' (Sir 22[18]), 'How beautiful is the wisdom of old men, And *thought* and counsel to the honoured' (Sir 25[5]; cf. 22[16], 23[2], 32[18], 42[20]). Of course it may be said that the strong tendency to ascribe morality to the exercise of the mind springs from the nature of the Wisdom books, but this yields the point, for it only raises the question: 'Why did the Hellenistic Jews select *these* books for their Canon?' The Jew, unlike the ancient Greek or the modern Englishman, habitually conceived 'mind' in ethical terms. The Wisdom books give another example in the use of *nouthetein*, 'to set another mind in the right direction' (e.g. Job 43; Wis 11[10]). The Revised Version rendering of some passages is not happy.

Such a concept clearly leads to the doctrine of conscience. Of course, from the first there were examples of the *phenomenon* without the *word* in Israel, as in all races—for instance, Adam and Eve suffered from a stricken conscience in the story of the Fall, as did David when Nathan cried: 'Thou art the man!' (cf. Ps 51[4], 119[51]). Again, it has already been shown that the *concept* is sometimes *implied* where *psyche* is used, and there are many examples under *nous* and its cognates, as just examined. But the question here is: 'When did the Hebrew begin to think of "conscience" as a kind of separate faculty in a man's make-up?' Probably not until the Hellenistic period. Here the relevant words are the verb *suneidenai* and the noun *suneidesis*. These Greek words, taken literally, describe 'consciousness' in general, and not 'moral consciousness' or 'conscience' in particular. The verb occurs twice in the Old Testament (Lv 5[1]; Job 27[6]), and the noun once (Ec 10[20]). Here one of the texts, in a late book, approaches the concept of 'conscience'—'My heart shall not *reproach* me as long as I live' (Job 27[6]). The connexion with 'heart' may be noted. The verb is found twice in the Apocrypha but without moral reference (1 Mac 4[21]; 2 Mac 4[41]). The noun occurs once in Sirach in one of the principal manuscripts, the others reading 'knowledge' (Sir 42[18]). It only occurs once elsewhere, but then in a very significant passage—'Wickedness, condemned by a witness within, is a coward thing, And, being pressed hard by conscience, always forecasteth the worst lot' (Wis 17[11]). While there is some doubt about the Greek text here, there is no doubt that *suneidesis* occurs, nor is the general sense of the passage doubtful. It is the climax of the long development of the Hebrew postulate that the chief use of thought is moral.

If it be asked where the writer of Wisdom found the word *suneidesis*, it is preferable to trace it to ordinary Greek use rather than to any particular philosophical school. This means that the ordinary Greek, as he became introspective, coined the term, just as the Roman coined *conscientia* and the medieval Englishman coined 'in-wit'. It has sometimes been said that the Stoics invented the Greek term, but in fact the Epicureans used it more often. Its usual meaning is 'the *feeling* of shame' and the Stoics discounted feeling. In the passage in Wisdom, as the context shows, the writer was thinking, not primarily of the shame of doing wrong, but of the *fear* of its consequences. While this 'fear' too is germane to Epicureanism rather than to Stoicism—for the true Stoic feared nothing—it needed neither to discover it. The Stoics did, indeed, teach that 'right reason' (*logos*) ought to direct a man's life, and, considering their emphasis on ethics, this, no doubt, required the idea of 'conscience' as well as 'conscious-ness'. Unlike other Greek philosophers they might even have called 'conscience' 'the voice of god', but only in their own sense of 'god'. The writer of Wisdom gives no hint of the origin of the 'conscience' that even the heathen share, but being a Jew, he no doubt would relate it in some way to 'God' in the Hebrew sense of the word. The passage shows no sign of distinctively Stoic influence. The writer seems to have used the word in the way in which ordinary men used it every day. His use of 'convict' or 'convince' (*elengchein*), both of the good and the bad, which involves the concept of 'conscience', agrees with this (1[3, 5, 8], 2[11], 4[20], 12[2]; cf. 5[1ff.]; Sir 18[13], 37[17]). Experience precedes theory, and words are often coined to express experience before they pass into theology or philosophy. When the writer of Wisdom spoke of a coward conscience, he was using significant everyday speech.[8]

In LXX, as in the Hebrew Old Testament, it is everywhere *assumed* that, within limits, men can *choose* what they will do, and so have some degree of true *freedom*. The same Old Testament

---

[8] For the evidence concerning Stoics and Epicureans, see Article, 'Conscience (Greek and Roman)', *ERE*, IV. 37–41.

passages might be quoted as earlier. In the Apocrypha Sirach bears witness that in his day there were those who professed determinism in the sense that God ordains that men should do wrong as well as that they should do right, but he mentions this only to repudiate it (15^{11-20}). He says that God 'made man from the beginning, And left him in the hand of his own counsel' (v. 14). Elsewhere, however, he implies that men can only do right if they accept the help of God (23^{1-6}). For him the secret of the right kind of life lies in the 'fear' and the 'love' of God ($2^{15f.}$). He does indeed recognize the power of evil habits, saying that 'a plant of wickedness hath taken root in the proud' (3^{28}), yet he admits that there may be an effective repentance (17^{24}, 18^{14}, 21^{1-3}). It is true again, that he has the text 'If ye (ungodly men) be born, ye shall be born with a curse' (41^9), but this seems to mean that God *foresees* that some men will be wicked—not that He pre-ordains it. In the Book of Wisdom there is a passage, already quoted, where the writer teaches that some men are born with 'good souls' and 'undefiled bodies', but in the same passage he implies that even such men are only able to live the good life if they pray 'Give me wisdom' ($8^{19}-9^{18}$). Under bad men there is a passage where the writer declares that even to 'the old inhabitants of (God's) holy land', whose 'nature by birth was evil, and their wickedness inborn' and who 'were a seed accursed from the beginning' (cf. Gn 9^{25}), God gave 'a place of repentance' though He knew beforehand that 'their manner of life would in no wise ever be changed' (12^3, $^{10f.}$). Elsewhere this writer declares that all men are *born* helpless and that it is for each man to 'call upon God' for wisdom (7^{1-14}). This means that they need not sin. There is also an interesting passage where it is stated that when men use wood to build ships, it is by the help of the Wisdom of God, but when they use it to make idols, it is through their own folly (14^{1-11}). This means that this writer, in a thoroughly Hebrew fashion, divides all the acts of men—even within the practical arts—into good and bad according as the acts are acceptable to God. In both Wisdom books there is the doctrine that men can and must choose between 'wisdom' and 'folly'—that is, they can and must choose whether they will obey or disobey God. For these writers this is the fundamental and pervasive choice. If they choose aright, God will help them to be righteous. The postulate that man is free is nowhere abandoned—not even in the two or three passages where it is asserted or implied that some men are born prone to good and some to evil.

In the first chapter certain Hebrew words were examined at this point, for, while the Hebrews had no verb to mean 'to will' '*simpliciter*', certain terms approximate to this. The first word was *bachar* 'to choose'. In LXX this is usually rendered by *eklegein* 'to pick out' (*108*), with *epilegein* as a variant (*7*). It is under this term that the problem of Election, which is considered in *The Bible Doctrine of Grace*, arises. As with *bachar*, *eklegein* is far more commonly used of God's choice than of man's. Examples of the latter, however, occur in such texts as Gn 13[11]; Dt 30[19]; 1 S 8[18]; Is 7[15], 40[20]; Job 29[25], and 1 Mac 6[35]. They suffice to show that the Hellenistic Jews, like all other peoples, just took it for granted that, within given limits, men are free to choose. Another rendering of *bachar* is *hairein* (*4*), literally 'to grasp', with *hairetizein* (*13*) as a variant (e.g. Jer 8[3], Ps 119[30]). Under the renderings of the next word, '*abah*, the two common Greek verbs for 'to will' emerge. *Boulesthai* renders '*abah* seventeen times (e.g. Gn 24[5]; 2 S 6[10]; Is 30[9]), and *thelein* (or *ethelein*) thirty-one times (e.g. Gn 24[8]; Dt 1[26]; 2 S 13[14]; Is 1[19]; Ezk 3[7]). For the Hebrew word for 'refuse' (*ma'en*) renderings like 'they would not' occur with *boulesthai* thirteen times (e.g. Ex 7[27]; 1 S 28[23]; Jer 13[10]; Pr 21[7]), and with *thelein* eighteen times (e.g. Gn 39[8]; Dt 25[7]; 2 S 13[9]; Is 1[20]; Ps 78[10]). Jeremiah has the phrase 'and ye would not' (with *thelein*) or its equivalent seven times (e.g. Jer 5[3]). It is remarkable that both words render the Hebrew verb *chaphetz* more often than any other term, for this means, not 'to will', but 'to take pleasure in'. There are examples for *boulesthai* (*24*) in Dt 25[7f.]; 1 K 13[33]; Jer 6[10]; Job 21[14]; Ps 70[2], and for *thelein* (*44*) in Dt 21[14]; 1 S 18[22]; Is 66[3]; Mal 3[1]; Ps 34[12]. This seems to show that, at least sometimes, both *boulesthai* and *thelein* denoted the 'pleasure' that accompanies the unhindered exercise of will rather than 'will' *simpliciter*. While both words are used far more often of the 'will' of God than of man, all the texts given above illustrate the latter. In the Apocrypha there are examples for *boulesthai* in To 5[11]; Jth 5[7]; Wis 14[19]; 1 Mac 5[48], and for *thelein* in Jth 8[15]; Sir 6[32]; Wis 13[6]; 2 Mac 13[25]. Texts that use the terms for the 'will' of *man* are remarkably few in the Psalter and the whole Wisdom Literature. Neither verb seems to be used to mean no more than 'to wish'. For the third word, *nadab*, the commonest renderings are *hekousios* and its cognates (*22*). These words derive from *hekōn*, which denotes 'willing' *simpliciter*, but in LXX they follow the use of *nadab* and denote *free gifts to*

God. Most of the examples are in Ezra-Nehemiah (e.g. Ezr 1⁴, 2⁶⁸, 7¹⁶; Neh 11²), but there are other instances (Lv 23³⁸; Ps 54⁶, 119¹⁰⁸). The terms are rare in the Apocrypha (*4*), but follow the Old Testament use. In Jth 4¹⁴ and 16¹⁸ they are used of 'freewill-offerings.' A notable text exhibits the way in which the Chasidim chose to serve the LORD unto war and death in the Maccabean days (1 Mac 2⁴²), while another describes a High Priest who, on the other hand, had 'willingly polluted himself' in the same crisis (2 Mac 14³). In passing it may be noted that *akousiŏs* (*4*), 'unwilling', and *akousiōs* (*15*), 'unwillingly', usually render *shagag* (*16*), which is discussed in another book. This verb relates to 'sins of ignorance' (which are not willed). The only other rendering of *nadab* that is at all frequent is by *prothumein*, 'to be eager' (*9*), and its adjective *prothumos* (*2*), which are confined to Chronicles (e.g. 1 Ch 29⁵; 2 Ch 29³¹) and always denote eagerness *in the service of God*. One of the three instances in the Apocrypha (2 Mac 15⁹) follows suit, the two others pointing the contrast (1 Mac 1¹³; 2 Mac 4¹⁴), as under *hekousios*.

The rendering of *mā'ēn* by *boulesthai* and *thelein* with a negative raises a nice point. In the English versions the Hebrew word is regularly and rightly rendered 'refuse'—and not 'be unwilling'— for *ma'en* is not a negative verb. It denotes a *positive* decision *not* to do something. There is a good example in the phrase 'But he refused, and said, I will not eat' (1 S 28²³; cf. 8¹⁹; Ex 4²³). In these particular texts LXX has *boulesthai*, but parallels under *thelein* are found—for instance, in Gn 37³⁵; Dt 25⁷; Hos 11⁵. In the three Hebrew poetical books there are only two examples— 'They refused to walk in his law' (Ps 78¹⁰—where the LXX manuscripts vary between *boulesthai* and *thelein*), and 'They refuse to do judgement' (Pr 21⁷), where LXX has *boulesthai*. It seems to follow that, when either of the two Greek terms occurs with the negative in the Apocrypha, it should be rendered 'refuse', or, as an alternative, 'will not' (which, unlike 'is not willing', denotes a positive act of will). There are examples for *boulesthai* in First Maccabees (e.g. 5⁴⁸, 7³⁰, 15²⁷), and it would have been better to render 1 Mac 12¹⁴ by 'We refused to be troublesome' rather than 'We were not minded'. Examples of *thelein* with the negative are rarer in the Apocrypha, but 'Refuse to sin' is preferable to 'Let not thy will be set' in To 4⁵, and 'Refuse to lie a lie' to 'Love not to make any manner of lie' in Sir 7¹³. Even in Wis 11²⁵ probably the meaning is 'How would anything have endured, if thou hadst willed that it should not?' It is likely that for the Hebrew mind the action of the will was *always positive*.

The two Greek verbs have cognate nouns, and under these the Greek use of abstract ideas is quite clear in secular literature. It has two nouns which, in their exact sense, express the mere *act* of willing, *boulēsis* and *thelēsis*, and two which denote the *outcome* of the process, *boulēma* and *thelēma*—all four without any consideration of the particular thing willed. But this is not so with the Jew, however 'Hellenized'. *Boulesis* does not occur anywhere in the whole of LXX and *boulema* only in one passage, and there the adjective 'miserable' implies the *kind* of act in view (2 Mac 15⁵; cf. Pr 9¹⁰, where *boulema* occurs as a variant reading). *Thelesis* occurs six times in the Old Testament, but then it renders such terms as *chaphets* ('pleasure'—Ezk 18²³) and *ratson* ('favour'—Pr 8³⁵; 2 Ch 15¹⁵). It has similar meanings in the Apocrypha, where it occurs three times (To 12¹⁸; Wis 16²⁵; 2 Mac 12¹⁶). *Thelema* occurs twenty-one times for *chaphets* (e.g. Ps 1²), and thirteen for *ratson* (e.g. Ps 30⁵, ⁷). It is found eight times in the Apocrypha—for instance, of the *'purpose'* of the 'rash', of the sinful, and of God (in the weather) (Sir 8¹⁵, 32¹⁷, 43¹⁶). In the Apocrypha, as in the Hebrew and Greek Old Testament, 'will' is never an abstraction, even though some of the Greek terms would admit this use.

Another word of some importance may be mentioned here. This is the verb *eudokein* (with its noun *eudokia*). It usually means not only 'to feel goodwill toward' but also to act accordingly. The verb renders nine Hebrew terms, the most frequent being *'abah* (*4*—all in Judges, e.g. 11¹⁷), *chaphetz* (*2*—e.g. Ps 51¹⁹), and *ratzah* (*17*, including eleven examples in the Psalms—e.g. Lv 26³⁴; Ps 40¹³, 68¹⁶, 85¹, 102¹⁴). It does not occur in the Book of Wisdom, but is found seven times in Sirach (e.g. 9¹², 45¹⁹). The noun *eudokia* always renders *ratson* in the Old Testament. Of its ten uses eight occur in the Psalms (e.g. 5¹², 51¹⁸, 145¹⁶). In the Apocrypha it is confined to Sirach, where it occurs sixteen times (e.g. 2¹⁶, 11¹⁷, 29²³). These two Greek words are used more frequently of the will of God than of man. They don't denote 'will' in the abstract, but a good kind of will.

Does LXX suggest that there was any difference between the meanings of *boulesthai* and *thelein*? Here the first thing to note is that the former is used in a few passages to render a Hebrew word (*ya'ats*) which means 'to advise' or 'counsel' (1 K 12⁶;

2 Ch 10⁶, ⁹, 25¹⁶), and that *thelein* is never so used. The regular
Greek word for 'counsel' is *bouleuein*. This occurs for *ya'ats* forty
times (e.g. 2 S 17⁷; Ps 31¹³). In two passages (Jer 42²²; Ezr 4⁵)
the Greek manuscripts vary between *bouleuein* and *boulesthai*—
which suggests that sometimes no clear distinction was made
between them. Again, *boulē* is the regular term for 'counsel' in
LXX. It renders twelve Hebrew terms, but nearly all these derive
from *ya'ats*, and it never renders words derived from *chaphets* or
ratzah, where the root ideas are not 'counsel', but 'delight' and
'pleasure'. *Boule* also occurs a number of times as a correlative of
bouleuein—e.g. in 'They counselled wicked counsel' (Is 7⁵) and
'The counsel which ye counselled the Lord shall scatter' (Is 8¹⁰;
cf. 14²⁶, 31⁶, 32⁷; Pr 25²²). It looks, therefore, as if in LXX all
Greek words from the root *boul* have a reference to counsel or
thought as well as to *will*, and this is not so with *thelein*. There is
even a passage where the Greek word for 'willingly' (*hekousiōs*),
is *added* to *boulesthai*, the phrase meaning 'willingly purposed'
(Ex 34²)! With *bouleuein* the combination of the two ideas of
thought and will continues in the Apocrypha. It occurs twice in
Wisdom (4¹⁷, 18⁵), five times in Sirach (9¹⁴, 12¹⁶, 37⁸, ¹⁸, 44³),
and frequently in First Maccabees. At least sometimes *boule* too
denotes choice, as well as thought. This word is found forty times
—of which four examples fall in Wisdom (6³ᶠ·, 8¹³, ¹⁷) and nineteen in Sirach (e.g. 6², 19²², 24²⁹, 37⁷, ¹³). In one passage, for
instance, *boule* is used of the *plans* for *action* of those that have
'dominion' (Wis 6³), and Sirach declares that a wise man's
'counsel' is like 'a fountain of life' (21¹³)—that is, it is a true guide
to action. The distinction, on this showing, between *boulesthai*
and *thelein* would be something like that between the two English
phrases: 'We decided (and willed) to go' and 'We wanted (and
willed) to go.' Yet it is likely enough that in common speech
there was often no consciousness of any difference in meaning.
The use of *both* verbs to render '*abah*, *ma'en* and *chaphets* suggests this.
Current speech often disregards the distinctions of exact thought.

Under the doctrine of man's 'dominion' over nature it may
first be noted that in the Apocrypha, as in the Old Testament and
indeed among all men, it is usually just assumed that men are
in some degree masters of things. For instance, the writer of
Wisdom assumes that a carpenter can, if he likes, use wood to
make an idol (14¹⁻¹¹), and he says that a potter is 'himself the
judge' of 'the use of each vessel' that he moulds—he may make

good vessels 'for our service' or, from the same clay, 'a vain god' (Wis 15⁷ᶠ·; cf. Sir 33¹³). Sirach, while he protests that 'the scribe' is superior to an 'artificer', none the less admits the value of the toil of the latter, even saying that such people as plough-men, smiths, and potters 'maintain the fabric of the age, And in the handywork of their craft is their prayer' (38²⁴⁻³⁴). On the other hand, 'the ungodly (carpenter) and his ungodliness are alike hateful to God' (Wis 14⁸ᶠ·). This shows that there may be a right and wrong use of 'dominion' as of freedom.

There are two passages in the Apocrypha where 'dominion' is not just assumed but mentioned (Sir 17²⁻⁴; Wis 9²ᶠ·; cf. 2 Es 6⁵⁴). If these passages are taken with the LXX renderings of the two relevant Old Testament passages (Gn 1²⁶⁻⁸; Ps 8⁶), several terms are found to express 'dominion'. In Genesis *archein* and *katakurieuein* occur, in the Psalm *hypotassein*, in Sirach *exousia* and *katakurieuein*, and in Wisdom *despozein* and *diepein*. The original meanings are 'to act as leader', 'to exercise lordship', 'to arrange under', 'authority', 'to be master of', and 'to arrange'. One term, *exousia*, denotes a *delegated* authority, and this is implied in all the texts. Even *despozein*, while it generally denotes *absolute* power (e.g. Ps 22²⁸; Wis 12¹⁶, ¹⁸), cannot mean this in Wis 9²ᶠ·, as the context shows. *Hypotassein* is perhaps better rendered by 'bring into submission' than 'bring into subjection', for it may refer to a voluntary subordination (e.g. Ps 62¹, ⁵), or to a submission (not by force but) through 'fear' (Sir 17⁴; Wis 18²²). In Gn 1²⁸ *katakurieuein* renders *kabash* ('subdue'); in Gn 9¹ LXX adds it to the Hebrew. The passage in Wisdom (9¹⁻⁴) shows that man's sway is meant to be exercised 'in holiness and righteousness', justice, 'uprightness', and 'wisdom'. He is to 'rule the world' with these—for their writ runs in the control of animals and things. Here, of course, there is the doctrine that man has no right to 'do just what *he* likes' with any of 'the creatures that were made by' God. He is to do what God wills. There is a hint of the idea, perhaps already implicit in Gn 1²⁶, that man should use his small control of animals and things with a 'goodness' *like* God's in the universe.[9]

⁹ The idea that God gave a Hebrew king his power is, of course, found in the Old Testament from the story of Saul onward. Later it was extended to Gentile kings, or at least to some of them (e.g. 1 K 19¹⁵; Ezr 1²; Dn 2³⁷, 5¹⁸). The word *exousia* occurs eight times in Sirach and twice in Wisdom—of God's power (Sir 10⁴; Wis 16¹³), of a ruler's authority (Sir 9¹³, 24¹¹, 45¹⁷; Wis 10¹⁴), of man's 'dominion' (Sir 17²; cf. v. 1-24), and of certain people who ought not to have authority, such as a wicked woman or a child (Sir 25²⁵, 30¹¹, 33¹⁹).

There remain the questions: 'How does LXX render Gn 1²⁶ᶠ·?' and 'How do the Apocryphal writers deal with the doctrine that man is "made in the image of GOD"?' The two may be discussed together, beginning with the second. There are two texts where Gn 1²⁶ᶠ· is quoted in the Apocrypha. In both, 'image' is rendered by *eikōn*, but other points may be taken first. One passage is in Sirach (17²ᶠ·). The general theme of the passage, as of the eighth Psalm, is the wonder that frail man should be given control over so many of the works of God. The term *exousia*, 'authority', renders the Hebrew word for 'dominion'. Man has 'strength' to exercise 'authority', the idea of freedom being implied. The other text is in the Book of Wisdom (2²³). The burden of this passage is that man was made to be immortal, and this belongs to the subject of the Hereafter. Here, however, it may be noted that the latter part of the phrase in question (as found in some manuscripts)—'an image *of his own proper being*'—is unique. The Greek term rendered 'proper being' (*idiōtēs*) means 'distinctive character', being derived from a word meaning 'one's own'. The commoner meaning of *idiotes* in ordinary Greek is 'a private person' (who keeps to his own affairs), and the term is found in this sense in Pr 6⁸ LXX, where 'kings and private persons' both find it 'healthy' to eat honey. In the passage in Wisdom the idea is that man shares in the 'idiosyncrasy' of God, in the original sense of that word. Outside the English Apocrypha the term is used of the distinctive character of a country (3 Mac 7¹⁷).

What is meant by *eikon*? Here it will be best to take the three Hebrew terms discussed earlier and to give lists of their Greek translations. The term *tzelem* is usually rendered by *eikon* (26), but it is also rendered once each by *morphē* (Dn 3¹⁹), *homoiōma* (1 S 6⁵), and *tupos* (Am 5²⁶). *Demuth* (and its verb) is translated by *homoiōsis* in Gn 1²⁶ and in five other places (Ps 58⁴; Ezk 1¹⁰, 10²²; Dn 7⁵, 10¹⁶), but in fourteen by *homoioma* (e.g. 2 K 16¹⁰; Is 40¹⁸)—notably in the first chapter of Ezekiel (v. 5, 16, 22, 26, 28; cf. 10¹, ⁸, ¹⁰, ²¹ᶠ·). The adjective *homoios* renders the root *dmth* four times (Is 13⁴; Ez 31⁸; Pr 26⁸; Ca 2⁹), and the verb *homoioun* renders it twenty times (e.g. Hos 4⁵ᶠ·; Is 1⁹; Ps 49¹², 10²⁰; Ca 1⁹). *Demuth* is also turned once by *eidea* or *idea* (Gn 5³). The third term, *temunah*, is rendered seven times by *homoioma* (Ex 20⁴; Dt 5⁸), five occurring in a single Deuteronomic passage (4¹²⁻²⁵). It is turned twice by *doxa* (Nu 12⁸; Ps 17¹⁵), and once by *morphē* (Job 4¹⁶). It will be noticed that *homoioma* renders all three terms, and *morphe* two. This suggests that for the LXX translators the three *Hebrew* terms were synonyms. *Homoioma* denotes a 'thing that is made like' another, and can be *seen* to be like it—that is, it is used in the way in which a photograph may be called 'a likeness'. It is true that in Gn 1²⁶ the Greek word is *homoiosis*, but in LXX this word and *homoioma* are mere alternatives, as appears particularly from the use of both in Ezk 1. This suggests that by 'the likeness of God' the LXX translators understood something visible, and not merely a 'spiritual' likeness. It is the same with *eikon*. The word is used both of God (Gn 1²⁷, 5¹, 9⁶), and of man (Gn 5³). In the Book of Wisdom it also occurs of 'effulgent' Wisdom herself (7²⁶), of animals (13¹³ᶠ·), and of sudden darkness (Wis 17²¹). It may be used for an idol (e.g. Dn 3¹, etc.), but also for an 'image' that is not an idol (e.g. Dn 2³¹ᶠ·). It is probably implied in Gn 1²⁶ that angels have an *eikon* ('Let *us* make man'— cf. Ps 8⁵ LXX). It is clear that *eikon* means something visible. It is the same with the other renderings of the three Hebrew terms. *Morphe* means 'shape', *tupos* 'figure', *doxa* a visible 'glory', and *eidea* 'appearance'. It seems plain that the Greek-speaking Jews, like the earlier Hebrews, thought of God as having an *eikon* or *morphe*. As already suggested, this does not require that God had a 'body', but it does mean that He was not thought of as 'wholly spiritual'. This is borne out by the uses in the Apocrypha of the other terms so far as they appear: *homoioma* in Sir 34³, 38²⁸; 1 Mac 3⁴⁸; *eidea* in Bar 6⁶³; 2 Mac 3¹⁶; *morphe* in To 1¹³; Wis 18¹. The use of the verb from *tupos* may be added (Sir 38³⁰; Wis 13¹³). *Homoiosis* does not occur in the Apocrypha. *Doxa* is considered elsewhere. For a higher notion of man's likeness to God, in the Apocrypha as well as in the Old Testament, we need to turn away from these *terms* to a consideration of certain ruling *ideas*. This is attempted in the next chapter. But the addition of *idiotes* to *eikon* in Wis 2²³, suggests that these other ideas were being applied to the *interpretation* of Gn 1²⁶ᶠ·. The phrase 'the image of his own proper being' describes the outward 'form' that expresses inward character. It recalls the term 'glory'.

The chief findings of this chapter may now be summarized. The Greek-speaking Jews inherited the Hebrew idea that man is made of two things—life and flesh. The latter was made of 'dust' or earth. The former did not wholly escape a physical reference, for it was still more or less clearly connected with 'breath'. The Hebrew idea that a man's 'flesh' consists of a number of parts, such as hand and heart, each having its own share of the 'life' that permeates a man, now largely gave way to the concept that everything made of 'flesh' goes together in a unit called 'the body' (*soma*). The four principal terms are *psyche, pneuma, kardia,* and *nous.* The first three seem, at least sometimes, to denote three aspects of one unit, for the whole range of experience is ascribed alike to them all, and *kardia* sometimes lost its reference to a particular physical organ. Yet *psyche* and *pneuma* are distinguished by the ascription of the first to animals and men, but of the second to men and God. It is under *pneuma* that the thought of the Jews has its *differentia* among Hellenists. A new set of terms emerges, *nous* and its derivatives, which interpret rather than translate the Hebrew original. Under *nous* the Greek-speaking Jew perhaps reached the idea of the wholly immaterial. The same may be true of the 'conscience', and also of the 'will', for it seems to be implied that the 'will' was now thought of as a distinct faculty in human nature, even though it is never conceived in an altogether abstract way. On the whole, it seems likely that, if the Hellenistic Jew ever considered the relation of *psyche* and *pneuma* and *kardia* and *nous* and 'will' to each other, he thought of the first four at any rate as different apects of a single unit, and, if we like, *we* can identify this with what *we* call 'personality' or 'the self', and put it over against what *we* call 'the physical'. If the Jew of the centuries before Christ thought of 'will' as a synonym for the other four terms, *we* should call him a 'dichotomist'; if he distinguished it from them, *our* term would be 'trichotomist'. Probably, however, he would have been very surprised to hear that he was either. Philo, as we have seen, made a somewhat unsuccessful attempt at the analysis that such terms pre-suppose, but there is no trace at any such attempt at precision in LXX—not even in the Book of Wisdom, where it would be most likely to occur. Sirach, who represents the ordinary devout Jew, is quite innocent of it. It is, of course, common for popular thought vaguely to grope after distinctions of which it is not clearly aware and which it does not consistently maintain. The Hellenistic Jew, like ordinary men in many lands and ages, would think of a man as a particular kind of living being, who exercised a variety of functions—and not as a bi-partite being, consisting of two disparate and wholly separable things, one belonging to a psychical and the other to a physical realm. In brief, he would think of a living man in the unitary way in which most men still think of a living animal. To discuss whether he modified this concept when he thought of a dead man belongs to another book. It seems possible that modern psychology will return more or less to the common opinion that man *is* the unit which he *seems* to be. Finally, except for one phrase in the Book of Wisdom, the doctrine that man is 'made in the image of God' is the same in LXX as in the Hebrew Old Testament.

CHAPTER FOUR

WHAT A MAN OUGHT TO BE

IN THE Apocrypha, under the question 'What ought a man to be?', by far the most important term is *sophia* ('wisdom') This occurs in the Old Testament to render *chokmah* more than a hundred and thirty times, and only ten for other terms (including five for *bīnah.*). It is the same with other words of the same Greek root as *sophia*. *Sophos* occurs over a hundred and twenty times for *chakam*, and only once each for four other words. *Sophōs* ('wisely') is found for *chokmah* or its adjective in Pr 31²⁶ and Isa 40²⁰, but it does not happen to occur in the Apocrypha. In the Old Testament *sŏphizein* ('be wise') occurs nine times for *chakam* (e.g. 1 K 5¹¹; Ps 19⁷; Ec 2¹⁵) and only once beside. In the Apocrypha it occurs ten times in Sirach (e.g. 7⁵, 10²⁶, 18²⁹), but nowhere else. *Sŏphistes* ('wise man') is found in Ex 7¹¹ and seven times in Daniel (e.g. 2¹⁴, 4¹⁵), but not in the Apocrypha. The regular use of *sophia* and *sophos* for *chokmah* and *chakam* shows that under the Greek words as under the Hebrew, there was no question of any merely intellectual or theoretical knowledge or even of mere meditation. For the Jew *sophia* was right knowledge *in right action*. Many illustrations will be found below. It may be added that the passages where *chokmah* is rendered by other terms than *sophia*— Ex 28³, 36²; Ezk 28⁴, ⁵, ⁷, ¹⁷; Pr 18⁴ (?), 31²⁶; 1 K 7¹⁴; Dn 1¹⁷— bear the same witness, as do the texts, discussed below, where *phronēsis* and *sunēsis* occur.

In the Apocrypha it is chiefly in the two 'Books of Wisdom' that the concept of *sophia* is expounded, and it will be best to take them first. The stand-point of the writer (or rather the translator) of Sirach appears in his prologue. Certain sacred books, he says, notably 'the law', have been given to Israel, and from these books men may learn the right way of life. There are students who, through *paideia* ('instruction' or 'education'), become masters in *sophia*. It is these men's business, not only to learn the ways of 'wisdom' for themselves, but to hand it on to 'them which are without'. The translator's grandfather learnt these ways and wrote them down in the Hebrew tongue, and his grandson sets himself to open this treasure of wisdom to Jews who

speak, not Hebrew, but Greek. The ruling idea is clear—'wisdom'
is given to the wise man in the Law, and it may pass from him to
others. Since there are many things in the book of Sirach of
which the Law says nothing, this implies that scribes were
already claiming that its precepts might be extended by analogy
to the whole of life, but to use a phrase from the prologue, the
main point is that the way to 'make progress' is to 'live according
to the law'.

The grandfather begins his book with an account of Wisdom,
using the term twelve times (Sir 1). He personifies her, as in
Pr 1–9. The chapter falls into three parts. In the first (v. 1–9)
he declares that 'There is (but) one wise . . . the Lord sitting
upon His throne'; that Wisdom is the first of His creatures, whom
He 'poured out upon all His works'; that it is as impossible for
man to discover Wisdom for himself as to unravel the secrets of
the sea, the heaven, and the deep; and that 'all wisdom cometh
from the Lord'. It is God's gift (cf. 6³⁷, 43³³). In the second part
(v. 10–20) Sirach declares that God gives Wisdom to man if only
he will receive her. He offers her in some degree to 'all flesh', but
'lavishes' (v. 10) the gift on 'them that love him'. She has the
secret of all health and wealth. There is but one condition of the
gift—'The fear of the Lord'. This phrase tolls through the
second part of the passage like a great bell. By 'fear' Sirach,
like Old Testament writers, does not mean fright, but awe and
worship and humility and obedience. If a man 'fear the Lord'
in this sense Wisdom is his. In the third part (v. 22–30) Sirach
describes the temper of a wise man as he teaches and the temper
of a learner as he listens. The former is not irritable and, if need
be, he can be silent for a while, for he knows that his opportunity
will come. The true disciple must be trustful and meek, obedient
and sincere. The sin of *pretending* to seek Wisdom is specially
stressed. But if a man has a true desire for her, God will 'lavish'
her on him. The ruling idea of the passage is that God is like a
great Rabbi, who, in the way and degree that He thinks well,
passes on His wisdom to His disciples—and the disciples become
a little wise too. Though the writer does not say so, there is here
the doctrine that in the realm of 'wisdom' a man may be a little
like God.

There are other passages besides Chapter 1 were Sirach speaks
at some length about Wisdom, and each adds something to his
account of her. In one (Sir 4¹¹⁻¹⁹) he describes her 'discipline' or

HBM

'way of education' (v. 17f.; cf. 6^{18-22}, 23^{1-6}). At the first she
leads a man by 'twisting' ways until she fairly 'torments' him,
but this is only to 'put him to the test'. If he will not follow her
path she will 'give him over to the hands of his (inevitable) fall';
if, on the other hand, she finds that she may 'trust his soul', she
will lead him to 'the straight way' and gladden him with her
secrets. To 'love her' is to 'love life', to 'inherit glory', and to
'minister to the Holy One', for God 'loves' them that 'love'
Wisdom. In the end the wise shall 'judge the nations'—for it is
they who already begin to know the mind of the final Judge. In
a second passage (14^{20}–15^{10}), which begins with a promise of
'happiness' or 'blessedness' to the man who lives his life to the
end 'in wisdom', there is an account, under an Eastern picture,
of his assiduity. First, he tracks Sophia down in the streets, then
follows her home, eavesdrops at her windows and doors, makes
his home next door to hers, and finally finds his way into her
home so often that he 'fastens a nail' for his cloak to hang on in
the walls of her guest-room. She welcomes him at last as a mother
welcomes her son or a bride her bridegroom. In this passage, as
elsewhere, to 'fear the Lord' is the same thing as to 'possess the
law' (cf. 21^{11}) and to 'obtain' Wisdom. As everywhere else, it
is taken for granted that, if any man *will*, he *can* be 'wise'.
On the one hand, if a man chooses to be a 'sinner' and a 'fool',
if he is proud and a liar, Wisdom will have nothing to do
with him; on the other hand, to the man who chooses her she
will give glory and joy and 'an everlasting name'.

Another passage (Sir 24) falls into four parts. In the first two
Wisdom 'praises her own soul'. She delights first (v. 3–7) because,
at the creation, 'coming forth from the mouth of the Most High'
she and she alone 'circled' the universe and 'got a possession in
every people and nation'. Yet, second, she sought a tabernacle of
rest, and found it, at God's behest, in Israel and in Zion (v. 7–17).
There Wisdom has flourished like a fair tree, with perfume and
flower and fruit. Thirdly (v. 19–29), she calls everyone who
'desires' her to a feast that never satiates, for her bounty is the
'book of the covenant of the Most High God', given in 'the law
of Moses' for a 'heritage to Jacob'. Her wealth is the wealth of
the Rivers of Paradise, as in the beginning—and of Jordan, the
river of Israel. While the first man *began* to 'know her', the last
will not be able to 'trace her (fully) out' any more than a man can
exhaust the sea. In the fourth part (v. 30–4) the wise man stands

amazed at himself. Has he not led a little 'conduit' from a water-
course and has it not swollen, first to a stream, then to a river,
and then to a sea? Further, not for himself only has he 'laboured!'
In this passage the connexion of Wisdom with the Law is peculiarly clear. For Sirach, again, there was no 'great gulf fixed'
between nature and revelation for it was *through the Law* in
Genesis that he learnt the truth that *God made the universe*—a creed
unique in his world.

Two other passages describe the wise man. The first (38²⁴–
39¹¹) spends itself upon the pre-eminence of 'the scribe'. Unlike
the husbandman, the artificer, the smith, and the potter, he has
'leisure' to 'become wise'. It is true that they 'uphold the fabric
of the age', but he does a greater thing—by the study of the
'wisdom of the ancients', by sorting the good from the bad in the
ways of 'strange nations', and most of all by learning through
prayer, he 'pours forth the words of his wisdom', and 'leaves a
greater name than a thousand' (cf. 25⁷⁻¹²). The scribe is man
par excellence, for his 'glory' is 'the law of the covenant of the Lord'.
In the other passage (51¹³⁻³⁰; cf. 50²⁷⁻⁹), Sirach first describes his
own life. From youth to age he has sought Wisdom and found her.
Purposing to practice wisdom, he has 'wrestled in her', yet still
'bewailed his ignorance of her'. He has been given 'a heart joined
with her from the beginning' and a 'tongue' wherewith to 'praise
the Lord'. He turns, therefore, as is his duty, to 'the unlearned',
calling them to 'put their neck under (her) yoke' (cf. 20³⁰ᶠ·). Is
she not 'close at hand to find', and worth any man's wealth? An
earlier sage's text is also Sirach's—'Wisdom is the principal thing;
therefore get wisdom' (Pr 4⁷).

Other passages deal more closely with the *practice* of wisdom.
Here comes the hypocrite, who pretends to practise it when he
doesn't. He is 'like a ship in a storm' (33²; cf. 1²⁹, 32¹⁵). A
second passage (15¹¹⁻²⁰) declares roundly what, as we have seen,
is everywhere assumed, that a man can be good or bad as he
chooses. God, in His wisdom, has set 'fire and water', 'life and
death', before every man, and He does not 'cause him to err' in
his choice. 'To perform faithfulness is of (a man's) own good
pleasure.' Again, mere knowledge, as such, is no wisdom, but
babble (21¹⁸⁻²⁰)—that is, wisdom unused is not wisdom. It
is the same with knowledge misused (37¹⁹⁻²²). The 'shrewd'
fellow, who misleads by 'subtil words', is 'unprofitable to his
own soul'.

It is plain that everything that Sirach says about Wisdom is
just an exposition of his account of her in his first chapter. One
series of ideas—God, Wisdom, the Law, the wise man, the younger
man seeking wisdom—is constant. 'The congregation' is mentioned several times. The Greek word is 'synagogue', and, while
it is applied more than once to gatherings in Israel's past, it is
difficult to resist the impression that Sirach himself attended a
synagogue of a more or less formal kind. Indeed, in many a
passage one can all but hear the old man talking to a gathering
of Jews. To discuss the virtues and deficiencies of his *social* teaching is outside our present subject. His motto and the synagogue's
is 'Know the Law of the Lord, for in its practice is wisdom'. In
Sirach there may be a Sadducean flavour here and there, but its
writer is a precursor of such honest Pharisees as Saul of Tarsus.
Finally, it is clear that in the main Sirach repeats and expands
the teaching of the Book of Proverbs.

The writer of the Book of Wisdom lived a couple of centuries,
more or less, later than Sirach. He shows that he is aware, as
Sirach does not, of a challenge to Judaism from the Gentiles. His
book, therefore, is an *apologia* as well as an exhortation. It falls
into three parts. First, the writer defends the practice of righteousness, whatever betide, because it leads to immortality (1–4).
Next, he tells of the origin and nature of Wisdom, using the word
twenty-five times (Wis 6^1–11^1). Thirdly, he describes the ways of
God with the Israelites, the Canaanites, and most of all with the
idolatrous Egyptians, spending himself on a description of the
horrors of the Ten Plagues (11^2–19^{22}). While there is a formal
connexion between the three parts—for, speaking in the name of
Solomon, the writer links the assurance of immortality with the
urgent recommendation of Wisdom to kings (1^1, 6^1), and he pre-
faces his account of the Exodus with a chapter that describes
Wisdom's work in still earlier days (10)—yet the connexion is not
very close. At 11^2 the writer practically drops the mask of
Solomon and in his third part he only mentions 'wisdom' in one
passage ($14^{2,\ 5}$), though he would no doubt have maintained
that God's ways with the Egyptians were a manifestation of His
wisdom. The subject of his first part, immortality, belongs to
another book. It is chiefly the second part that is pertinent here.
In it some have traced the influence of Stoicism, but, whether
they are right or not, there can be no doubt that this writer was a
loyal Jew. The basis of his teaching is not, as with the Stoics, a

belief in an almighty and deterministic Something, but in the righteous God who has made Himself known to Israel (e.g. 5^{15-23}, 9^{1-8}, 11^{2-20}, 19^{22}). For him 'wisdom' is no impersonal 'ultimate' but the 'wisdom of God'.

It will be convenient to compare the teaching of this writer with that of Sirach, attending chiefly to the likenesses first and then to the differences. The later writer, like the earlier, holds that 'wisdom cometh from the Lord'—and from no other source, whether within or without man. This appears, for instance, in the emphasis on the need for a man to *pray* that he may be given wisdom (7^7, 9^{1-18}), and in the declaration that God is the 'One that guideth even wisdom and that correcteth the wise' (7^{15}). Again, as with Sirach, Wisdom is the first of God's creatures, for she 'was present when (God) was making the world' (9^9), and it is Wisdom that permeates and holds together the universe (e.g. 7^{24}, 8^1). With both writers the wisdom manifest in creation is the same as the wisdom given to man for the right ordering of life (9^{1-18}). With both Wisdom comes from God, and she is altogether His gift (8^{21}, 9^4). It is true that in the later book Wisdom is ostensibly offered to 'rulers' only, for the form of the book requires this— the idealized Solomon commending the true secret of rule to other rulers—but in reality Wisdom is open to all men. This is asserted, in effect, in a passage that speaks of *man's* 'dominion over the creatures that were made by' God (9^2), and, as matter of fact, kings have no monopoly of the characteristics that the book ascribes to Wisdom. Again, for this writer, as for Sirach, the 'wise man' is the perfect man. Yet again, the formal address to *all* 'kings' implies that even *Gentiles* may learn wisdom. It may be recalled that for Sirach 'the wise' were ultimately to 'judge the nations' (Sir 4^{15}; cf. Wis 6^{21}). Again, for the later writer, as for Sirach, Wisdom is pre-eminently 'teacher' (e.g. 7^{22}), and the way to learn from her is to 'love her' (6^{12}), for 'love of her is observance of her laws' (6^{18}). Similarly, this writer declares that 'they that use (the treasure) of Wisdom prepare for themselves friendship with God' (7^{14}). Here, of course, some degree of likeness to God is implied by the terms 'love' and 'friendship', for lovers and friends must 'have something in common'. Again, the humility of the seeker after wisdom and his assiduity in his search are both illustrated—for instance, in 'Solomon's' description of his own early days (7^{1-14}, 9^{4-18}). It is the humble and persistent search for wisdom every day that is the high calling of man. Again, for this writer, as for Sirach, it is the duty of a wise man to pass on his wisdom to others. To do anything else were 'pining envy', which has no 'fellowship with wisdom', for 'a multitude of wise men is salvation to the world' (7²²⁻⁵). Finally, it is everywhere an axiom with the later writer, as with the earlier, that a man *can* be 'wise' and so live the right kind of life, if he *will*.

Turning to the differences between the writers of Wisdom and Sirach, we may note first two variations in emphasis. There were certain ideas that no sincere Jew could escape, but some of these, in the foreground with Sirach, are in the background with the later exponent of Wisdom. The latter never uses the term synagogue or 'congregation', and, while he recognizes that God is 'God of the fathers' of Israel, that the Hebrews are 'his people', and that the Jews are His 'sons and daughters' (Wis 9¹, ⁷, ¹², 10¹⁵), he does not as nearly as Sirach treat 'wisdom' as the monopoly of the Jew. As we have seen, he depicts 'Solomon' as offering her to heathen kings. While, similarly, he assumed that 'the Law' has been given to Israel (16⁶, 18⁴, ⁹)—and what Jew would or could deny it?—it is not a leading concept in the part of his book in which he spends himself in describing Wisdom. Indeed, there the word for 'law' (*nŏmos*) only occurs three times—once in an address to kings (where the word probably means 'law', not 'the Law'), once of 'the laws of wisdom', and once of Solomon's 'small power to understand judgement and laws' (6⁴, ¹⁸, 9⁵). In other words, for this writer, in his most characteristic section, 'law' is something wider than 'the Law'. It is consonant with this that the term 'righteousness', as will appear later, bulks more largely in his teaching than in that of Sirach. His list of the heroes of Israel in Chapter 10, stretches, not, like Sirach's list of famous men (Sir 49⁴), from Enoch to Simon the High Priest, but from Adam to Joseph—that is, it describes men who lived before the Law was given. The list does indeed include Moses but here Moses is leader rather than teacher (Wis 11¹). While the difference from Sirach here is only a matter of perspective, the perspective of a man's mind denotes a great deal.

A second difference between the two writers appears in their account of the ways of Wisdom with men. It is true, indeed, that for both she must be 'sought' and for both she gives herself to the sincere seeker, but, while in Sirach the emphasis is on her devotee's search for her, in the Book of Wisdom it is on her search for him. Indeed, she comes to meet him and her brightness is so 'radiant' that she is 'easily beheld' by 'them that love her' ($6^{12ff.}$). The later writer says nothing of her 'twisting ways'. This too, however, is only a difference of emphasis, for the writer of Wisdom, like Sirach, speaks of a *paideia* that is 'discipline' and not mere teaching (1^5, 2^{12}, 3^{11}, 6^{17}, 7^{14}), and of the way in which God 'chasteneth', or rather 'disciplines', men (3^5, $6^{11, 25}$, 11^9, 12^{22}).

This difference in emphasis and perspective reaches its climax in this writer's definition of 'wisdom' as '*spirit*'. Even this idea had *some* anticipation, for there is one Old Testament passage where 'the spirit of the LORD' is called 'the spirit of wisdom' (Is 11^2; cf. 61^1), and another where Wisdom herself speaks of 'my spirit' (Pr 1^{23}). Sirach too says once that the 'wise man' is 'filled with the spirit of understanding' (Sir 39^6). But the writer of Wisdom makes the concept dominant. He uses the word *pneuma* in relation to Wisdom in three ways—first, she is called 'the spirit of the Lord' (1^7), God's 'holy spirit' (9^{17}), and His 'incorruptible spirit' (12^1); next, she is called 'a spirit' (1^6); lastly, there is said to be 'a spirit in her' (7^{22}; cf. v. 7). The greatest passage in the book (7^{22}–8^1) is divided formally between a description of the 'spirit' that is in Wisdom ($7^{22f.}$) and a description of Wisdom herself (7^{24}–8^1), but in reality the two are one. The passage has the splendour of a galaxy, and to anatomize a galaxy is ill work, but the following seem to be the chief ideas: (*a*) Wisdom is to God as light is to the sun, but *this* sun never sets ($7^{25f., 29f.}$); (*b*) the 'spirit in wisdom' has certain negative splendours—it cannot be sullied or polluted; it is invulnerable and irresistible; it cannot be 'tripped up'; it is never anxious. The Revised Version renders some of these words as past participles (e.g. 'unpolluted', 'unharmed',) but they seem rather to fall under the list of adjectives that 'answer to Latin words in—*bilis*';[1] (*c*) of positive adjectives some chiefly describe the 'spirit in wisdom' *per se*—it is intelligent, holy, only-begotten (*monogenēs*), manifold, tenuous, inerrant, and steadfast; some describe its relation to the universe—it is mobile, keen or sharp, almighty, all-overseeing; and some its relation to man—it is easy to discern; it loves what is good; it is beneficent; it loves man; it makes its way through all 'spirits' that are intelligent and pure and very tenuous. Perhaps the last phrase implies that the spirit of Wisdom is ready to *make* the spirit of man intelligent, pure, and tenuous—like itself. While the verses that formally describe Wisdom herself (and not her 'spirit') repeat

[1] J. H. Moulton, *Grammar of New Testament Greek*, I. p. 222.

some of these ideas, their chief subject is a climacteric marvel—
Wisdom, being an 'outflowing' of God's glory, an 'effulgence' of
His light, a 'mirror' of His activity, and an 'image' of His goodness, passes, wonder beyond belief!, into 'holy souls' and makes
them 'friends of God and prophets'. In the sequel ($8^{2\,\text{ff.}}$) 'Solomon'
tells how he has loved Wisdom and made her his bride, and how
'she teacheth soberness and sagacity, righteousness and courage'.
So this cosmic 'spirit' is ethical too. In the last quotation there
seems to be an echo of the four-fold doctrine of *sophia* in Plato,
(with variations) just as the description of the 'spirit of wisdom'
recalls the teaching of the Stoics—but both are 'baptized into'
Hebraism. Elsewhere the writer adds a second marvel—there are
men who *refuse* the gift of Wisdom (e.g. 1^{16}, $2^{21\text{f.}}$; cf. 7^{28})! The
will of man can and does resist the irresistible! Even man's sin,
therefore, testifies to his greatness. This creature can say 'no' to
God. On the other hand, if he will, he may share in the wisdom,
and so in the righteousness, of God Himself. Two other passages
about Wisdom follow (8^2, 9^{18}, 10^1–11^1), but they hardly do more
than illustrate what has already been said. In the first, 'Solomon'
describes his life-long zest in the pursuit of Wisdom and her
treasures, and then falls to prayer that she may still be given him.
The second shows Wisdom at work, in this episode and that,
from Adam to Moses. The ruling idea in both is that Wisdom is
man's God-given guide to the good life and therefore 'the one
thing needful'.

It is sometimes said that the doctrine of Wisdom in the inter-
Testamental period is equivalent to the doctrine of 'The Spirit of
the Lord' in the Old Testament, but, apart from the Book of
Wisdom, this is scarcely so. There are clear differences. First,
in the Old Testament, the Spirit of the Lord is either a special
gift to a *few*, or a gift promised to *all* in the *future*, but in the
Apocrypha, Wisdom is offered to *all now*. Next, in the Old
Testament the Spirit sweeps down upon a man and masters him
willy-nilly, but in the Apocrypha man is free to take or leave
Wisdom. Thirdly, of the two concepts power and knowledge it
is the first that is dominant in the Old Testament doctrine of the
Spirit of God, but the second in the concept of Wisdom. Fourthly,
while man has a 'spirit' of his own as over against the Spirit of
God, this is not so with 'wisdom'. Man has and can have no
'wisdom' of his own. Similarly, while a man's 'spirit' may be
evil, there is no such thing as a sinful wisdom. As has been seen,

the term 'spirit' is only once connected with Wisdom in Sirach. In Philo (omitting the use of the word for literal 'air') it is not frequent; indeed he only uses it 'under the suggestion of some passage of Scripture'.[2] It is in the Book of Wisdom, and there only, that the doctrines of 'the Spirit of God' and His 'Wisdom' tend to be the same. Yet, as its writer ascribes a distinct *pneuma* to man (2³, 5³, 15¹¹, ¹⁶, 16¹⁴), even there it is impossible to equate 'spirit' and 'wisdom'. Again, God's *pneuma* and man's are not related to each other as in Ps 51. It is elsewhere that the writer of Wisdom makes his special contribution. With him the Spirit of God is *now* offered to *every* man who is *willing* to receive the gift. This was a great advance upon the teaching of Ezekiel and Joel, for that only promised a future gift, given only to Israelites. In the Book of Wisdom God offers His Spirit, which is Wisdom, to every man, and if a man accepts the gift, he thereby becomes a 'wise' man and like God.

The term *sophia* only occurs nine times in the Apocrypha outside the two Wisdom books, and *sophos* only in three passages, all in First Esdras (3⁵, ⁹, 4⁴², 5⁶), and none of the twelve passages does more than repeat, incidentally, some of the ideas already described. For instance, God is called 'the fountain of wisdom' (Bar 3¹²; cf. 1 Es 4⁵⁹ᶠ·, 8²³), and Judith's 'wisdom' clearly belongs, not to the realm of theory, but of practice (Jth 8²⁹, 11⁸, ²⁰).

Some mention may be made of three groups of words which are used as synonyms for 'wisdom' and 'wise'. They all describe wisdom in practical life. The first consists of words derived from a Greek term for 'mind' (*phrēn*) (originally 'midriff'). It is not itself found in the Apocrypha, and the verb *phronein*, 'to take thought how to act', is also rare (8–e.g. 1 Mac 10²⁰). It occurs in the opening sentence of Wisdom where 'to take thought' about God is the key to life (1¹). The derived adjective, *phronimos*, and the abstract noun, *phronēsis*, usually translate either *bīn* and *bīnah* (or *tebūnah*), with the meaning 'discern' and 'discernment' (e.g. Pr 1², 8¹⁴, 14⁶, 20⁶), or *chakam* and *chokmah* (e.g. 1 K 3²⁸, 10⁴; Job 34²⁴; Pr 11²⁹). Perhaps the nearest English terms are 'skill' and 'sagacity'. In the Old Testament there is a good instance of *phronesis* (*39*) in the skill to rule that God gave Solomon (1 K 3²⁸, 10⁴). God Himself shows *phronesis* in creation (Jer 10¹²) and in history (Is 40²⁸), and Wisdom says 'I am *phronesis*' (Pr 8¹⁴). The

[2] See *HDB*, Extra Vol., p. 206.

rendering 'prudence' therefore, with its merely utilitarian suggestion, is not happy. *Phronimos* (*30*) can be used in a bad sense
to mean 'subtil' (e.g. Gn 3¹), but a man is truly 'sagacious' when
he understands the ways of God (Dt 32²⁹; cf. Ps 94⁸). There is a
cognate word *phrontis* (*3*) for the 'anxiety' of a sinner (Job 15²⁰).

In the Apocrypha *phronesis* (*18*) is almost confined to Sirach (*5*)
and Wisdom (*10*). Like *sophia* it is the antecedent of God's creation (Sir 1⁴), and among men the monopoly of those that 'fear the
Lord' (Sir 19²⁰ᶠ·; cf. 25⁹). In the book of Wisdom it is the product
of *sophia* (6¹⁵, 7⁷; cf. 17⁷). The adjective *phronimos* (*12*) is commonest in Sirach (*9*), who uses it five times in a passage where he
contrasts the wise man and the fool (21¹⁵⁻²⁸). *Phrontizein* (*10*)
denotes for him 'anxiety' (e.g. 8¹³, 32¹), but the writer of Wisdom
uses its noun *phrontis* (*5*) for God's 'care' of the righteous (5¹⁵),
and the wise man's 'care' for 'discipline' (6¹⁹), as well as for a
potter's 'care' as he moulds an idol (15⁹).

The second group of words consists of three terms: *sunienai*
(which means literally 'put together') and its derivatives, the
adjective *sunetos*, and the verbal noun *sunesis*. Perhaps the nearest
English equivalents are 'understand' and 'understanding' (adjective and noun). *Sunienai* is often used in LXX to render *bin* (e.g.
Neh 8²ᶠ·; Ps 19¹²; Pr 2⁵), but in the Apocrypha it is confined to
the Book of Wisdom and there it only occurs three times (3⁹, 6¹,
9¹¹). The adjective *sunĕtos* is found in LXX both for *bin* (e.g.
Job 34¹⁰; Pr 17²⁴; Is 29¹⁴) and for *chakam* (e.g. Gn 41³³; Is 5²¹).
In the Apocrypha it is confined to Sirach, where it occurs eighteen
times (e.g. 3²⁹, 7²⁵, 10²³). The abstract noun *sunĕsis* renders seven
Hebrew terms, of which the commonest is *bin* (e.g. Ex 31³;
Pr 2²ᶠ·), but it is used six times for *chokmah* (e.g. Ex 31⁶; Is 49¹⁰).
In the Apocrypha it is found thirty times in Sirach (e.g. 1⁴, 6³⁵,
24²⁶, 44⁴; cf. Bar 3¹⁴). The third group also has three terms—
the noun *epistēmē*, the adjective *epistēmōn*, and the verb *epistasthai*.
They all run back to a verb meaning 'to set (one's mind) on (a
thing)' and refer to the resultant 'experience'. In the Old Testament the verb *epistasthai* (*51*) almost always renders the common
Hebrew word for 'know' (*yada'*). Though it had a religious use,
it was the word that a Jew used when he was not thinking of
religious knowledge. It is therefore rare in the Apocrypha (*3*—
Wis 8⁸, 9⁹, 15³), but the last of these passages shows what a Jew
could do even with a 'neutral' word—'To set the mind on thee is
entire righteousness'. The adjective *epistemon*, which describes a

'man of experience' is rare in LXX (*13*), as, apart from Sirach (*17*), is the noun *epistēmē* (*9*). There are passages under both that show the Hebrew attitude to experience divorced from religion (e.g. Is 5²¹; Ez 28⁴⁻⁷). Sirach, who can ascribe *episteme* to God (33¹¹), teaches that 'experience' justifies 'wisdom' (e.g. 1¹⁹, 16²⁴, 17⁷). He declares that 'the *experience* of wickedness is not *wisdom*, And where there is the counsel of sinners there is no *sagacity*' (19²²). The whole range of the vocabulary of knowledge in the Old Testament, whether in Hebrew or Greek, shows that from first to last an 'Israelite indeed' set no value upon knowledge apart from will and ethics—or apart from God.

From the consideration of the words 'wisdom' and 'spirit' it appears, then, that man in his diminutive way is or may be like God. The Greek renderings of the other terms named in Chapter 2 may now be examined. The first of these is 'righteousness', for *tsedaqah* (or *tsedeq*). With this there goes the adjective *tzaddiq* ('righteous'). In the Old Testament the two terms are in an overwhelming number of texts rendered by *dikaiŏsunē* and *dikaios*. In the Apocrypha these Greek words are commonest in Wisdom, then in Sirach, and then in Tobit and First Maccabees. There is not a single passage in the whole list that does not express or imply the idea that there is some link between the righteous God and the righteous man. Of course, too, the mere use of the word for both (and for no other being) itself implies a likeness between them.[3] The truth is that in and after the Exile the whole world was for the Jew a vast battle-ground betwee righteousness and iniquity, in which the former usually seem to be being worsted, but in which the victory of the righteous v ultimately sure because God is righteous. It is true that in or two texts (e.g. Sir 35¹⁸; Wis 18⁷, ²⁰) there is the particulari idea that Israel is righteous and the Gentiles sinful, and prob this notion was very prevalent among the Jews. But it h large amount of truth in it. In the Dispersion, to which m

---

[3] In Sirach, *dikaiosune* occurs in the following passages: 16²², 26²⁸, 38³³, 44¹⁰ and *dikaios* in 9¹⁶, 10²³, 27⁸, 33³, 35⁶ᶠ·,¹⁸, 44¹⁷. In Wisdom, *dikaiosune* occurs i 2¹¹, 5⁶, ¹⁸, 8⁷, 9³, 12¹⁶, 14⁷, 15³; and *dikaios* in 2¹⁰, ¹², ¹⁶, ¹⁸, 3¹, ¹⁰, 4⁷, 16 10⁴, ⁵, ⁶, ¹⁰, ¹³, ²⁰, 11¹⁴, 12⁹, ¹⁵, ¹⁹, 14³⁰, 16¹⁷, ²³, 18⁷, ²⁰, 19¹⁷. There are e for Tobit in 2¹⁴, 3², 4⁵, ¹⁷, 13⁶, ⁹, ¹³, 14⁷. In First Maccabees the words 2²⁹, ⁵², 7¹², 11³³, 14³⁵. The adverb *dikaios* which occurs three times in the G Testament for *tsedek* (e.g. Dt 1¹⁶) is found in Sir 35¹⁸; Wis 9¹², 12¹⁵, 19¹³; 2 9⁶, 13⁷. There are two other terms here—the verb *dikaioun*, discussed in *Doctrine of Sin*, and the noun *dikaioma*. The latter is only used for *tsedaqah* in the Old Testament (2 S 19²⁹, Ezk 13²¹, Pr 8²⁰); it occurs in the Apocr 8⁷; Sir 4¹⁷, 32¹⁶; Bar 2¹², ¹⁷, ¹⁹, 4¹³; 1 Mac 1¹³, ⁴⁹, 2²¹, ⁴⁰.

the Apocryphal books belong, only *faithful* Jews would remain Jews, and there can be no doubt that the level of the life that centred in the Synagogue was much higher than in its Hellenistic environment. Broadly speaking, the Jews *were* righteous and the Gentiles sinners. Two texts from Wisdom are representative of the whole teaching: 'To be acquainted with (God) is entire righteousness' (15³), '(The righteous man) shall put on righteousness as a breast-plate' (6¹⁸).

The synonym *yashar* ('straight') has some twenty-five Greek renderings, the commonest being *euthus* (*86*), with its noun *euthutēs* (*20*) and its verb *kata-euthunein* (*9*). While *euthus* can be used of God (Ps 25⁸), these words are not of much importance either in the Apocrypha (*22*) or the New Testament. In the former the verb is commonest (*10*) and always means 'to make a *path* straight'. God 'makes straight the path' both of exiled Israel and of every Jew if they are faithful (Jth 8²³, 12⁸, 13¹⁸). Judith 'walked a straight way before God' (Jth 13²⁰). In Sirach to pursue 'wisdom' is to 'set the heart straight' (51¹⁵, ²⁰; cf. 49²ᶠ·), for, however perplexing her ways are at first, she ends with 'the straight way' (4¹⁷ᶠ·). The Book of Wisdom has only three passages—'wisdom knows . . . what is straight' (9⁹; cf. 10¹⁰), as man did when God made him (9³). These words only repeat the doctrine of righteousness under the metaphor of a straight path.

While the Hebrew word for 'good' (*tob*) and its cognates have about forty Greek renderings, the commonest are *agathos* and *kalos*. The former occurs over three hundred times and the latter over a hundred. It is *agathos* that is used for the 'goodness' of God, and under it a man too may be 'good'. An examination of ⸦p⸧assages would repeat what was said under the Hebrew term. ⸦A⸧nother translation of *tob*, *chrēstos* (*28*)—with its noun *chrēstotēs* ⸦5⸧)—may be mentioned. In the Old Testament the phrases ⸦Go⸧d is good' and 'Thou art good' occur twenty-one times; in ⸦twel⸧ve the rendering is *chrestos* (e.g. Nah 1⁷; Ps 25⁸, 34⁸, 86⁵), and ⸦i⸧n ⸦ni⸧ne *agathos* (e.g. 1 Ch 16³⁴; 2 Ch 30¹⁸). While the latter only ⸦occ⸧urs once in the Psalms, there are parallel phrases (54⁶, 118²⁹, 143⸦⸧. *Chrestos* originally meant 'serviceable', and 'kindly' is a good ⸦re⸧ndering. 'O give thanks unto the Lord, for He is kindly, for Hi⸦s⸧ mercy endureth for ever' is the typical text. The adjective *chrestos*, ⸦h⸧owever, is only used three times about man (Ps 112⁵; Pr 2²¹; J⸦e⸧ 44¹⁷). It is under the noun *chrestotes*, which is confined

to the Psalms and is used ten times of God and five of man, that
the idea clearly appears that man is to be 'kindly' because God
is. Three phrases in Ps 119 (v. 65–8) are good examples: 'Thou
hast wrought kindliness, O Lord, with thy servant according to
thy word. Teach me kindliness . . . because I have believed in
thy commandments. . . . Kindly art thou, O Lord, and in thy
kindliness teach me thy judgements' (cf. Ps 37³, 85¹²). In the few
uses of *chrestos* (*6*) and *chrestotes* (*3*) in the Apocrypha (e.g. Wis 8¹,
15¹) there is nothing noteworthy.

The next word used both for God and man is 'holy'. In the
translation of the Old Testament there are some twenty-five
Greek renderings for the Hebrew term *qadosh* and its cognates.
Most of these, however, are very rarely used and only a few are
relevant here. By far the commonest are *hagios* (*557*) and terms
of the same root. The translation is a good one, for the original
idea of the Greek root is 'awe'. The terms in question are *hagios*
('holy' or 'saint'), *hagiazein* and *kathagiazein* ('hallow' or 'sanctify'),
hagiasmos ('holiness' or 'sanctification'), *hagiasma* (a thing sanctified), *hagiosunē* ('holiness'), and a term only found in the
Apocrypha, *hagiotēs* ('holiness'). The fundamental idea throughout, of course, is that *God* is holy. In the Apocrypha, where
hagios (*135*) is commonest in the two Wisdom books (*32*) and
Maccabees (*61*), the phrase 'the Holy One' is an alternative for
word 'God' itself (e.g. To 12¹²; Sir 4¹⁴, 23⁹, 43¹⁰, 47⁸, 48¹⁰;
Bar 4²², ³⁷, 5⁵¹). The word is also used of God's 'holy name'
(To 3¹¹, 8⁵; Sir 47¹⁰; Wis 10²⁰), of the 'spirit' of God (Sir 48¹²;
Wis 9¹⁷), and of the 'spirit of wisdom' (Wis 7²²). It may also be
used of angels (To 11¹⁴, 12¹⁵). The most frequent use of *hagios*,
however, is to describe *things* 'sanctified' through their connexion
with God. Here the predominant use is of the Temple and things
belonging to it. For the Temple itself there are examples in 1 Es
1⁵³; Jth 4¹²ᶠ·, 8²¹, ²⁴; Sir 24¹⁰; Wis 9⁸. In the First Book of Maccabees, where this use is very frequent, the word is rendered 'sanctuary' (e.g. 4⁴²⁻⁵¹, 10³⁹⁻⁴⁴, 14²⁷⁻⁴⁹; cf. 2 Mac 15¹⁴). Of things
belonging to the Temple, the ark, for instance, is called 'holy'
(1 Es 1³), as also the first-fruits (Sir 7³¹), the candlestick (Sir
26¹⁷), the high-priest's garment (Sir 45¹⁰), the oil (Sir 45¹⁵), the
altar (Sir 50¹¹). Similarly the word is used of the Sabbath
(1 Es 9⁵⁰), and of a feast (To 2¹), of the 'holy city' (To 13⁹),
'mountain' (Wis 9⁸), and 'land' (Wis 12³). It may be used too
of the 'heavens' as the abode of God (Wis 9¹⁰), of His laws (2 Mac

6²³, ²⁸), and His 'knowledge' (2 Mac 6³⁰). It is used of the 'sword' (2 Mac 15¹⁶). It goes without saying that when used of *things* the term is altogether ritualistic, or, if it be held that some concept such as *mana* still clung to the word, at least that no moral idea is involved. While the passages where the term is used of *God* do not plainly express the idea that His 'righteousness' is a part of His 'holiness', yet, in view of the movement of later Old Testament thought, this may safely be assumed in the Apocrypha. The word is used to describe *men* less frequently (*14*). It is applied to priests (1 Es 8⁵⁸; Sir 45⁶) and to all Israel (1 Es 8⁷⁰; Sir 49¹²; Wis 17²). It may be noted that, where the Hebrew uses *qadesh* and *qedeshah* to denote a sacred prostitute, the Greek avoids *hagios*, *pornē* being used—for instance, in Gn 38²¹ and Dt 23¹⁸ (and *angelos* in Job 26¹⁴). In all these uses the Apocrypha repeats the ideas of the Old Testament—God is holy and the one source of holiness; whatever belongs to Him, whether it be a thing or man or nation, is thereby holy; the holiness of the Temple and all that goes with it is specially prominent; while God's 'holiness' still includes the concepts of the numinous and the righteous and the separate, the 'holiness' of men and things is a *ritual* separateness. In particular, the 'holiness' of the priests was still predominantly or even altogether ritual. There were good priests, for one was called 'Simon the Just', perhaps with implications about some others! Mattathias, too, who led the Maccabean revolt, was a priest. No doubt both these were loyal to the whole Law, alike on its ethical and ritual sides. Indeed, the interweaving of these two elements would be specially easy in Maccabean times, for the ethics of the Hellenistic *cultus* were notoriously low. Yet such men as Jason and Alexander Jannaeus and Caiaphas were also High Priests, and presumably, since they passed into the Holy of Holies on the Day of Atonement, they were ritually 'holy'! The people's reaction to this appears in Josephus' story that once they pelted Alexander with citrons as he stood at the altar. But, whether the people would or not, he was the ritually 'holy man'. The way in which the term was wedded to ritual appears indirectly under two other words. The term *chasid*, transliterated from the Psalms, appears to describe those who led the godly Jews in their opposition to Hellenism (e.g. 1 Mac 2⁴²), and 'Pharisee', a term meaning 'separated', sprang up later. Both the *chasidim* and the Pharisees kept the *whole* Law, and not only its ritual commands, and the term *hagios*, in its common connotation, was not suitable to describe them.

The use of the other Greek words of the same root as *hagios* does not contradict this, for they almost always refer to *things*. In the Old Testament they render Hebrew terms of the same root as *qadosh* in an overwhelming number of their instances. The verbs *hagiazein* and *kathagiazein* are used of the Temple and its accompaniments in a variety of Apocryphal books (e.g. 1 Es 1[3]; To 1[4]; Jth 9[13]; Sir 35[9]; 1 Mac 4[48]; 2 Mac 1[26]). *Hagiasmos* occurs of the sacrifices in Sir 7[31] and 2 Mac 2[17], *hagiasma* some twenty times of the Temple in Sirach and First Maccabees (e.g. Sir 47[10, 13]; 1 Mac 1[37-46]; cf. Jth 5[19]), and *hagiosune*, also of the Temple, in 2 Mac 3[12]. *Hagiotes* is used of the Sabbath in a passage unique in LXX (2 Mac 15[2]). Of these terms only *hagiazein* is applied to *men*—twice to Israel (Jth 6[19], Sir 33[12]), and once each to Moses and Jeremiah (Sir 45[4], 49[6]). There is one passage where God is said to be 'sanctified' (Sir 36[4]) and one where *hagiasmos* occurs about Him (Sir 17[10]). There is a passage in Sirach (33[7ff.]) where God's hallowing of a selected day is compared to His hallowing of a selected people. The key to the whole subject is found in the phrase 'O holy Lord of all hallowing' (2 Mac 14[36]). But the emphasis is still chiefly on the *things* that He hallows.

Another group of terms under renderings of *qadosh* consists of *hieros* ('sacred') and its cognates. Here, while the commonest Old Testament word, *hiereus* ('priest'), always stands for *kōhēn*, the adjective is used seven times as a cognate of *qadosh* (e.g. Ez 28[18]). In First Esdras (e.g. 1[2, 8]) and in the Books of Maccabees (e.g. 1 Mac 6[2]; 2 Mac 2[9, 19]), it is often used in its neuter forms for the Temple, the 'sacred (place)'. In one passage it occurs of heathen shrines (2 Mac 1[13-18]). *Hierosunē* is used once in the Old Testament for the 'high-priesthood' (1 Ch 29[22]), a use repeated, along with that of *archierosunē*, in First Maccabees (2[54], 3[49], 7[9, 21]; cf. 2 Mac 4[7]; Sir 45[24]), even when such a sinner as Alcimus is in question. Other words from the same root are found—for instance, in 1 Es 5[46]; 2 Mac 12[40]. All the evidence points the same way: this root denotes no more than the 'sacred' *status* of men and things. The Jews did not deny that Alexander Jannaeus, the libertine, and Annas, the crafty, *were* priests.

Two other words, *semnos* and *hosios*, though neither ever renders *qadosh*, may conveniently be mentioned here. *Semnos* is intruded on the Hebrew in one manuscript of Jg 11[35], and occurs

three times in Proverbs (6^8, 8^6, 15^{26}) and three in Second Maccabees ($6^{11,\ 28}$, 8^{15}), with the cognate noun once (3^{12}). Its original
meaning was 'august', describing the aspect or mien of the gods
and god-like men. In Second Maccabees it retains this meaning,
but in Proverbs it hardly means more than 'seemly'. The term
hosios, often rendered 'holy', is discussed later, but it is once
used to translate a participle from the cognate verb in the phrase
'sacred places' (Ps 68^{35}).

Before leaving the terms that denote 'holiness', we may ask the
question, 'Was holiness aggressive?', since some seem to claim that
the 'holy' was always 'catching'. There is no doubt that this
idea belonged to the concept, in Israel as elsewhere, in ancient
times. Achan, for instance, having taken a 'devoted thing',
becomes *ipso facto* 'devoted' himself. This idea is found after the
Exile (Lv $6^{27f.}$), but it was not consistently applied, as a passage
in Haggai shows (2^{12}). To speak of 'the holy city' or 'the holy
mountain' no doubt implies that the Temple to some degree
hallowed its surroundings and the context in Haggai requires
the concept of a 'holy land', yet the ruling idea in 'holiness' was
now *separation*, as the very buildings of the Temple itself showed.
Here barrier after barrier shut off first one kind of men and then
another from the Holy One, who, save when one man entered
once a year, dwelt alone in the Holy of Holies. The Jew, too, on
the whole sought to separate himself from the Gentiles. The
Book of Jonah remained an ineffective protest. There were pro-
selytes, of course, but, in spite of one New Testament passage, the
future proselyte was usually left to come to the Synagogue for
himself; the Jew did not seek him.[4] This, of course, has been the
dominant phenomenon in Judaism ever since. It is a mistake to
think that the typical Jew of the centuries now in question thought
of 'holiness' as 'catching'. For him it was seclusive, not aggressive.
Even the 'wise' man, who urged others to learn wisdom, did not
seek disciples among the Gentiles. From the time of the Code of
Holiness the 'holy' people has been a 'separated' people (Lv 20^{26}).

Throughout LXX the idea of 'purity' goes closely with that of
'holiness'. This appears from the use of the first of the common
Greek words for 'pure', *hagnos*, for it and its cognates render
qadosh some twenty times and the commonest Hebrew word for
'pure' (*tahor*) and its cognates about seventeen times. The use of
hagnos, etc., is almost always ritualist (e.g. Ex 19^{10}; Nu 8^7, 19^{17};

[4] See Article, 'Proselyte', *HDB* IV. 132–7.

Lv 14^{49}; Is 66^{17}). There are, however, four texts in the Old Testament where a moral significance may be traced. The word occurs once of God (Ps 12^6), once of man (Pr 21^8), and twice it connects man with God (Ps 19^9; Pr 15^{26}). This group of words is rare in the Apocrypha. There is one instance in First Esdras (7^{10}), and five in the Books of Maccabees (1 Mac 14^{36}; 2 Mac 1^{33}, 4^{13}, 13^{38}), but only once is there any moral significance (2 Mac 4^{13}). There are three passages where *tahor* is rendered by words of the root of *hagios*, all with a ritual meaning: Lv 10^{14}; Nu 8^7, 19^{17}. It is rendered once by *dikaios* (Pr 30^{12}), once by *dokimos* (2 Ch 9^{17}), once by *amemptos* (Job 4^{17}), and once by *hosios* (Pr 22^{11}).

Another rendering of *tahor* and its cognates, *katharos* and its derivatives, is much commoner. The adjective itself occurs about seventy times for *tahor*, over forty being found in the Priestly Code (e.g. Ex 25$^{11-39}$). Similarly the verb *katharizein* is found about the same number of times, thirty-one of them occurring in Leviticus (e.g. 12^7). It does not seem possible to draw any precise distinction between the meanings of *katharos* and *hagnos*, though it is true that the former and its verb only occur three times for words of the root *qdsh* (Nu 5^{17}; Lv 27^{26}; 1 Ch 29^{20}). The use of both words for *tahor* (and for two other Hebrew roots—*chtt* and *zkk*) seems to show that they are altogether synonymous. Again, *katharos*, like *hagnos*, is used predominantly of ritual purity, and it is difficult to suppose therefore that they were not synonyms. *Katharos*, etc., however, are used frequently to describe cleansing by the use of water, and there seems to be only one doubtful instance of this for the *hagnos* group (Nu 8^7). There are examples of the ritual use of *katharos* and its verb in Gn 7$^{2f.}$; Lv 12$^{4f.}$; Nu 19^{19}; Dt 12^{15}; 1 S 20^{26}; Neh 12^{30}; Mal 1^{11} (cf. Ex 24^{10}). The ethical idea has comparatively few illustrations. The verb occurs in the Decalogue in relation to God's condemnation of a false oath (Ex 20^7), in Jeremiah's phrase 'Woe unto thee, Jerusalem! thou wilt not be made clean' (13^{27}), and of the Lord's 'messenger' as a 'purifier of silver' (Mal 3^3). In Ezekiel the adjective and verb occur thirteen times in all—characteristically both in a ritual (22^{26}) and a moral sense (36^{25}). The fifty-first Psalm provides a classic example of the religious and moral use (v. 2, 7, 10; cf. Ec 9^2). Job puts a man 'with clean hands' alongside the 'righteous' (17^9; cf. 14^4, 28^{19}).

Similar phenomena recur in the Apocrypha on a smaller scale.
IBM

As the Books of Maccabees deal largely with the 'cleansing' of the Temple, the verb to 'purify' or 'cleanse' (*katharizein*) occurs there nine times in a ritual sense (e.g. 1 Mac 4[36]; 2 Mac 2[18]). 'Unclean' may be added (1 Mac 1[48], 4[43]) and 'cleansing' (e.g. 2 Mac 1[13]). As the other books in the Apocrypha say little of ritual, they have no parallels for the ritual use. Sirach uses *katharizein* both for literal 'cleansing' (34[4], 38[30]; cf. Wis 15[7]), and of 'cleansing' from sin (23[10], 38[10]). The adjective *katharos* (*10*), 'clean', is nowhere used in a ritual sense in the Apocrypha, unless it be in 2 Mac 7[40]. It is used literally sometimes (To 13[16]; Jth 10[5], 12[9]; cf. Sir 43[1]). In the ethical sense it occurs of God in the phrase 'Blessed art thou, O God, with all pure and holy blessing' (To 8[15]), and of man in the phrase 'I am pure from all sin with man' (To 3[14]; cf. Sus [46]). Sirach speaks of the 'purity' (*kathariotes*) both of 'the firmament' (43[1]; cf. Ex 24[10]), and of 'wisdom' (*katharismos*—51[20]). It is not easy to define 'purity' except negatively, but it is clear that for the Jew God was 'pure' and man ought to be. There is a significant text in the Book of Wisdom. There, while Wisdom is said to 'penetrate *all things* by reason of her purity' (*kathariotes*), yet in the realm of the '*spirits*' of *men* she keeps to the 'pure' (7[23f.]). Another Hebrew term for 'pure', *barar*, is rendered by *katharos* in 'He that hath clean hands and a pure heart' (Ps 24[4]; cf. Job 9[30], 22[30]), and its noun, rendered by *kathariotes*, is set alongside 'righteousness' in Ps 18[20, 24]. While both *hagnos* and *katharos* are used throughout LXX in a ritual sense more often than in a moral one, the latter sense clearly occurs. But, on a review of the uses of the whole series of terms denoting 'holy' and 'pure', it is obvious that in the overwhelming majority of the texts where they occur, it is ritual that they refer to and ritual only. As in the post-Exilic books of the Hebrew Bible, the teaching of the three great Prophets of Holiness bears little fruit.

The next pertinent term is 'glory'. In LXX the Hebrew word *kabod* is rendered by no less than twenty-five Greek words, but in by far the majority of passages the word *doxa* is the translation. With this there goes the verb *doxazein* ('glorify'), which is used eighteen times to render *kabod* or its cognates. The Greek terms derive from a verb (*dokein*), which sometimes means 'to think' and sometimes 'to seem'. *Doxa* and its verb go back to the former of these. The noun's original meaning had been 'opinion'; then it came to mean 'good opinion' or 'good reputation', and so 'glory'. The last is the regular meaning both in the Old Testament and the Apocrypha. In the latter, *doxa* occurs a hundred and twenty-four times (of which fifty-one are in Sirach and thirty-three in Maccabees); *doxazein* fifty-eight times (including thirty-one in Sirach and twenty in Maccabees). The secular use of *doxa*, under which it might denote mere 'pomp', is illustrated, for instance, in the Books of Maccabees (e.g. 1 Mac 10[58, 60, 64]). There may also be a false kind of 'glory' (e.g. Sir 8[14], 9[11]). But the subject of the Apocryphal books being religion, their characteristic and normal use of *doxa* is to denote, as *kabod* does in Hebrew, the manifestation of true worth. Similarly they use *doxazein* for its recognition. To 'glorify' is to recognize worth.

The primary idea, of course, is that God is 'glorious' and should be 'glorified'. In the Apocrypha, however, the phrase 'the glory of God' is not used to denote a literal flame, as so often in the Old Testament, except in retrospect (Sir 45[3], 49[8]) and prospect (Bar 5[9], 2 Mac 2[8]). There was no such 'flame' now. As the Rabbis said, there was no (ark or) *shekīnah* in the Second Temple. In its literal meaning *doxa*, like *kabod*, has no reference to 'flame' or 'light'. The 'glory of God' was indeed splendid, but the splendour was not now visual. The two chief Apocryphal ideas of the 'glory of God' find expression in both parts of the Song of the Three Holy Children. In the Song of Azarias (v. 3–22) the chief 'glory' of God is the manifestation of His *righteousness and holiness* in His *historical* ways with Israel—not least in His judgements. Here the term 'name' occurs, in the Hebrew way, to denote God's character so far as He has been pleased to make it known (v. 3). It is 'for thy name's sake'— that is, 'because of what Thou art'—that Azarias prays for deliverance, for so will God 'glorify (his) name' (v. 20). The theme, on the other hand, of the Song of all the Three (v. 29–68) is the 'glory' of God in the immense gamut of *creation*. The whole song just exhibits the range of the meaning of the one cry: 'Blessed is thy glorious and holy name' (v. 30). It is a type of the right way to 'glorify' God. The joyful iteration of the cry, 'Hymn and exalt Him above all for ever', shows how the true Jew exulted in the true God, come what may. Elsewhere in the Apocrypha the same two concepts of God's 'glory' recur. Sirach tells of 'the majesty' of (God's) glory, in creation (17[8]; cf. 43[1-12]) and Esdras of His 'goodness and glory' in His dealings with Israel (1 Es 5[61]). Similarly, 'they that love God' are to see 'all (God's) glory' when

Jerusalem is rebuilt (To 14[14ff.]; cf. Bar 4[37], 2 Mac 2[8]). God's 'glory' shows forth His righteousness, for instance, in the Prayer of Manasses when the penitent king sees 'the majesty of (God's) glory' alike in His justice and His mercy and ends his prayer with the famous phrase: 'Thine is the glory for ever and ever.' In Sirach, Wisdom, 'glorying' in the midst of her people, cries to men: ' "Come unto me", and so learn to practise the law of *righteousness*' (Sir 24[1, 19, 24]). In the Book of Wisdom she is 'a clear effluence of the glory of the Almighty', 'renewing' and 'ordering all things' (7[25, 27], 8[1]), whom 'Solomon' beseeches God to 'send forth . . . from the throne of (his) glory' (9[10]) in order that he may learn to judge and rule righteously. Similarly she 'forsook not' the 'righteous' Joseph but 'gave him eternal glory' (10[13f.]). These texts show that the Old Testament blending of the concepts of creation and righteousness in the character of God under the term 'glory' continues in the Apocrypha. One or other of the two ideas is illustrated in all the other passages that speak of the 'glory' of God. For instance, Baruch declares that it is the living who 'give (God) glory and righteousness' (2[18]), Tobit says that it is those who 'love' God, even in His judgements, who shall 'see all (his) glory' (14[14]), Esdras, calling Israel to confess her sins and to 'do (God's) will', tells her that so she will 'give glory unto the Lord' (1 Es 9[8f.]), Judith, in her song of thanksgiving, speaking of God as 'great, glorious, and invincible', calls on all His *creation* to 'serve' Him (16[13ff.]), and Tobias, appealing to God's 'holy and glorious name', makes the same kind of connexion in his marriage song (To 8[5f.]). As in the Old Testament, to 'glorify' God is to recognize and exult in His 'glory' in worship.

While it was for Israel to 'glorify' God, He too 'glorified' *Israel*. The writer of Wisdom summarizes his whole book in this phrase (19[22]; cf. Sir 24[12]). But the ruling idea is rather that God 'glorifies' *the right kind of man*. This is the theme of the long but sustained passage in which Sirach 'praises famous (*endoxos*) men' (44[1]–50[24]). The ruling idea appears at the beginning of the exordium—'The Lord created in them great glory'—and so they were 'a glory in their days' (44[2, 7]). In other words their 'glory' among men comes from Him, and is therefore true glory. Similarly, just as God is said to 'glorify' them, so they are said to 'glorify' God (e.g. 45[3], 46[2, 12], 47[6], 48[4], 49[16]). In the exordium, too, Sirach describes the uniform character of these very various

men. With all their variety they all work the works of God—they
are all merciful and righteous (44¹⁰); they are men of 'power',
but still more of 'understanding' (v. 3). Even those whose names
are now forgotten have a 'glory' in their 'seed' that 'shall not be
blotted out' (v. 9ff.). It is clear that, for Sirach, without character
there is no 'glory'. Yet in the series of portraits itself a further
idea appears. It is upon those heroes of Hebrew annals who
succeeded that the writer spends his descriptions. For instance, he
says much of Moses and of David but he passes quickly by
Jeremiah and 'the twelve prophets', for these had seemed to fail.
Similarly Isaiah is subordinated to Hezekiah, and with Ezekiel,
whose achievement seemed to be small, the writer falls back upon
the 'vision of glory' (48²⁰–49¹⁰). In other words, Sirach celebrates the *achievements* of God through men. Their deeds are His
deeds. The writer cannot put Solomon whole-heartedly into his
list, for, while he was 'wise in his youth', he headed the long line
of sinful Davidic kings (47¹²⁻²⁵; cf. 49⁴). In Sirach's leading
examples a 'glorious' man has three characteristics—he is a man
who serves God with all his heart; he is a man, therefore, who is
righteous; and he is a man who succeeds. It is true that the terms
'righteous' and 'righteousness' do not occur often, but Sirach, of
course, assumes that his heroes 'wrought righteousness', for did
they not work the works of God? For instance, in his exultant
description of the glory of Simon the high-priest on some great
day in the Temple (50¹⁻²¹) the writer does not say that Simon was
righteous, but no Jew could have written in the same way of
Jason or Menelaus, though no doubt the same splendid ceremonial
attended their ministration. Again, Sirach's concept of 'success'
needs noting. It was success in the serving of the people of God
through the 'power' of God (44²). It is for this that they now
have 'good reputation' in Israel. In contrast with an earlier
period, their *wealth* is only named in the instance of Solomon
(47¹⁸). In the Hellenistic period, with its continual confusion and
war, as over against the days of the Persian peace, even a quiet,
God-fearing peasant could not be sure that his toil would bring
prosperity, and this reflects itself in the books of the time. It is
true that the idea persisted that in the *future* God will surely give
prosperity, as appears particularly in Baruch's account of the
future 'glory' of Jerusalem (4³⁶–5⁹; cf. Sir 10⁵, 36¹²⁻¹⁷), but for
the *present* there might be 'glory' without it. Sirach, indeed,
asserts at length that 'the fear of the Lord' is the true 'glory' of a

man, whether he be rich or poor (10¹⁹⁻³¹).⁵ The emphasis on
wealth has gone. It lies now on the recognition of the *worth* of a
man in the true sense of the word. There are other examples in
such passages as 1 Es 8³ᶠ·, Sir 3¹⁸, ²⁰, 35⁸, and 1 Mac 2¹⁷, ⁵¹, ⁶²,
9¹⁰. Sirach roundly declares that 'there is a shame that is glory
and grace' (4²¹).

'Glory' is not confined to heroes. Ordinary men too may have
it. For instance, Sirach, offering 'wisdom' to *every* man, declares
that 'the fear of the Lord is glory and exultation' (1¹¹; cf. 1¹⁹,
4¹³). While the writer of Wisdom does not say much about the
glory of men, in Sirach there is a close connexion between 'glory'
and 'wisdom'. For instance, he tells his 'son' that wisdom's
'fetters shall be for a covering of strength, and her chains for a
robe of glory' (6²⁹; cf. v. 31); he declares that 'the man that shall
meditate in wisdom' shall 'lodge in her glory' (14²⁰, ²⁷); he
promises a man 'If thou followest righteousness, thou shalt obtain
(wisdom) and put her on, as a long robe of glory' (27⁸; cf. Wis
10¹⁴). Here it may be noted that Sirach everywhere takes it for
granted that he himself is 'honoured' or 'glorified' in the Jewish
community (cf. 37²⁶, 39⁴, ⁹, Wis 8¹⁰). In this period, indeed, the
'wise man'—the man who both knew and practised righteousness
as taught in the Law (e.g. Sir 37⁸; cf. 1 Es 4³³)—was himself the
'glory' of Israel, for his kind of life, however inconsiderably (cf.
Sir 43³⁰⁻³), manifested the glory of the wisdom of God. For the
Jew the 'glory' of the Wisdom of God was a true man's 'robe' and
the 'beauty' of his old age (Sir 25⁵).

Another set of Greek words, *timē*—('honour'), with its verb
(*timān*), its adjectives (*timios* and *entimos*), and its adverb (*timiōs*),
are used twenty-four times in the Greek Old Testament to render
kabod and its cognates (e.g. Ex 20¹², 26²; Nu 22¹⁷; Dt 28⁵⁸; Is 3⁵;
10¹⁹; Pr 3⁸, ¹⁵, 6¹). They stand, however, more frequently for two
other Hebrew roots—*vqr*, whose meaning is 'precious', its noun
denoting 'price' (e.g. Lv 27², ¹²; Ps 19¹¹), and *'rk*, which denotes
'value' (e.g. Lv 27⁸). This set of Greek terms, therefore, denotes
true 'worth' as ground of proper 'honour'. In the Apocrypha, it
is true, the terms may be used of the 'honour' paid to *things*—such
as idols (Wis 14¹⁵), the Temple and City (1 Mac 1³⁹; 2 Mac 3²),
and the High Priest's breast-plate (Sir 45¹²)—yet their chief use is

---

⁵ When it is remembered that this is the period of Ecclesiastes it is remarkable how
small a part the problem 'Why do the righteous suffer?' plays in the pre-Christian
Apocrypha. Later, however, it appears again in full vigour in Second Esdras.

to describe *men*. There is a secular use, under which the 'glory
and honour' of rulers appears as an almost conventional phrase
(1 Mac 14²¹; 2 Mac 4¹⁵; cf. Dn 4²⁷), but here they concern us as
giving a Jewish account of the right kind of man. It is perhaps
an accident that in the Apocrypha a term of this class is only
once used to describe the character of God (To 3¹¹; cf. 12⁶)—for
there is mention of the 'honouring' of Wisdom (Wis 6²¹) and there
are a few examples of this use in the Greek Old Testament (e.g.
Is 29¹⁸, 3⁹, 7²)—but in the main these terms describe the 'value'
set *by men* upon *a man*. There is only one passage where *God* is
said to 'honour' a man (1 Es 8²⁶), and this is an exception that
proves the rule, for it means that God has led the *man* Artaxerxes
to 'honour' Esdras. The leading passage is in Sirach (10¹⁹⁻³¹).
It begins: 'What manner of seed hath worth? The seed of man'
(cf. Ps 8, where LXX uses both *doxa* and *time* of man's 'dominion').
It implies that *time* is a kind of *doxa* (10²²), and its theme is the
truth that only a man who 'fears the Lord'—of course in the wide
Hebrew sense of 'fear'—is a man of true 'worth' and therefore
worthy of honour among *men*. Similarly, in the Book of Wisdom
'Solomon' declares: 'Because of (wisdom) I shall have glory
among multitudes, and honour in the sight of elders, though I be
young' (8¹⁰; cf. 4⁸). Tobit emphasizes the 'honour' due to
parents (4³, 10¹¹), and Sirach has a long passage (3¹⁻¹⁶; cf.
7²⁷, 30¹⁻¹³) in which he lays out the meaning of the Fourth Commandment (Ex 20¹² LXX), no doubt because parents had small
'honour' in the Hellenistic world. The parallelism with 'glory'
appears here too. Sirach, of course, does not base filial duty on
any vague 'nature' but on the ordinance of God (v. 2, 6, 16).
Outside the family the 'physician' is singled out for honour, for
his skill derives from God (38¹, ¹²). Was the Son of Sirach himself a physician? 'Honour' is no more to be denied to a 'poor
man that hath understanding' than 'glory' is to be given to 'a
sinner' (10²³). A man may 'honour himself' so long as he takes
the measure of his own 'worth' (*axia*) 'in meekness' (10²⁸). It is
clear that *time* is normally a species within the genus 'glory',
denoting the 'honour' due from man to man. The dominant
idea is that only a man who wills what God wills is worthy of
honour among men.

There is truth in the saying 'Like father, like son', and the
doctrine of a true man's likeness to God requires an examination
of the doctrine of the Fatherhood of God. The Old Testament

preparation for this was postponed to this point. It had taught that God chose the *people* Israel to be His son—'Israel is my son, my first-born' (Ex 4²²), 'first-born' meaning 'beloved' as a first-born son is beloved. Clearly here sonship is by adoption, not by birth. A ritual passage does indeed use the phrase 'Ye are the children of the LORD your God' but only as equivalent to 'Thou art an holy *people*' (Dt 14¹ᶠ·). Again, every king of the Davidic line, as representing his people, is called God's son—'I will be his father and he shall be my son' (2 S 7¹⁴ D). Here too sonship came by adoption, as the context (v. 8 ff.) implies. In neither case did this sonship imply any inevitable likeness between God and His 'son', as history abundantly showed. The adopted race 'rebelled against' its 'father' (Is 1²). As to the line of David, the passage in Samuel in set terms faces the question: 'What if a Davidic king sin?' The answer is that God will 'chasten him'. The Prophets and Deutero-nomists, of course, have the doctrine that God similarly chastened His people. But, at any rate outside one or two Prophetic com-minations, they teach too that He will not abandon or repudiate His 'son' Israel. Even when Northern Israel went into captivity, the hope of its repentance and return was never altogether lost. The metaphor of sonship is not very frequent, but certain ideas are constant—it is the people (or the Davidic king as ruling and representing the people) that is called God's 'son'; sonship is by adoption; the great Father is always faithful; when Israel or a Davidic king sins, God disciplines him; the discipline will at last succeed, and Israel will be righteous like his 'father'. In all this there is no suggestion that every ordinary Hebrew is a 'son of God' even if he is righteous. There is just one text that anticipates this idea, though in it God is not called 'father' but said to be 'like a father'—'Like as a father pitieth his children so the LORD pitieth them that fear him', with a love that is everlasting (Ps 103¹³, ¹⁷). Here it is not *every* Hebrew who is treated as if he were a beloved 'child', still less *every man*, but the Hebrew who 'fears' God—i.e. worships Him and walks in His ways. There is no suggestion that God is a sinner's father.

The doctrine that God is not only 'like' an *individual's* father, but *is* his father, appears first in the Apocrypha. In a moving passage the Son of Sirach, pleading for help, cries first 'O Lord, Father and Master of my life' and then 'O Lord, God and Father of my life' (23¹, ⁴). The writer of the Book of Wisdom depicts the unrighteous Gentiles as jeering at the righteous Jew because 'he vaunteth that God is his father' (2¹⁶); elsewhere he praises God as 'father' when picturing Him as the steersman of Noah's Ark, the 'wood through which cometh righteousness' (14³, ⁷). In these four passages the concept is that God is the Father of *righteous Jews*. Even in the last the writer is thinking, not of the Gentiles, but of the righteous 'seed' (14⁶ᶠ·). In another passage, however, the writer describes the journeying of the Children of Israel in the Wilderness as 'a father's chastening' and 'admonishing' of *wayward* children (11⁹ᶠ·). In a book written in the days of the Apostles and surviving in Latin there is a passage of retrospection in which God, having vainly pleaded with Israel century after century to be His 'sons' so that He might be their 'father', declares that at long last He will 'cast (them) out' (2 Es 1²⁸⁻³²). Under the word 'father', therefore, it appears that God is the 'father' of every Jew, but that sinful Jews are not His true 'sons'.

Under the term 'son' (*huios*), however, we sometimes find the idea that *all* Jews, good or bad, are 'sons of God'. In the Greek Esther, for instance, the Jews as a whole are called 'children of the most high and most mighty living God' (16¹⁶). So too the writer of Wisdom calls the Israelites of Solomon's day God's 'sons and daughters' (9⁷), and declares that at the Exodus God 'judged' His 'sons with great carefulness' (12²¹; cf. 16¹⁰, 18⁴, ¹³). It is clear that here Israelites are God's sons merely because they are of 'the seed of Israel'. On the other hand, there are texts under 'son', as under 'father', which imply that it is the *righteous* Jew who is the true 'son of the Most High' (Sir 4¹⁰; Wis 2¹⁸, 5⁵).

An examination of the few relevant passages where 'child' occurs as a variant for 'son' gives the same results. There are three terms for 'child', the first being *teknon*. Hosea calls the people Israel a 'son' and 'child' in one text—'When Israel was a child, then I loved him, and called my son out of Egypt' (Hos 11¹). The passage is a prelude to a poignant account of the child's disobedience (cf. 13¹³), but it ends with a promise that the repentant 'children' shall return 'trembling' from exile (v. 10). In both parts of Isaiah there are passages about God's 'rebellious children' (30¹, 63⁸, ¹⁰), and a Deuteronomic song declares indignantly to a 'foolish and unwise people' that they are *not* their Father's children (Dt 32⁵ᶠ·). Of the other two terms for 'child', *pais* and *paidion*, the second is not used either in the Old Testament or the Apocrypha for a 'child' of God. In the Old Testament it is *pais* that renders the Hebrew terms. Of these by far the most frequent is *'ebed* ('bond-man'), and after it *na'ar* ('young man'). It only occurs once for *yeled* ('child'—Ec 4¹³) and twice for *bēn* ('son'— Pr 4¹, 20⁷), and in all three of *men's* children. In the great majority of the passages where *pais* occurs in the Apocrypha (*45*), apart from Wisdom, the meaning is either certainly or probably 'servant'. In Wisdom there are texts where *all* Jews are called the *paidēs* of God. In one of these the context seems to require the rendering 'servant' (9⁴ᶠ·). In four others the rendering may be either 'servants' or 'children' (12⁷, ²⁰, 16²⁶, 19⁶). In yet others the meaning 'child' is either certain or likely (8¹⁹, 12²⁵ᶠ·, 18⁹). There remains one passage (2¹⁰⁻¹⁸). In it *pais* seems certainly to mean 'child' (v. 13), for the context speaks of 'son' and 'father' (v. 16, 18). The passage teaches that 'the righteous man'—i.e. the faithful Jew—has the right to call himself a 'child of God'. In view of some New Testament passages it may be added that in LXX God is twice said to have 'begotten' (*gennan*) a Davidic king (Ps 2⁷, 110³) and once to have 'begotten' children who go on to rebel (Is 1²). Only the first of these follows the Hebrew, and in none of them, of course, is there any idea of physical birth.

Taken altogether, the evidence suggests two conclusions—that *every* Jew was *born* a 'son' or 'child' of God, but that this sonship was only *realized* by righteous Jews. There was a birth-right which belonged to every member of the race because God had chosen to adopt the race (cf. Sir 36¹²), but the birth-right might be 'despised'. 'Like father, like son' was only true of an obedient *huios* or *pais*. To use a paradox, God was every Jew's father, but not every Jew was His son.

The next term is 'perfect'. Each of the two Hebrew words for 'perfect' named earlier has about forty Greek renderings in the Septuagint! Few of these, however, are relevant here. Of the renderings of the root *shlm* only *teleios* is in point, and under *shlm* it only has eight Old Testament examples. Of these, four refer either to ritual or the 'completing' of an enterprise (Jg 20²⁶, 21⁴; 1 K 8⁶¹; Jer 13¹⁹; cf. 2 Ch 8¹⁶). The remaining four (1 K 11⁴, 15³, ¹⁴; 1 Ch 28⁹) ascribe either a 'perfect' or an 'imperfect heart' to Kings of Judah, and, as in the Old Testament, denote no more than a king's general 'loyalty' to the LORD, particularly in the realm of the *cultus*. The meaning of *teleios* elsewhere is discussed below.

When we turn to the other Hebrew root, *tmm*, we find that it is sometimes rendered in LXX by one or other of three *negative* adjectives. The first of these is *amōmos* ('blameless'). This is used for the root *tmm* over sixty times in the Greek Old Testament, but it only occurs four times in the Apocrypha. In three it describes people who are 'blameless' in a limited realm—a rich man in the use of wealth (Sir 31⁸), a wife in loyalty to her husband (Sir 40¹⁹), and priests in faithfulness to the ritual law (1 Mac 4⁴²). It is only used to describe blamelessness in the *whole* of life once— 'There is a prize for blameless souls' (Wis 2²²). The second adjective is *amemptos*, a synonym for *amomos*. In the Old Testament it renders *tmm* six times—once in Genesis (17¹) and five times in Job (e.g. 1⁸, 12⁴). In the Apocrypha it is found only in Wisdom—to describe Abraham (10⁵), Phineas (18²¹), and the Children of Israel at the time of the Exodus (10¹⁵). The last passage vividly illustrates this writer's concept of ancient Israel. In all the three passages the writer is speaking of men in the distant past, not of contemporaries, and even in them 'blameless' may only be a synonym for 'righteous' and 'holy', as, indeed, the context suggests. The corresponding adverb is rendered 'honourably' in its single example (Est 13⁴). In these passages 'blameless' does not seem to mean 'sinless', but only to refer to special excellence, as in such an English phrase as 'a man of blameless life'. The third adjective is *akakos*, which with its noun *akakia* renders *tmm* fifteen times in the Old Testament. It suggests 'guilelessness' rather than 'sinlessness'. Only the adjective is found in the Apocrypha and that only once—in the phrase 'an *innocent* mind' (Wis 4¹²). The word 'sinless' (*anamartētos*) occurs once in the Old Testament—not to render *tmm*, but to suggest that a certain Hebrew phrase means that the sinful are 'wet' and the sinless 'dry' (Dt 29¹⁹)! In the Apocrypha it is found twice—in the phrase 'innocent babes' and with special reference to abstinence from secret idolatry (2 Mac 8⁴, 12⁴²). Under all these negative terms there is little to suggest that anyone, at least apart from certain 'men of old time', was, in the absolute sense, 'sinless'. The term *athōos* might be added, for it occurs once in the Old Testament for *tmm* (Ps 18²⁵) and eight times in the Apocrypha, but it too does not denote absolute sinlessness, its meaning being illustrated by the phrase 'innocent blood' (Est 16⁵; 1 Mac 1³⁷; cf. Sir 7⁸; Sus 46, 53).

Turning from negative to positive words, we find that *tmm* is rendered by two Greek terms with their cognates. The first of these is *haplous*. Its primary meaning is 'simple'—or, in the moral realm, 'single', in its old sense. Words of this group render *tmm* three times in the Old Testament (2 S 15¹¹; Pr 10⁹; and, as a variant, Job 22³), and there is a fourth passage where LXX perhaps does not follow the present Hebrew text (Pr 11²⁵). In all these cases the idea is 'singleness of heart', which is the rendering in the chief instance in the Apocrypha (Wis 1¹; cf. Sus ⁶³). There these words occur six times in all—two of the remaining four carrying the idea of 'innocence' (1 Mac 2³⁷, ⁶⁰), and two the meaning 'merely', which is irrelevant here (Wis 16²⁷; 2 Mac 6⁶). When a man is called 'single-minded', it need not be meant that he is sinless.

Before turning to *teleios*, the second positive term, two other words may be mentioned. The first is *katartizein* (*19*). While this renders nine Hebrew terms, neither *shalem* nor *tamam* is among them. The word, however, denotes 'to complete' a thing in all its parts, and so to make it perfect. It is used in Ezra (7) of the 'completing' of the Temple walls (e.g. 4¹²), and in the Psalms (*11*) of the 'perfecting' of 'steps', of a 'body', of 'strength' (18³³, 40⁶, 68²⁸), and so on. The other term is *holokleros* (*9*), which renders *shalem* and *tamim* twice each. It denotes, not something that is made complete, but that *is* complete—as an 'unhewn' stone (e.g. Dt 27⁶; 1 Mac 4⁴⁷), or a 'complete' week (Lv 23¹⁵), or a 'sound' body (Is 1⁶). Under it there is one pertinent and pregnant text—'But we shall not sin, knowing that we have been accounted thine. For to be acquainted with thee is *complete* righteousness, And to know thy dominion is the root of immortality' (Wis 15²ᶠ·).

The second important positive term that renders *tmm* is *teleios*. The relevant cognates are the verb *teleioun* and the nouns *teleiotes* and *teleiōsis*. (The verb *suntelein* and its noun *sunteleia* are not used of human perfection.) The fundamental idea of these words is an 'accomplished end'. Anything may be called *teleios* when it fulfils its purpose. When used of *growing* things—whether plants, animals or men—it means 'full-grown' or 'mature', though instances of this use are rare in LXX. In the Old Testament a few 'men of old time' are called 'perfect' as well as blameless—e.g. Noah and Job (Gn 6⁹; Job 1¹) and Abraham by implication (Gn 17¹). The accompanying phrases in the first two texts indicate the realm in which a Hebrew is called to be perfect, for Noah is said to be 'right-

eous' and 'well-pleasing to God', and Job 'true', 'blameless', and
'righteous'. The latter 'kept himself from every wicked act'. In
a passage where God and man are put side by side the parallel
terms 'holy' (*hosios*) and 'elect' occur (2 S 22²⁶). In two passages
in Proverbs (11³, 13⁶) the adjectives 'upright' and 'guileless'
(*akakos*) accompany 'perfect'. Two leading concepts emerge—
that a 'perfect' man is one who is 'right *with God*', and that his
'perfection' is *moral* perfection. This, of course, is just one more
example of the perennial Hebrew emphasis.⁶ The passage
'There is none that doeth good, no, not one' (Ps 14¹⁻³) need not
mean more than that there was no perfect or even righteous man
among the writer's contemporaries. An unpractised standard
need not be an impracticable one.

There are many passages in the Apocrypha, as in the Old
Testament, where *teleios* and its cognates describe the end or completion of a process or enterprise (e.g. 1 Es 6⁴, 8⁶⁸; Jth 8³⁴; Sir
7⁴⁵; Wis 12¹⁷; 1 Mac 4⁵¹), but the number that speak of perfect
men is rather meagre. All the pertinent texts occur in the two
Wisdom Books. Sirach has one passage where Noah is called
'perfect, righteous' (44¹⁷), a second which may mean that a man
may be perfect in the realm of almsgiving, and a third that
denies that any man has been found 'perfect' in the use of wealth
(31¹⁰). There is a passage in Wisdom about 'a righteous man'
who is 'quickly perfected' (3¹⁶) in his youth, which may denote
'perfection' by 'maturity' (cf. Sir 12¹¹), though it may also merely
mean 'quickly ends his life'! Finally, there are three passages
which relate 'perfection' to 'wisdom'. The first (Sir 34⁸) declares
that if a man is truthful he keeps (the) law perfectly, and that
'wisdom is perfection to a faithful mouth'. This means, not that
perfection is possible in the one realm of truth, but that truthfulness is a warrant of perfection in the whole of life. The second
passage (Wis 6¹⁵) runs, 'To ponder about (wisdom) is perfection
of sagacity, and he that keeps vigil on her account shall quickly
be rid of anxiety'—i.e. he will always know his way (cf. 7²³).
The third passage implies that God's standard of human perfection differs from that current among men—'Even if anyone be

---

⁶ In the Old Testament *teleios* is also used to render words from *shlm*, as already
noted. In addition it occurs five times for words from *qdsh*—four times for sacred
prostitutes (Dt 23¹⁷; 1 K 15¹²; Hos 4¹⁴) and once for the shrines of Amos' day (7¹⁹),
perhaps because they were the haunts of these unfortunates. Possibly this use of
teleios is a Hellenistic euphemism for the 'paid' sodomite and the harlot (cf. Dt 23¹⁸),
for one of the meanings of *telos* is 'pay'.

(reckoned) perfect among (the) sons of men, the wisdom (that cometh) from thee being absent, he shall be accounted nothing' (Wis 9⁶). The three passages, taken together, practically say 'Wisdom *is* perfection'. In the culminant account of Wisdom (Wis 7²²ᶠ·) the term *teleios* does not happen to occur, but who can doubt that the writer believed in her perfectness? It follows that God, offering 'wisdom' to man, offers him perfection. At least it is to be his goal.

A summary may be attempted, which, in effect, not only describes the teaching of the writers of the Apocrypha about perfection, but gives their answer to the question asked in the whole of this chapter—'What ought a man to be?' It is clear, first, that they held that a man would be 'perfect' if he fulfilled his high calling and were, in his derivative, creaturely, and slight way, like God Himself. God offers him this perfection. Next, it is clear that it is in the moral (that is, for the Jew, the religious) realm that men are called to be perfect. Thirdly, a true man, since he is loyal to God, will always be zealously *seeking* perfection. This appears, for instance, in two passionate accounts of this search (Sir 51¹³ᶠᶠ·; Wis 8²ᶠᶠ·). Fourthly, there is no hint so far that perfection is 'an impracticable ideal'. As already suggested, under the Old Testament, the typical Jew believed that a man *could* practise the ideal, even though none of his contemporaries *did* practise it. The choice of the word 'wisdom' to describe perfection shows this. As already noted, it implies the belief that if a man *knows* what is right, he is able to practise it. This idea, of course, was also dominant in Greek thought. For this reason, indeed, Philo was able to marry it to the Jewish theology of his time. The idea has often recurred. It is the assumption and defect of much of the laudable enthusiasm for education today. It is true that the Jew could only harbour the concept by ignoring certain passages in Jeremiah and Ezekiel and the fifty-first Psalm[7]—but what generation of any people with a Canon has not ignored parts of it in practice? The assumption, even if it were subconscious, was that, if a man knew God's will for men fully, he could fulfil it perfectly. It does not necessarily follow that the Jew still believed that a man could be perfect by 'keeping the letter of the law' just as it stood. There were problems of conduct that all its six hundred commandments did not cover. The reach of the concept of 'wisdom' was wider than their compass, for it covered

[7] cf. p. 64 *supra.*

the whole of life. Indeed, the Rabbis had already begun the task, which they have pursued ever since, of showing by analogy how the implied meaning of this command and that could be applied to every detail in life. There were 'scribes' who knew that the Two Great Commandments cover the whole of life, and that the rules of the Law do no more than apply them to details (Mk 12²⁸⁻³⁴). However closely 'wisdom' might be related to law, it now over-stepped its limits. The defect of the thought of the generations immediately before Christ was that it did not ade-quately allow for the truth that it is possible to *know* what is right and yet to find oneself unable completely to *practise* it. There were multitudes who *would* not do so—as the pleadings of the writers of Proverbs, Sirach, and Wisdom all show—but were there any who *could* not? It would have been admitted, no doubt, that the Gentiles could not be perfect, for they had not the needed knowledge, but the books of the Apocrypha were written for Jews and it is assumed that every Jew could fulfil God's will if he would. 'To the godly' God had 'given wisdom' enough for all their needs (Sir 43²⁷⁻³³). In other words, the problem 'What I *would* not, *that* I practise' was not faced. Both the Sages and the Rabbis were primarily teachers, and it is a teacher's postulate that his hearers *can* do what he tells them to do.

A note needs to be added here about the teaching of Second Esdras, a book that belongs to the first Christian century, even though to discuss it belongs to the volume on Sin. It is in this book that the Jewish doctrine of the *Yetser Hara* finds its best exposition. Under this the Rabbis taught that there is 'an evil seed' in every man's heart from creation onward, and it might be argued that this means that in every man's life there must be some sin, and that therefore it is impossible to be perfect. But, to summarize a conclusion whose grounds are explored elsewhere, Esdras does not teach that the *Yetzer Hara*, or 'Evil Impulse', is sinful *per se*. It denotes, not sinfulness in the strict sense, but the propensity to sin, and this writer confines 'sin' to sin *in act*. It is true that he argues poignantly that because of this propensity, almost every man does in fact sin, and asks almost broken-heartedly: 'Why, O God, dost Thou punish men when it is all but impossible that they should not sin?'! No adequate answer is given to the question—yet even this writer does not declare that sin is quite inevitable. He believes that there have been and are a very few perfect men (e.g. 2 Es 3³⁶).

PART THREE—THE NEW TESTAMENT

CHAPTER FIVE

WHAT A MAN IS

IN STUDYING the Septuagint it would be evident to the reader more than once that in examining the meaning of terms it is hardly possible to separate the answers to the questions 'What is a Man?' and 'What ought a Man to be?' This is still more difficult in the New Testament. When a term occurs whose meaning begins with an answer to the first question but leads on to an answer to the second, it is best to take the two together. This applies to some of the chief terms in this chapter. In it words are dealt with that occur in the corresponding chapters on the Old Testament and LXX.

The first term is *zoe*. As in LXX this is rendered in the English versions by 'life' (*127*), a word that is also used for *bios* (*10*) and *psyche* (*41*). The latter is discussed later. *Bios* is sometimes rendered 'substance' (e.g. Lk 15³⁰). Half its instances occur in Luke. It always refers to what we call 'this life' or its furnishings (e.g. Mk 12⁴⁴; Lk 8¹⁴; 2 Ti 2⁴; 1 Jn 3¹⁷). It may be good or bad (1 Ti 2²; 1 Jn 2¹⁶). It refers to the surface of life and is not important for the present subject.

As in LXX, *zoe* too can be used to mean 'this life'—e.g. in the phrases 'in thy life-time' (Lk 16³⁵), '(God) giveth to all life and breath and all things' (Ac 17²⁵), 'in this life only' (1 Co 15¹⁹; cf. Ro 8³⁸; Ph 1²⁰), 'What is your life? For ye are a vapour' (Ja 4¹⁴), and 'The breath of life from God entered into them' (Rev 11¹¹). Even fishes have *zoe* in this sense (Rev 16³). Another use of *zoe*, however, already foreshadowed in LXX, begins in the Synoptic Gospels and thereafter is *dominant* in the New Testament. Some passages where the verb *zēn* ('live') occurs, are also pertinent. *Zoe* is found in two passages that are common to Mark, Luke, and Matthew. The first is about *skandala*, 'stumbling-blocks' (Mk 9⁴³⁻⁵). Here 'to enter into life' and 'to enter into the kingdom of God' are equated and both are set over against being 'cast into Gehenna'. In the other passage the Young Ruler asks: 'What shall I do that I may inherit eternal life?' (Mk 10¹⁷⁻²²). Here 'to be saved' and 'to enter into the kingdom of God' (v. 24, 26) are used as equivalents to 'inherit eternal life'. The phrases relate to the future, for the words 'inherit' and 'enter into' require this.

Other Synoptic texts, however, relate to the present. When Jesus, speaking of the resurrection, says 'God is not God of dead men but of living ones' (Mk 12²⁷), He means that the righteous dead will 'rise again' because, in some sense, they are alive now. Luke adds the explanatory phrase 'For all live unto him' (20²⁸)— i.e. true life, whether here or hereafter, depends on a right relation to *God*. Another text expresses the same idea—'Man shall not live by bread alone, but by every word that proceedeth out of the mouth of God' (Mt 4⁴). In both passages Jesus, quoting the Old Testament, shows its ultimate teaching about 'life'. But in the passage about the Young Ruler there is a significant sequel. Jesus not only tells him that 'to inherit eternal life' he must keep the latter part of the Decalogue and do his duty to *men*, and sell all that he has (since wealth is his *skandalon*), but adds: 'Follow *me*.' So he will 'fulfil' his duty to *God* as foreshadowed in the *first* part of the Decalogue. He had not noticed that Jesus had omitted this in His quotation! He was not doing his duty to God and this is the root of his restlessness. In the words 'Follow *me*' Jesus claims that *He* teaches and practises the true kind of *zoe*. It is *His* disciples who will 'enter into *life*'.

Seven of the eight uses of *zoe* in the Acts refer to the true kind of 'life'. Three denote the 'life' of the Risen Chirst, as over against existence in Hades (Ac 2²⁷ᶠ·, 3¹⁵, 8³³). It was 'not possible that death should hold' *Him* (2²⁴). While two other passages require that it is believers in Him who will live in the coming Age (13⁴⁶, ⁴⁸), there are also two which imply that 'believers' in Him *begin* to live the true kind of 'life' *now* (5²⁰, 11¹⁸). He is the 'pioneer' (3¹⁵) who opens this way of life for others, and the Apostles' new teaching can be summarized as 'this Life' (5²⁰). 'Life', here and hereafter, *through Christ* was part and parcel of the Kerugma from the first.

Underlying all Paul's writings there is the axiom: 'Christians live and other people are dead.' The meaning of 'dead' will be discussed in another book. As to the noun 'life' (*36*) and its verb 'live' (*51*), it is true that Paul frequently uses them in the ordinary sense, but it is always easy to see whether he means this or 'the Christian kind of life'. One of the key passages here is: 'The first man Adam became a living soul (Gn 2⁷); the second Adam became a spirit that makes (men) live' (1 Co 15⁴⁵). Here both senses occur in one verse. The relevant passages fall readily into a Trinitarian pattern. Paul, of course, starts from the Old Testament—'As it

is written, But the righteous shall live by (*ek*) faith' (Ro 1[17]; cf.
Hab 2[4]). The Man of Tarsus had been striving in vain to be
'righteous', as God demands—that is God is his *terminus a quo*.
Similarly, sinners are sinners because they are 'alienated from *the
life of God*' (Eph 4[18]). But God the Father is also the Christians'
terminus ad quem. When God gives 'righteous judgement' He will
give the believer the 'free gift' of 'eternal life' (Ro 2[5, 7], 6[23]).
Again, all the texts in which Paul speaks of 'the living God' imply
in one way or another that God is the source of the true kind of
life (Ro 9[26]; 2 Co 3[3], 6[16]; 1 Th 1[9]; 2 Ti 3[15], 4[10]). Both Christ
and Christians 'live by the power of God' (2 Co 13[4]). This true
life comes through faith in *Christ*. Here, of course, is Paul's main
theme. Christ Himself 'now liveth unto God' and therefore the
Christian too is 'alive unto God' (Ro 6[10f.]; cf. Gal 2[19]). Only a
few texts need to be quoted out of many. Believers are 'saved by
(Christ's) life', and through Him 'reign in life', and 'walk in
newness of life' (Ro 5[10, 17], 6[4]). For a Christian 'to live is Christ',
and so he 'holds forth the word of life' to others (Ph 1[21], 2[16]).
Christ, indeed, '*is* (his) life' (Col 3[4]), for he 'lives together with
him' (1 Th 5[10]), and therefore 'lives (a) godly (life) in him'
(2 Ti 3[12]). The Law had offered 'life' in vain (Ro 7[18]). It will
be seen that examples have been chosen from all the groups of
Paul's Epistles. One famous text is the best summary—'It is no
longer I that live, but Christ liveth in me: and that life which I
now live in the flesh I live in faith, the faith which is in the Son
of God, who loved me, and gave himself up for me' (Gal 2[20]). But
'life' is also related to the Holy Spirit. For instance, Paul has the
phrases: 'The law of the Spirit of life in Christ Jesus' (Ro 8[2]), 'Ye
are an epistle of Christ . . . written with the Spirit of the living
God' (2 Co 3[3]), and 'We live by the Spirit' (Gal 5[25]). Obviously
the Christians' kind of life is the right kind. Other men do not
really 'live'. Behind all Paul's writings there throbs the conviction: 'We were dead and are alive again!' 'In *Christ*' through the
Spirit Christians live unto *God*.

Yet this 'newness of life' is still to be consummated. Paul presupposes that there are two Ages. Christian life cannot find full
scope in the present 'evil' Age (e.g. Ro 12[2]; 1 Co 2[6-8]; 2 Co 4[4];
Gal 1[4]). To render *aion* by 'world' is inaccurate, for the Greek
term relates primarily to time and not to space. The true life
has indeed begun, but there are phrases that imply its present
limitations—e.g. 'That life which I now live *in the flesh*' (Gal 2[20]),

'Your life is *hid with Christ in God*', 'When Christ, our life, shall be manifested, then shall ye also with him be manifested in glory' (Col 3[3f.]), 'to depart and be with Christ . . . is very far better, yet to abide *in the flesh* is more needful for your sake' (Ph 1[23f.]). Life needs its proper environment to be consummate, and a sinful world is not its proper environment. Paul expresses this by keeping the phrase 'eternal life' (*9*) for the future Age (e.g. Ro 2[7]; Gal 6[8]; 2 Ti 2[10]). For him life after death is not mere survival but has its own quality which may be called 'glory' (2 Co 4[17]; 2 Th 2[10]).[1] It is 'life indeed'—life that *is* life (1 Ti 2[19]).

The writer to the Hebrews says the same things but in his own way. He uses 'live' (*12*) more frequently than 'life' (*2*). While it is 'a fearful thing to fall into the hands of the living God', Christians come without 'fear or quaking' to His 'city' (10[31], 12[21f.]). Jesus is the Christian Melchizedek who, unlike the Levitical priests, '*ever* liveth to make intercession for us' (7[3, 25]). He gives Christians 'boldness' to take the 'new and living way' that He has 'inaugurated' for them by His 'blood' (10[19f.]). This Epistle is the Epistle of 'indissoluble life' (7[16]). None of the phrases quoted is Pauline, but the underlying experience is the same. It is the Christian who '*lives*' (12[9]). Similarly, in the First Epistle of Peter, where 'live' occurs seven times and 'life' twice, much of the phraseology is distinctive, but the ideas are the same. God 'begets (Christians) again' of 'incorruptible seed' unto 'a living hope by the resurrection of Jesus Christ' (1[3, 23]). They are 'living stones' in the same 'spiritual house' as their Lord (2[4f.]). They 'live unto righteousness' and are 'heirs of the grace of life' (2[24], 3[7, 10-12]). There is one pertinent passage in each of three other Epistles (Ja 1[12], 2 P 1[3], Jude [21]). In the Apocalypse Christ's message to His martyrs is 'I am the first and last, and the Living One; and I was dead, and behold, I am alive for evermore, and I have the keys of death and Hades' (1[17f.]; cf. 2[8]). This writer's uses of 'life' (*17*) and 'live' (*12*) almost all fall under four phrases —God is 'the living God' (*5*, e.g. 4[9f.], 7[2]), i.e. the only Being who ultimately 'counts'; the names of Christians are written in the Lamb's book of life (*6*, e.g. 3[5], 21[27]); the Lamb gives them to 'eat of the tree of life' (*4*, e.g. 2[7], 22[2]), and to 'drink of the water of life' (*4*, e.g. 7[17], 21[6]). All the symbols are derived from the Old Testament; they are all 'completed' in Christ.

---

[1] It is curious that the word 'eternal' (*aionios*) does not occur in Ephesians, Colossians, and Philippians.

In the Johannine books the use of 'life' (*44*) and 'live' (*15*) is as significant as it is simple. Except in a passage that describes a miracle (Jn 4⁵⁰⁻³), the two terms *always* denote the kind of 'life' that passes from Christ to 'believers'. Only a few of the most familiar texts need be quoted: 'In him was life, and the life was the light of men' (Jn 1⁴), 'Whosoever believeth on him hath eternal life' (3¹⁶), 'I am the bread of life' (6³⁵), 'I came that they might have life' (10¹⁰), 'I am the resurrection and the life' (11²⁵), 'I am the way, the truth, and the life' (14⁶); 'The Word of life' (1 Jn 1¹), 'He that hath the Son hath the life' (1 Jn 5¹²). As usual, the Fourth Gospel epitomizes the teaching of the whole New Testament. It is the Gospel of Life.

The fourth Gospel is also the climax of the doctrine of life in the whole Bible. If one text were to be chosen as the quintessence of John's teaching it would be, 'This is life eternal, that they should know thee, the only true God, and him whom thou didst send, Jesus Christ' (17³). The whole of the Old Testament is in the first phrase and the whole of the New in the second. Again, as this text shows, in John, as over against Paul, *aionios* (*23*) relates primarily to the *kind* of life that 'believers' begin to live *now*. The noun 'life', indeed, has no need of the adjective 'eternal'. By its very nature it puts time and Ages under its feet. The one passage where *zoe* clearly refers to the future life as separate from this one (5²⁹) is thereby suspect. To say that a 'believer' 'lives, though he die' and 'never dies' is to say the same thing (11²⁵f.). 'Eternal life' begins here, and physical death only consummates it (14²f.). Finally, while John says so much of the Son's gift of 'life', he insists that he only gives it as the Father's agent (e.g. 5²⁴f., 6⁵⁷, 12⁵⁰; 1 Jn 4⁹, 5¹¹), and, while he does not antedate Pentecost, he has a parenthesis to show the Spirit's part in the complete experience (7³⁹). At the beginning of the Bible man shares 'life' with animals; at the end he shares it with the Triune God.

In tracing the answer to the question 'What is man?' from 'God breathed into his nostrils the breath of life' to 'I am the life' we have reached, in effect, the conclusion that apart from Christ a man is not a man. In Him is life and only the living *are* men. Yet it is also true that, as under LXX, we have passed from the question 'What is a man?' to the question 'What ought a man to be?' Already in the Old Testament the ordinary meaning oɪ 'life' began to pass into a higher one, and the transition is completed in the New. This overlapping of chapters brings out clearly three architectonic truths. First, it illustrates the way in which the New Testament completes a development that begins in the Old. Next, it shows how the New Testament writers say the same thing in different ways. Third, and most of all, it brings out clearly the pervasive *differentia* of the New Testament —that on this subject, as on every other, it 'brings all things to a head in Christ' (Eph 1¹⁰). Without Him the New Testament has nothing unique to say at all.

The next term *pnoe* only occurs twice in the New Testament— once to describe the 'sound from heaven' at Pentecost and once of God's gift of the 'breath' of life 'to all' (Ac 2², 17²⁵). This brings us to *psyche* (*104*). In AV it is rendered 'soul' fifty-eight times and 'life' forty. In two passages there is mention of *God's psyche* (Mt 12¹⁸; He 10³⁸), but both are quotations from the Old Testament. The writers of the New Testament, as of the Apocrypha, do not spontaneously speak of 'the *psyche* of God'. On the other hand the Seer ascribes *psyche* to *animals* (Rev 8⁹, 16³), and when Jesus told men not to be 'anxious for their *psyche*', He took an example from the birds (Lk 12²²⁻⁴). But, as with *nephesh*, in Hebrew, and *psyche* itself in LXX, the vast majority of the passages refer to the 'life' or 'soul' of *man*. When Paul says 'the first Adam became a *living psyche*' (1 Co 15⁴⁵) he unites the words 'life' and '*psyche*' to define man just as his far-away fathers had done (Gn 2⁷).

All the three Septuagintal uses of *psyche* have examples in the New. A few instances may be given from the various parts of the New Testament. For the meaning of '(a man's) life', Mk 3⁴, 10⁴⁵; Ac 15²⁶, 27²²; Ro 16⁴; Ph 1²⁷; Jn 13³⁷; Rev 12¹¹ will serve. Secondly, *psyche*, like *nephesh*, stands for the personal or reflexive pronouns in Mk 13³⁴; Lk 1⁴⁶; Ac 2²⁷; Ja 5²⁰; 1 P 1¹⁹; Jn 10²⁴. With this use, as with *nephesh*, there go the texts where *psyche* means 'a man', e.g. Ac 2⁴¹, ⁴³, 7¹⁴; Ro 13¹; Rev 18¹³. The third use, where 'soul' is used as if·it were the element in human nature that has experiences, is not very common, but it is found, for example, in Mk 12³⁰; Lk 2³⁵; Ac 3²³, 14²; Eph 6⁶; He 12³; Rev 18¹⁴. These passages show that the three various meanings overlap, as in the Old Testament, and that the New, like the Old, sometimes speaks as if man *is* a soul, and sometimes as if man *has* a soul. So far, under *psyche* the New Testament repeats LXX. As to the use of *psyche* with *moral* adjectives, found in Sirach and Wisdom, it is remarkable that, apart from 1 Co 15⁴⁵ (which is an exception that 'proves the rule'), the word *psyche* never once has an adjective of any sort in the New Testament, except in a second-century passage (2 P 2¹⁴), where the phrase 'unsteadfast souls' occurs. Similarly, there are hardly any passages that require that a *psyche* is *already* either good or bad (1 P 1²²; 3 Jn ²; cf. Rev 18¹⁴). The prevalent New Testament question about the *psyche* is not 'What of its present?' but 'What of its future?' It is a thing to 'save' or 'lose', and, to quote the fontal passage, 'What doth it profit a man,' asked Jesus, 'to gain the whole world and forfeit his *psyche*?' (Mk 8³⁵ᶠ·). Similarly, the *psyche* is a thing to 'gain'— 'In your patience ye shall gain your souls' (Lk 21¹⁹). This is an entirely new perspective, for in the Old Testament and Apocrypha, apart from the few passages that hope for a resurrection, the emphasis, under *psyche*, is on 'life' *now and here*. All the later New Testament writers, in their several ways, follow Jesus' lead here. Paul, in a long sentence that describe God's judgement on 'every *soul* of man' (Ro 2⁹), declares that the judgement falls for woe or weal according as a man 'worketh'; the writer to the Hebrews speaks of 'an anchor of the *psyche* within the veil' (6¹⁹), and 'of them that have faith unto the winning of the *psyche* for their own possession' (10³⁹; cf. Lk 17³³); James bids his readers 'Receive with meekness the inborn word, which is able to save your *souls*' (1²¹); Peter calls 'the salvation of your souls' the 'end of your faith' (1 P 1⁹; cf. 2¹¹); and John the Seer describes the martyrs as those who 'loved not their *life* even unto death' (Rev 12¹¹). The believer in Christ is the opposite of the Rich Fool with his short-sighted apostrophe of his 'Soul' (Lk 12¹⁹) for every man is trustee for his 'soul' and, if he keeps his trust, he is 'rich toward God' (v. 21) and will live for ever (Jn 12²⁵). All this suggests that man's *psyche* is not morally good or morally bad *per se*, though it may *become*—indeed is becoming—one or the other. Man begins with a *psyche*, as animals do, but his *psyche* becomes something different in accordance with his way of life. More will be said of this under *pneuma*.

What then is a man's right way with his *psyche* or 'life' or 'soul'? He is forbidden 'to be anxious' about it, not because it is worthless, but because God will take care of it for him. Does not his 'Father' know his needs? It is for a man to 'seek', not his own *psyche*, but God's 'kingdom', and if he does so, his 'Father' will give him both (Lk 12²²⁻⁴, ³⁰⁻²). This leads to Jesus' great paradox—'Whosoever would save his *psyche* shall lose it; and whosoever shall lose his *psyche* for my sake and the gospel's shall save it' (Mk 8³⁵). Here, as always, Jesus' psychology is accurate. All thinkers agree that the way to 'enjoy life' is to forget it in some enterprise outside oneself, and that any hard enterprise demands self-denial and self-sacrifice. Jesus pushes this principle to its limit. Facing death Himself, He declares that every disciple of His must 'take up his cross'. This, of course, does not mean that every Christian will die for his faith, but that, in Paul's phrase, he will not 'count his life dear' unto himself (Ac 20²⁴), but will hold it in pawn for Christ. This leads to the full Christian *differentia* under *psyche*. The subject of the whole pregnant paragraph (Mk 8²⁷–11¹) is 'the Son of Man' (cf. Mt 16¹³). At the beginning Peter declares that Jesus is the Christ to whom every Jew owes allegiance; next, Jesus, while accepting this name, introduces another, and declares that '*the Son of Man*' must Himself die to live—lose His life to save it;[2] finally, 'the Son of Man', when He comes in judgement, will be 'ashamed' of any disciple who has been 'ashamed' to lose his life for His sake. Elsewhere the reason why 'the Son of Man gives his life' appears—it is as 'a ransom for many' (Mk 10⁴⁵). Like the Servant of the Lord, He 'pours out his *soul* unto death' and so 'sees of the travail of his *soul*' (Is 53¹¹ᶠ.). He died for others, and *thereby* Himself lives for ever. But His followers are not to 'lose their souls' primarily for 'many' but *for Him*. This is the Christian *differentia* in the doctrine of the *psyche* (cf. Mt 10³⁷⁻⁹). The Fourth Gospel repeats the phrase, as it does others, in another context (Jn 12²⁴⁻⁶). Other New Testament writers have the *idea* without the phrase (e.g. Ph 3¹⁰ᶠ.; He 13¹³; 1 P 2²¹; Rev 20⁴). The Christian holds his 'soul' in trust *for Christ*, and *thereby* for God. To 'lose' it for Christ is to 'gain' it for ever. 'Life' lost *for Him* is 'life' won. To 'gain' one's *psyche*' is to 'enter into *zoe*'.

The next term is *pneuma* or 'spirit'. The New Testament instances may be classified in the same way as the Old. First, the term is very often used of *God* (*214*). Here there are three subdivisions—there are such phrases as 'the Spirit of God' or 'the Lord' (*29*); the phrases 'the Spirit' *simpliciter* and 'Spirit of truth', 'of holiness', and so on, are frequent (*102*); 'Holy Spirit' is common (*83*). While all the phrases are used much more often in the New Testament than in the Old, this is particularly true of the phrase

---

[2] The writer has discussed the reason for Jesus' use of 'Son of Man' here (and elsewhere) in *The Bible Doctrine of Salvation*, pp. 150 ff.

'Holy Spirit', which occurs in only two Old Testament passages (Is 63[10f.]; Ps 51[11]), and only three times (once of the *pneuma* of a man) in the Apocrypha. Second, *pneuma* is used of *supernatural beings*, both bad and good. Here the most frequent phrase is 'unclean spirits', which occurs, for instance, eleven times in Mark as a synonym for 'demons'. Wicked 'spirits' are mentioned under other phrases in the later books (e.g. Ac 16[18]; 1 Co 2[12], 12[10]; Eph 2[2], 6[12]; 2 Th 2[2]; 1 Jn 4[1-6]; Rev 16[14]). This use too is much more common in the New Testament than in LXX. References to good 'spirits' are rare, but there are some (Ac 23[8f.]; He 1[7, 14]). Third, *pneuma* is used of the 'spirit' of *man* (*93*). In the New Testament, as in LXX, the word is never used of an animal, but only of beings that we should call 'persons'. There are some twenty-five texts where it is doubtful whether the reference is to God or to man and which therefore are not included under the figures above (e.g. Ac 6[10]; Ro 8[4f.]; 2 Co 3[6, 8]; Gal 5[5]; Eph 6[18]; 1 P 1[2]; Jude [19]; Jn 4[23f.]). Our immediate subject is the use of *pneuma* to denote the 'spirit' of *man*.

In the New Testament, as in LXX, *pneuma* and *psyche* are sometimes synonyms. The first sentence in the Magnificat, 'My soul doth magnify the Lord, And my spirit hath rejoiced in God, my Saviour' (Lk 1[46f.]), is an illustration. It shows too how both may stand for a personal pronoun—though this is rare with *pneuma*— and how both may describe the organ of experience. The last use is common in Paul (e.g. Ro 7[6], 12[11]; 1 Co 2[11], 5[3-5]; Eph 4[23]; Col 2[5]; 2 Th 2[13]). Perhaps some slight distinction between *psyche* and *pneuma* may be gathered from the use of the phrase 'in spirit' (e.g. Mt 5[3]; Mk 2[8]; Ac 16[18], 19[21]; Ro 1[9]; 1 Co 5[3-5], 14[2, 14]; 2 Co 2[13]; Col 2[5]; 1 Ti 3[16]; 1 P 3[18]; Jn 4[23]; cf. Jn 13[21]), for it appears to stress the *inward* aspect of experience. There is a more marked difference in the phrases used about a man's death. As we have seen, a dying man 'gains' or 'loses' his *psyche*, but he 'yields' or 'gives up' his *pneuma*—i.e. it leaves his body (Mt 27[50]; Jn 19[30]; cf. Lk 8[55], 23[46]; Ac 7[59]). *Pneuma*, again, can be used to describe the part of a man that survives death (Lk 24[37]; He 12[23]). The writer of Wisdom had used *psyche* for this (3[1]), and the Seer of the Apocalypse does the same (6[3], 20[4]; cf. Ac 2[27]), but here he is peculiar. It is consonant with this that he never uses *pneuma* (*18*) for the 'spirit' of *man*.[3] The 'spirit' of a dead man, sometimes at

---

[3] In Rev 22[6] (cf. 19[10]) probably 'the spirits of the prophets' are 'the seven spirits of God' (1[4], 3[1]), and not the prophets' own 'spirits' as in 1 Co 14[32].

least, could be seen (Lk 24³⁹). It had a 'form', therefore, though not the 'flesh and bones' of a body. This suggests that, as in the Apocrypha, the concept of 'immateriality' had not even yet been fully reached, at any rate when the 'spirits' of men, as distinct from God, were in question. As it happens, all the relevant passages here refer to the survival of the *pneuma* of *good* men, whose 'spirit' is 'saved' (e.g. 1 Co 5⁵). For them *zoe* and *psyche* and *pneuma* go indissolubly together after death, as for all men before it. What befell the *pneuma* of a bad man is not clear. In view of the whole history both of *ruach* and *pneuma* with its constant emphasis on 'life', it is not likely that the inhabitants of Hades were counted to be 'spirits'.⁴ The regular New Testament name for the dead is *nekros*, and *nekros* and *pneuma* are opposites (cf. Ja 2²⁶; Rev 11¹¹, 13¹⁵). To turn to another point, it is remarkable that in the New Testament, as in LXX, the use of adjectives with *pneuma*, when it describes a *man's* 'spirit', hardly occurs. There is a notable instance, however, in the phrase 'the spirit indeed is willing, but the flesh is weak' (Mk 14³⁸). This introduces the New Testament contrast of 'flesh' and 'spirit', which will be taken under *sarx* ('flesh'). The only other adjective is *poios* ('what sort of') which is found once in some manuscripts (Lk 9⁵⁵). Its use implies that a man's *pneuma* may be either good or bad. *Per se* it is neither. It is true that God is called 'Father of spirits' (He 12⁹), and that, if this meant 'Father of all men's spirits', it would imply that they are good, but the interpretation 'Father of the spirits of Christians' suits the context better, for the writer (v. 3–13) is speaking of the way in which God 'chastens every son whom he receiveth'. He is 'master' of *all* 'spirits' (Nu 16²²; 2 Mac 3²⁴), but not 'Father'. A man, like God, has a *pneuma*, for he is not a mere animal, but his *pneuma*, unlike God's, is not intrinsically 'holy'. If the term *pneuma per se* implied such an idea, it could not be used of 'unclean spirits'.

The *differentia* of the New Testament, however, under the doctrine of the 'spirit' of a man does not appear so long as the *pneuma* of man is considered alone, but only when it is related to the *pneuma* of God. The doctrine of the Spirit of God needs, therefore, to be examined at some length. The discussion falls into two parts. There are the references to the Spirit *before* Pentecost, and the references *after* Pentecost. The first set,

---

⁴ The phrase 'the spirits in prison' therefore (1 P 3¹⁹), is not likely to mean 'spirits in Hades'. The passage will be discussed in *The Bible Doctrine of the Hereafter*.

though not very numerous, are various, yet they have a unity,
for in one way or another they all relate to Jesus. To begin with
the few instances of the use of 'the Spirit' in references to the Old
Testament, Jesus Himself led the way by ascribing 'the Spirit' to
'David' in a passage from the Psalms (Mk 12³⁶) *which He applies
to Himself.* Peter does the same (Ac 1¹⁷, cf. 4²⁵), and, by implication, so does the writer to the Hebrews (3⁷). No doubt the idea
that David was 'a man of the Spirit' lies behind other quotations,
at and after Pentecost (Ac 2²⁵, ³⁰, 13²², ³⁴; Ro 11⁹). In one of
these David is called a 'prophet' (Ac 2³⁰), and, as the current
belief was that every 'prophet' was 'a man of the Spirit', all the
texts relating to Old Testament Prophets belong here. In these
passages the old Prophets are always men who looked for the
coming of the Christ. Here again Jesus Himself led the way
(Lk 10²⁴) and the early Church followed (e.g. Mk 1²; Lk 1⁷⁰;
Ac 2²²ᶠ.; Ro 1²; He 1¹; 2 P 3²) though the explicit ascription of the
Spirit to ancient Prophets is rare (Ac 18²⁵; He 10¹⁵; 1 P 1¹⁰⁻¹²;
2 P 1¹⁹⁻²¹). Peter has a passage (Ac 3²²⁻⁵) in which he says that
all the Prophets, from Moses onward, foretold Pentecost, and that
Christians are their 'sons'. All the references to the Old Testament, whether under the word 'Spirit' or the word 'prophet',
focus in Christ.

To turn next to texts about the gift of the Spirit, not 'of old
time', but in the days of Jesus, there are first the passages where
Luke, following the Old Testament fashion of ascribing the gift
of the Spirit to particular people, ascribes it to the Baptist, to
Elisabeth, to Zacharias, and to Simeon, the context in every case
relating to Jesus (Lk 1¹⁵, ¹⁷, ⁴¹, ⁴⁷, 2²⁵⁻⁷). Then there come the
texts where the Spirit is related to Jesus Himself. They are few
but decisive. Both Luke and Matthew testify that Jesus was
'conceived by the Holy Ghost' (Lk 1³⁵; Mt 1¹⁸, ²⁰). Then, the
'people' called Him a 'prophet' and He accepted the name
(Mk 6¹⁵; Lk 4²⁴). But for Christians Jesus was not just '*a* man of
the Spirit' but '*the* Man of the Spirit'. At His Baptism the Spirit
descended upon Him 'as a dove' and God declared Him to be
His 'beloved Son' (Mk 1¹⁰ᶠ.). There is no parallel to either phrase.
Then the Spirit 'drives' Him 'full of the Holy Spirit' to His
ordeal in the Wilderness (Lk 4¹; Mk 1¹²), an ordeal that pressed
upon Him all His ministry (cf. Mk 8³³) and culminated in Gethsemane. Next there are two complementary passages. In the
first, Jesus, speaking to His neighbours at Nazareth, risks His life

by declaring that God has 'anointed' Him with the Spirit for a ministry like Deutero-Isaiah's but transcending it (Lk 4[16-30]). In the second, when 'the scribes from Jerusalem' declare that 'he hath Beelzebub', Jesus retorts that those who so withstand Him are 'blaspheming' unforgivably against the Holy Spirit (Mk 3[22-30]; cf. Ac 7[51]). He and the Spirit go together. Luke has a second passage of a like kind (11[20]) that relates the Spirit to the Kingdom. All these texts show that our Lord fulfilled His ministry 'in the power of the Spirit' (Lk 4[14]). In later parts of the New Testament there are brief references which show that this was taken for granted in the early Church (Ac 10[38]; Ro 1[4]; He 9[14]; Rev 5[6]; Jn 1[32f.], 4[23-6], 6[63]). The first distinctive element in the New Testament doctrine of the relation of the Spirit of God to men is that to *Jesus* God 'gave not the Spirit by measure' (Jn 3[34]), or, on the less likely exegesis, that Jesus was Himself so filled with the Spirit of God that He could give Him to others without 'measure'. To return to the Synoptic Gospels, there is only one passage where the Spirit is named without evident relation to Jesus (Lk 11[13]) and there the reading is doubtful and probably embodies an early Christian interpretation of our Lord's own phrase, 'good things' (Mt 7[11]). The first *differentia* of the passages that speak of 'the Spirit' before Pentecost is that they concentrate on Jesus.

One text, however, has not yet been quoted. It introduces the second distinctive element in the New Testament doctrine. Mark tells that John the Baptist foretold that a 'mightier' than himself was coming who would '*baptize with Holy Spirit*', Luke and Matthew adding 'and with fire' (Mk 1[8]; Lk 3[16]; Mt 3[11]; cf. Jn 1[33], 3[5]). This teaching has no Old Testament antecedent. But after John's message a silence falls. There is no suggestion that Jesus, 'in the days of His flesh', gave the Spirit to anyone, not even to the Eleven. He had the Spirit but did not give Him. The Fourth Gospel gives the reason, which is perhaps implied in Luke (Jn 7[39]; Lk 12[50]). Jesus was not yet 'glorified'. His gift of the Spirit awaited His 'lifting up' in death and resurrection. *Then* the idea occurs immediately (Ac 1[2-8]; cf. 24[49]; Jn 20[22]), and the Spirit is forthwith given at Pentecost.

This leads to the second class of passages. In Acts Peter at once relates the gift of the Spirit *to Jesus*. While His phrase 'he hath poured forth this' (Ac 2[33]) is borrowed from the Old Testament (e.g. Jl 2[28f.]; Ezk 36[27]; Is 44[3]), there is an amazing difference. Peter ascribes to the Risen Jesus the prerogative of God. No doubt there is here one of the beliefs that within a few decades led ineluctably to the assertion of our Lord's divinity. From Pentecost onward Christ is the active Lord of the Church through the Spirit. It is true that the phrase 'the Spirit of Christ' only appears three times (Ro 8⁹; Ph 1¹⁹; 1 P 1¹¹) and 'the Spirit of Jesus' only once (Ac 16⁷), but this only brings out the fact that in the New Testament the Spirit of God 'proceedeth *from* the Father *through* the Son', as, for instance, the phrase 'God sent forth the Spirit of His Son into our hearts' (Gal 4⁶) shows. The last paragraph in the first Gospel may be a summary of the later doctrine of the Church (Mt 28¹⁸⁻²⁰), but in it the Church summarized the facts of its experience. Jesus, now equipped with 'all authority', issues His command to His disciples, and this is rightly gathered up in His commission to 'baptize into' the name of the Trinity—'the Father, the Son, *and the Holy Spirit*'.

To complete the New Testament doctrine an interpretative phrase must be added to the Matthæan epitome. Only *believers* were baptized. The Spirit 'proceedeth from the Father through the Son' *to the Christian*. This leads to the third and fourth distinctive notes in the New Testament teaching. The Spirit is *offered* to all *men*, and *given* to all *Christians*. At Pentecost, Peter, quoting Joel's forecast of the *future*, declared that any Jew might *now* receive the Spirit and soon the Church learnt that this is true of any Gentile too (Ac 2¹⁷, ³⁸, 10⁴⁴⁻⁶, 11¹⁸). God, through Christ, now gives His Spirit, not to a chosen few, as in the Old Testament, but to every man who will accept the gift. What Joel said of the future is now present. It is Paul, of course, who works out the implications of this universal offer (e.g. Gal 3¹⁴). It is he too who enunciates the complementary truth 'If any man hath not the Spirit of Christ, he is none of his' (Ro 8⁹), and who teaches that, since every Christian has the Spirit, every Christian has a ministry (1 Co 12¹³ff.). The Christian is 'a man of the Spirit'. This is his mark (e.g. Ac 10⁴⁷, 19¹⁻⁷).

Further, in the New Testament every Christian *knows* that he has the Spirit. While this had been true of prophets in the Old Testament, it is now true of 'all the Lord's people'. A text from Paul again epitomizes a truth that pervades the New Testament after Pentecost—'the Spirit himself beareth witness with our spirit that we are children of God' (Ro 8¹⁶). Or again, he teaches that through the indwelling Spirit the indwelt Christian cries 'Abba! Father!' (Gal 4⁶, 8¹⁵). The New Testament teaches

that *every* Christian lives in conscious fellowship with the Spirit
This doctrine raises difficult questions, but what doctrine does
not? Again, fellowship between the Spirit and the Christian is
surpassingly intimate. This comes out, for instance, in Paul's
doctrine that in prayer itself the Spirit is on the Christian's side,
difficult though He finds the partnership (Ro 7²⁶ᶠ.). His 'groan-
ings which cannot be uttered' spring, not from the reluctance of God,
but from the recalcitrance of man. Yet He persists in the fellowship, and this is well, for *He* knows what to ask. In the New Testament Christians do not pray *to* the Spirit for He prays *with* them.

A comparison may now be made between the doctrine of the
work of the Spirit of God in the Old Testament and the Apocrypha
on the one hand and the New Testament on the other. First,
throughout the Bible the Spirit is a *gift* of God to certain men.
This means that He is not immanent in *all* men but given to some
men—in the New Testament to Christians. After He is given He
might be called immanent, but *per se* He is transcendant. Second,
in the New Testament, as in the Old, the most prominent characteristic of the Spirit is *power*. This is sometimes asserted and sometimes assumed, but the idea is always present. In the Acts of the
Apostles, though not only there, this power is power to *witness* for
Christ, as the Prophets had power to witness for God, and this
carries with it the ideas that a witness can and will 'endure hard-
ship', face persecution, run the risk of martyrdom, and sometimes
suffer it. The words 'Ye shall receive *power* when the Holy Spirit
is come upon you, and ye shall be my witnesses' (Ac 1⁸) is the
watchword of the whole of the Acts of the Apostles. Quite in the
Old Testament way, the story of Pentecost tells of 'the rushing of
a wind' that 'bears' all before it (2²). While there is only one
later parallel to this (4³¹), and while, no doubt, 'the fruit of the
Spirit' often grew quietly, growth is as much an instance of quiet
power as gravitation. Again, John's word 'Paraclete' does not
mean 'Comforter' in the modern sense, but 'Strengthener'.
Modern Christianity, with its emphasis on the soothing power of
the Holy Spirit, has made a mistake in emphasis—and mistakes
in emphasis may be as perilous as downright error, for they are
more subtle. Outside the Acts of the Apostles the New Testament
writers speak chiefly, not of the Spirit's power in Christian witness,
but of His power to turn bad men into good men, as in Psalm 51.
This needs omnipotence. In the New Testament the Spirit is
strong, both against sin without and sin within.

Third, next after power there comes *wisdom*. This appears first in an immediately practical way. Again and again in the Acts the Spirit guides Christians in their enterprise (e.g. 6^{10}, 8^{10}, 11^{12}, 13^{2}, 16^{7}). Once, indeed, He does not guide but 'catches away' a witness (8^{39}), as sometimes in the Old Testament (e.g. 1 K 17^{12}), but this is exceptional. The concept of guidance broadens and deepens in the Epistles. When Paul says ironically 'I think that I also have the Spirit of God' (1 Co 7^{40}), he implies that the Holy Spirit is the regular *teacher* of Christians. The Council at Jerusalem says without argument 'It seemed good unto the Holy Spirit and to us' (Ac 15^{28}). This, again, raises serious questions and they begin to appear in the New Testament itself. Both Paul and John give directions which imply that there were those who claimed to have received the Spirit and had not. Paul's instance (1 Co 12^{3}) seems to illustrate the possible extravagances of those who 'spoke with tongues', but John's reference requires something less crude (1 Jn 4$^{1-6}$). Yet the difficulties did not lead to the practical abandonment of the doctrine, as they have sometimes done in later times, for in the Fourth Gospel the doctrine rises to its climax. There 'the Paraclete' is 'the Spirit of truth', who is to guide Christians 'into all truth' (16^{13}; cf. 15^{26}). While the Spirit meets every need of the Christian, as Paul's list under the 'fruit of the Spirit' (Gal 5^{22}), for instance, implies, He does this through His power and through His wisdom.

The doctrine of the Spirit's wisdom, as of His power, had Old Testament antecedents. This appears if the development of the doctrine of the relation of the Spirit to 'prophets' in the older book is recalled. At first the gift showed itself in ecstasy. At Pentecost this, or something like it, recurred, under the term '*glossolalia*', or 'speaking with tongues' (Ac 2^{4}). This seems to have been universal at Pentecost but later it was not uniformly so (1 Co 12^{10}). Three things at least are clear about it. First, there was very great excitement. This was so great that an outsider might suppose that the 'speaker with tongues' was either 'drunken' or 'mad' (Ac 2^{15}; 1 Co 14^{23}). Was it unnatural that a man who was suddenly aware that he had received the Spirit of God should be carried off his feet? Excitement in various forms has naturally marked later 'revivals'. Second, there was more or less articulate speech, as the word *glossolalia* itself requires. Paul says that the ecstatics spoke in an 'unknown tongue', while Luke supposes that the 'tongues' were known in other parts of the world (Ac 2$^{6ff.}$).

LBM

Third, the phrase 'the Spirit gave them utterance' (v. 4) implies that He had something to say even through these men. Soon there were Christians to whom He gave the power to 'interpret' their message (1 Co 12¹⁰). In the broader sense of the word, even through these excited men He was 'teaching' the Church. Yet there is always the danger that *glossolalia* should be taken to be intrinsically valuable. Paul showed the Christian way here (1 Co 12–14). He does not deny some value to the phenomenon but puts it in its place. It is not unnatural, when a young fellow 'falls in love' that he should be excited, but human nature does not allow of perpetual excitement, and if his 'love' is genuine, he will learn in the years of married life that his excitement was only a symptom of a love that is quieter and deeper and continuous. Paul taught the Corinthian Christians a similar lesson. It looks as if the phenomena grew less frequent until they revived in Montanism. Perhaps something better took their place, for when Paul bids the Ephesians 'Be filled with the Spirit', he adds 'speaking one to another in psalms and hymns and *spiritual* songs, singing and making melody with your heart to the Lord' (Eph 5¹⁸ᶠ·; cf. 1 Co 14¹⁶). The use of the term *pneumatika* is significant (cf. 1 Co 12¹). Yet, just as ecstasy was not the *chief* mark of the great Old Testament Prophets, so it was not the *chief* mark of the 'apostles, prophets, and teachers' of the New Testament. They too, speaking under the sway of the Spirit, said 'Thus saith the Lord', and it was their *message* that counted. More, *every* Christian said 'Thus saith the Lord' either by word or deed or both (1 Co 12⁴⁻¹¹), for every Christian wielded 'the sword of the Spirit', and so spoke a 'word of God' (Eph 6¹⁷; cf. 1¹⁷). No wonder that there needed to be a 'gift' for 'discernings of spirits' (1 Co 12¹⁰)!

The New Testament leaves no doubt about the nature of the relation between the *pneuma* of God and the *pneuma* of man. Here the most famous text is: 'The Spirit himself *beareth witness with* our spirit that we are children of God' (Ro 8¹⁶), but this text is by no means singular. For instance, Paul has a considerable passage (1 Co 2⁶⁻¹⁶) in which he argues from the *likeness* of *pneuma* in God to *pneuma* in man, and declares that by *psyche* a man 'receiveth not the things of the Spirit of God'—that, indeed, he 'cannot know them' in that way because they need to be 'examined *spiritually*' by 'the *spiritual* man'. Similarly, as we have seen, in Hebrews it is 'the *spirits* of just men made perfect' who are the sons of 'the Father of (their) *spirits*' (He 12⁹, ²³), and in Peter it is a 'meek and quiet *pneuma*' that God values (1 P 3⁴). Such phrases would not be natural with men who identified man's *pneuma* with God's. Here too John sums all up—for him the Christian, since he is 'born of the Spirit', will 'worship God', who is Himself 'spirit', 'in spirit and (so) in truth (Jn 3⁵, 4²⁴). The relation between the *pneuma* of God and the *pneuma* of man in the New Testament is fellowship, not absorption. Paul has indeed a text that says 'he that is joined (*kollasthai*) unto the Lord is one spirit' (1 Co 6¹⁷), but, as the context suggests, he is thinking of the unity within duality in marriage (cf. Mt 19⁵). 'Unity within duality' is a definition of 'fellowship'. Similarly, Paul speaks of the Spirit as 'making his home' in Christians (Ro 8⁹, ¹¹; 1 Co 3⁶), and John of the Paraclete's 'dwelling' in them (Jn 14¹⁷; cf. 1 Jn 4¹³), both terms suggesting the intimate fellowship of family life. What is sometimes called 'Christian mysticism' is dualistic, not monistic.

While the *pneuma* of God is most often related to the *pneuma* in man, there are texts that relate the former also to the 'heart' of the believer (Ro 2²⁹, 5⁵, 8²⁷; 2 Co 1²²), to his 'mind' (1 Co 2¹⁶; Eph 4²³), and to his 'conscience' (Ro 9¹). The elements in human nature are not separable, like the lifeless parts of a machine, but integrated in a living organism. The Spirit, when once in fellowship with a man's *pneuma*, will thereby be related, in appropriate ways, to everything in him. While it is true that in one passage (1 Co 14¹⁻¹⁹) Paul says that in *glossolalia* the speaker's 'mind' and 'understanding' were often separated from his *pneuma*, it is on this very ground that the Apostle declares that this 'gift' is both incomplete, needing the 'understanding' of another to supplement it, and inferior, for instance, to prophecy (v. 31 f.), for the 'spirits' of prophets do not escape the control of their understanding. None the less, it is primarily through a man's *pneuma* that the Spirit has fellowship with him.

A question, of course, arises from all this: 'Is the Holy Spirit *the monopoly of Christians*?' A Johannine text seems to say that this is so—'The Spirit was not yet given, because Jesus was not yet glorified' (Jn 7³⁹). The preceding clause, however, perhaps suggests that this may only mean that the *disciples* had not yet received the Spirit. Yet, even so, had the Holy Spirit nothing to do with the Eleven or 'the Women' before the Resurrection? Or does John mean that they did not *consciously* receive the Spirit earlier? At least he implies that *Jesus* did not, or even could not, give the Spirit until He was 'glorified'. But on any showing a *lacuna* in

explicit New Testament teaching appears here. Whence came
Paul's '*will*' to do good and 'delight in the law of God after the
inward man' '*before* the Spirit set him free (Ro 7[15-23], 8[2])? Why
were such men as Cornelius called 'devout' (Ac 10[2]) *before* conversion? Of course, such questions lead to a wider one: 'Has the
Spirit of God nothing to do with *all* men?' The New Testament
gives no *direct* answer, though there is some indirect evidence of
what the answer of the first Christians may have been. The subject is discussed in *The Bible Doctrine of Grace*. It will be seen that
in the New Testament doctrine of man *pneuma* is the architectonic
term.

As to the *outward and visible organs* of the body, the eye and ear,
the hand and foot, the tongue, mouth, and lips, may all be taken
together. As already shown, the sense of the unity of the body
was now fully developed. This meant that its various parts were
now conceived as its 'members' or organs (1 Co 12[12ff.]). There
is no passage that, on examination, requires the notion that any
organ is itself conscious. 'He that hath ears, let *him* hear' (e.g.
Mk 4[9]) illustrates the uniform concept. Of the passages sometimes quoted on the other side two may be taken as samples. The
first is Jesus' teaching about 'the evil' and 'the single eye' (Lk
11[34-6]). Here He assumes, like Sirach, that the man himself
decides which he shall have—contradicting the age-long notion
that a man cannot help having an 'evil' eye and that its glance
curses, whether he will or not—that is, Jesus denies 'the eye' any
approximation to 'autonomy'.[5] The 'evil eye' can even appear
in a list of the 'evil thoughts that proceed out of *the heart* of men'
(Mk 7[21f.])—that is, that spring from the *will*. The other use of
the phrase is in James' warning about 'the tongue' (3[1-12])—that
is, about a man's use of speech. While in some of James' phrases
'the little member' seems itself to act, it is like the 'rudder' that
is swung by a 'helmsman' and like a 'bridle' that a rider holds—
i.e. the will controls it. In the New Testament the outward
members are not themselves seats of consciousness or originators
of action.

There remains 'the head' (*kephalē*, *72*). Among the phrases (*18*)
where it is used in a more than merely physical sense, the phrase
'head of the corner' is fairly common. It is quoted from Ps 117[22],

---

[5] Jesus adds to Sirach. Speaking of the 'whole body', He says that (whatever good
or evil the motives behind benignant or malignant looks may do to others) the 'single'
or the 'evil eye' blesses or curses the man *himself*.

and rightly interpreted as '*chief* corner stone' (1 P 2⁶ᶠ·). Again, the Hebrew use of *ro'sh* for the head of a *community* has a parallel in Paul's teaching that Christ is 'the *head* of the Church' (Eph 5²³; cf. 1²², 4¹⁵; Col 1¹⁸, 2¹⁹). It is unlikely that the Apostle believed that Christ, being the member called 'the head,' controls 'his body', the Church, in the same way as a man's 'head' is *now* said to control his members, for this idea is derived from our knowledge of the nervous system. The Jews had no knowledge of this and the claim that ordinary Greeks had it cannot be made good.⁶ Even the text 'that we . . . may grow (not 'grow up') unto him in all things, which is the head, even Christ' (Eph 4¹⁴ᶠ·) cannot mean 'that we may grow unto (or 'into') the head as the other parts of a man's body do', for even under the modern concept this is hardly a natural account of growth, and Paul's readers had no such concept. Here, as in the Old Testament, the analogy is with the head (ruler) of a *community*. The Christian Church (and every believer) has a living unity with its 'head' that far transcends, though it includes, the unity of any other community with *its* poor 'head'. The unity is through the Spirit, which is related to the 'heart', not the 'head', as is shown below. Similarly, *this* community '*grows* into a holy sanctuary in the Lord' (Eph 2²¹)—as a building grows under the hand of its 'architect and builder' (He 11¹⁰). Paul's other uses of *kephale* in metaphor support this (1 Co 11³; Col 2¹⁰). The New Testament agrees with the Old in attaching small importance to the 'head' as an outward organ of an individual's body.

Of the *internal* organs the 'heart' (*kardia, 154*) is by far the most important, as in LXX. It does not, however, need a long discussion, for, except at the usual but crucial point, it follows LXX use. It does not altogether lose its physical reference, for it is made of 'flesh' (2 Co 3³), but it is the seat of the will (e.g. Mk 3⁵; Mt 5⁸; Ro 6¹⁷; 1 Co 4⁵; He 10²²), of the intellect (e.g. Mk 2⁶, ⁸; Lk 2³⁵; Ro 1²²; Eph 1¹⁸; He 8¹⁰; Jn 12⁴⁰), and of feeling (e.g. Lk 24³²; Rom 1²⁴; Col 3¹⁶; Jn 14¹). This means that 'heart' comes the nearest of the New Testament terms to mean 'person', but also, as usual in Bible psychology, that 'will' takes precedence over intellect and emotion. *Kardia* can be used to mean 'the inward man' considered as a whole (e.g. Lk 16¹⁵; Mt 12³⁴; Ro 8²⁷; He 13⁹; 1 P 3⁴; Ja 4⁸) and hence it sometimes means 'conscience' (e.g. Ro 2¹⁵; He 10²²; 1 Jn 3¹⁹⁻²¹). The First great Commandment

⁶ Article 'Head', Hastings' *Dictionary of the Apostolic Church.*

probably means 'Thou shalt love (*agapein*) the Lord thy God with all thy heart—that is, with all thy soul and with all thy mind and with all thy strength' (e.g. Mk 12³⁰, ³³). But how shall a sinner do this? It is here that the distinctive New Testament teaching under 'heart' emerges. There is a 'circumcision of *Christ*' which is a 'circumcision of the heart' 'in the spirit' (Col 2¹¹; Ro 2²⁹). In the believer the 'heart' is the seat of the Spirit of God (e.g. 2 Co 1²²; Gal 4⁶). His 'heart', like other men's, had been the seat of sin (e.g. Mk 7²¹), 'darkened' and 'hard' and 'impenitent' and so on. The writer of Hebrews lays special stress on 'hardness' (3⁸–4⁷). Now, 'the love of God has been poured out in (the believer's) heart through the Holy Spirit' (Ro 5⁵), and so he is 'obedient from the heart' (Ro 6¹⁷), 'sings in (his) heart' (Col 3¹⁵), and so on, for, God having written (His) laws 'upon (the believer's) heart' (He 8¹⁰), he can 'sanctify Christ as Lord in his heart' (1 P 3¹⁵), for there 'the peace of God keeps guard' (Ph 4⁷). In the New Testament, it is the heart, not the head, that rules the body, and it is 'in the heart' that Christ 'dwells' (Eph 3¹⁷; cf. 3⁶, 4¹²).

The word for one other of the internal organs occurs with some frequency in the New Testament. This is *splangchna* (*11*), literally 'bowels' or 'intestines'—with its verb *splangchnizesthai* (*12*). It is once used physically (Ac 1¹⁸), but, when it is used of God (Lk 1⁷⁸), or of the risen Christ (Ph 1⁸), or when Paul exhorts the Colossians to '*put on splangchna*' (Col 3¹²), the physical reference has clearly been completely lost. The Revised Version, therefore, rightly renders it by such terms as 'tender mercy' (Lk 1⁷⁸; cf. Ph 2¹), 'affections' (2 Co 6¹²; cf. 7¹⁵), 'compassion' (1 Jn 3¹⁷). 'Compassion' might have been used everywhere, for the reference is always to strongly sympathetic feeling. For the verb, which is confined to the Synoptic Gospels (e.g. Mk 6³⁴; Lk 10³³; Mt 18²⁷), RV always has 'moved with compassion'. Usually the verb is used of *Jesus*' 'compassion' and, correspondingly, the noun always alludes, however silently, to 'the compassion of Christ Jesus' (Ph 1⁸). This word too has been 'baptized into Christ', and this is why it is more frequent than in the Apocrypha.

As in the Apocrypha, the use of the Greek names of the other internal organs, except in their purely physical sense, is rare. Two, '*epar*' ('liver') and *stear* ('hard fat'), do not occur at all. *Nephros* ('reins') is only found once and then in a phrase from the Old Testament (Rev 2²³; cf. Jer 11²⁰, etc.). Of the two words for 'belly', one, *gaster* (*9*), usually means the literal 'womb' (e.g. Mk 13¹⁷; Lk 1¹⁵). It occurs otherwise once, in a quotation about the Cretans (Tit 1¹²). The other, *koilia* (*22*), which can be used for 'womb' (Lk 1¹⁵), has a purely physical sense except in three passages. In two of these it is a contemptuous term for the god of 'earthly things' (Ro 16⁸, 3¹⁹). The third, a quotation from 'scripture', which perhaps combines Ezk 3³ and 47¹, runs: 'He that believeth on me . . . out of his belly shall flow rivers of living water' (Jn 7³⁸; cf. 4¹⁴). Here the Revisers might have rendered by 'heart', as is done with the Hebrew term in Ps 40⁸, both in LXX and English. It will be noticed that when the New Testament varies from LXX in its use of a term for an internal organ, it is *always* in reference either to Christ or to those who believe on Him.

Under the two LXX terms for *the whole body*, *sōma* and *sarx* ('body' and 'flesh'), there is a large and distinctive development in the New Testament, which needs extensive examination. For that book it is best to take *sarx* (*142*) before *soma*. The former is very frequent in Paul (*84*), but it occurs in every kind of book. It will be found that while the term is sometimes used, as in LXX, for the whole 'body', there are Christian uses that are *sui generis*.

While no rigid classification is possible, since one meaning passes insensibly into another, four stages may be distinguished. First, *sarx* may be used in a purely physical way. This is so in the Apocalypse (*6*), where the word only occurs in the plural—for instance, in 'The birds eat the fleshes of kings', of 'captains', of 'mighty men', of 'horses' and of 'all men' (Rev 19¹⁸). There are also passages in Luke (24³) and James (5³) where a psychological reference is wholly absent, and there are Pauline texts where the phrase 'according to the flesh' at any rate comes very near it (e.g. Ro 1³, 9³, ⁵; Eph 6⁵). When used in this sense 'flesh' is 'good' for, as in the Old Testament, it is one of the things that God made. The New Testament, however, has its own culminant expression of this truth. This is in the doctrine of the Incarnation, stated once for all in the phrase, 'The Word became flesh' (Jn 1¹⁴; cf. He 10²⁰). By the time the Johannine books were written the first heresy, Docetism—which borrowed the Eastern idea that 'matter' is bad *per se*, and which therefore deduced that our Lord's 'flesh' was a mere 'appearance'—was beginning to creep into the Church. The writer of the First Epistle of John therefore declares that 'He who does not confess that Jesus Christ cometh in the flesh is deceiver and antichrist' (2 Jn [7]; cf. 1 Jn 4[2]). This shows decisively that 'flesh' in the physical sense is 'good' in the sense in which all the creation is 'good' (Gn 1)—that is, it is one of God's bounties but ethically neutral. It can therefore be used of animals (1 Co 15[39]).

The second meaning of *sarx*, to denote man in his *weakness*, begins to appear in the Synoptic Gospels. In them, when parallel passages are allowed for, the word is only found six times, and it has only three instances in Acts. In these books it always illustrates an Old Testament use of *basar* and LXX use of *sarx*. Under this use *sarx* is not merely physical. As we have seen, the Hebrew never adopted Aristotelian dichotomy but normally thought of man as a unit, and this appears under *sarx* in this New Testament sense. Two phrases illustrate this. When Jesus said to Peter, 'Flesh and blood hath not revealed it unto thee' (Mt 16[17]), He meant 'No *man* hath revealed it' (cf. Gal 1[16]; Eph 6[1]). Here again, however, the New Testament has its unique contribution to make, for, as the writer to the Hebrews says, at the Incarnation the Son of God 'partook' of 'flesh and blood' (He 2[14])—i.e. became a man. The New Testament uses another Old Testament phrase 'All flesh' to denote 'all men' (Mk 13[20]; Ac 2[17]; 1 Co 1[28]; 1 P 1[24]; Jn 17[2]). Both phrases illustrate the Hebrew use of 'flesh' to imply the frailty or weakness of man as over against God. In the passage in Matthew, for instance, 'flesh and blood' is set over against 'My Father', and in Mark 'all flesh' needs God's help against the 'tribulation' that is coming. The latter passage shows how 'weak' man is, not only as over against God, but against the troubles of 'this life', and especially against death. Here, again, the New Testament has its own word to say and it relates it to Jesus. *His* 'flesh' survives death (Ac 2[31]). The idea of 'human weakness' marks the second stage in the teaching of the New Testament.

Under the third meaning 'the flesh' is weak *against sin*. One text in the Synoptic Gospels illustrates this. On the one hand it relates 'flesh' to Christ; on the other to sin. It also introduces the New Testament contrast between 'flesh' and 'spirit'. The text is 'The spirit, indeed, is eager (*prothumos*), but the flesh is weak' (Mk 14[38]). These words are spoken to Peter, James, and John in Gethsemane, and it is possible to take them to mean no more than 'I know that you wanted to keep awake, but you are very tired, and the drowsiness of your bodies has overcome you' (cf. v. 40), but the context allows, or perhaps demands, a deeper meaning too. Jesus, when He says to Peter, 'Couldst thou not watch with me one hour?', is surely referring back to Peter's boast that he was ready to 'die with (Jesus)' (v. 31). Peter had not believed that he needed to 'watch and pray lest (he) enter into trial (*peirasmos*)' (13³⁷), but it quickly appeared that there was a 'trial' for which he was not 'ready' and which was to test, not his power to keep awake, but his 'faith' (Lk 22³²). He was weak, and not, as he thought, strong, against temptation to a great sin. But was not our Lord also describing what had just been *His own* experience under the quiet olives and the ordeal that had now begun and was presently to be consummated *for Him*? Had He not begun to experience, as never before, that, while His own 'spirit' was eager to do God's will, His own 'flesh' was 'weak'? The writer to the Hebrews (6) seems to have interpreted Gethsemane in this way, for he has a passage (4¹⁴–5¹⁰) where he says that Christ 'in the days of his *flesh*' 'offered up prayers and supplications with strong crying and tears unto him that was able to save him from death' and was 'heard for his godly fear' (5⁷). In this passage the writer had already said that our Lord 'shared the experience (*sumpathein*) of our *weaknesses*' (4¹⁵), and so he connects 'weakness' with 'the flesh', as our Lord had done. Probably the Synoptic passage marks the origin of the New Testament doctrine that it is through 'the flesh' that man lies open to the temptation to sin. For Jesus to refuse to die would have been to refuse to do His Father's will—that is, to sin. Under this use 'the flesh' is still not itself sinful, for, though Jesus knew, as other men do, the '*weakness*' of 'the flesh', and was 'tempted like as we are', yet it was 'without *sin*' (or, if the alternative rendering is preferred, 'apart from sin'). Here the word 'tempt' links with 'temptation' in the Marcan passage. While it is the writer to the Hebrews who works out this idea most fully, Paul has a compact phrase that summarizes the same teaching, for he says that because of the '*weakness*' of the Law 'through the *flesh*' God 'sent His own Son in a state like (*homoiōma*) that of (the) *flesh* of sin' (Ro 8³; cf. Col 1²²; 1 Ti 3¹⁶). Peter expresses the same idea in his own way when he says that 'He that hath suffered in the *flesh* (in the same way as Christ) hath ceased from sin' (1 P 4¹; cf. 2 Co 13⁴). There have been those who have interpreted Gethsemane as nothing more than a shrinking from the terrible physical sufferings of crucifixion, but this is hardly credible. It is not heartless to suggest that, among the many thousands who were crucified by the Romans, there would be some who bore the physical agony without any need to appeal to God for help. For Jesus there was a more terrible *spiritual* trial, whose mysterious expression was the cry: 'My God, my God, why hast thou forsaken me?'[7] God 'saved' Him (He 5[7]) from a worse 'death' than a merely physical one.

From the story of Gethsemane onward, then, three ideas go together—'flesh', 'weakness', and 'test'. The writer to the Hebrews uses the plural 'weaknesses' (5[15]; cf. Mt 8[17]), taking the trials of need, trouble, and death along with the temptation to sin, because it is through these other 'weaknesses of the flesh' that temptation comes. This idea had some Old Testament anticipations, especially in Job. Again, all three of the meanings of *sarx* so far distinguished go together in what Paul says about his 'thorn in the flesh'—or rather about the sharp stake that caught in his flesh as he made his way through the thicket of life.[8] The 'stake' stuck into his physical 'flesh'; it was a source of 'weakness'; it was a 'messenger of Satan'—the phrase probably referring to the story of Job—that 'fisticuffed' and so 'tested' him (2 Co 12[7-10]; cf. Gal 4[13f.]). At the end of this passage he catalogues a series of his trials or tests: 'weaknesses, injuries, necessities, persecutions, distresses.' It was through the 'flesh' that all these came upon him (cf. 2 Co 4[7-11], 1[22, 24]; Col 1[24]). But by the 'weakness' of 'the flesh' he did not mean merely physical 'weakness', for in his list of reasons why he 'might have confidence in the flesh' (Ph 3[4-6]) he includes the 'zeal' and 'righteousness' of the Pharisee, and these were not physical qualities. Or again, he mentions Christians who have a 'weak *conscience*' (1 Co 8[7, 12]). If a Christian uses his 'freedom' under *any* impulse other than 'love', 'the flesh' has found a way to 'assault' him (Gal 5[13]). Under this third sense *sarx* is anything and everything in his nature, whether physical or not, through which sin can attack him.

But Paul uses *sarx* also in a fourth sense. He gathers up his Master's teaching that sins come 'from within' and that 'out of the heart of men evil things proceed' (Mk 7[21-3]) under this one word. Here *sarx* is no longer merely the element in human nature that sin finds it easiest to attack, but something that is *itself sinful*.

[7] For the writer's attempt to show how the New Testament writers interpret this, see *The Bible Doctrine of Salvation*, pp. 198 ff., 260 f., 268, 300 ff. In that book he also defends his translation of Romans 8[3f.] on the next page.
[8] The term 'stake' (*skolops*) is used in LXX of the way in which God disciplined Israel (Nu 33[55]; Hos 2[6]; Ezk 28[24]).

This does not mean, however, that there is an element in man's nature that is intrinsically bad, for all the passages where *sarx* occurs in this fourth sense relate to men *after* they have *begun* to sin. It is when men have disobeyed God again and again that they 'walk in the desires of (their) flesh' and 'do the things that the flesh and the mind will' (Eph 2²ᶠ·). It is the 'flesh' of men *who have sinned* that needs to be 'destroyed' (1 Co 5⁵) or 'crucified' (Gal 5²⁴). The term occurs outside Paul in the same sense (1 P 3²¹; Jude 7ᶠ·, ²³), but it is in the Pauline passages where 'law' occurs alongside 'flesh' that the idea is clearest. For Paul, 'law', whether the Hebrew law or the 'law written in (the Gentiles') hearts' (Ro 2¹⁵), teaches men what sin is, but gives them no power to resist its temptations. They are sure to break it through the weakness of the 'flesh' and so the 'flesh' itself will become sinful. There are illustrations in the earlier chapters of Romans (2²⁷⁻⁹, 3²⁰ᶠ·, 6¹⁴, ¹⁹), but it is enough to quote from Chapters 7 and 8. Here Paul declares: 'When we were in the *flesh*, the (evil) passions (*pathemata*) (that were the effects) of sin, (and) which came through (the breaking of) the *law*, wrought in our members to bring forth fruit unto death' (7⁵). Again, the Apostle says that when he sins in spite of his knowledge of the *law* and his will to keep it, 'it is no longer I that work (such works), but sin that makes its home in me'—or rather, 'in my (weak) *flesh*' (7¹⁶⁻¹⁸; cf. v. 25). This complex of ideas culminates in the Chapter 8 (v. 1–13), where Paul sums up his subject in the sentence: 'What the *law* could not do, in that it was *weak* through the *flesh*, God, sending His own Son in the likeness of (the) *flesh* of *sin*, and as an offering for *sin*, passed the death sentence on *sin* in the *flesh*, that the requirement of the *law* might be fulfilled in us, who walk not after the *flesh*, but after the spirit' (v. 3f.). Here the 'flesh' is first 'weak' and then sinful. There are similar passages in Galatians (2¹⁶, ¹⁹⁻²¹, 4²¹⁻³, 5¹⁸ᶠ·) and Philippians (3¹⁻¹¹).

The way in which the 'flesh' is sometimes only 'weak' and sometimes sinful too may also be illustrated by the varying meanings of the phrase '*in* the flesh'. Examples of the second idea are found in the passages just quoted; there are instances of the first in 2 Co 4¹¹, 10³; Gal 2²⁰; Ph 1²², ²⁴ (cf. 1 P 4²). There is a distinctive New Testament doctrine under the fourth meaning of *sarx* as under the other three. Christ 'was crucified through weakness' (2 Co 13⁴), in order that believers in Him, though still 'in the (weak) flesh', may be able to 'crucify the (sinful) flesh'

(Gal 2[20], 5[24]). That 'flesh' in the fourth sense is not limited to the physical appears, for instance, in Paul's list of 'the works of the flesh' (Gal 5[19-21]), for it includes sins that are not sensual. While the latter bulk largely in the list because they were sins to which Gentile converts had been specially prone, Paul includes also 'idolatry', 'sorcery', and various forms of 'strife'. For him a *full* list of 'the works of the flesh' would have included the whole gamut of sin.

It is under the fourth sense of 'flesh' that Paul's account of the conflict between a man's 'flesh' and 'spirit' falls. While even this pair of words can be put over against each other without any suggestion that 'flesh' is sinful (Col 2[5]; 1 Ti 3[16]), the Apostle uses them together some sixteen times to denote a *moral* conflict. There are two passages where he draws out the contrast at some length. The first of these is Ro 8[5-17], or rather, the whole of Ro 7 and 8. In the first of these chapters he only uses *pneuma* once (v. 6) and *sarx* three times (v. 5, 18, 25). Here one phrase, 'I know that in me, that is in my flesh, dwelleth no good thing', is the key to the chapter. The Apostle does not stay to say how, in that case, he could long and struggle to be good. There is here a leading instance of an omission in Paul's teaching, as far as it has survived. This is discussed in *The Bible Doctrine of Grace*. Here the pertinent point is the contrast between the sinful 'flesh' and the 'spirit'. This is explicitly drawn out at some length in 8[5-17] —under a contrast between 'the mind' of the 'flesh' and 'spirit', between being 'in the flesh' and 'in the Spirit', and between the 'life after the flesh' and, by implication, 'the life of the spirit'. As has been seen, the relation between the Spirit of God and the spirit of the Christian is here peculiarly close. The other passage is Gal 5[16-25]. In it Paul draws his famous contrast between 'the works of the flesh' and 'the fruit of the Spirit'. The ruling idea appears in the phrase: 'The flesh lusteth against the Spirit, and the Spirit against the flesh.' It may be debated whether *pneuma* here means the Spirit of God or the spirit of the Christian. The contrast between the *terms*, as distinct from the ideas, is probably peculiar to Paul, for, as will be argued in the book on Sin, the Johannine phrase, 'That which is born of the flesh is flesh, and that which is born of the Spirit is spirit' (Jn 3[6]), relates to the physical transmission, not of sinfulness, but of weakness, as the parallel text shows (Jn 6[63]). When Peter, however, says that Christ was 'put to death in flesh but made to live in spirit'

(1 P 3¹⁸), he may be giving his version of what Paul says in 2 Co 5²¹. In its fourth use, *sarx* is no longer weak *against* sin, as in the third, but sin is strong *in it*.

As the phrase just quoted, 'the flesh lusteth (*epithumein*) against the Spirit and the Spirit against the flesh', shows, there is an easy transition from *sarx* to *epithumein* (*17*) and *epithumia* (*37*), two other relevant Greek terms. The verb appears in Paul's quotation of the Tenth Commandment, 'Thou shalt not *covet*' (Ro 7⁷ᶠ·). Unlike most of the other commandments, this forbids, not an evil *act*, but an evil *desire*, and the Apostle is true to the spirit both of the Hebrew and Greek terms when he extends the prohibition to cover '*all* coveting'. In this commandment, taken in this universal way, Paul says that 'sin' (practically personified) found and took its 'opportunity'. *Epithumein* means 'desire' or 'crave' (not 'lust' in the modern sense). As in LXX it can denote either a non-moral 'desire' (e.g. Lk 15¹⁶; Mt 13¹⁷; 1 P 1²; Rev 9⁶), or a 'good desire' (1 Tim 3¹; He 6¹¹), or a 'bad desire' (*7*—e.g. Mt 5²⁸; Ac 20³³; 1 Co 10⁶; Ja 4²). The noun 'cravers' appears once, in 'cravers of evil' (1 Co 10⁶). But the significant New Testament use appears under the noun *epithumia* ('desire' or 'craving'). While it occurs three times of a non-moral 'desire' (Lk 22¹⁵; Ph 1²³; 1 Th 2⁷), it never describes a good desire, and it occurs thirty-four times of a bad one. There is no such predominance of one meaning in LXX. 'The craving of the *sarx*' occurs seven times (Ro 13¹⁴; Gal 5¹⁶ᶠ·, ²⁴; Eph 2³; 2 P 2¹⁸; 1 Jn 2¹⁶), and 'fleshly cravings' three times (1 P 2¹¹, 4²; 2 P 2¹⁰). The phrases 'craving of deceit' (Eph 4²²), 'of defilement' (2 P 2¹⁰), 'of the world' (1 Jn 2¹⁷; cf. Tit 2¹²; 2 P 1⁴), and 'of the devil' (Jn 8⁴) also occur. In the use of the phrases 'the craving of the heart' (Ro 1²⁴), 'of the body' (Ro 6¹²), 'of the eyes' (1 Jn 2¹⁶; cf. Gn 3⁶), and 'of the *psyche*' (Rev 18¹⁴), there is evidence that *epithumia* now meant 'a *bad* desire' *per se* when ethics were in question, for the notion of sin is not inherent in the nouns 'heart', 'body', and so on.⁹ What the phrases show is that when sin has once mastered the 'flesh', it goes on to master the whole man, including even the *pneuma* (2 Co 7¹).

It has sometimes been suggested that Paul's and James' (1¹⁴ᶠ·) teaching about *epithumia* is derived from the Rabbinic doctrine that in every man there are 'impulses', one 'good' and the other

---

⁹ Even when *John* speaks of 'the craving of the *sarx*' (1 Jn 2¹⁶), he need not mean that the *sarx* is itself evil, for the parallel words are 'eyes' and (outward) 'life' (*bios*) and these are not inherently bad.

'bad' (*yetzer hatob* and *yetzer hara'*). This is hardly likely for several reasons. First, in the passages from which the Rabbis derived their doctrine (Gn 6⁵, 8²¹), *yetzer* (which there means 'purpose') is not rendered in LXX by *epithumia*, but by *dianoia* and its verb. Second, in the Rabbinic phrases it is the adjective, 'good' or 'bad', and not the noun, that has the ethical implication, whereas the relevant New Testament texts *epithumia*, used alone, means 'an *evil* desire'. Third, the Rabbis taught that God planted both *yetzers* in man *at the Creation*, but Paul believed that 'through one man sin entered into the world and death through sin' (Ro 5¹²)— that is, he ascribed the beginning of sin to *the temptation in Eden*.¹⁰ Fourth, and chiefly, the logic of the belief that God created the two *yetzers* requires either that the 'Evil Impulse' was not itself sinful (a conclusion which, as will be shown in *The Bible Doctrine of Sin*, is drawn in Second Esdras), or that God is the author of sin— and either conclusion would be anathema to Paul. He almost certainly knew of the Rabbinic doctrine, and seems deliberately to have rejected it. As to Ja 1¹⁴ᶠ·, it is a very apt summary of the story in Genesis—first 'craving', next 'sin', finally 'death'. James would believe that if Adam had never sinned, he would never have died. In him sin took some nine hundred years to be 'perfected', but it killed him at the last! Where the Rabbis refer to the creation, the Apostles refer to the first sin. The use of *epithumia* in the specifically Christian sense seems to have begun with Paul. The Apostle, wishing to epitomize his Master's teaching that an evil *desire* is sinful as well as an evil *act* (e.g. in Mt 5²⁰⁻⁴⁸), laid hold of the verb in the apposite Commandment and used its noun for *inward* sin. Jude (v. 16, 18), Peter (1 P 1¹⁴, 2¹¹, 4²ᶠ·), and John (Jn 8⁴⁴; 1 Jn 2¹⁶ᶠ·), as well as James, followed his example. On the other hand, it is Paul—and probably Paul alone, for the one apparent parallel in John (3⁶) is at least questionable—who portrays the struggle between good and evil in man as a conflict between two pairs of allies—the Spirit of God and the spirit of man fronting and fighting 'Sin' and the 'flesh' of man. If one searches the Old Testament for an anticipation there is only the appeal of Wisdom against Folly in the Book of Proverbs (e.g. Chapter 8), and there is no inward agony in Proverbs.

---

¹⁰ As has been seen, Paul grounds his doctrine of *epithumia* upon the Tenth Commandment. Here LXX has *epithumein* in both versions of the Decalogue (Ex 20¹⁷; Dt 5²¹), but the Hebrew terms are different (*chamad* and *'avah*). Both these roots occur in the story of the temptation of Eve (Gn 3⁶), though there LXX does not use *epithumein* or *epithumia*.

Pneuma and *psyche* have each its adjective and *sarx* has two. Apart from one passage where Paul is speaking of evil spirits (Eph 6¹²) and another that relates to the Law (Ro 7¹⁴), *pneumatikos (22)*, a word that Paul uses twenty times, always refers to those who are 'spiritual' because they have received the Holy Spirit. The word is used sometimes to name them (e.g. 1 Co 2¹³⁻¹⁵; Gal 6¹; 1 P 2⁵), and sometimes to describe their 'grace-gifts' (e.g. 1 Co 12¹, 14¹) or message (e.g. Ro 15²⁷) or blessings (Eph 1³) or songs (Col 3¹⁶). Paul also uses the word in a passage in which he refers the manna and water of the Wilderness to Christ (1 Co 10³ᶠ·). John the Seer uses the adverb to mean 'in the speech of spiritual men' (Rev 11⁸). The other three adjectives are always used, explicitly or implicitly, in contrast to *pneumatikos*. *Psychikos (5)* differs from it as *psyche* from *pneuma*. Except in 1 Co 2¹⁴, it can be rendered 'animal'. For instance, Paul sets the 'animal body' over against 'the spiritual body' (1 Co 15⁴⁴, ⁴⁶), and Jude calls those who 'have not the Spirit' 'animal' (Jude ¹⁹; cf. Ja 3⁵). Of the two adjectives from *sarx* one, *sarkinos (4)*, can perhaps always be interpreted to correspond to the passages where 'the flesh' is 'weak' as in LXX (Ro 7¹⁴; 1 Co 3¹; 2 Co 3³; He 7¹⁶), but its meaning may vary with the context, like that of its fellow adjective, *sarkikos (7)*, which three times means 'physical' (Ro 15²⁷; 1 Co 9¹¹; 2 Co 10⁴), and in four instances may refer either to the weakness or the sinfulness of the 'flesh' (1 Co 3³ *bis*; 2 Co 1¹²; 1 P 2¹¹). In 1 Co 3¹⁻³ Paul may be suggesting first that the Corinthians are weak and then that they are sinful.

Under *soma*, the other LXX term for the whole 'body', it may first be noted briefly that all the phenomena found in LXX recur in the New Testament. Unlike the rare Hebrew term for 'body', *soma* occurs often *(135)*, as in the Apocrypha. It is specially frequent in Paul *(86)*, and the idea of its unity, probably borrowed from the Greeks, is particularly clear in his comparison of the Church with the body of Christ (1 Co 12¹²⁻²⁶). It is used of the dead, as equivalent to *ptōma* ('corpse'—e.g. Mk 15⁴³; Lk 17³⁷; Ac 9⁴⁰), and there is a text which seems to suggest that for a body to remain unburied was still counted a disaster (Rev 11⁸⁻¹⁰). It was at any rate a dishonour (Mk 15⁴²ᶠᶠ·; Ac 8²). 'Body and soul' is still a phrase for the whole man (e.g. Lk 12²²ᶠ·; Mt 10²⁸), but so are 'body and spirit' (1 Co 7³⁴; Ja 2²⁶) and 'spirit and soul and body' (1 Th 5²³). *Phthartos*, which means 'destructible' rather

side of this ultimate antinomy in another way. It was on Calvary
that the Son of God redeemed man from 'the body of sin'. The
believer, thereby, 'puts off the body of the (sinful) flesh' (Col 2[11]),
and for him 'the body of sin is done away' (Ro 6[6]).[12]

But what about the body after a man has been saved? For him
Christ is 'the saviour of the body' (Eph 5[23]), both here and hereafter. For the believer's *present* body the pivotal phrase is 'the
body of humiliation' (*tapeinōsis*). It occurs, indeed, under the
form 'the body of *our* humiliation' (Ph 3[21]), and is not used directly
to describe Jesus' body 'in the days of his flesh', but Paul uses the
cognate verb when he says that Christ, 'being found in fashion
as a man', '*humbled* himself, becoming obedient unto death, yea,
the death of the cross' (Ph 2[8]). It was there that He perfected
His sufferings for others. For Christians 'the body of sin' is now
inoperative (*katargeisthai*, Ro 6[6]). In defiance of it they 'fill up the
remainder of the afflictions of the Christ in (their) flesh' (Col 1[24]).
They are still 'in the flesh' of weakness (e.g. Gal 2[20]), but they are
not 'in the flesh' in its sinfulness (e.g. Ro 8[9]). They are 'in the
body', always 'bearing about the dying (*nekrosis*) of Jesus' in it
that His 'life' too 'may be manifested' in it (2 Co 4[10]; cf. 5[6],
Gal 4[7]). Just as the phrase 'the body of sin' goes with 'flesh' in
the sinful sense of the last word, so the phrase 'the body of humiliation' goes with 'flesh' when it means 'weak'. The two words
'body' and 'flesh' have not yet parted company.

They go together, again, in another part of Paul's doctrine,
a part which, as appeared under the discussion of 'flesh', he nowhere works fully out—the doctrine of possible (and often actual)
'sin in believers'. There is need here only to name texts under the
word 'body' that illustrate what has already been said under
'flesh'. 'By the spirit' Christians are to 'put to death the doings of
the body' (Ro 8[13]). This implies that the Roman believers have
not been innocent of such 'doings'. Similarly, even Paul himself
needs to 'bruise' his 'body', lest even he should 'become reprobate'
(1 Co 9[27])—that is, the struggle against sin is not yet over. The
'body of humiliation' is weak—and, therefore, may once more
become sinful. Again, 'body' and 'flesh' still go together when
Paul declares that a true Christian, far from yielding to new
temptations, 'manifests the life of Jesus' in his 'body' or 'mortal
flesh' (2 Co 4[10f.]). The distinction between them begins to appear
when Paul bids believers to 'glorify God in (their) body' because it is

[12] For discussion of the antinomy here named see *The Bible Doctrine of Salvation*.

'a sanctuary of the Holy Spirit' (1 Co 6¹⁹ᶠ.) and to 'present (their) bodies a living sacrifice, holy, well-pleasing to God' (Ro 12¹), or prays that their 'spirit and soul and body may be preserved entire' at the Parousia (1 Th 5²³). These texts seem to imply that the 'body' has permanent worth, and this is not so with the 'flesh'.

There is no doubt about the distinction when Paul speaks of the hereafter. Then Christ 'shall fashion anew the body of our humiliation (that it may become) of like form with the body of his glory' (Ph 3²¹). Paul could not have said 'the *flesh* of his glory', for 'flesh and blood cannot inherit the kingdom of God' since they are 'destructible' (1 Co 15⁵⁰). The word 'form' too occurs in the passage from Philippians and, as will appear later, the 'body', unlike 'the flesh', had a 'form'. The Apostle says elsewhere that the 'bodies' of Christians are already being 'transfigured' (2 Co 3¹⁸; cf. Mk 9²) from a present 'glory' unto a perfect 'glory'. The meaning of 'glory' is discussed later. To sum up the New Testament doctrine of the 'body'—there is first a 'body of sin', with which Christ's 'own body on the tree' is one in a way past man's comprehension; then for believers there is a 'body of humiliation', which they share with Jesus; finally, they are to share with Him in the 'body of glory'.¹³ The whole teaching just applies to the 'body' (which, once again, is not merely material so long as it is alive with *psyche*) the ideas that underlie the text: 'Him who knew no sin (God), made to be sin on our behalf; that we might become the righteousness of God in him' (2 Co 5²¹). Again, Paul's teaching might be approximately summarized under the term 'organ'—'the body of sin' is the organ of sin; 'the body of humiliation' is the organ both of temptation and of the sharing of the sufferings of Christ; 'the body of glory' is the organ of the life to come.

As under the LXX *nous* and its cognates are taken at this point. It is not a name for an internal organ, but it belongs to the discussion of the nature of the 'inward' man. Of the terms named under LXX the following occur in the New Testament: *nous* (*23*), *noein* (*13*), *noēma* (*6*), *anoētos* (*6*), *anoia* (*2*), *dianoia* (*11*), *dianoēma* (*1*), *annoia*, (*2*), *eunoia* (*1*), *eunoein* (*1*), *noēma* (*6*), *nouthesia* (*3*), *and nouthetein* (*8*); *nounechos* being added (*1*, Mk 12³⁴). More than half the passages are Pauline. Eight of the terms named occur in the

¹³ Lk 24³⁹⁻⁴³ is, of course, a difficulty here, for it ascribes 'flesh and bones' to the Risen Christ, but to discuss it lies outside the present subject. It has been suggested that the transformation of our Lord's body was not complete till the Ascension, when He was fully 'glorified' (1 Ti 3¹⁶).

Synoptic Gospels, most frequently in Luke. Here already the texts show that in the New Testament there are three ideas under these terms—'to perceive', to 'understand', and to 'consider what to do'. One text may contain more than one of the ideas. There is an example of each of these meanings in 'Do ye not yet *perceive* nor put things together (*sunienai*)?' (Mk 8¹⁷), 'He answered *understandingly*' (Mk 12³⁴), and 'He hath scattered the proud in the *counsel* of their heart' (Lk 1⁵¹; cf. Ps 33¹⁰). Though *dianoia* hardly stands out as in LXX, 'Thou shalt love the Lord thy God ... with all thy mind (*dianoia*)' (Mk 12³⁰) shows how 'understand' is the central idea. A man 'perceives' that he may 'understand', and he thereby takes 'counsel' with himself what to do and how to live. The New Testament, like the Old, has nothing to say of the merely 'academic mind'. Even 'let him that readeth understand' (Mk 13¹⁴; cf. Rev 13¹⁸, 17⁹) has a practical reference. Further, as the New Testament, like the Old, is a Book of Religion (and of the outcome of religion in ethics), the uniform and integrating idea under this group of words is that man has a 'mind' in order that he may 'perceive' and 'understand' *how God wills that he should live* and 'take counsel' with himself accordingly. The first Great Commandment sums up the doctrine of 'mind', not only for the Synoptic Gospels, but for the whole New Testament.

Under this group of words, however, the usual distinctive New Testament doctrine begins to appear in the Synoptists. Jesus knows the 'thoughts' of His enemies (Lk 11¹⁵; cf. 6⁸) and, when He baffles them, they are 'filled with' the *anoia* of men who do not know what to do (Lk 6¹¹). On the other hand, His disciples are disciples just in order that they may 'understand' *Him* (Mk 8¹⁷), and, before He leaves them, He '*opens their mind* that they may understand ... in all the Scriptures the things concerning himself ... that the Christ should suffer, and rise again from the dead the third day; and that repentance and remission of sins should be preached in his name unto all nations' (Lk 24²⁷, ⁴⁵⁻⁷). Whether Jesus literally taught in the Forty Days or not, this is an accurate summary of the climax of His message to the 'mind'.

Paul uses the verb *noein* rarely (*4*), but the passages illustrate the three notions named—'perceive' (Eph 3⁴), 'understand' (1 Ti 1⁷), 'consider' (2 Ti 2⁷). It is under the noun, *nous*, however, which he almost monopolizes (*20* instances out of *23*), that the Christian *differentia* stands starkly out. One text (1 Co 2¹⁶) gives the dominant idea. Deutero-Isaiah (40¹³ LXX) had asked 'Who knoweth the mind of the Lord?', meaning that it is inscrutable. 'Not so true now', says Paul, for '*we* have *Christ's* mind.' The believer knows enough of the unsearchable mind of God to live by. Men divide for Paul into those who have 'the mind of their flesh' (Col 2¹⁸), and those who have 'the mind of Christ'. The latter are 'renewed in the spirit of (their) mind' (Eph 4²³). When the Apostle speaks of those who have 'the mind of the flesh', he is apt to let himself go. In two passages he passionately expounds its horrors (Ro 1²⁸⁻³²; Eph 4¹⁷ᶠ·; cf. 1 Ti 6³⁻⁵; 2 Ti 4⁸ᶠ·). The 'mind' of the sinful is 'reprobate', 'vain', 'defiled', 'corrupted', 'darkened'. The passage in Ephesians includes *anoia*, 'senseless-ness'. Paul only uses *dianoia* three times, and then of the heathen (Eph 2³, 4¹⁸; Col 1²¹). It is with them, rather than the Jew, that he deals in his doctrine of the sinful mind. Knowledge *per se*, of course, is not within his 'universe of discourse'. The Gentiles did not know *how to live*, for they have 'no sense' (*anoetos*—e.g. Ro 1¹⁴; Gal 3¹, ³). Paul has two passages that expound the *Christian* mind (2 Th 2¹⁻³; Eph 4²⁰⁻⁴). He alone uses three terms in the group. One of these is *noēma* (*6*), the resolve that is the product of thought. It may be either bad or good (e.g. 2 Co 2¹¹, 11³). The other two terms, *nouthetein* (*8*) and *nouthesia* (*3*), denote 'putting in mind'. Christians are so 'filled with all knowledge' that they can 'put one another in mind' how to live (Ro 15¹⁴), as Paul says he had done to the Ephesians for three years (Ac 20³¹); Christian fathers are to practise 'the admonition (*nouthesia*) of the Lord' (Eph 4⁴). Christ is the master of a believer's mind.

Outside the Synoptists and Paul words of this group are rare (*9*). *Noein* and *ennoia* ('intent') occur twice each (He 4¹², 11³; 1 P 4¹; Jn 12⁴⁰), and *dianoia* five times—always of *Christian* 'understanding' (He 8¹⁰, 10¹⁶; 1 P 1¹³; 2 P 3¹; 1 Jn 5²⁰). The last passage gives the key to the whole New Testament doctrine of the mind: 'The Son of God . . . hath given us an *understanding* that we know him that is true.' There is no doctrine of an impartial mind. In the New Testament, *phronein*, a synonym for *noein*, 'suffers' the same 'sea-change', but it is taken later under *sophia*, 'wisdom', as in LXX. There is a distinctively Christian 'mind', for a Christian having 'the mind of Christ' knows how to live.

The next term is *suneidēsis*, 'conscience' (*30*). While its verb *suneidenai* (*4*) may refer primarily to 'consciousness' (e.g. Acts

12¹²), it may also denote 'consciousness *of right and wrong*' (1 Co 4⁴), and this is always so with the noun. *Suneidesis*, therefore, may safely be rendered 'conscience'. That there is such a thing is, of course, often implied even where the word does not occur. No New Testament book would make sense if a man does not know that there is a difference between right and wrong. The phrases '(Peter) went out and wept bitterly' and '(Judas) went away and hanged himself' belong to the most famous of all stories of conscience, and Paul wrote the classical account of its struggles without naming it (Ro 7⁷⁻²⁵). Here, however, the use of the Greek *word* is in question. It is confined to three writers—Paul (*20* instances in the Epistles and *2* in Acts), the writer of Hebrews (*5*), and Peter (*3*). In Hebrews, while there is one reference to the writer's own 'good conscience' (13¹⁸), the other four passages all claim that 'the blood of Christ', unlike the impotent blood of the Day of Atonement, 'cleanses' and 'perfects' conscience (9⁹, ¹⁴, 10², ²²). Here, while it is implied that every man knows that he has often done wrong, and that this has befouled his very consciousness, the emphasis is upon the fact that the Christian knows that Christ takes away this foulness and enables him, if he is faithful, to sin no more. This, *the* miracle of Christ, is not described under this word elsewhere, unless it be in a difficult text in First Peter (3²¹). This, however, is more likely to mean that in baptism a convert 'appealed' to God to witness that his confession was sincere. Peter's other two texts (1 P 2¹⁹, 3¹⁶) refer to a Christian's consciousness that he is 'suffering wrongfully'—like Christ Himself. *Then* his 'conscience' is clear. Paul's uses are more various. They fall into three classes. First, he refers five times to his own 'conscience'—four times in claiming that, both before and after his conversion, he has been loyal to his own people (Ac 23¹, 24¹⁶; Ro 9¹; 2 Ti 1³); and once in claiming that he is now loyal to 'the grace of God' (2 Co 1¹²). Second, there is the passage where he speaks of the 'conscience' of the Gentiles, relating it to 'the law written in their hearts' (Ro 2¹²⁻¹⁶; cf. 2 Co 4²). Third, he refers sixteen times to the 'conscience' of Christians. Among these, eight occur in the discussion of the question 'Ought a believer to eat meat that has been sacrificed to idols?', either by going to a restaurant 'in an idol's temple' (1 Co 8¹⁻¹³), or because butchers, when killing an animal to 'sell in the shambles', sometimes invoked a god (1 Co 10²³–11¹)—a relic of the days when meat was only eaten in sacred festivals. Of the other eight instances one calls on Christians to obey 'the higher powers' of the State, not only because they will be punished if they do not, but because they know it is right (Ro 13⁵). The other seven passages all refer to Christian preaching and teaching. In two Paul claims that while other hearers may not have admitted that his 'gospel' is 'the manifestation of the truth' his converts do admit this (2 Co 4²⁻⁴, 5¹¹). The last five texts, all in the Pastoral Epistles, refer to two kinds of people within certain churches— those who, knowing that their teaching and practice is right, have a good conscience; and those who, knowing that their teaching is evil, have a bad conscience—until at last it has become so seared that even the sense of wrong-doing is gone. *Suneidesis*, therefore, is a word of wide range. Its 'universe of discourse' is the whole realm of ethics. While many of the passages raise questions about the Christian doctrine of society, in the New Testament 'conscience' is always the 'conscience' of *one man*. Some results of a study of all the passages from this angle may be named.

First, *every* man has a conscience (2 Co 4²)—that is, he knows that there is a difference between right and wrong. Conscience, again, is the proper arbiter of one's own conduct (Ro 2¹⁵). As it relates to knowledge, it is a function of the *mind* (cf. Tit 1¹⁵), rather than a separate element in human nature. Second, every man sometimes obeys and sometimes disobeys its behests (Ro 2¹⁵). When he obeys, he does so 'for conscience sake'—that is, just because he knows that an act is right, and not because he fears the results of doing it (Ro 13⁵; 1 Co 10²⁵, ²⁷). Third, if he does what he thinks to be right, he has the approval of a 'good' or 'pure' conscience (Ac 23¹; 1 Ti 1⁵, ¹⁹, 3⁹; 2 Ti 1³; 1 P 3¹⁶, ²¹; He 13¹⁸); and if he does what he thinks to be wrong, he has the disapproval of an 'evil' conscience (He 10²²)—that is, conscience may either 'defend' or accuse him (Ro 2¹⁵). As it happens all these passages except the last refer, not to particular acts, but to a course of conduct in a given 'universe of discourse'. Fourth, persistent sin brings a 'searing' of conscience (1 Ti 4²), and a 'staining' of 'mind and conscience' (Tit 1¹⁵)—that is, to use a third figure, the 'heart is hardened' and conscience atrophies. Fifth, while every man's conscience is authoritative for him, it is not infallible, for, when one man's conscience may allow what another's forbids (1 Co 8⁷), both cannot be inerrant. Such differences arise, in part, from differences in knowledge—the 'law written in' a Gentile's heart, for instance, being of smaller scope than the law given to the Jews (Ro 2^{12}); and, in part, from differences in insight—there being Christians of 'strong conscience' who see that, since 'the earth is the Lord's', no meats 'offered to idols' can thereby be 'unclean', and Christians of 'weak conscience' to whom to eat them is sin (1 Co 8$^{7-13}$, 10$^{23-33}$). Sixth, while 'conscience' is 'individual' in the sense that every man has his own, it is not 'individual' in the sense that the only question that he ought to ask it is 'What is right *for me*?'. He ought also to ask 'What result will my action have for others?' In 'things indifferent', therefore, a man of 'strong conscience' will not always insist on following it, for thereby he may make his weak brother to 'stumble' (1 Co 10^{32}). Here, from a particular instance Paul, as so often, passes to the underlying principle. Within the wide realm of things that he may either do or leave undone, the true Christian 'seeks to please all men in all things' for this will help his witness (1 Co 10$^{23, 33}$). Further, he seeks so to live as to 'commend himself to every man's conscience' (2 Co 4^2; cf. 5^{11}; Ac 24^{16})—that is, he wants every man to say to himself, when he meets him: 'This man is honest through and through.' He will then be more likely to add 'And his message is true'. Conscience ought to be altruistic, for a man ought to 'love his neighbour as himself'.

But what about God and conscience? In many of the passages there is explicit reference to God, and it is implicit in the rest. First, God is the *origin* of conscience—whether it acts under 'the law written' on the Gentile's 'heart', or the law given to the Jew through Moses, or 'the law of the Spirit of life in Christ Jesus' (Ro 2^{15}, 9^4, 8^2; Gal 4^6). Second, the true Jew and the true Christian both 'live before God in all good conscience' (Ac 23^1; cf. 24^{16}). This is how a man should 'behave himself in the world' (2 Co 1^{12}; cf. 4^2; 2 Ti 1^3; 1 P 2^{19}). He is continually answerable, not to any impersonal 'ethical ideal', still less 'to himself', but to God. Third, while he will usually obey other authorities 'for conscience sake', what authority they have is not absolute and ultimate but derives from God (Ro 13$^{1-7}$), and it is not to be obeyed when it clashes with *His* authority (cf. Ac 4^{19}, 5^{29}; Rev 2$^{12f.}$). Fourth, when at last God judges every man, it will be according to the 'law' that He has given each man to know (Ro 2^{12}), and the Gentile, the Jew, and the Christian will each stand at the bar of *his own* conscience. It follows that, while a man may not know all God's will and may even misunderstand it, God asks no more of him than that he be honest with himself—i.e. with what he does know of God's will. For the New Testament God and conscience are correlative from first to last.

Are Christ and the Spirit related to conscience? There are texts in Hebrews that define salvation as the 'cleansing' and 'perfecting' of the conscience by 'the blood of Christ' (9¹⁴, 10², ²²). In other passages a manifold relation to Christ is suggested rather than defined—under 'faith' (1 Ti 1⁵, 3⁹); under Christ's 'lordship' (1 P 3¹⁵ᶠ·); and under His 'resurrection' (1 P 3²¹). The passage where the Prologue of the Fourth Gospel speaks of the Logos as 'the light of men', that 'shines' invincibly 'in the darkness', and that 'lighteth every man', seems to make the Son the mediator of conscience in *every* man, whether Christian or not (Jn 1³⁻⁵, ⁹), though the word 'conscience' is not used.

There are only two passages where the Holy Spirit is specifically related to 'conscience'—once in reference to His 'signifying' that Jewish ritual was helpless in face of conscience (He 9⁸ᶠ·), and once in the phrase 'my conscience *bearing witness* with me in the Holy Spirit' (Ro 9¹). The verb 'to bear witness with' (*summarturein*) only occurs twice elsewhere, both times in Romans. In one of them 'the Spirit himself beareth witness with (the) spirit (of Christians)' (8¹⁶); in the other 'conscience bears witness with the law written in (Gentiles') hearts' (2¹⁵). God 'writes' *something* on every man's heart. Here Paul has the phrase that Hebrews, quoting Jeremiah, uses of the New Covenant in Christ (8¹⁰). Is it through the Spirit that God 'writes on' Gentiles' hearts? He is not indeed immanent in every man, but He does tell every man something of what God wants him to do.

The next subject is *liberty*. Here there is a distinctive Christian use of the term, but there are two preliminaries to its discussion. First, in the New Testament, as in the Old, it is just assumed that for every man, whether Christian or not, there is a realm within which he can do as he chooses. God is indeed sovereign (e.g. 1 Ti 6¹⁵; Rev 11¹⁷, 19⁶), as is Christ His vicegerent (e.g. Ro 14⁹; 1 Co 15²⁵), but this sovereign, like earthly rulers, leaves His subjects some scope for freedom. For instance, a man decides what and how he will eat (Mk 7¹ᶠᶠ·) and whether he will marry or not (1 Co 7¹ᶠᶠ·). James insists on the limits of this freedom (4¹³⁻¹⁷), but, while limited, it includes *moral* choice as the last verse in this passage implies. Many other passages also presuppose this. Paul seems to deny it in his account of the moral

impotence of the sinner (Ro 7¹⁵ff.; cf. Jn 8³⁴), and the term 'elect'
too seems to contradict it, but it will be claimed in a later book
that these are not true exceptions. Everywhere else the postulate
that every man has a real, though limited, area of freedom, is
taken to be too obvious to need stating. This, of course, is the
universal postulate of men's daily lives. Today, if anyone says
'man is not free', he means that, though a man *thinks* he can
choose, he is really a machine. In ancient times, however, no one
(except philosophical Epicureans) said 'man is not free'. The
phrase would be '*This* man is not free'—the corresponding noun
being, not 'robot', but 'slave'. This difference in mental background needs to be remembered wherever the subject of freedom
emerges in the New Testament. Even a slave was not a person
who had no will of his own. There were things about which he
could do as he liked. Otherwise what would have been the use,
for instance, of warning Christian slaves against 'eye-service'
(Eph 6⁶)? The same is true of the subjects of any king, however
absolute, and throughout the Bible God is not 'fate' but a king.
He never robs a man *wholly* of freedom. Man, again, cannot
altogether rob a fellow-man of freedom except by killing him. Even
a man on a cross could look and speak—and writhe. There is
always a realm of choice.

This postulate may be further illustrated from the New Testament use of the Greek terms that emerged under LXX when its
renderings of the Hebrew words that most closely approximate
to the meaning 'to will' were noted. Of these *eklegein* always
appears in the New Testament as *eklegesthai* (*21*), 'to choose out
for oneself'. It is most frequently used of God's choice, but,
apart from the seven times where it denotes Christ's choice of
the Apostles (e.g. Mk 13²⁰; Jn 6⁷⁰; Ac 1²), it is used six times of
human choice (Lk 10⁴², 14⁷; Ac 6⁵, 15²², ²⁵; Jn 15¹⁶). Of the
other words, *haireisthai* (*3*) is used twice of human choice (Ph 1²²,
He 11²⁵), and *hekōn* (*2*) occurs once of Paul's choice (1 Co 9¹⁷)—
where *akon* in its only example accompanies it—and once of the
'creation's' lack of choice (Ro 8²⁰). The other words *always* refer
to human choice—*hekousiŏs* and *hekousiōs* in Philem ¹⁴; He 10²⁶;
and 1 P 5², and *prothumŏs* and *prothumōs* in Mk 14³⁸ (with a parallel
in Matthew); Ro 1¹⁵, and 1 P 5². The last terms denote 'eagerness' rather than mere 'willingness'.

There remain *boulesthai* and (*e*)*thelein*. As in LXX these are
far the commonest terms to denote 'to will'. The second pre-

liminary note falls under them. Is the LXX distinction between the two verbs maintained in the New Testament? As the common word for will is *thelein* (*208*) and *boulesthai* is relatively rare (*37*), the question becomes 'where *boulesthai* occurs, does it imply that *thought has preceded choice?*' The evidence suggests that it does, and that *boulesthai* may be rendered by such terms as 'be minded' and 'determine'. In Paul (*9*), for instance, there are six passages where 'determine' suits (2 Co 1¹⁵, ¹⁷; 1 Ti 2⁸, 5¹⁴; Tit 3⁸; Philem ¹³), and the other three at least admit this rendering (1 Co 12¹¹; Ph 1¹²; 1 Ti 6⁹); while in Acts (*14*) the translation 'to be minded' is everywhere apt (e.g. 5²⁸, 15³⁷, 18¹⁵, 25²⁵). Correspondingly, one cognate noun, *boulē* (*13*), always means 'counsel', and another, *boulēma* (*3*) always means 'plan'. It does not follow that *thelein* cannot be used when a *considered* choice is made, but only that, unlike *boulesthai*, it does not always imply this. In English the verb 'to want' is often used to express an act of will in which the element of deliberate thought is absent. There are passages where this suits *thelein* (e.g. Lk 5³⁹, 9²⁴; Ac 10¹⁰; 1 Co 4²¹, 7³⁹; 1 P 3¹⁰; Rev 11⁶), but none where it suits *boulesthai*. Many passages where *thelein* is used have no relation to Christian freedom—e.g. 'If any man *will* sue thee at the law' (Mt 5⁴⁰), or 'What *will* this babbler say?' (Ac 17¹⁸). To illustrate its scope it is only necessary to give a handful of texts chosen from different parts of the New Testament. *God* is said to 'will' in Mt 9¹³; Ro 9¹⁸; 1 Ti 2⁴; Ja 4¹⁵; Jn 7¹⁷; the verb is used of *Christ* in Mk 1⁴⁰ᶠ·; 1 Co 4¹⁹; Jn 17²⁴; of *His followers* in Mk 9³⁵⁻⁴⁴; 2 Ti 3¹²; 1 P 3¹⁰; Jn 7¹⁷; and of *other men* in Mk 8³⁴ᶠ·; Gal 5¹⁷; Rev 22¹⁷; Jn 5⁴⁰. It may be added that both verbs have a positive meaning when used with a negative, as in LXX. Paul's 'I would not have you ignorant', for instance, means 'I have made up my mind that you shall not be ignorant'. To render either verb by 'would' is misleading because in English 'would' is often no more than an auxiliary verb. Usually 'to be unwilling' is the best rendering of either verb with the negative, for in English 'unwilling' denotes some degree of 'decision against', but there are passages that demand 'refuse'—e.g. for *ou boulesthai* (*3*), Ac 18¹⁵; and for *ou thelein* (*36*), Lk 15²⁸; Mt 22³, 23³⁷; Ac 7³⁹; Ro 1¹³, 7¹⁶; 2 Th 3¹⁰. The wide variety in the use of the *verb thelein* does not recur under its noun, *thelēma*. This word is found sixty-four times and in fifty-five it is used of the will of *God*. Of the exceptions (Lk 23²⁵; 1 Co 7³⁷, 16¹²; Eph 2³; 2 P 1²¹; Jn 1¹³ *bis*) the most notable is Paul's phrase 'the will of the flesh' (Eph 2³).

The word is rarely used even of Christ (Lk 22⁴²; Eph 6⁶). The master phrase is 'the will of God'. Where it occurs, it is always assumed that it is the ultimate and final guide for man. Instances will appear at different points below. The one use of another noun, *thelēsis* (He 2⁴), illustrates the same truth. This, of course, draws to its climax an idea that dominates the Bible (cf. Jn 9³¹). Man's duty and privilege is to know and do 'the will of God'. It may be added that a characteristic use of 'must' (*dei*) in the New Testament illustrates the same point. It often means 'It is the will of God that I (or he or they) should do so and so' (e.g. Mk 8³¹; Ac 4¹²; 1 Co 15²⁵; Rev 4¹; Jn 20⁹). At any rate, usually the analogy for New Testament thought about the relation between God's will and man's is not, as often today, with the relation between inexorable 'laws of nature' and human freedom, but between the lordship of a king or master and the freedom of a subject or slave.

We can now turn to the distinctive Christian doctrine of freedom. The Christian, like the Jew, called God 'Lord' and believed, therefore, that he should be God's slave—adding that Christ is 'Lord', as God's Son, and he himself Christ's slave. As just suggested, therefore, in the New Testament, the question 'Is there a *Christian* freedom?' runs up into the question 'How can a Christian be free when he himself declares that he is and ought to be a slave?'

The paradox of Jesus' life appears here. On the one hand, He was wholly obedient to God; on the other, He was wholly free. The Synoptics everywhere imply the first idea. As usual, John sums it up in a phrase or two—'I seek not mine own will, but the will of him that sent me', 'My meat is to do the will of him that sent me and to accomplish his work' (Jn 5³⁰, 4³⁴). That Jesus always and everywhere served God was obvious to all who had eyes to see—as it has been ever since. Yet throughout the Gospels Jesus is also *the* free man. This, in turn, is obvious—so obvious that it is often missed! In every story Jesus does what He chooses. His life is the unique instance of the 'service' that is 'perfect freedom'. As it happens the word for 'free' (*eleutheros*) only occurs once in the Synoptic Gospels (and its cognates not at all), but the one instance, though it occurs in a seemingly insignificant little story (Mt 17²⁶), gives the key to the paradox. Jews who were careful to keep the Law, paid a poll-tax twice—once, of *necessity*, to Rome or Herod, and once *voluntarily* to the Temple treasury

(Ex 30¹³). But there were Jews who omitted to pay the latter or only paid under pressure. When challenged by the Temple agents through Peter, Jesus paid it but claimed that the King of kings did not *demand* it from His 'children'. They give freely. Jesus was teaching Peter a great truth through a small incident. This is expounded in the passage where He names a 'yoke' (Mt 11²⁹ᶠ·). To be 'under the yoke' was to be a slave (1 Ti 6¹). Yet Jesus, who had made many yokes at Nazareth, knew that a well-made yoke eases a burden by adding to it! It is paradoxical. When Jesus said 'take my yoke upon you', He was not inviting others to submit to a yoke that He imposed, but to carry the same kind of yoke that He carried. It was a yoke that emancipated! He was utterly obedient and utterly free! The explanation is given in the context—from which the great invitation 'Come unto *me*' is too often severed (Mt 11²⁵⁻³⁰)—'All things have been delivered unto me of my Father'—that is, He has told me to do whatever I will. The reason for this is then given—'No one knoweth the Son save the Father; neither doth any know the Father save the Son'—that is, He and I are in complete fellowship, and this means that I always will what He wills, not by compulsion, but because I myself want to do it. A servant cannot be a perfect servant unless he is utterly free! At Jesus' baptism God had said, 'Thou art my beloved Son, in thee I am well pleased' (Mk 1¹¹). Such a 'son' is free to do as He will. This 'word from heaven' came with the gift of the Spirit. Its second clause recalls a phrase from Deutero-Isaiah (Is 42¹). Matthew, summarizing Jesus' ministry by quoting the passage more fully, puts three ideas together—'Behold, my *servant* whom I have chosen; My beloved in whom my soul is *well pleased*; I will put my *Spirit* upon him' (Mt 12¹⁸). In Jesus' life it was obvious that 'where the Spirit of the Lord is, there is liberty' (2 Co 3¹⁷)—and service. Because He 'loved God . . . with all (his) soul', He did 'the will of God from the soul' (Eph 6⁶).

Yet no one text, however great, tells the whole truth about Jesus. From the First Commandment there sprang a second, 'Thou shalt love thy neighbour as thyself', and for Jesus this meant the Cross. The 'yoke' that He bore was not 'easy' nor His burden 'light' in Gethsemane. 'Abba, Father,' He cried, 'all things are possible unto thee; remove this cup from me: howbeit not what *I* will but what *thou* wilt' (Mk 14³⁶). He took the cup. John gives the reason—'The cup that my Father hath given me, shall I not drink it?' (Jn 18¹¹). An imperfect slave, like an imperfect son, might drink because he feared punishment, but not the perfect 'Servant of the Lord', for He was the perfect 'Son'. Jesus could not leave Gethsemane until He was Himself willing to die. This was the final test of the 'love' that cannot come by coercion. In order that a man may love, he must be free. If a man 'loves God with all his heart', and therefore 'loves his neighbour as himself', *because he wants to do so*, He is free in the Christian sense. It is this, His own liberty that Jesus gives to other men. The one passage in the Fourth Gospel where the word 'free' occurs says just this (8³¹⁻⁶): 'If the Son shall make you free, ye shall be free indeed.' Or, as Matthew puts it, 'neither doth any know the Father save the Son, *and* he to whomsoever the Son determines to reveal him' (Mt 11²⁷). The secret of liberty as over against 'the will of God' is 'sonship'. The idea of *irresponsible* liberty is not Christian. The English word that best describes Jesus' liberty is 'loyalty'. He willingly did the will of God. He offers this kind of liberty to all who will accept Him as Lord. It is the freedom of the Kingdom of God. 'To do the will of God' is Jesus' own account of the mark of His 'brother and sister and mother'(Mk 3³⁵; cf. Mt 7²¹).

After Pentecost the idea that the Christian is a man who does or seeks to do God's will as manifested by Christ is a universal postulate. It only emerges in set terms incidentally, but it does so in significant ways. First, the 'will of God' is the rule of a believer's *whole life*. To him *it* is, of course, says St. Paul, the thing that is 'good and well-pleasing and perfect' (Ro 12²). It is his lot 'to be filled with the knowledge of his will' so that he may 'walk worthily of the Lord' (Col 1⁹; cf. 4²; 2 Ti 2²⁶). Even slaves may do this (Eph 6⁶). The writer to the Hebrews tells his readers that they need 'patience' that they may 'do the will of God' till death (He 10³⁶). Peter insists that it is for Christians to suffer 'according to the will of God', as Christ did (1 P 3¹⁷, 4², ¹⁹). For John a Christian is a 'man who willeth to do his will' (Jn 7¹⁷), and who, doing it, 'abideth for ever' (1 Jn 2¹⁷). Second, God wills *particular ministries* for particular Christians. At the beginning of five epistles Paul insists that he is 'an apostle by the will of God' (e.g. 1 Co 1¹; cf. Ac 22¹⁴). As it happens, Paul is the only explicit example of this idea under this phrase, but it is, of course, silently applied to all Christians in such passages as Ro 12³ᶠᶠ·; 1 Co 12⁴⁻¹¹, ²⁷⁻³¹. It had anticipations in Jesus' parables of the large liberty of *responsible* slaves (Lk 19¹²⁻²⁷; Mt 25¹⁴⁻³⁰; Mk 13³⁴). Third, there are passages where *particular acts* are related to 'the will of God'—the route of Paul's journeyings (Ro 1¹⁰, 15³²), the liberality of the Macedonian Churches on Paul's appeal for gifts (2 Co 8⁵), the obedience of Christians to the State (1 P 2¹⁵), and the prayers of Christians (1 Jn 5¹⁴). The word *thelema* is only used twice of a believer's own will, and then of practical decisions (1 Co 8³⁷, 16¹²).

The doctrine of Christian liberty was elaborated through controversy, with Paul as its protagonist. The noun for 'liberty', *eleutheria* (*11*), is always used of *Christian* freedom, as is the verb for 'set at liberty' or emancipate' (*eleutheroun, 7*). The adjective 'free', *eleutheros* (*23*), while generally used in a broader sense, occurs ten times to describe the freedom of believers. Of the twenty-eight texts involved twenty are Pauline, and it is probable that the other eight refer back to Paul's use of the three terms. The idea appears first in the controversy about circumcision— and therefore about the whole ritual law of the Jews. At the Council of Jerusalem Peter calls this a '*yoke*' that 'neither our fathers nor we were able to bear'. Paul gives his own version of the controversy in Galatians and it is here that Christian 'liberty' is first mentioned (Gal 2⁴). In this passage 'liberty' is freedom from the Jewish ritual law. Paul adds the instance of the commensality of Christian Jews and Gentiles (v. 11 ff.). But the believer is a man who has been set free from much more than ritual law. This appears in a later passage in Galatians (4²¹–5¹). Here Paul exhibits his doctrine of Christian liberty by allegorizing the story of Hagar and Sarah, comparing them to 'two covenants', and adding a comparison between 'the Jerusalem that now is'— which corresponds to 'Mount Sinai' and is a city of slaves—and 'the Jerusalem that is above', which is a city of free men. The passage gathers to the assertion 'For freedom did Christ emancipate us' (and not for a second slavery). In this passage there are three leading phrases—'*yoke*' of bondage', 'born after *the Spirit*', '*children* of the freewoman'. It may be noticed that the three words in italics also occurred in the discussion of the freedom of Jesus, except that 'child' is used instead of 'son'.

Did Paul then teach that the Christian is 'set free' from *all* the law given on 'Sinai', whether ritual or *moral*? The first point is that the Bible knows nothing of an *autonomous* 'moral law' or 'imperative'. The New Testament term is 'ought' '*opheilein*' (*35*), and both this word and its derivatives always denote a debt *to a*

person—never a responsibility to a moral ideal that exists *per se*.[14]
In particular, they are used of 'debts' to God. Since these cannot
be wholly paid (cf. Mt 18[24]), a man needs to ask that God will
'forgive' his unpaid debts (Mt 6[12]). A debtor who cannot pay his
debts lives in 'fear'. He has 'the spirit of bondage unto fear'
(Ro 8[15]). The believer is 'emancipated' from 'fear' because God
has freely forgiven his debts for Christ's sake. But what about
keeping the moral law in the future? According to Paul's argument, a true believer will always keep it—not because he is afraid
of God—still less because of any 'moral imperative'—but because
he is now not a 'slave' but a 'son', and a true son does his father's
will, not because he 'owes' this to Him, but because he himself
wants to do it. He is loyal—i.e. that paradoxical thing a 'willing
slave'. His is not the Covenant of the Law but the Covenant of
Love. He soars above the realm of 'ought' in the imperative
sense of the word. He has the Spirit and 'the Lord is the Spirit:
and where the Spirit of the Lord is, there is *liberty*' (2 Co 3[17]).
Here, with deliberate paradox Paul puts the term 'Lord' alongside 'liberty' for in his time the universal idea was 'where there is
a Lord, there is a slave'. The Apostle says 'where Christ is Lord,
there is a free slave, for this slave shares His master's Spirit, and
therefore there is no clash of will'. Or again, where there was a
slave there was fear, but, as John puts it, 'perfect love casteth out
fear' (1 Jn 4[18]).

But it had to be '*perfect* love'. This leads to Paul's ultimate
doctrine of 'emancipation'. Like many another Jew, he had
'loved (God's) law' and it had been his 'meditation all the day'
(Ps 119[97])—or, to use his own phrase, he had 'delighted in the law
of God after the inward man' (Ro 7[22]). But he had discovered that,
rightly pondered, this law pierced to motive—as Jesus had taught
in the Sermon on the Mount—and he had discovered that he did
not always keep it in *that* realm, and that, try as he would, he
could not. The seventh chapter of Romans describes the 'wretched-
ness' of the man who, having discovered the range of the Law that
he loves, has thereby discovered his impotence to obey it 'with
all his heart and mind and soul and strength'. To this Jew the
very Law in which the Jews boasted had become the 'occasion'
of greater sin, for 'to whom much is given of him shall much be
required'. Unlike the writer of Second Esdras, Paul knows better

---

[14] *Ōphelon* (*4*), though from this verb, has neither connotation, meaning, as in LXX,
'would that'.

than to confine sin to sinful *act*. For him inward sin is fundamental sin—and sin leads to death. He puts the three words together in a famous phrase, 'the *law* of *sin* and *death*'. It is from this that 'the *law* of the *Spirit* of *life* in Christ Jesus'—a phrase that encounters word with word—has 'emancipated' him (Ro 8²). 'Being made free from sin' he is the enthusiastic 'slave of God' and of 'righteousness' (Ro 6¹⁸, ²⁰, ²²). He has entered into 'the liberty of the glory of the children of God' (Ro 8²¹). Here, as 2 Co 3¹⁷ᶠ· shows, it denotes a 'transfiguration' into the splendour of the liberty for which man was made. The Christian is 'really free' for he shares the liberty of the Son (Jn 8³⁶) and lives by the 'Spirit' (Gal 5²⁵). He is emancipated at last. He can do as he will.

The last phrase quoted, however, is only part of a sentence of Paul's. What he says is: '*If* we live by the Spirit, by the Spirit let us also walk.' The text is the conclusion of a passage (Gal 5¹³⁻²⁵) in which the Apostle warns his readers against the abuse of 'freedom', and it occurs in the very Epistle in which he most ardently claims it! The implication is that some of his converts do still sometimes 'fulfil the desires of the flesh'. In other words, he has to do with *imperfect* Christians—men who are not '*filled* with the Spirit'. His uncompromising assertion of Christian liberty presupposes a believer who 'loves the Lord (his) God with all his heart' and *therefore* 'loves his neighbour as himself'. It is no accident that Paul needs to quote the Second Great Commandment at the beginning of this passage. The Galatians did not always so 'love' as to 'be slaves one to another'. They were not all apt to 'wash one another's feet'. The three references to Christian freedom in other Epistles than Paul's repeat his warning. When James (2⁸⁻¹²), quoting the same Commandment, speaks of a 'kingly law'—that is, the law of the 'kingdom of God' (v. 5)—which is also 'the perfect law' and the 'law of liberty' (1²⁵, 2¹²)—he is arraigning Christians who despise the poor! Peter needs to remind believers that to be 'free' is to be a 'willing slave of God' (1 P 2¹⁶). By the second century outright Antinomianism had invaded the Church (2 P 2¹⁸ᶠ·). There were men who said that a Christian was 'free' to be lascivious! Underlying all three passages there is the paradox of Christian loyalty—'free' because *perfect* 'slave'. Imperfect Christians were in a kind of 'intermediate state' and with them New Testament writers do not hesitate to appeal to 'fear' (e.g. 2 Co 7¹; 1 P 1¹⁷; He 10³¹; Jude ¹⁷). Christian 'teachers' (*didaskalos*) must sometimes needs be

NBM

'disciplinarians' (*paidagogos*) appealing to the 'rod' (1 Co 4²¹), as 'the law' had done (Gal 3²⁴ᶠ·). Paul's argument about 'liberty', like some of his other arguments, presupposes that a Christian *is* all that 'in Christ' he *may be*. Similarly, when Augustine said 'Love God and do what you will', his emphasis was on the first phrase. When a man 'loves' utterly his 'service is perfect freedom'. Only when an emancipated slave is '*filled* with' his Master's Spirit can he be trusted to do whatever he will—but then he is so trusted, and this freedom is his 'glory'. It is a freedom like Jesus' own; in such a Christian God is 'well pleased' (Lk 12³²; Ph 2¹³; 2 Th 1¹¹).

As has been shown above, in the Old Testament man's 'dominion' is the complement of his 'freedom'. It is a limited yet a real control of some of God's creatures. In the New Testament it is assumed, as will appear below, that at the creation God put '*all* things under (man's) feet'. It is assumed too, and once all but asserted (Ro 8²⁰), that any evils in the creation are the results of man's sin. To discuss the difficulties of this doctrine is no part of the present subject, though it may be noted that such phenomena as earthquakes and avalanches are only reckoned disasters when they harm men or their property. In the New Testament there are two distinctive doctrines—of *believers'* ultimate and complete 'dominion', and of their partial 'dominion' now. The evidence for this follows.

Of the Greek verbs mentioned under this subject in LXX two, *diepein* and *despozein*, do not occur in the New Testament. A third, *archein*, only means 'rule' twice (Mk 10⁴²; Ro 15¹²), in texts that are not pertinent. A fourth, *kathistanai* (*22*), is only relevant in one phrase, which some of the best manuscripts omit (He 2⁷). This leaves *hypotassein* (*38*), *exousiazein* (*4*) with its noun *exousia* (*102*), and *katakurieuein* (*4*). *Hypotassein* may be taken first.

When this word relates to *persons*, it seems always to denote a voluntary 'submission', not a coercive 'subjection', even though this is not so in such a phrase as 'Thou didst put all *things* in subjection under his feet' (He 2⁸). It is noteworthy that under this subject Paul (1 Co 15²⁷; Eph 1²²; Ph 3²¹), the writer of Hebrews (2⁵⁻⁸), and Peter (1 P 3²²), all refer to the eighth Psalm and not to the first chapter of Genesis. The reason is that the Psalm uses the phrase 'the son of man'. The writer to the Hebrews works out the Christian exposition at some length. He is 'speaking' of the 'coming world' as the habitat of man (He 2⁵, *oikoumenē*). As always in the New Testament this is the present universe, not a distant

region 'in heaven', though it includes the sky (e.g. Rev 21$^{1f.}$).
It is 'not yet under (man's) feet', but already 'Jesus'—by which
term this writer always means 'the Son of Man'—is 'crowned with
glory and honour' (v. 8$^{f.}$). *He* is already master of the universe.
Paul (Ro 8$^{19-22}$), referring to the 'curse' (Gn 3$^{17-19}$) by which
Adam had lost his primal 'dominion' over nature and become a
'toiler' (Gn 3^{23}—*'ebed*, the word for 'slave'), says that 'the whole
creation' had been 'made subject to vanity' because of man's sin,
that with him it lies under 'the bondage of corruption', and is
therefore now 'groaning and travailing together in pain'. But, like
all 'travail', this 'travail' is 'in hope'. As nature was 'cursed'
because man sinned, so it will be 'emancipated' with him. For
Paul, as for the writer to the Hebrews, this emancipation began
with Christ's resurrection. 'All things', defined with magnificent
scope, are *already* in subjection under (Christ's) feet (Eph 1$^{20-2}$;
cf. 1 P 3$^{21f.}$). *He* is already master both of a sinful mankind and
a recalcitrant universe. He is king of 'all things', even though
the 'curse' of toil has not yet been lifted, and even though man's
body, good as it is, is not what it ought to be and will be, but 'a
body of humiliation' (Ph 3^{21}), under whose burden even Christians 'groan' (Ro 8^{23}). Since it is through the body that men
'partake' of the universe of things (cf. He 2^{14}), the 'redemption'
of this universe awaits the day when God will make 'the heaven
and the earth' anew (Rev 21^1; 2 P 3^{13}). Then there will be a
'restitution (*apokatastasis*) of all things' (Ac 3^{21}) and 'no more
curse' (Rev 22^3). Then Christ, having completed His work, will
hand back His 'kingship' to the Father and Himself 'be set in
submission' to the God who is to be 'all in all' (1 Co 15$^{23-8}$).
When that happens, God will restore man's primal 'dominion'
over 'all things' (cf. He 2^8), for this is the Creator's will. This
means that man's freedom will then have complete scope, since,
as already seen, for a true man 'service is perfect freedom'. Under
hypotassein, therefore, there are three doctrines—that at present
for all men, even believers, *complete* 'dominion' is lost (with
consequent ills); that Christ already controls the imperfect
universe; and that at the end 'dominion' will be restored to
redeemed man.

Meanwhile it is assumed, of course, that every man has a right
to use 'things' for his own purposes, so long as the purposes are
good. He may, for instance, sow corn or catch fish or kill sheep.
Spite the 'curse', man has still some degree of 'dominion' or

control. But the New Testament has here an additional and distinctive doctrine, and, as elsewhere, it relates, not to all men, but to believers. As already seen, Christ is ruling the world *now*. This idea is expressed, not only under *hypotassein*, but under *exousia* ('authority'—e.g. Mt 28[18]; Eph 1[21]; Col 2[10, 15]; 1 P 3[22]; Rev 12[10]). While 'the Lamb' is patient in His 'kingship' (Rev 1[9], 5[9]), He sees to it that even now 'all things work together for good to them that love God' and that 'no creature' shall 'separate' one of them from His 'love' (Ro 8[28, 39]). Under this text Paul, using the terms of his time, enumerates the mightiest 'creatures' in the universe. Elsewhere he even says to believers '*all things* are yours' —because 'ye are Christ's' and 'Christ is God's' (1 Co 3[21-3]). The true Church has always known that, as she is one with her 'head' and as He has 'all things under His feet', in her there is already 'the working of the strength of the might' of God (Eph 1[19-23]). 'In the world ye have tribulation; but courage! *I* have conquered the world' (Jn 16[33]). Christians 'groan' but conquer.

The few New Testament uses of the remaining term *kata-kurieuein* are not pertinent here, for they relate to authority over *persons* (Mk 10[42]; Ac 19[16]; 1 P 5[3]). The same is true of its synonym, *basileuein* (*21*), 'to exercise kingship' (e.g. Rev 1[9], 5[10], 22[5]; cf. Ro 5[17]). Under it there is a doctrine of the saints' kingship in history that completes the doctrine of 'dominion' over things.

It has several times appeared in this chapter that the Christian man has begun to be like Christ and therefore like God. The next chapter pursues this teaching farther. There it will be found that in most of the passages where the phrases 'the likeness' and 'the image of God' occur in the New Testament the emphasis is not on what man was 'in the beginning' but on what *the Christian* has already begun to be and what he is to be in the end through Christ.

In the New Testament, however, there are two passages where Gn 1[26f.] is directly quoted and these refer to *every man* as he *is now*. This introduces the question 'What is meant by the *phrase* "the image of God" in the New Testament, when it refers to *all* men?' In one passage (1 Co 11[7f.]) Paul unites the text where God is said to 'make man (male and female) in his own image' (*eikon*) with the text where He is said to 'build' one of Adam's ribs 'into a woman' (Gn 1[26f.], 2[21f.]). Here the Apostle is clearly speaking of *every* man, good or bad. To interpret 'image' of anything like 'moral and spiritual likeness' would be quite alien to a passage where the Apostle is defending the contemporary custom by which men went unveiled and women veiled in public. His argument bases on the *physical* difference between men and women, and while he silently admits that women share God's *eikōn* with men, he discriminates between the sexes under 'glory'. As in LXX *eikon* means a 'form' that can be seen. This interpretation involves the continuance of the belief that God Himself has a 'form'. Today this idea is supposed to be confined to the less intellectual kind of men, but the present writer believes that it was universal among the first Christians. It would be out of place here to discuss the subject but there seems to be no Biblical text that says that God is invisible—in the sense that there is in Him nothing that can be seen. As has been shown, in the Old Testament the Deuteronomist says that at Sinai the Israelites had not 'seen any form' (4¹², LXX *homoioma*), but exceptions occur for Moses, Isaiah, and Ezekiel. John follows the Deuteronomist (1¹⁸), though it is not impossible that he made the same exception (5³⁷, ¹⁰⁻¹). It is indeed true that he wrote 'God is spirit' (4²⁴), but he also refers to God's *eidos* (5³⁷), and in the New Testament, as in LXX, *eidos* means something that can be seen (e.g. Gn 29¹⁷; Is 53²ᶠ·; Lk 3²²; 2 Co 5⁷). Similarly, the phrase 'the unseen (*aoratos*) God' can be taken to mean, not that God is invisible, but that no man has ever seen Him (Col 1¹⁵; 1 Ti 1¹⁷; He 11²⁷). It is as though the sun, whose light is everywhere, were never seen. The interpretation of *eikon* as something visible, though never seen, is possible also in the phrase 'the image of him that created him' (Col 3¹⁰) which refers to Gn 1²⁶ᶠ· without quite quoting it. The second direct quotation is in the text 'With (the tongue) we bless the Lord and Father, and with it we curse men, who have been made after God's likeness (*homoiosis*)' (Ja 3⁹). This Greek term does not occur elsewhere in the New Testament, but 'moral and spiritual likeness' does not suit the context, for James does not mean 'We curse men although they are good'! As will appear in the next chapter, the New Testament teaches that men ought to be like God in *character*, and that, when a man begins, through faith, to be like Him in this way, there begin to be changes in his 'form' too, but this does not appear in the passages that refer Gn 1²⁶ᶠ· to *all* men, whether believers or not, as they are *now*. The passages interpret the text, like LXX, to refer to man's outward form; and this 'form', which was originally like God's, has not been altogether lost through sin.

It may be said that the doctrine that God, like man, has a

'form' is to imply that He has a 'body' and belongs to the material universe. This, however, is to thrust modern ideas on ancient thought. Perhaps the difference under this subject is most nearly stated if we say that the Hebrews and early Christians believed that 'form' is 'physical' but not 'material'. Probably the opinion of ordinary men in many ages, on analysis, would be found to imply just this. They believe that 'form' belongs to the physical world, for it can be seen, but they do not believe that it is made of 'matter'. Probably they would say, if pressed to elucidate what they mean, that a man's 'body', for instance, is 'flesh' *plus* 'form', and that the former alone is material. At any rate this is what the Biblical writers suggest wherever they refer to the subject. Since ordinary men ascribe the same 'form' to all men or all horses or all roses and so on—even though there are differences in every individual case—it follows, though they would be surprised to hear it, that they do not think that 'form' and size go together. This means that in some strange way 'form' is independent of space. The Greeks shared these opinions almost certainly, for it was surely from common speech that Plato and Aristotle—or the latter at any rate—started when they elaborated their philosophy of 'form'. Experts seem still to differ about the exact nature of their doctrines, or at least of Plato's, but these differences do not concern the present subject, which relates to the beliefs of ordinary men. It is at least possible that Paul would know something of Greek philosophy, for it would be discussed in the schools of Tarsus, but, when he wrote his Epistles, he could assume that any Hellenistic reader had a concept of 'form' that was sufficiently like the Jewish concept for his purpose. The passage from the Epistle of James sustains this, for James was no philosopher and he is certainly writing to 'ordinary men'.[15]

It is sometimes asked whether the New Testament doctrine of man is dichotomist or trichotomist—that is, whether man consists of 'body and soul' or of 'body, soul, and spirit'. The truth is that the question was not one that the New Testament writers either asked or answered. If one were driven to describe them by a word of this kind, one would have to coin some such word as 'poly-merotomist'! The evidence given above shows that the conclusions reached earlier for the books of the Apocrypha apply also to the New Testament. As contrasted with the Old Testament the term

[15] For some comments on the doctrine of God here involved see the Additional Note at the end of the volume.

for 'body' (*soma*) is much more frequent both in the Apocrypha and New Testament. Terms that are not related to any particular bodily organ, especially *nous* and its cognates, are borrowed from Greek. *Kardia* no longer always describes the physical 'heart'. *Nous* and *kardia* and *pneuma*, and even *psyche* and *thelema*, seem sometimes to be synonyms, but the Aristotelian idea that man consists of two disparate elements cannot be deduced from the manifold evidence. For Paul, it might, indeed, be claimed that in man there are two disparate things, but these would be 'flesh and spirit', not 'body and soul', and, as has been seen, *sarx* is by no means wholly physical and even *pneuma* has probably not altogether lost its connexion with 'wind'. The truth is that the New Testament writers, like their contemporaries—and like most men always—were not scientific psychologists. For them man was both unitary and manifold. None the less, here as elsewhere, the New Testament has its own *differentia*. It related everything to Christ. If Paul were confronted with the questions on which modern psychologists, after all their careful scrutiny of man's nature, by no means wholly agree, he would have said: 'I do not know what may be true or untrue in your various theories, but one thing I know—that there is a "new man" *in Christ Jesus*. "Christ! I am Christ's! and let the word suffice you." '

CHAPTER SIX

WHAT A MAN OUGHT TO BE

In this chapter the question 'What ought a *man* to be?' becomes, in effect, 'What ought a *Christian* to be?', and even 'What *is* a Christian man beginning to be?', for it is the message of the New Testament that Christ has revealed the final answers both to the question '*What* is God's purpose for man?' and to the question '*How* is man to fulfil that purpose?'

As intimated in the Introduction, this book is a sequel to *The Bible Doctrine of Salvation*. The latter, of course, involved the answer to the question 'What is a Christian man?', for it discussed 'faith', and the primary answer to this question is 'A believer in Christ'. The whole of this chapter could be described as 'the outcome of faith'. It pursues the method of examining the use of the chief terms that describe this outcome.

It may be useful to begin by indicating the arrangement of the chapter. It falls into four main divisions. In the first (A) the New Testament use of a long series of adjectives and their cognates is examined. There are three leading adjectives—'holy', 'righteous', and 'wise'. Under each of these a number of synonyms are discussed. The adjective 'perfect' is reserved for the fourth division. The second subject is the sonship of man and the fatherhood of God (B). The third is the 'glory' of man and related doctrines, including the 'image' of God (C). This involves a discussion of Paul's doctrines both of the 'outward' and 'inward' man, and of 'the old man' and 'the new man'. The fourth subject is Christian perfection (D). Under this subject certain other terms are taken before the word 'perfect' itself, and finally there is a discussion of a passage about sinlessness.

A

The commonest word for a Christian in the New Testament is *hagios*, a 'holy one' or 'saint'. This marked a revolution. It will be recalled that in the Old Testament and Apocrypha the use of the Hebrew and Greek words for 'holy' to describe a *man* is rare, by far the commonest use relating to the *ritualistic* holiness of *things*. It is true that sometimes the nation is called 'holy' and sometimes it is assumed that certain men, notably priests, are 'holy', but there was no such assumption about *every* individual Jew. In the New Testament the word, on the other hand, is used for *ordinary men*, scattered in small communities in many parts of the Roman Empire. Any man, whatever his place in society, who 'believes on the Lord Jesus Christ', is a 'saint'. The word did not mean, as today, that he was a man who stood out in the Christian community as a specially good man. *Every* Christian was *hagios*. When this distinctive but common New Testament use is compared with the use of 'holy' among the Jews at the time, the change is startling. At first sight it is startling too that the new use did not appear before Pentecost. After the gift of the Holy Spirit there were men who found themselves using the name 'holy ones' for themselves. In other words it was a derivative use. Its antecedents need to be examined.

In the New Testament, as in the Old, it is a postulate that God is 'holy'—so much so that usually it is a silent postulate, only finding expression for some special purpose (Lk 1⁴⁹; 1 P 1¹⁵ᶠ·; Rev 4⁸; Jn 17¹¹; 1 Jn 2²⁰; cf. He 12¹⁰). But among the Jews it had become an inoperative postulate at the critical point. This will appear if the use of the terms in the Synoptic Gospels is examined.

In them the term *hagios* occurs thirty-seven times. Of these twenty-two illustrate the phrase 'Holy Spirit'. This is considered later. As in other New Testament books, some texts illustrate the common use of *hagios* at the time for *things* ritually 'holy'. The Temple (and Tabernacle) are 'holy' (e.g. Mt 24¹⁵; Ac 6¹³; He 9¹⁻³); Jerusalem is 'the holy city' (e.g. Mt 4⁵, 27⁵³). A 'first-born' son is ritually 'holy' (Lk 2²³). Again, the Old Testament 'prophets' are 'holy' (Lk 1⁷⁰; Ac 3²¹; 2 P 3²), and with them the Baptist (Mk 6²⁰), as are the 'covenant' and 'angels' and the Law (Lk 1⁷²; Mk 8³⁸; Ac 10²²; Jude ¹⁴; Rev 14¹⁰; Ro 7⁷). So far there is nothing distinctive in the use. In the Synoptic Gospels the word is only twice used to describe Jesus Himself. Luke calls the Babe 'holy' before He is born (1³⁵), and a demon cries out 'I know thee who thou art, the Holy One of God' (Mk 1²⁴). This introduces the question of Jesus' own use of the term and His attitude to it. Apart from the texts where He speaks of 'the Holy Spirit' (Mk 3²⁹, 12³⁶, 13¹¹; Mt 28¹⁹), He only uses *hagios* three times—once of the 'angels' (Mk 8³⁸), once of 'the holy place' (Mt 24¹⁵), and once in the sentence 'give not the holy unto the dogs' (Mt 7⁶). With these texts there go His three uses of the verb *hagiazein*, 'hallow'. One of these is in the Lord's Prayer (Lk 11²) and is

discussed below. The other two examples occur in one passage
(Mt 23[16-22]). Here Jesus illustrates and vindicates the right use
of ritual, His indignant argument being that everything that is
'holy' is ultimately so because God is holy. Ritual is nothing
apart from God. In the saying 'Give not the holy to the dogs' He
also *starts* from current ritual, for of course no worshipper ever
did this. But what does He mean by 'holy' here? He has just been
speaking of the 'hypocrite' who *will* not see (Mt 7[3-5]). This recalls
another passage where He speaks of men who 'have eyes but see
not' and 'have ears but hear not' (Mt 13[10-16]; cf. Mk 4[23-5]).
Jesus had further teaching for those who were willing to see and
to hear, and who had an appetite for what He had to give. Those
who had no such appetite He compares to 'dogs'. As will appear
in the next book, they are committing the ultimate 'sin against the
Holy Spirit'. On this showing, by 'holy' He here means His own
teaching. Why did He not elsewhere call it 'holy' but explain it
under the term 'righteousness'? This leads back to the Old
Testament concept of the holiness of God. It was shown that under
this idea God was numinous, righteous, and separate (yet not
separate). There is no doubt that 'the people' took Jesus for a
numinous man. This is implied when they called Him 'a prophet',
and His 'mighty works' would reinforce the belief, for, as was seen
under the Old Testament, God's holiness appeared especially in
his 'mighty works'. In other words, when the people called a
man holy, the emphasis lay upon the numinous element (cf. Mk
6[14f., 20]). So long as this was so Jesus would not permit the word
to be used about Himself. When a demon cried out 'I know thee
who thou art', it is implied that the people were asking 'What and
who is this?' (Mk 1[24, 27], 8[27f.]). Jesus does not deny the demon's
assertion that He is 'the holy one of God', but bids the demon 'Be
muzzled'. Except under the name 'Son of Man' our Lord left
men to find out for themselves who He was—and this required
that before they used current words about Him, they must learn
what *He* meant by the words. This has its most famous example
under the name 'the Christ'. In the passage now in question Jesus
refuses to be reduced to a merely numinous miracle-worker, as
happened when other Jews cast out demons (Lk 11[19]; cf. Ac
8[9-11]). In His teaching He did not deny the numinousness of God,
but He would not let it be separated from righteousness. When
Peter, awed by an early miracle, cried 'Depart from me, for I am
a sinful man, O Lord', he was afraid of what this numinous man

might do to a sinner, until Jesus said 'Fear not' (Lk 5⁸⁻¹⁰). This 'fear' of the numinous in a miracle-worker appears also in the Gadarenes, who did not want to risk a second such incident as the drowning of pigs (Mk 5¹⁶ᶠ.). It appears also in the shrinking back of the crowd in the Garden when Jesus fronted it, until the healing of Malchus showed them that He would do them no harm (Jn 18⁶; Lk 22⁵¹). *We* take it for granted that Jesus would work no miracle that would harm a man, but His contemporaries—with some of the stories of Old Testament prophets in mind (2 K 2²³⁻⁵, 5²⁷, 7², ²⁰; Jer 28¹⁶ᶠ.)—were far from sure of this. Jesus was 'the holy one of God', but He did not use or allow the phrase until men had at least begun to learn what He Himself, focusing the complex idea of holiness in righteousness, meant by the word. He was far from rejecting the numinous or 'aweful', but He would not be *merely* numinous. The infrequency of the use of the term *hagios* in the Synoptic Gospels, as compared with the Epistles, reflects the historical situation. John, as usual, epitomizes what resulted sooner rather than later, for the disciples say 'We know and have believed that thou art the Holy One of God' (Jn 6⁶⁹). *They* had learnt the right meaning of the word.

Jesus' teaching about the holiness, not of Himself, but of men is implied in His remaining use of one of the terms. The first petition in the Lord's Prayer is the much neglected phrase '*Hallowed* be thy name' (Mt 6⁹). In reality it is only one part of a threefold prayer, for 'Thy kingdom come' and 'Thy will be done' are synonyms for it and, like all true synonyms, they express the same idea in other and distinctively significant ways. Here Jesus, in effect, recalls and epitomizes the teaching of the three great Prophets of Holiness: Isaiah, Deutero-Isaiah, and Ezekiel. For instance, the very phrase 'Hallowed be thy name' recalls its opposite, 'They have profaned thy holy name'. All the elements in these Prophets' teaching recur. The element of awe is there for the petition is offered to one who is 'in heaven'. But awe is not isolated. God is separate, for He is 'in heaven'—yet not separate, for He is 'Father'. To 'hallow God's name' is to reverence Him and therefore to worship Him and therefore to follow a given way of life. If His name is 'hallowed', *ipso facto* His kingdom (kingly rule) has come and His will is done. His Kingdom is a kingdom of righteousness—hence men are to pray for the 'forgiveness' of past 'trespasses' and 'deliverance' from future sins. His 'will is done' only when men are willing to do it, for righteousness cannot be enforced. The biblical phrase 'The heaven(s) and the earth' describes the universe. Now sin has parted earth from heaven, but earth is to rejoin heaven in the hallowing of God's name, the coming of His kingdom, and the doing of His will—for Jesus prescribes no prayer that is not to be answered. If it be asked whether the three phrases mean 'Do *thou* hallow thy name', 'Do *thou* bring thy kingdom', and 'Do *thou* do thy will', or 'May *men* hallow thy name', 'May *men* submit to thy rule', and 'May *men* do thy will', the answer is 'both', in the sense 'May men let God do what He alone can do'. Under holiness, as under other doctrines, the Lord's Prayer looks back to the Old Testament at its best and looks forward to the Church of the future. It is the prelude to Pentecost, for the gift of the Holy Spirit is its only adequate answer. Our Lord's own account of holiness is 'as in heaven, so on earth'.

After the Resurrection appearances, which were numinous indeed, Peter quickly hailed Christ as 'the Holy and Righteous One' (Ac 3[14]), and, when the disciples presently applied the greatest of Deutero-Isaiah's prophecies about God's 'righteous Servant' (Is 53[11]) to their Risen Lord, they changed the phrase to 'thy holy Servant' (Ac 4[27, 30]), preferring the wider word for, as in the three Prophets, holiness includes righteousness. After Pentecost, however, the term is rarely used of Christ (Rev 3[7], 6[10]), for 'the Lord', now 'seated at the right hand of God in power', was *of course* holy. Paul gives an instance of this universal postulate when he declares that 'in Christ Jesus, the chief cornerstone' every church 'groweth into a holy temple in the Lord' (Eph 2[20f.]), as does the writer to the Hebrews when he calls Jesus the true 'high *priest*' and 'minister of the true tabernacle' (8[1f.]). The Holiness of the Son of God is an axiom that needs no stating. The contrast when the New Testament writers speak of the Spirit is striking, especially when the rarity of the phrase 'holy Spirit' in the Old Testament is remembered. But it is none the less true that, even when the name 'the Spirit' is used without the adjective, the concept 'holy' is implied, for He is the Spirit of *God*. Whenever the adjective is added, it is probable that there is a reference, however indirect, to the way in which the Spirit 'hallows' Christians. This leads to a consideration of the use of *hagios* in the distinctive Christian way.

Of the many instances of the use of the term *hagios* in the New Testament (*228*), two-thirds fall under two phrases—'the Holy

Spirit' (*88*) and 'the saints' (*67*). In the Synoptic Gospels Jesus Himself speaks of 'the Holy Spirit' six times—twice of those who blaspheme against the Spirit (Mk 3²⁹; Lk 12¹⁰), and four times of a gift that the disciples are to receive, and are sure to receive, but which they have not yet received (Mk 13¹¹; Lk 11¹³, 12¹²; Mt 28¹⁹). As John summarizes, 'the Spirit was not yet given because Jesus was not yet glorified' (7³⁹). At Pentecost the gift was given. There was no doubt that those who received it were numinous men, as the 'speaking with tongues' and the ecstasy showed—and as Peter, in effect, said when he quoted Joel. Paul, who himself knew what ecstasy was and himself 'spoke with tongues', does not deny the numinous but, like Jesus, puts the *merely* numinous in its right place (1 Co 14). Of course, from the first, Christians were not *permanently* ecstatic, and the Book of Acts, which uses the term 'Holy Spirit' often (*40*), while it sometimes asserts and sometimes assumes that it is Christians, and Christians only, who are 'men of the Spirit', does not mean that the numinous was a permanent characteristic. In that book 'saints' slips quietly into use to describe Christians *in their daily life* (e.g. Ac 9¹³, ³², ⁴¹, 26¹⁰). Paul uses 'saints' (i.e. 'holy ones') over forty times as the Christians' *normal* name for themselves (e.g. Ro 1⁷; 1 Co 1²; Eph 5³; Ph 4²¹ᶠ·; Col 1¹²; 1 Th 3¹³; 1 Ti 5¹⁰). The writer of the Epistles of John prefers to say 'we' when he means 'Christians'. His one text, however, is significant—'Ye have an anointing (of the Spirit) from the Holy One' (1 Jn 2²⁰). In other Epistles Christians are rarely called 'holy' (*6*—e.g. He 6¹⁰; 1 P 2⁵; Jude ³), but this is only because the writers do not happen to want to speak often of Christians as such. In the Apocalypse the phrase 'the saints' is more frequent (*16*—e.g. 5⁸, 13⁷, 18²⁰, 22²¹), the reference usually being to the *suffering* 'saints'.

The significance of the two commonest uses of *hagios* now emerges. The Christian, since he is 'a man of the Spirit' and knows that he is, is *ipso facto* 'holy'. To explore all that this means would be to repeat much in this and the preceding chapter, particularly the discussion under *pneuma*. But, if the doctrine of the Holiness of God is recalled, it will be seen that the fundamental concept is that Christians are 'holy' because, through Christ by the Spirit, they are *in fellowship* with God and therefore, in their small and imperfect way, *like* Him. This leads to the *separateness* of Christians. It had its pronouncedly *ritualistic* side, for they had the Sacraments. But it also had its *ethical* side. Christians were separate, yet not separate—'in the world' but not 'of' it, like their master (Jn 17[11, 14]). Because they were 'holy' they were beginning to be righteous as 'the world' was not. As already suggested, the Christian use of the term, as over against the current Jewish use, related principally to men and not to things. In these 'holy' men righteousness is not the origin of their holiness, but its result. This relation between the two terms is important. To illustrate the dual concept fully would be to quote most of the passages where the Epistles teach ethics. For instance, when Paul or Peter speaks of a Christian's 'conversation' or way-of-life (*anastrophē*—e.g. Eph 4[22]; 1 Ti 4[12]; 1 P 1[15, 18], 2[12]), he refers to the higher moral life of the *hagios*. The Seer of the Apocalypse says this at some length in his own way. For him the 'nations' are to teem into God's 'holy city', yet it is reserved for those whose 'names are written in the Lamb's book of life' (Rev 21[10, 25-7]). In it there is 'no temple', for the whole of it is a Holy of Holies (Rev 21[22]; cf. 1 K 6[20])— that is, in it there is no need to separate God from His people, for they too are 'holy'. Or again, Peter, urging Christians to 'put away all wickedness', quotes about them one of the chief Old Testament passages under the word, calling them a 'holy priesthood' and a 'holy nation' (1 P 2[1, 5, 9]). Similarly, quoting the great text in Leviticus (19[2]), 'Ye shall be holy, for I the LORD your God am holy', he says 'like as he which called you is holy, be ye yourselves also holy in all manner of living' (1 P 2[15f.]). This text epitomizes the whole Christian doctrine of a holiness that issues in righteousness. If it does not so issue, it is not holiness. Through the Holy Spirit every 'saint' is beginning, in some elementary and far-off way, to be *like God*.

Two points perhaps need to be emphasized. First, this use of 'saint' to mean 'Christian' does not mean, as under the modern use of 'saint', that a man has gone far toward perfection, still less that he has reached it For instance, Paul calls the Christians at Corinth 'saints', though his Epistles to them are largely about their imperfections. Similarly, he speaks of 'the perfecting of the (imperfect) saints' (Eph 4[12]; cf 2 Co 13[9]; 1 Th 3[10]), and implies that they are not yet 'blameless' (Ph 2[15]; 1 Th 3[13], 5[23]). There is the same implication in the few places where the term 'holy' is used of the Christian community as a whole (Eph 5[27]; 1 P 2[5, 9]). Indeed, every ethical exhortation in every Epistle implies that perfection still lies ahead. So too, while at certain times the disciples were 'all *filled* with the Holy Spirit' (Ac 2[4], 4[31], 13[51])—

and while particular leaders on particular occasions are said to be '*full* of the Holy Spirit' (e.g. Ac 4[8], 6[5], 9[17], 11[24])—Paul needs to bid Christians *to be* '*filled* with the Spirit' (Eph 5[18]), and Peter to tell them *to be* 'children of obedience' who are to be 'holy in all manner of living' 'like as he which called' them (1 P 1[14-16]). The New Testament 'saint' is an imperfect 'saint'. But, secondly, the 'saint' has *begun* to be like God, for he is through the Spirit a 'child of God' (Ro 8[16]). For Peter Christians are 'a holy nation' that they 'may show forth the excellencies' of God (1 P 2[9]). In the New Testament every believer is in some degree 'godly', in the literal sense of that word. There is at least some hint of the divine about him.

Similar results follow if the use of the four cognates of *hagios*—*hagiazein* (*27*), *hagiasmos* (*10*), *hagiōsunē* (*3*), and *hagiōtes* (*2*)—is examined. The first of these means 'to sanctify' or 'hallow', and the other three mean 'sanctification'—the first tending to stress the process, the second the result, and the third the quality of 'holiness' itself. Only the last necessarily implies *entire* sanctity. Some texts require that Christians are already 'sanctified' (e.g. Ac 20[32]; 1 Co 1[2], 6[11]; He 10[10]) and others that the process is still going on (e.g. Ro 6[19, 22]; Eph 5[26]; 1 Th 5[23]; He 2[11], 12[14]). In the Fourth Gospel 'the Father' being determined to save 'the world', 'sanctified' the Son to this end (10[36]; cf. Ro 1[4]; 1 Co 1[30])—the Son in turn 'sanctifies' Himself for His disciples' sake when He chooses to die—and thereby God 'sanctifies' them (17[17, 19]). In the Epistle to the Hebrews it is always the High Priest, Jesus, who 'sanctifies' (2[11], 10[14]) through His own 'blood' (9[13], 10[29], 13[12]). None the less a Christian's consent has a share in the process of his own sanctification (2 Co 7[1]; 1 Th 4[3, 7]; 2 Ti 2[21]; 1 P 3[15]) and a Christian's ministry whether it be an Apostle's (Ro 15[16]) or any convert's (1 Co 7[14])[1] seeks the 'sanctification' of others. Again, every 'creature of God' is sanctified by Christian use (1 Ti 4[5]; cf. Lk 11[2]). The ultimate end of the whole correlated process is that believers may be 'unblameable in sanctification before God' at the Parousia (1 Th 3[13]; cf. He 10[14]), or, in a phrase that sums the whole subject, 'partakers of (God's) holiness' (He 12[10]). Holiness passes *from* the Father *by* the Son *through* the Spirit *to* the Christian.

Under the Old Testament discussion the question 'Is the holiness

[1] In this passage Paul presupposes that the home is, of course, to be Christian, not heathen.

The terms 'unclean' and 'uncleanness' belong to the book that deals with Sin, but another term, 'common' (*koinos*), which appears as a synonym for 'unclean' (Ac 10¹⁴), may be taken here. The phrase occurs in the vision where Peter is bidden to break the Jewish dietary laws (Dt 14¹⁻²¹; cf. Lv 11), and so to ignore a distinction between Jew and Gentile that was as full of meaning as that between Brahmin and pariah or Nordic and negro today. In the Old Testament the Greek term *koinos* only occurs in Proverbs (4—e.g. 1¹⁴), and there only one text is apposite, and in it the Greek departs from the Hebrew (Pr 15²³). Here *koinos* means 'a profane man' and perhaps a Gentile. In two texts in First Maccabees (1⁴⁷, ⁶²) it is used of the sacrificing and eating of such 'profane' things as Gentiles ate, particularly 'swine's flesh'. Apparently this use of *koinos* and its verb *koinoun* had become general among the Jews by the first century, for it is found in the Synoptists, in Acts, in Paul, in Hebrews, and in the Apocalypse. While *koinos* can mean 'common' in the broad sense (4—e.g. Ac 2⁴⁴, Tit 1⁴), its religious use is more frequent (9), and its verb (14) is always used in this way. Here 'profane', in its literal meaning, is an exact rendering. The word is used, for instance, of the 'profaning' of the Temple by Gentile feet, the terms *hieros* and *hagios* expressing its opposite (Ac 21²⁸; cf. He 9¹³). The Pharisaic 'tradition' carried the dietary law to extreme limits, Pharisees always washing their hands before eating even a cake of bread, apparently lest any 'profane' particle should enter their mouths. Jesus and His disciples, and probably others, did not follow this 'tradition' (Mk 7¹⁻⁷, ¹⁴⁻²³). Mark seems to give so much space to this incident because, when he wrote, the controversy about the commensality of Jewish and Gentiles had not yet been finally settled, for he adds the triumphant comment 'cleansing all foods' (v. 19). Even earlier, at the time that Paul wrote to the Romans, it was the general Christian belief that 'nothing is profane of itself' and he needed to warn his readers that in practice this principle might prove a *skandalon*—i.e. a good thing misused (Ro 14¹³⁻²¹). Alongside the belief that certain 'meats' were 'profane' there lay the belief that an 'uncircumcized' Gentile was 'profane and unclean' *per se* (Ac 10²⁸, 11³, ⁸). The writer to the Hebrews sets a backslider's previous 'sanctification' (*hagiazein*) by the 'blood of the covenant' over against the enormity of his present 'profaning' of it (10²⁹). On the other hand, John the Seer, when he says that (men) shall 'bring the glory and the

honour of the (Gentile) *nations* into' the Holy City, deliberately
adds that these are no longer 'profane' (Rev 21²⁶ᶠ·). Behind the
scattered instances of the use of the term in the New Testament
there is the story of the revolution by which Christianity broke
away from Judaism, and the revolution was implicit when Peter
broke bread with Cornelius. Of course where the first-century
Christian said 'nothing is profane', for 'to the clean all things are
clean' (Tit 1¹⁵), his twentieth-century brother says 'Nothing is
secular for to the Christian all the things that God made are holy'.

The examination of the Marcan passage exhibits Jesus' doctrine
of 'cleanness'. Sin alone profanes, and, as it comes 'from within',
a sinner profanes himself. On the other hand, God, through the
Holy Spirit, 'cleanses (men's) *hearts* by faith' in Christ (Ac 15⁸ᶠ·),
for it is only 'the clean in heart' that 'see God' (Mt 5⁸; cf. 23²⁶).
Loyal disciples, however they may stumble, are 'already clean'
(Jn 15³; cf. 13¹⁰ᶠ·), yet the process of 'cleansing', as of sanctification, is incomplete. While it begins with the 'cleansing' of the
'heart' from 'an evil conscience' expressed in baptism (He 10²²),
the 'cleansing' of the 'heart' (1 Ti 1⁵; 2 Ti 2²²), of the 'conscience'
(1 Ti 3⁹; 2 Ti 1³; cf. He 10²), and of 'the flesh (in the Pauline
sense) and spirit unto holiness' (2 Co 7¹), must proceed until a
man is 'cleansed from all unrighteousness' (1 Jn 1⁹). The whole discussion of *hagios* and the terms that go with it shows the scope of
the command and promise 'Ye shall be holy, for I, the Lord your
God, am holy'.

If then a Christian man is both holy and becoming holy (and
pure and clean), what kind of life will he live? The chief term
here is the Prophetic word 'righteous' (*dikaios*), with its cognates.
This introduces the second principal word. Under the Old
Testament, 'righteousness' was discussed before 'holiness' because
at the end of its story the prevalent concept was that a man must
be 'righteous' *before* he could 'dwell in (God's) holy hill' (Ps 15¹ᶠ·).
In the New Testament this is reversed. A Christian is first 'a holy
one' because the Holy Spirit links him with God—and then and
thereby he goes on to become 'righteous'. Of the six words that
form a group here only four—*dikaios* itself, *dikaiosunē*, *dikaiōma*,
and *dikaiokrisia*—are pertinent now, the other two—*dikaioun* and
dikaiōsis—belonging to the book on Sin. No attempt is made here
to develop the full meaning of 'righteousness' in the New Testament for it belongs to social rather than individual ethics. The
writer has attempted to describe this in earlier books. Here, so

far as possible, the doctrine of the *individual* man is being isolated. The immediate subject is the relation of one man to God. Under these terms it will be found that Old Testament ideas underlie the uses of the New except at two architectonic points.

The two most frequent of the terms, *dikaios* (79) with its adverb *dikaiōs* (5) and *dikaiosune* (91), 'righteous' and 'righteousness', are found in all parts of the New Testament. The latter is very frequent in Paul (57) because he argues at length about it. *Dikaios* is most frequent in his Epistles (*17*) and Matthew (*17*).

God is rarely called 'righteous' (2 Ti 4[8]; Rev 16[5]; Jn 17[25]; 1 Jn 1[9]; cf. Ro 3[26]; He 6[10]), for those whose holy book was the Old Testament took this for granted. This comes out in the use of *dikaioma* (*10*), which always denotes some expression of God's righteousness, whether in the Law (e.g. Lk 1[6]; Ro 2[26]; He 9[1]), in creation (Ro 1[20, 32]), in God's 'righteous acts' (Rev 15[4]), or in the 'obedience' of Christ, which made His whole life, and will make the life of Christians, a single expression of God's righteousness (Ro 5[16-19]; cf. Rev 19[9]). The one use of *dikaiokrisia* (Ro 2[5]; cf. Ac 17[31]; 2 Th 1[5]) asserts what is everywhere assumed—that God's 'judgement' is of course 'righteous'. The phrase 'the righteousness of God', similarly, only appears two or three times outside Paul (Mt 6[33]; Ja 1[20]; 2 P 1[1]). Matthew's text 'Seek ye first the kingdom (of God) and his righteousness' leads to Paul's use of the phrase. He has it seven times (Ro 3[5, 21, 25], 10[3] *bis*; 2 Co 5[21], 9[9]; cf. Eph 4[24]), which all imply that 'the righteousness of *God*' surpasses far what *men* call 'righteousness'. This subject will recur below. There are things about which every man is so sure that he rarely mentions them and for all believers in a personal God one of these is 'God is righteous'. When Paul asks 'Is God unrighteous?' (Ro 3[5]) it is a question that needs no answer.

When these words are used in relation to *men*, something is taken for granted also, as being obvious for those whose Bible was the Old Testament. This is that the word 'righteousness' denotes the right way of human life—that is, what God expects and requires of men. It is used to name the rule of life in the Synoptics (e.g. Lk 1[75]; Mt. 21[32]), in Acts (13[10], 24[25]), in Paul's Epistles (e.g. 2 Co 3[9], 6[14]; Gal 2[21]), in Hebrews (5[13], 11[33]), in other Epistles (Ja 2[18]; 1 P 3[14]), in the Apocalypse (22[11]), and in the Johannine books (Jn 16[8]; 1 Jn 2[29], 3[7]). Parallel to this use of the noun 'righteousness' there is that of the neuter adjective, 'that which is righteous' (*dikaion*). This parallelism can be illustrated from most parts of the New Testament (e.g. Lk 12⁵⁷, Mt 20⁴; Ac 4¹⁹; Eph 6¹; Ph 1⁷; 2 Th 1⁹; 1 Ti 1⁹; 1 P 2²³; 2 P 1¹³; cf. Jn 7²⁴). Just as the Christian inherited from the Old Testament the axiom 'God *is* righteous', so he inherited too the axiom 'Man *ought to be* righteous'—i.e. at this point men ought to be like God.

But *is* any *man* 'righteous'? In the New Testament there are here two seemingly contradictory phenomena. Particular persons, both past and present are said to be 'righteous' (e.g. Mk 6²⁰; Lk 1⁶; Ac 10²²; He 11⁴; Ja 5¹⁶f.; 1 Jn 3¹²), men being divided into two classes, 'the righteous and the unrighteous' or 'the evil and the good'. Jesus Himself uses these current phrases (Mt 5⁴⁵) and speaks of 'righteous' men (Mt 10⁴¹, 13¹⁷, 23²⁹, ³⁵). Paul, though rarely, has similar passages (Ac 24¹⁵; Ro 5⁷; cf. Tit 1⁸), as have other Apostolic writers (He 12²³; 1 P 3¹²; 2 P 2⁸; Rev 22¹¹). There are parallel passages under the use of the noun (e.g. Mt 21³²; Ac 10³⁵; He 11⁷, ³³, 12¹¹; Ja 2²³; Rev 22¹¹). On the other hand Paul declares roundly 'There is none righteous, no, not one' (Ro 3¹⁰). The seeming contradiction is resolved when *Jesus'* account of 'righteousness', best exhibited in the Sermon on the Mount, is considered. He allows that 'the Law and the Prophets' had begun to teach 'righteousness' but adds that He had come to 'complete' them and demands that men shall practise a 'righteousness' that exceeds 'the righteousness of the scribes and Pharisees', even at its best (Mt 5¹⁷, ²⁰). The latter did not teach that a man is unrighteous if he is guilty of such a 'jot' as an angry word or such a 'tittle' as a lustful look (v. 18, 22, 28)—but *Jesus* taught just this. In other words, for Him 'righteousness' was sinlessness. Men who are 'seeking the kingdom of God' are, of course, seeking '*his* righteousness' (6³³; cf. 5¹⁰), and how could this be less than sinless (cf. 5²⁰)? This is why Jesus was on occasion ironical about 'the righteous' (Mt 9¹³; Lk 15⁷). Sometimes the word is used in the way current at the time, but at other times Jesus gives it His own higher and deeper meaning, which starts, not from the practice of the better kind of man, but from the character of God.

Paul has the same dual use. There is a 'righteousness of the law' to which he had himself attained (Ph 3⁶). 'The Law' is good as far as it goes, for it is 'righteous' (Ro 7¹²; cf. Gal 3²¹), but it is insufficient, for 'if righteousness is of the law, Christ died for nought' (Gal 2²¹; cf. Ph 3⁹; Tit 3⁵). *He* is 'the end of the law unto righteousness' (Ro 10³⁻⁵). Paul has learnt this because, as he says in a compressed passage (3²¹⁻⁶), 'a righteousness of God hath been manifested apart from the law'. Underlying these pregnant verses there are several ideas—(a) that God requires in a man a righteousness like His own; (b) that, as all men have sinned, no man can attain His righteousness; (c) that God would not Himself be righteous if He had left man in this hopeless dilemma; (d) that through Christ man may begin to attain this kind of righteousness—to 'become the righteousness of God *in him*' (2 Co 5²¹; cf. Eph 4²⁴). There is yet another idea, that of justification, which is crucial, but this belongs to another book. In effect both Jesus and His great disciple say: 'Ye shall be *altogether* righteous after the manner in which God is *altogether* righteous.' This resolves the seeming contradiction in the use of the terms.

Has anyone ever been altogether 'righteous'? The Christian answer is 'Yes, Jesus'. In the New Testament Jesus does not Himself claim to be 'righteous' (except by implication—Mt 3¹⁵; cf. Jn 8⁴⁶), for, as noted earlier, apart from His exposition of the meaning of the name 'Son of Man' He left men to discover for themselves the truth about Him. In the Synoptics, again, the disciples do not use the adjective of Him, for they are discovering what He is and they do not use adjectives in the process. But after the Resurrection Peter, Stephen, and Paul all call Jesus '*the* Righteous One' (Ac 3¹⁴, 7⁵², 22¹⁴; cf. 1 Jn 2²⁹, 3⁷; He 10³⁸). Again, the adjective occurs in references to Jesus as 'the Righteous Servant' of Is 53¹¹ (Ac 3¹³ᶠ·; 1 P 3¹⁸; 1 Jn 2¹; cf. Mt 3¹⁵; 1 P 2²³), for to suffer in order to save others is part of the New Testament account of 'righteousness'. All these texts *assume* that Jesus 'fulfilled all righteousness'. This was a Christian axiom, and, like other axioms, it was usually just taken for granted. Not one man in a million defines or even articulates the axioms by which he lives. As with *dikaios*, so with *dikaiosune*. In the New Testament direct references to the 'righteousness' of Jesus are few (1 Co 1³⁰; He 1⁹; 2 P 1¹), but the doctrine is axiomatic in every passage which teaches that men are to become righteous *through Him* (e.g. Ro 3²¹⁻⁶, 10⁴⁻¹⁰). Under the noun, as under the adjective, the 'righteousness' of Jesus is indirectly asserted (e.g. Ac 17³¹; Ro 5¹⁷, ²¹; He 7²ᶠ·; Rev 19¹¹; Jn 6⁸⁻¹¹). Without this axiom there would have been no Christianity either in the first century or any other. In Jesus the Kingdom began and the Kingdom *is* righteousness (Mt 6³³; Ro 14¹⁷; cf. 1 Co 6⁹).

What is the relation of Christians to this climacteric 'righteousness of God'? Of 'the disciples' in the Synoptists we do not know much except that, having consented to 'leave all and follow' Jesus, they went on following. Surely, however, this implies both that they had begun to 'hunger and thirst after' the righteousness that He exemplified and taught, and that they at least hoped that by following Him this 'hunger' would, as He promised, be 'satisfied', even though it would be at the price of persecution (Mt 5[6, 10]). But here, as elsewhere, there was much more after Pentecost. Paul has a text that sums up the difference in the situation—'Him who knew no sin he made to be sin on our behalf *that we might become the righteousness of God* in him' (2 Co 5[1]). Two parallel texts may be added—'Of God are ye in Christ Jesus, who was made unto us . . . righteousness' (1 Co 1[30]); 'the ministration (*diakonia*) of the Spirit' and 'of righteousness' 'exceeds in glory' (2 Co 3[8f.]). The three texts taken together state that, inasmuch as a Christian is 'in Christ', he begins, through the indwelling Spirit of Christ, to 'become the righteousness' of God Himself! This is the ultimate account of what might be expected from the intimate fellowship of Christ and the 'believer'. It is true that at the beginning of this fellowship 'faith' is *'reckoned* for righteousness', a phrase that belongs to a later book, but in every fellowship the 'stronger personality', to use a rather ugly phrase, moulds the character of 'the weaker personality', more or less gradually, into its own likeness—a phenomenon that comes to its matchless zenith in the fellowship of Christ with the Christian. If it were not so—if the 'righteousness' of Christ were never anything more than 'imputed' to the Christian—the Antinomians would be right (cf. 1 Ti 1[9]). Wherever the New Testament writers speak of 'righteousness' in connexion with Christians, they mean a righteousness that 'exceeds the righteousness' of 'respectable' people in every age (cf. Ro 10[3f.]). Paul has a lengthy account of it—which includes the ministry of suffering for others, as Christ's did—in 2 Co 6[3-10]. Here he calls 'righteousness' the Christian's 'armour' (cf. Ro 6[13]; Eph 6[14]). In Christians 'grace reigns through righteousness unto eternal life' (Ro 5[17]), for they 'believe unto righteousness' (Ro 10[10]; cf. 4[13], 10[6]; Ph 3[9]). If their 'body is dead because of sin', their 'spirit is life because of righteousness' (Ro 8[10]; cf. Eph 4[23f.]). In their lives they bring forth the 'products of righteousness' (2 Co 9[10]; Eph 5[9]; Ph 1[11]; cf. Gal 5[22]). While all this does not mean that a Christian has already altogether 'become the righteousness of God', it does mean that he is 'becoming' it. He is 'following after' it (1 Ti 6[11]; 2 Ti 2[22]; cf. 3[16]); he can already be said to be 'living righteously' (Tit 2¹²; cf. 1 Th 2¹⁰; 1 Co 15³⁴; 2 Co 6¹⁴); and he hopes for Christ's 'appearing' because he expects that 'at that day the righteous Judge' will give him 'the crown of righteousness' (2 Ti 4⁸; cf. Gal 5⁵). His is 'the righteousness that issues from faith' (Ro 9³⁰), and it begins, continues and ends 'in Christ'. It is derivative, but it is not fictitious. It is derivative, and *therefore* dominant in life.

In the remaining New Testament books *dikaios* and its cognates are not often used, but when they occur, it is assumed that there was a well-known Christian doctrine of 'righteousness'. The writer of Hebrews speaks of 'the word of righteousness', 'the righteousness which is according to faith', and 'the fruit of righteousness' (5¹³, 11⁷, 12¹¹). Peter reminds his readers both that Christ died that they might 'live unto righteousness' and that there is a beatitude for those who 'suffer for righteousness' sake' (1 P 2²⁴, 3¹⁴). John, in whose time there seem to have been Christian Pharisees who said that they 'had no sin', sums up the Christian doctrine in a few verses (1 Jn 1⁵–2⁶)—God, who would not be 'faithful and righteous' if He did not forgive the penitent, 'cleanses them from all unrighteousness'; He does this because 'Jesus Christ, the Righteous One', is their 'Atonement'; they 'know' Christ—that is, they 'have fellowship with him' and so with 'the Father'; in consequence they inevitably 'keep his commandments', or, as the same idea is phrased later, 'do righteousness', for this is the mark of those who are 'begotten of him' and 'abide in him' (2²⁸ᶠ·; cf. 3¹⁰). John practically defines Christian 'righteousness' as a 'love' like that of the Christ who 'laid down his life' for others (3¹⁰, ¹⁶). For the present purpose he has the key phrase, 'He that doeth righteousness is righteous *even as he is righteous*' (3⁷). Christ came in order that men may be like God.

One of the other two translations of the Hebrew word for 'righteous' (*tzaddiq*) noted under LXX, the adjective *euthus* ('straight'), is rare in the New Testament (8), though the adverb of the same form ('straightway') is common. All the three passages relevant here declare that some enemy of the faith is *not* 'straight' (Ac 8²¹, 13¹⁰; 2 P 2¹⁵). In the one text where *euthutes* occurs (He 1⁸) and in the three that use *kateuthunein* (Lk 1⁷⁹; 1 Th 3¹¹; 2 Th 3⁵) it is *Christ* who 'makes straight' the way of the faithful. *Chrēstos* ('kindly') is also rare (7), but more significant. In a Lucan passage it is used along with the words 'love' and 'pitiful' to describe God —and therefore His 'children' (Lk 6³⁵ᶠ·; cf 1 P 2³). Similarly,

Paul tells the Ephesians to be 'kindly', like Christ, and so to 'imitate' their Father (Eph 4³²ᶠ·). The corresponding noun *chrēstotēs* (*10*) is wholly Pauline. Twice the Apostle speaks of God's 'kindliness' to all men as opposed to 'judgement' and 'severity' (Ro 2⁴, 11²²), and twice of His 'kindliness' in Christ (Eph 2⁷; Tit 3⁴). Once he uses the word of man's 'kindliness' to deny that sinners are 'kindly' (Ro 3¹²), and in three passages he claims that 'kindliness' is a Christian virtue—in two closely relating it to the Spirit (2 Co 6⁶; Gal 5²²), and in the other comparing it to Christ's 'forgiveness' (Col 3¹²). Christians are to be 'kindly' because God is.

Both the usual LXX renderings of *tob* ('good'), *agathos* and *kalos*, are common in the New Testament. Where their meaning is distinguishable, *agathos* (*99*) refers to inherent character and *kalos* (*98*) to its expression in life. God is only once called 'good', but then in the phrase 'None is good (*agathos*) save one, God' (Mk 10¹⁸; cf. Ro 12²). The implication is that goodness has only one exemplar and source (cf. Ja 1¹⁷). While there are a few passages which require that there may be *some* goodness in a man who is not a Christian (e.g. Ac 23¹; Ro 5⁷), the overwhelming majority of passages where *agathos* is used in the Epistles relate to the Christian character. Christians are 'created in Christ Jesus for good works' (Eph 2¹⁰; cf. Ro 7¹⁸ᶠ·). The noun *agathōsunē* (*4*) is confined to Paul and always describes Christians. It is part of 'the fruit of the Spirit' (Gal 5²²), and 'the fruit of light in the Lord' (Eph 5⁷⁻⁹; cf. Ro 15⁴), whereby Christians may 'fulfil all (God's) good pleasure' (2 Th 1¹¹). *Kalos*, which occurs some fifty times in the Epistles, is *never* used in any of them except with reference, explicit or implicit, to Christian behaviour. This is so even when the 'law' is called 'good' (Ro 7¹⁶; 1 Ti 1⁸), for only Christians can fulfil it. Probably there is not one of the fifty texts whose meaning cannot be illustrated from the life of Jesus. Christians have a degree of 'goodness', but it derives from God through Christ. In New Testament times there was a distinctive kind of Christian 'behaviour' (*anastrophē*—e.g. Gal 1¹³; 1 Ti 4¹²; He 13⁷), whose mark was a distinctive kind of 'goodness' (Ja 3¹³; 1 P 2¹²), that could be defined as 'good behaviour in Christ' (1 P 3¹⁶). While God is not Himself called *kalos* in the New Testament, John calls Christ 'the good shepherd' who manifests 'good works from the Father' (Jn 10¹¹, ¹⁴, ³²). The whole evidence, when gathered together, under these two words, illustrates the customary sequence—from God, through Christ, unto men.

The third leading adjective is *sophos*, 'wise', which has four synonyms—*phronimos, sōphrōn, sunetos,* and *epistēmōn.* The doctrine of 'wisdom' does not dominate the New Testament as it dominated Alexandrian Judaism, but it is not unimportant. With the adjective *sophos* (*19*) there go the cognates *sophia* ('wisdom'—*51*) and *sophizein* ('make wise'—*2*). *Sophia* still denotes the principle of the practice of the true kind of life. Further, what was implied in the Wisdom Literature is now explicit—God offers 'wisdom' to *every* man, Gentile as well as Jew. Yet this term did not best suit the Christian message, for it is specifically the word of a *teacher*, and of a teacher who assumes that a disciple or pupil *can* do what he is told if he *will.* As has been shown, this is an axiom with all the Wisdom writers. Paul, of course—both because he knew the impotence of his own will, and because he had learned how Jesus lived and taught—explicitly denied this. Christ did indeed teach the right way to live, but with the Apostles teaching is ancillary to grace. It is only through the latter that a Christian *can* do all that he learns he *ought* to do. 'With all thy getting, get wisdom', said the Wise Man, and left it there; he had no 'gospel' for the man who *knows* what is right but can't *do* it. In the New Testament 'power' is emphasized more than knowledge. None the less it has a distinctive doctrine of 'wisdom'.

Under the use of *sophia* in the Synoptic Gospels (*10*) and Acts (*4*) this begins to emerge. In the Lucan writings there are passages that reflect the use of the Wisdom Books (Lk 2[40, 52], 11[49]; Ac 7[10, 22]), but elsewhere the term is specially connected first with Jesus and then with His disciples. Jesus' hearers ask 'What is the wisdom that is given unto *this man?*', its evidence being His 'mighty works' (Mk 6[2]). Jesus Himself claims that 'the Son of Man' has a greater 'wisdom' than Solomon (Lk 11[31]), and promises to 'give wisdom' to His disciples (Lk 21[15]). In a passage in Acts 'wisdom and the Spirit' go together, alike in the serving of tables and the argument of Stephen (Ac 6[3, 10]). Another passage anticipates Paul's distinction between true and false wisdom (Lk 7[29-35]). In it the Pharisees 'reject the counsel of God' and so show that they are not the 'children of wisdom'. The same contrast appears under the term 'wise' (Lk 10[21], 23[34]). In the passage in Matthew beginning 'Come unto me' (11[28-30]) Jesus again anticipates Paul, for, by adapting some verses in Sirach (51[23-7]), He claims Himself to be the 'wisdom of God'.

Of the uses of *sophia* in Paul (*28*) about half appear in one passage (1 Co 1^{17}–2^{16}). Here it looks as if he used the term, not spontaneously, but under challenge. Similarly, two-thirds of the texts where he uses 'wise' (*15*) appear in the same argument with his critics at Corinth (1 Co 1$^{19-27}$, 3$^{18-20}$). There is throughout a contrast between 'the wisdom of this world' or 'of men' or 'of the flesh' and 'the wisdom of God', which *is* Christ (1^{24}). This was a new distinction, for in the Old Testament and Apocrypha there is no sinful 'wisdom'. It is no accident that a discussion of 'power' intertwines with that of 'wisdom', for Paul is maintaining that 'Christ crucified' *is* 'the wisdom of God' precisely because He *is* 'the power of God', Wisdom without power is vain, for the true definition of 'wisdom' is not mere knowledge but 'righteousness and sanctification and redemption' (1^{30}). Similarly, it is the Spirit that 'reveals God's hidden wisdom' to Christians, for they alone are 'spiritual' and 'have the mind of Christ' (2$^{6-16}$), and Paul's preaching (*kerugma*) is true wisdom just because it is 'in demonstration of the Spirit *and* power' (2^4). There is just one passage where Paul follows the contemporary division of men into 'wise and foolish' according to their culture (Ro 1^{14}), but there the phrase is practically a quotation from current speech. For Paul only a Christian is a wise man, for only he both *knows* the true way of life *and can* tread it. For him such a phrase as 'impotent wisdom' would have been a contradiction in terms. Outside this long passage Paul's use of the terms 'wisdom' and 'wise' is sporadic, but it illustrates the ideas found at the beginning of First Corinthians, as do other writers' Epistles and the Apocalypse. There is a true and a false wisdom (Ro 1^{22}; 2 Co 1^{12}; Col 1^{28}, 2^{23}; Ja 3$^{13-17}$); the source of the true wisdom is God (Ro 11^{33}, 16^{27}; Eph 3^{10}; Ja 1^5, 3$^{13, 17}$; Rev 7^{12}); it is 'hidden in Christ' (Col 2^3), and is given through Him to Christians (Eph 1^8; Col 1$^{9, 28}$), who are the truly wise (Ro 16^{19}; 1 Co 6^5; Eph 5^{15}; Ja 3^{15}), for 'to know Christ' is to have 'the spirit of wisdom' (Eph 1^{17}); it is closely related to 'power' (Col 1$^{9-11}$) and to 'the word of Christ' (Col 3^{16}). The two texts where the verb *sophizein* occurs illustrate the two kinds of wisdom (2 Ti 3^5; 2 P 1^{16}). It is remarkable that none of the three words occurs either in the Epistle to the Hebrews or the Fourth Gospel, the two books where the influence of the Wisdom Literature is otherwise clearest. In particular, the teaching of the Book of Wisdom which identifies the Spirit with Wisdom in creation is altogether absent. In the New Testament it is the Son who is the agent of creation (Col 1^{16}; He 1^2; Jn 1^3).

The key to Paul's doctrine is the phrase 'we speak God's wisdom in a mystery' (1 Co 2⁷). God, having kept His deepest secret 'hidden' through the ages past, has now revealed it through Christ. For the Apostle there is no wisdom apart from Christ, and therefore there are no wise men except Christians. Here there is an implicit doctrine that through Christ believers share in the wisdom of God, and so are like Him, as an atom is like a universe.

Of the three synonyms for *sophia* the first is *phronēsis*. It belongs to a group of six words derived from *phrēn*, 'mind' (*2*—1 Co 14²⁰), of which two—*phronein* (*25*) and *phronimos* (*16*)—are fairly frequent, and four—*phronēsis* itself (*2*) *phronēma* (*4*) *phrontizein* (*1*), and *phronimōs* (*1*)—are rare. *Phronein* occurs twice without any reference to the distinctively Christian 'mind' (Ac 28²²; 1 Co 13¹¹), but elsewhere all these words refer to the 'craft' of the Christian life. Almost always there is an explicit or implicit contrast between this 'craft' and the 'craft' of the men of this world. The key here is in Jesus' saying: 'Be ye crafty as snakes but harmless as doves' (Mt 10¹⁶). The Christian's 'wisdom' shows itself in the true 'art' of daily life. The distinction between 'wisdom' and 'craftsmanship', however, can hardly be maintained under all these terms, especially *phronein*. Paul, who almost monopolizes it (*22*), practically uses it as the verb of *sophos*. The one phrase 'Have this *mind* among yourselves which ye have in Christ Jesus' (Ph 2⁵) contains his whole doctrine. The *differentia* of the 'mind' of the Christian comes out also in the antithesis between 'the mind of the Spirit and the mind of the flesh' (Ro 8⁵⁻⁷, ²⁷). Or again, it is involved whenever Paul uses *phronimos* (*5*—Ro 11²⁵, 12¹⁶; 1 Co 4¹⁰, 10¹⁵; 2 Co 11¹⁹). This use of the adjective had been anticipated in the parable of the Wise and Foolish Virgins (Mt 25²⁻⁹; cf. Lk 16⁸). Paul teaches that to 'have the same mind' is the secret of Christian unity (Ro 15⁵; 2 Co 13¹¹; Ph 1⁷, 2², 4², ¹⁰). The term *sophrōn*, 'sound of mind', and its cognates are not infrequent (*16*). Words of this group are very rare in LXX (*4*), but twice they describe 'wisdom' (Wis 8⁷, 9¹¹). They are particularly frequent in Timothy and Titus (*10*). Originally they denoted literal 'sanity' (Mk 5¹⁵; Ac 26²⁵; 2 Co 5¹³). God gives Christians 'a spirit . . . of power and love and sanity' (2 Ti 1⁷; cf. 1 P 4⁷). While this 'sanity' is peculiarly necessary in 'bishops' (1 Ti 3²; Tit 1⁸), in a passage that uses the terms often (Tit 2¹⁻¹⁴) it is commended to 'aged men' and 'young women'!

The next group of words consists of *sunienai* (*27*), *sunesis* (*7*), and

sunetos (*4*), the usual renderings being 'understand' and its cognates. For once a group of words of this type is more frequent in
the Synoptics (*23*) than elsewhere. While these terms can be used
without any reference to the specifically Christian kind of 'understanding' (e.g. Lk 2⁵⁰; Ac 13⁷), here again it is the 'understanding'
of *disciples* that is emphasized, in contrast with that of others. In
Mk 4⁹ an early copyist interprets the phrase 'Who hath ears to
hear, let him hear' by 'Let the understanding man understand',
and this gives the ruling idea. Matthew illustrates this when, on
quoting Is 6⁹ᶠ·, he points the contrast between those who 'understand' and those who do not in the interpretation of the Parable
of the Sower (13¹³⁻¹⁹; cf. Mk 7¹⁴; Ac 28²⁶ᶠ·). Paul has a like
contrast (1 Co 1¹⁹), and relates Christian 'understanding' both
to the Spirit and 'the mystery' of Christ (Col 1⁹, 2²). With him,
as with the Synoptists, 'understanding' depends, not upon an
acute mind, but a right will (Ro 3¹¹, 15²¹; Eph 5¹⁷), for God 'gives
understanding' to the willing (2 Ti 2⁷). If any man 'hath ears
to hear', that man *will* 'understand'. 'If any of you lack wisdom,
let him ask (it) from God who gives (it) to all single-mindedly and
does not reproach (the ignorant)' (Ja 1⁵). Prayer is the secret of
'wisdom'. Like the Sages the Apostles say 'If any man willeth
to do, he shall both know what to do, and be able to do it'—but the
Apostles add 'through Christ', and *only* through Him.

Of the next group of words the noun, *epistēmē*, does not occur
in the New Testament, and the adjective, *epistemōn*, only once
(Ja 3¹³), where James echoes Sirach except that he calls 'wisdom'
'meek'. The verb *epistasthai* (*14*) is most frequent in Acts (*9*),
where its uses show that it meant no more than 'to know that this
or that is so' (e.g. Ac 10²⁸, 15⁷). For the most part the use of this
word only brings out by contrast the Christian transfiguration of
its synonyms. Once, however, under it the babbler about
'logomachies' in the church is said 'to know nothing' (1 Ti 4⁴),
and once the 'knowledge' of certain 'railers' is compared to that
of 'animals' (Jude ¹⁰). It was not by the 'experience' of life *at
large* that the Christian learnt true 'wisdom' but by 'knowing
Christ'. The world knew not God 'through (its) wisdom' (1 Co 1²¹),
but through Christ the Christian has a wisdom that is like God's.

B

All that has so far been said, and much more, is gathered up
in the New Testament doctrine that 'believers' are 'sons' or

'children of God'. As has been shown, while the Old Testament prepared the way for the doctrine that the righteous Jew is 'a child of God', this only developed clearly in the Apocrypha, especially in the Book of Wisdom. Logically the doctrine of the 'fatherhood of God' is the same doctrine, put in its correlative form, but it was found that it is more correct to say that the teaching is that while God is every Jew's father, only a righteous Jew is His son. This has a bearing on the New Testament doctrine. Here the evidence of the Synoptic Gospels will be taken first; then that of the other books. In both cases the passages that speak of 'sonship' will be examined before those that speak of 'fatherhood'.

Of the three words in LXX for 'child' one, *pais*, is not relevant. In two passages in the Lucan Songs (Lk 1$^{54, 69}$) 'child' is a possible rendering, but there, as usually in LXX, the more likely meaning is 'servant'. Similarly *pais* is used in Matthew (12^{18}) in a quotation about 'the Servant of the Lord' (as in Ac 3^{13}, etc.). Under the second term, *paidion*, a 'little child', Jesus calls His disciples to be *like* 'little children' (Mk 10^{15}). He tests the Syro-Phoenician woman by using *teknon*, the third term, as though, like other Jews, He thought that Jews were God's 'children' and Gentiles were 'dogs' (Mk 7^{28}). Under the words that mean 'child' the one really relevant text in the Synoptists is the passage: 'If *ye* then, being evil, know how to give good gifts unto your *children*, how much more shall your Father in heaven give good things to them that ask him' (Mt 7^{11}). Luke changes Matthew's phrase '*your* Father' to '*the* Father' (as he changes 'good things' to 'the Holy Spirit'—11^{13}). These phrases are discussed later. The promise is 'to them that ask', which gives a hint of the idea that God cannot be fully Father to those who do not want His gifts. The Baptist had already told unrepentant Jews that they were not 'children (*teknon*) of Abraham' but the 'offspring of vipers' (Lk 3$^{7f.}$), and Matthew ascribes the latter phrase to Jesus also (12^{34}, 23^{33}).

The next term is *huios* ('son'). There are only three directly relevant texts in the Synoptics—in one of the Beatitudes Jesus says that 'the peace-makers shall be called sons of God' (Mt 5^9); He declares that those that are 'accounted worthy to attain to . . . the resurrection from the dead' are 'sons of God' (Lk 20^{36}); He pronounces that those who 'love their enemies' are 'sons of the Most High' (Lk 6^{35}) or of 'your Father in heaven' (Mt 5^{45}). The phrase 'the sons of the light' (Lk 16^8) may be added and there is a passage where Jesus implies that there are people, such as Himself and Peter, who are 'sons' of the heavenly King (Mt 17²⁶). Apart perhaps from the last passage the implication of the texts is that, not all Jews, but only people of a certain kind are true 'sons of God'. This is explicit in a text which declares that many Gentiles shall 'sit down with Abraham and Isaac in the kingdom of heaven; but the sons of the kingdom shall be cast forth into the outer darkness' (Mt 8¹¹ᶠ·; cf. 3⁸ᶠ·). Under one text (Lk 6³⁵; Mt 5⁴⁵) Jesus challenges men to behave as God behaves, and *so* to be His 'sons'. Sonship means likeness of character.

Jesus uses the term 'Father' for God much more often than He uses 'children' or 'sons' for men (Matthew, *45*; Mark, *5*; Luke, *17*). Under it He made two innovations. The first appears from His use of the phrase *'your* Father'. Here, except in the Matthean text quoted above (7¹¹), *'your'* refers to those who are willing to listen to Jesus. The phrase only occurs once in Mark (11²⁵), where Jesus is teaching the Twelve to 'forgive' since their 'Father' forgives. Luke has the phrase three times—once when Jesus teaches 'them that hear' to be 'merciful', like their Father (6²⁷, ³⁶); and twice when He tells the 'little flock' of His disciples that their 'Father' will not only feed and clothe them but 'give (them) the kingdom' (12²², ³⁰, ³²). In Matthew Jesus uses the phrase 'your Father' eighteen times, with *'our* Father' once as its equivalent (6⁸ᶠ·). Of these nineteen texts fifteen occur in the Sermon on the Mount, and eleven of these belong to the sixth chapter, 'the Chapter of the Father'. All nineteen refer to *the kind of life*, better than that of the Pharisees, that 'disciples' are to live. They are 'the light of the world' and, on seeing *their* lives, men will 'glorify' the God who is obviously *their* 'Father' (5¹⁶). They are to be 'perfect' like their 'Father' in the realm of love, loving their enemies as He does (5⁴⁵, ⁴⁸), and 'forgiving' as He does (6¹⁴ᶠ·). They are not to parade their alms and prayers and fastings 'before men', for this turns worship into pretence, but to remember that they are 'ever in their great Father's (not 'taskmaster's'!) eye' and that He has His own rewards (6¹, ⁴, ⁶, ¹⁸). They are to trust their Father to clothe and feed them (6²⁶), for He knows their 'needs' before they ask (6⁸, ³², 7¹¹). The last idea is repeated outside the Sermon (10²⁹), as is the warning against the Pharisees (23⁹), with the exposition 'One is your Father'. There remain two texts —a reference to the glory of the righteous in their Father's future 'kingdom' (13⁴³), and the phrase 'It is not ye that speak,

Jew's father, but every Jew is not his son', He 'fulfils' this creed
by showing that God is *every man's* father, but also by declaring
that only a man who lives according to *His* account of righteousness (and so, for instance, loves his enemies), is God's 'son'. In the
spiritual realm a son is only a son in so far as he is like his father.

The second distinctive element in Jesus' teaching in the Synoptic
Gospels relating to the word 'son' is His belief in His own unique
Sonship. Here this doctrine is only pertinent in so far as it is related
to *men's* sonship. As will appear presently, the two go together in the
later Apostolic teaching. But, as with the doctrine of the Spirit,
with which that of a Christian's sonship is organically connected,
the doctrine of sonship was only developed after Christians had
become aware that they were 'sons of God' through the Son of
God. In the Synoptic Gospels, however, there is an anticipation
of this doctrine and a preparation for it in Jesus' use of the phrase
'*My* Father'. Under it (except in Lk 2⁴⁹) He speaks of Himself as
the link between God and men. The phrase itself does not occur in
Mark (though it is implied in 14³⁶—where Matthew has 'my
Father'—and in 8³⁸). Luke's uses recur in Matthew except for
2⁴⁹, 22²⁹, and 23³⁴. Matthew has the phrase seventeen times.
They begin with the end of the Sermon on the Mount (7²¹).
Here Jesus, speaking of 'the will of my Father which is in heaven'
as described in the Sermon, declares that while He Himself is
'lord' of those who do it, He is 'lord' of none others. Later He
says that His true relatives are those who do His Father's will
(12⁵⁰). Several texts link God, Jesus, and Jesus' disciples. For
instance, Jesus tells Peter, the representative disciple, that 'my
Father' has revealed to him His Messiahship (16¹⁷). Again, in
Chapter 18, Jesus says 'my Father' four times—twice when
speaking of the 'little ones which believe on me' (v. 6, 10, 14),
once when He promises His disciples success in prayer when they
are gathered 'in (His) name', and once when He is teaching them
His way to forgive (v. 21, 35). There is a passage, too, where
He tells them that they need not fear 'plants' that 'my
Father' hath not 'planted' (15¹³), and one where He says that
the fate of every one of them will depend upon what *He* testifies
to '(His) Father' about him (10³²ᶠ·). In the story of the Last
Week Matthew has the phrase six times (20²³, 25³⁴, 26²⁹, ³⁹, ⁴², ⁵³) and Luke adds two (22²⁹, 24⁴⁹). In all eight Jesus, being
God's Son, is therefore related to men. Even in the difficult text,
Mt 20²³, *God* decides the precedence of *His Son's* disciples. Three

times Jesus speaks of the 'cup' that 'my Father' has given me to drink for men's salvation (Mt 20²³, 26³⁹, ⁴²), and three times of the 'kingdom' that 'my Father' will give 'to me' and so to them (Mt 25³⁴, 26²⁹; Lk 22²⁹). Luke has a passage where the Risen Christ says 'I send forth the promise of my Father upon you', heralding the Spirit. The burden of the whole series of passages is gathered in one text—'All things have been delivered unto me of my Father: and no one knoweth the Son, save the Father; neither doth any know the Father, save the Son, *and he to whom the Son willeth to reveal him*' (Mt 11²⁷). To 'know', of course, as in the Old Testament, describes intimate fellowship. It is this filial fellowship with God that Jesus promises when He goes on to cry 'Come unto me'. It is this that is the unique blessing that Jesus has brought to His 'disciples' (Lk 10²²⁻⁴). The blessing was the sonship of the true 'sons of God', rare though this phrase was on Jesus' lips. The way was open for Paul's 'Abba! Father!' and John's '*My* Father and *your* Father'. In the Synoptic Gospels, whenever Jesus says 'My Father' He is thinking of redemption.

In the later New Testament books Christians are called 'sons of God' in Paul (*7*), in Hebrews (*6*), and in the Apocalypse (*1*). The parallel phrase 'children of God' occurs in Paul (*4*), in 1 Peter (*1*), and in John (*6*). With these there go the passages where Christians are said to be 'born of God' (*gennasthai*). This phrase is sometimes rendered 'begotten of God' in the English versions, but the verb could be used to mean 'born' (Jn 16²¹) and this suits the passages in question better. While Paul once implies that he knew the phrase (Gal 4²⁹), and while Peter twice uses the synonym 'born again' (1 P 1³, ²³), it is peculiarly John's phrase. He uses it six times in his Gospel and nine in the First Epistle.

The dominant ideas in the post-Pentecostal New Testament appear in the Trinitarian text, 'And because ye are sons, God sent forth the Spirit of his Son into our hearts, crying, Abba, Father' (Gal 4⁶). Here Paul is speaking of the *knowledge* of sonship (cf. Ro 8¹⁶). He has just spoken of its *origin*—'God sent forth His Son . . . that we might receive the adoption of sons' (Gal 4⁴ᶠ.). Here, on the basis of the new Christian experience of the Spirit, the Apostle focuses all that Jesus had said when He spoke of 'my Father'. Christians are 'all sons of God through faith in Christ Jesus' (Gal 3²⁶). Christ is 'the first-born among many brethren' and they are to be 'joint-heirs' with Him (Ro 8¹⁷, ²⁹). The use of 'brethren', from Acts onward, to mean 'fellow Christians' derives from the consciousness of believers that they were all 'brethren *in the Lord*' (Ph 1¹⁴; cf. Gal 4²⁸⁻³¹; Col 1²). It was for this reason that they were a 'brotherhood' (1 P 2¹⁷, 5⁹). The writer to the Hebrews develops the idea at some length (2¹⁰⁻¹⁸). For him Christ, 'the first-born' (1⁶), is the 'file-leader' (2¹⁰) of the 'many sons' who are His brethren (2¹¹, ¹², ¹⁷), and to His care God has committed His 'children' (2¹³). Christian sonship springs from unity with the Son.

But, as already suggested, believers are also 'sons of God' and 'brethren' of the Son because they are the men of the Spirit. For Paul Christians are 'born after the Spirit' (Gal 4²⁹). He develops the idea in Ro 8¹⁴⁻¹⁷, where 'the Spirit of adoption' 'leads' the 'sons of God', and 'bears witness with (their) spirits that (they) are children of God'. Christian sonship is sonship of spirit through *the* Spirit. As 'the Spirit was not yet given' (Jn 7³⁹), John does not put his favourite phrase 'children of God' on Jesus' lips but keeps it for his Epistles (cf. Jn 9⁵²).

The word 'adoption' (*huiothesia*) occurs in two passages already quoted (Ro 8¹⁵, Gal 4⁵). It is not found in LXX, and in the New Testament it is peculiar to Paul (5). He uses it once (Ro 9⁴) as though it were a current phrase to describe the way in which God adopted the people Israel to be His 'son'. As already seen, the relevant Old Testament texts require the *idea* of adoption though they do not use the word. It was shown to be the same in the texts, particularly 2 S 7¹⁴, relating to the sonship of Davidic kings. There God *adopts* David's line. Paul applies this passage to Christians (2 Co 6¹⁸; cf. Rev 21⁷), and he quotes a text in Hosea in a way that means that God now adopts Gentiles as well as Jews (Ro 9²⁴⁻⁶). In one text he uses 'adoption', not of the beginning of the Christian life, but of its consummation in the coming 'redemption of the body' (Ro 8²³). In the other three passages (Ro 8¹⁵; Gal 4⁵; Eph 1⁵) 'adoption' describes the wonder of God's grace to sinners one by one. If the series of passages where the *idea* occurs in the Old Testament and the *word* in the New are taken together, it is obvious that in the Bible there is nothing formal or artificial or merely legal about 'adoption'. It is an experience that throbs with life and joy.[2] But 'adoption' does imply that those who had *not* been 'sons of God' *become* 'sons'. This one word, taken alone, precludes the doctrine that *all* men, sinners and saints, are children of the universal Father.

[2] cf. *The Bible Doctrine of Salvation*, pp. 243 f.

Where Paul speaks of 'adoption' John speaks of a new birth. This idea too, of course, requires that men are to become something that they have not been before. Indeed, John has the sentence 'as many as received him, to them he gave the right to *become* children of God' (Jn 1¹²). It is of Christians that he cries 'Behold what manner of love the Father hath bestowed upon us, that we should be called children of God: and such we are' (Jn 3¹). He adds significantly *'for this cause* the world knoweth us not'. Sonship is unity with God and therefore separation from sinners. The difficult passage that follows is discussed under 'perfection', but here it may be noted that John's starting-point (verses 3–6) is that 'he that is born of God' has nothing to do with sin. How then could John have believed that every sinful man, even when he 'abides' in sin, is God's 'child'? It is in his Gospel that the New Testament evidence on this point reaches its climax. There Jesus, replying to the Jews' claims 'Our father is Abraham' and 'We have one Father, God', retorts 'Ye are of your father the devil' (Jn 8³⁹, ⁴¹, ⁴⁴). In the New Testament the phrases 'sons of God' and 'children of God' are never used of *all* men. 'As many as are led by the Spirit of God, *these* are sons of God' (Ro 8¹⁴). God's 'fatherhood' is the type of all true fatherhood (Eph 3¹⁵), but it is only those who have 'received the spirit of adoption' who are 'joint heirs with Christ' and enjoy 'the liberty of the glory of the children of God' (Ro 8¹⁵, ¹⁷, ²¹; cf. Jn 8³⁶). Only those who have begun through the Spirit of Christ to be like the universal Father are His 'sons'. The paradox noted in Jesus' teaching reappears in the doctrine of 'the Son' and what He does. God is universal Father, but only believers are sons.

On a closer examination of the doctrine of God's Fatherhood in the later New Testament it may first be noted that the term 'Father' is now much more frequent than in the Synoptic Gospels. It is used of God a hundred and ninety-two times. Of these forty-two occur in Paul, and no less than a hundred and thirty-four in the Gospel (*118*) and Epistles (*16*) of John. While it is true that the Jews called God 'Father', and that the name is sometimes used in Gentile religions, it is only in Christianity that 'Father' is the dominant name for God.

There is no doubt about the origin of this Christian use. Today many Christians seem to think that *nature* clearly teaches that God is the Father of all men, but its testimony is ambiguous. One has to consider, for instance, the germ of cancer as well as 'the swelling grain', and the sun-stricken sands of the world's deserts as well as the blessings of light. In the New Testament while Jesus emphasizes the benefits of nature (e.g. Mt 6²⁶ff.), He also knows of its shortcomings (e.g. Mt 13⁵⁻⁷), and Paul, admitting its boons (Ac 14¹⁷), seems to have been more impressed by its terrible imperfections (Ro 8¹⁹⁻²²). Indeed, he could only explain these by describing them as the travail that leads to joy—and he derived this doctrine, not from observing nature, but from his doctrine of Christ. There is only one passage in the whole New Testament about nature that speaks of God as 'Father' (Mt 5⁴⁵) and even there Jesus does not say that 'all nature says that God is good' but that men may learn to forgive by noting God's more usual ways with the sunshine and the rain. He knew that the sun also helps thorns to grow (Mt 13⁷), and that there are such things as floods (Mt 7²⁴ff.). The truth is that Christians have learnt that 'God is love' and Father, not from nature, but through the Incarnation.

In the New Testament this is obvious. In almost every passage where an Apostolic writer calls God 'Father' the context relates the word in some way to Christ. There only seem to be three exceptions, which are discussed below. The term is rarely used for 'God' in the Acts (3) because it is rarely pertinent. The texts repeat the Synoptic teaching that 'the Father' has a mission to men through Christ, but make it explicit that this mission is to be carried on (and completed in God's chosen time) through the Spirit (Ac 1⁴, ⁷, 2³³). In the Apocalypse, when the word is used of God (5), it is always as the Father of *Christ*, who hands on kingship to Christians (1⁶, 2²⁷, 3²¹), marking them for His own (3⁵, 14¹). In James (3) two passages come among the exceptions discussed later. In the third 'our God and Father' seems to refer to the 'brethren' who 'hold the faith of our Lord Jesus Christ' (1¹⁹, ²⁷, 2¹). The texts in 1 Peter (3—1²ᶠ·, ¹⁷⁻¹⁹), 2 Peter (1—1¹⁷), and Jude (1—1), all illustrate the many-sided connexion of God with men through Christ. In Hebrews (1⁵) Christ has the mission of the Davidic 'son' of God (2 S 7¹⁴). Paul, writing to Christians, calls God 'our Father' nine times—eight of them at the opening of Epistles. The first paragraph in Romans (1¹⁻⁴), which ends with the phrase 'God our Father *and* the Lord Jesus Christ', is the Apostles' own exposition of the phrase. God is 'our Father' through the 'gospel' of 'his Son' to 'all the nations'. The Apostle gathers up this manifold idea in the phrase 'the God and Father of our Lord Jesus Christ' (Ro 15⁶; 2 Co 1³, 11³¹; Eph 1³; Col 1³).

Again, it is through the Spirit that Christians cry 'Abba, Father' (Ro 8[15]), and the Spirit is the Spirit of '(God's) Son' (Gal 4[6]; Eph 2[18], 3[14-17]). Paul denies that God is the 'Father' of unbelieving Jews (Ro 4[11f.]), but extends the ancient promise to David's line so as to include all Christians (2 Co 6[18]). These are a 'separated' people (verse 17). All this, taken together, suggests that through Christ God is the 'Father' of believers—but not of others.

The three exceptional passages are He 12[9]; Ja 1[17], 3[9]. In the first the phrase is 'the Father of *spirits*'. As, in the context, 'submission' to Him brings 'life' it seems that the writer is thinking of Gn 2[7], using *pneuma* for *pnoe* like the writer of Wisdom. Man's 'spirit', as distinct from his 'flesh', comes from God—i.e. 'father' here denotes source. In Ja 1[17] the phrase is 'Father of lights'. Here James seems to be symbolizing Gn 1[14ff.] and to mean 'Creator' by 'Father', but the following verse perhaps shows that this passage is not a real exception. In Ja 3[9], where there is an explicit reference to Gn 1[26f.], the phrase is 'the Lord and Father' (cf. Sir 23[1, 4]). In all three passages the writers are thinking of the story of Creation and mean 'Originator' by 'Father' (cf. Lk 3[38]). It is the same with Paul's quotation from Stoic poets at Athens, 'For we are also his offspring' (Ac 17[28]). He too was thinking of the story of creation (v. 24), but he would use 'offspring' (*genos*) in a sense that his hearers would understand and the Stoic philosophy knew nothing of the *personal* fatherhood of God. While these four passages directly teach that God is 'Father', not only of Christians, but of *all* men, by 'father' they mean no more than 'creator' or 'originator'. There remain two Pauline passages which are often quoted to support the doctrine of the universal fatherhood of God. One of them uses the phrase 'One God and Father of all', but the context at least admits the interpretation 'Father of all Christians' (Eph 4[4-6]; cf. 1 Co 12[6]). In the other passage the relevant phrase is 'the Father from whom every fatherhood in heaven and earth is named' (Eph 3[14])—i.e. man's fatherhood is in some degree like God's. This does not necessarily mean that all men are God's sons. It may mean that every human father ought to treat his children as God treats His (Christian) children. But these two passages do leave the way open to a doctrine of the universal Fatherhood of God. The Apostles have such a doctrine. Its basis is a phrase not yet considered, '*the* Father' *simpliciter*.

Outside the Johannine books this is commonest in Paul (*14*).

It is not found in Hebrews or the Apocalypse, and James only approximates to it (3⁹). It occurs in the salutation of First Peter (1²) and Jude (¹) as the recognized Christian account of God, and this has an instance in Second Peter (1¹⁷). In Mt 11²⁷ it occurs in Jesus' exposition of what He meant by 'my Father'.

While there are passages in Paul where the context implies that by 'the Father' the Apostle means 'the Father' of *Christians* (Eph 5²⁰; Col 3¹⁷; 2 Ti 1²), in most texts he is thinking of something wider. There are passages where he speaks in the context of 'all things' or 'all men' or both. In one 'the Son', having at last brought 'all things' into 'submission' to Himself, 'delivers up the kingdom to God,' even the Father' (1 Co 15²⁴), and in another 'every tongue' is at last to 'confess that Jesus Christ is Lord to the glory of God the Father' (Ph 2¹¹). In the context of both passages, as in two others, there is a reference to Christ's resurrection (1 Co 15²¹ᶠ·; Ph 2⁹; Ro 4⁴; Gal 1¹). Did not Paul believe that the Risen Christ had given him a 'gospel' to *all* men, and does not this mean that *any* man might cry 'Abba, Father!'? In another passage (1 Co 8⁵⁻⁷) Paul, speaking both of 'all things' and 'all men', declares that only Christians know that 'there is one God, the Father'—but was it not all Christians' business to pass on this truth to *all* men? Of the passages about 'all things' one (Eph 1¹⁵⁻²²) sums up everything that the others say. It is linked with a parallel passage (Eph 3¹⁴, ²¹) by the universal idea of the 'fullness of God', and in both Paul connects the phrase 'the Father' with the universal idea of God's 'glory'. In both the Apostle is praying for the Church, but is the Church always to monopolize the 'glory' of 'the fullness of God' and 'the love of Christ that passeth knowledge'? Does not the amplitude of the passages forbid a niggardly use of 'Father'? There are passages too where Paul uses 'the Father' when speaking of the 'grace' that 'redeems' (Gal 1³; Col 1¹²) and of the access both of Jews and Gentiles 'through (Christ) in one Spirit unto the Father' (Eph 2¹⁸). The last passage is Trinitarian and links with the passage in Peter (1 P 1¹ᶠ·). It is true that the last text speaks also of 'the elect', but it will be found in a later book that for the present writer this only illustrates the truth, already manifest in Jesus' use of the phrase 'my Father' in the Synoptic Gospels, that God is all men's Father but sinners *will* not be His 'sons'. There is an implicitly universal scope in Paul's use of the phrase 'the Father'. For him there is 'one God' who is *intrinsically* 'Father' even though men may not

so much as know it (1 Co 8⁵⁻⁷). It was because of this intrinsic
Fatherhood that He 'sent forth his Son, born of woman'—in
order that 'all of woman born', however sinful, might, if they
would, 'receive the adoption of sons' (Gal 4⁴ᶠ·). In Paul, as in the
whole of the New Testament, God 'takes the initiative', and He
does so because He has a father's heart. It is as if He said to *all*
men 'I am your Father; will you be My sons?'

As on so many other subjects, so on this one—indeed, pre-
eminently on this one—the Fourth Gospel is the final elucidation
of New Testament teaching. The distribution of the relevant
phrases is itself significant. In this Gospel God is never called
'*Our* Father', for, as already shown, this writer did not count even
the disciples to be God's 'children' till they received the Spirit.
The phrase '*your* Father' only occurs once (Jn 20¹⁷), and then in
the longer phrase 'my Father and your Father', for the Risen
Christ was now about to give His disciples the Spirit (v. 22).
The phrase '*my* Father' occurs twenty-five times, and it is implied
in the many others where 'the Father' and 'the Son' are named
together. '*The* Father' is found no less than seventy-three times.
Indeed, this is the key phrase of this Gospel. It is the writer's
account of the intrinsic nature of God. Three general remarks
may be made about it. First, Jesus uses it constantly in His
controversies with 'the Jews', assuming that it was a name that
they would accept—and they do accept it. In the light of the
evidence in the Apocrypha—and, as the experts tell us, in Rabbinic literature too—this might be expected. The writer, however, adds what no Jew added—that God, because He is intrinsically 'Father', 'so loved the world' of sinners that 'He gave His
only-begotten Son' that men might 'believe' in Him (3¹⁶) and
so 'become children of God' (1¹²ᶠ·). Secondly, John's Gospel was
written mainly for Gentiles—both 'believers' and unbelievers
(20³¹)—and it presupposes that for them too God is intrinsically
'Father'. Everything in the Christian Gospel springs from this
truth. It is architectonic. Thirdly, God's fatherhood is manifested—not in nature, for 'no man hath seen God at any time'—
but in 'the only-begotten Son who is in the bosom of the Father'
(1¹⁸). This, of course, is just an epitome of Jesus' teaching about
'my Father' in the Synoptic Gospels. The controversies in the
Fourth Gospel are not about the intrinsic Fatherhood of God, but
about the unique Sonship of Jesus and His claim to mediate
sonship to those who otherwise are not 'children of God'.

To pursue the use of the phrases passage by passage would be to write a commentary on a very large part of the Fourth Gospel. Examples may be taken from what Jesus says in four long passages of mingled conversation and discourse. Of these three are controversial. The first is presented as Jesus' answer to the Jews' charge that He 'called God His own Father, making himself equal with God' (5¹⁸, ⁴⁰). For the present purpose the verses which are the climax of Jesus' discourse in the passage are the most pertinent ones—'The Father which sent me, he hath borne witness of me . . . ye will not come to me' (v. 37–40)—that is, God is Father but you are not sons.

The next passage belongs to the Eighth Chapter (v. 12–59) but has antecedents in the Seventh (v. 37–52). Here, perhaps, the circumstances of the end of the first century have most influenced the writer's presentation of what Jesus said, but its teaching for the present purpose is clear. As in an earlier story (2²³⁻⁵), there are people who 'believe on him' (8³⁰), but to whom Jesus cannot 'trust himself'. In both contexts Nicodemus appears (3¹, 7⁵⁰), who, on the strength of Jesus' signs, was prepared to call Him 'a teacher come from God'. There were others who were ready to call him 'a good man', 'the prophet', or even 'the Christ' (7¹², ⁴⁰). But was He uniquely 'Son'? In John's account Jesus demands that the unsatisfactory believers *must* admit this with all its implications. 'I am not alone', He says, near the beginning of the discussion, 'but I and the Father that sent me' (8¹⁶); 'Ye have not known him, but I know him', He says at the end (8⁵⁵). In the discussion the word 'father' is central. 'Our father is Abraham', say the half-believers, and therefore 'God is our Father' (v. 39–41). Probably they claimed, not only descent from Abraham, but to 'do his works', and therefore to be true sons of God in the Jewish sense.[3] The dispute is about Jesus' unique Sonship—not about God's intrinsic Fatherhood. The belief in the latter is common ground. This finds strange expression in the use of 'the Father' in two senses in one sentence (v. 38)! In the end Jesus says 'Ye are of the father (who is) the devil' and they retort 'Thou . . . hast a devil' (v. 44, 52). Here again it is clear that the writer of the Fourth Gospel believed that God is 'the

---

[3] At the end of the century it is probable that the followers of the Baptist, with whom there was a controversy (Jn 1⁸, etc.), would at least admit that Jesus was a prophet. It would be about the Christian claim that Jesus was 'the Son' that they would dispute. Even if they were Gentiles, they might claim that they were 'children of Abraham' in the Baptist's sense (Lk 3⁸).

Father' but that all men are not His sons. Some men thwart His
fatherhood, for they are not willing to 'abide in (His) word' and
so His 'word hath not free course (*chōrein*—cf. Wis 7²³ᶠ)' in them
(v. 31, 37).

In the next passage (10¹⁻¹⁸, ²⁵⁻³⁹) the central idea appears in
the text 'the Father knoweth me, and I know the Father; and I
lay down my life for the sheep' (v. 15). It is the Father's 'commandment' to the Son that He should 'lay down (his) life and take
it again' and the Father 'loves' Him because He willingly con-
sents to do so (v. 17 f.). In this enterprise in particular '(He) and
the Father are one'—as He claims when He faces some who 'are
not (His) sheep' (v. 26, 30; cf. v. 35–8). Once more, the controversy is not about 'the Father' but 'the Son'. Jesus' opponents
take no objection to the first phrase; they accept it as common
ground. But they refuse to be His 'sheep'—that is, to 'know and
understand that the Father is in me and I in the Father' (v. 26,
38). They will not let Him save them. Here there is no explicit
statement that they are not God's children, but, in the light of
other passages the implication is clear. They 'believe not' (v. 38),
and it is those who 'believe' who 'become children of God' (1¹²).
Like the Prodigal's Elder Brother, these men refuse to be 'sons',
and so baffle the Fatherhood of God. It is not quite accurate to
say that in the New Testament God is 'potentially' Father of all
men, though it may be said that all men are 'potentially' His sons.
When men sin, God's intrinsic Fatherhood is not so much 'poten-
tial' as frustrate, and it is to overcome this frustration that the
Son lays down His life and takes it again. Christ died in order
that men might be 'sons'.

If these three passages are considered together it appears that
there is progress in the teaching. The first says 'ye will not'; the
second, 'ye will not fully'; the third, 'if ye will'. The fourth
(13–17) passes to 'ye that will'. It begins with a conversation,
not with 'the Jews', but with the disciples. The writer says, in
effect, that its subject is 'the Father' (13³). Yet he distributes the
phrase significantly. Jesus does not use it till Judas has gone out
into the night (13³⁰). In the prayer in which the passage culminates (17) Jesus, of course, says 'Father', not 'the Father', but it is
a prayer for His 'friends' and not for 'the world'—or rather for
'the world' through His 'friends' (15¹⁴, 17⁹, ²⁰ᶠ·). Twice there
is an adjective with 'Father', a very rare phenomenon. The first
adjective is 'holy' and leads to a prayer that God will 'hallow' the

group in the midst of an unholy 'world' (v. 11–17). The second
is 'righteous' and comes in the middle of the concluding passage
(v. 24–6) where Jesus, relying upon the righteousness of God's
love *for Him*, prays that those who 'know' God through Him shall
finally be 'with (Him) where (He) is' (cf. 1 Jn 1⁹). One text is
a final epitome, not only of the prayer, but of the whole New
Testament doctrine of the Fatherhood of God—'That they all
may be one; even as Thou, Father, art in me, and I in thee, that
they also may be in us, that the world may believe that thou didst
send me' (v. 21). The three preceding chapters (14–16) are just
a preparation for this. In them the phrase 'the Father' occurs
forty-two times. Two notes may be added. First, in three of the
four passages where Jesus promises the Paraclete, He calls Him
the gift of the Father through the Son (14¹⁶, ²⁶, 16²⁶) and this is
implied in the fourth (16⁷, ¹⁵). The Father gives the Spirit 'to
them that ask him' (Lk 11¹³) or He would not be 'Father'.
Second, John says '*the* Father' and not '*your* Father', partly
because 'the Spirit was not yet given' (7³⁹) and no one is son until
he knows that he has the Spirit, and partly because for John,
Fatherhood, however baffled by sin, belongs to the ultimate
nature of God. 'God is love', and therefore 'God so loved the
world that he gave his only-begotten Son' (1 Jn 4⁸, ¹⁶; Jn 3¹⁶).

The same set of ideas—that God is intrinsically Father, that
sin baffles His practice of Fatherhood, that He seeks to practise it
through the gift of His Son to sinners, and that He does practise
it by the Spirit in believers—appear also in the other passages in
the Fourth Gospel that speak of 'the Father' (e.g. 3³⁵, 4²³, 6³⁷⁻⁴⁶,
12²⁶⁻⁸). It is the same with the First and Second Epistles of John,
where 'the Father' occurs fifteen times—especially in 1 Jn 2¹³⁻¹⁶,
²²⁻⁴. This writer's love of the concept of the intrinsic Fatherhood
of God, with its implication that God longs to be Father of all
men, appears in his use of '*the* Father', and not '*your* Father', even
when he is writing to Christians. He has given his own definition
of the frequent phrase 'to know God' in the text 'Our fellowship
is with the Father, even with his Son Jesus Christ' (1 Jn 1³). It
is true, he adds, that the sinful can no more have 'fellowship' with
God than darkness with light, but 'the blood of Jesus Christ his
Son cleanseth us from all sin' (1 Jn 1³⁻⁷). In the New Testament
there is a development of the doctrine of the Fatherhood of God,
but it is *one* doctrine, for it grows out of the development of the
experience of the disciples of Jesus from the days when the few

'saw Him with their eyes' and even 'handled Him with their hands' to the days when the many began to 'abide in the Son and (so) in the Father' (1 Jn 1¹, 2²⁴). Then men are like God.

C

In the New Testament the 'glory' (*doxa*—*164*), both of God, of Christ, and of Christians, is often mentioned. In examining the use of the term it will be convenient to follow, in the main, the order of discussion under LXX expanding it at the significant point—the 'glory' of Christ. Almost half the texts occur in Paul (*74*). When the term is used *of God* it denotes *any* of His manifestations. It can be used of what we call a 'physical' light (e.g. Lk 2⁹; Ac 7⁵⁵; 2 Co 3⁷; Rev 21²³). Here, however, it is necessary to recall the so-called 'Philonic' use of 'allegory'. Under this a term may be used in more senses than one, which are all true, and which are not to be too strictly separated. In ancient days there was at least a partial parallel in the Platonic tenet that things that are seen participate imperfectly in things that are unseen, eternal, and real.

There is also at least a partial parallel today in the use of the terms 'symbolic' and 'sacramental'. The use of the word 'light' in the New Testament (*57*) is a good example. It is used seven times of the 'light' of a lamp or fire (e.g. Mk 15⁵⁴; Jn 11⁹; Ac 16²⁹) or 'the light of day' (e.g. Mt 10²⁷; Jn 11⁹), but the other fifty texts all illustrate in one way or another the relation of 'light' to God. It is not likely that to a Jew these passages would denote something 'merely physical'. Paul, for instance, in quite a 'Philonic' way, recalls the first of God's commands in the story of creation, 'Let there be light' (Gn 1³), when speaking of the 'light' that shines in the hearts of Christians (2 Co 4⁶). For him these were the same light in different manifestations. This is just another instance of the way in which the Jew refused to draw our sharp distinction between the physical and spiritual, already noted in his concept of the unity of human nature. 'Light' in the New Testament is *both* splendour *and* purity or holiness. The 'invisible things' of God blaze out in His visible 'glory' in creation (Ro 1²⁰⁻³). Similarly, God manifests one and the same 'glory' in such various things as the Call of Abraham (Ac 7²), the cherubim (He 9⁵), the Shekinah (Ro 9⁴), the giving of the Law (2 Co 3⁷), the reading of the Law in the Synagogue (2 Co 3¹⁵), 'the ministration of the Spirit' (2 Co 3⁸), and 'the glory of the gospel of the

blessed God' (1 Ti 1¹¹). Just as in LXX there is the complementary use of *doxa* to denote the recognition of God's 'glory' by
men—e.g. in the doxologies 'Thine is . . . the glory' (Mt 6¹⁵), and
'Worthy art thou, our Lord and God, to receive glory and
honour . . .' (Rev 4¹¹). The latter text illustrates the way in which
time ('honour') is a synonym for *doxa* under this use. The use of
the phrase 'to glorify God' links with it. The Greek verb *doxazein*
(59) is very commonly used of the recognition of the 'glory' of God
and men's delight in it (30). The distinctive New Testament use
begins in the Synoptics (especially Luke), where men 'glorify'
God because of *Jesus'* miracles of love (e.g. Mk 2¹²; Lk 5²⁵), and
even because of the way in which He died (Lk 23⁴⁷). Paul
illustrates the later Christian use when he draws his account of
the whole process of the Incarnation, Atonement, and Exaltation
of Christ to its climax in the phrase 'to the glory of God the
Father' (Ph 2¹¹). Similarly, for the writer of the Fourth Gospel
Jesus' work on earth was to 'glorify God' (e.g. 17⁴). In the Apocalypse (21²³) 'the glory of God' is the 'light' of the Holy City and
the Lamb is 'the lamp thereof'. The development of New Testament thought relates the 'glory of God' ever more and more
intimately to Jesus. This is the culmination of the Old Testament
teaching that the right kind of human life exhibits the 'glory' of
God. His 'glory' is much more than this but includes it.

The New Testament also speaks of the 'glory' of *Christ*. The
earliest use here is of the 'glory' of the Son of Man at the Parousia,
when He is to come 'in the glory of his Father with the holy
angels' (Mk 8³⁸). In this Apocalyptic passage two ideas are
implied—(*a*) that 'glory' is both 'light' and 'holiness', and (*b*) that
the 'glory' of the Son derives from the 'glory' of the Father. Luke
adds the belief that this kind of 'glory' was already manifested at
the Transfiguration and Ascension (Lk 9³¹ᶠ·, 24²⁶). Similarly,
in all three accounts of Paul's vision on the way to Damascus the
manifestation is through 'light' (e.g. Ac 22¹¹; cf. Ph 3²¹; Rev 1¹⁶).
Two New Testament writers go on to deduce that this 'glory'
belonged to the Son before the Incarnation—Hebrews calling
Him 'the effulgence of (God's) glory' (1³; cf. Wis 7²⁶), and John
speaking of 'the glory which I had with thee before the world was'
(17⁵). Finally John declares that during Jesus' life *on earth* the
disciples 'beheld his glory' (1¹⁴), though, as the 'tabernacle' and
Temple had hidden the Shekinah, so Christ's body had hidden
His glory from others (2²¹; cf. He 10²⁰; 1 Co 2⁸). So the final

concept of the 'glory' of the Son is four-fold—it had its manifestations before the Incarnation, during Jesus' life on earth, at the Ascension, and at the Parousia. For the present subject the important point is the New Testament doctrine of the manifestation of the 'glory' of *Christ*—or of the Father's 'glory' through Christ—*in the salvation of men*. Luke gives two instances, quoting the Servant Songs (Lk 2³²; Is 42⁶, 49⁶; cf. 52¹⁴ in LXX), and implying that the sufferings of the Christ lead to His 'glory' (24²⁶). In the Apocalypse the first doxology is to 'him that loved us and loosed us from our sins . . . to him be glory' (1⁵ᶠ·). In Hebrews 'Jesus' is 'crowned with glory and honour' 'because of the suffering and death' (2⁹). In First Peter 'the glories' of Christ 'follow' His 'sufferings' (1¹¹; cf. 1¹⁸ᶠᶠ·). John says that 'the Spirit' could not be given till Jesus was 'glorified' (7³⁹). Paul defines his 'gospel' in the phrase 'the illumination of the knowledge of the glory of God in the face of Jesus Christ' (2 Co 4⁶). The glory of Jesus is to save.

The New Testament often uses *doxa* and *doxazein*, not only of God and of Christ, but also *of Christians*. In Matthew Jesus says that His disciples are 'the *light* of the world' in order that by their 'good works' they may '*glorify*' their 'Father in heaven' (5¹⁴⁻¹⁸). Peter repeats this message and relates it to 'Jesus Christ' (1 P 2¹², 4⁸). Paul bids the Corinthians to 'glorify God in your body' because 'ye were bought with a price' (1 Co 6²⁰; cf. 2 Co 9¹³; Gal 1²⁴; 2 Th 3¹). John sums up the concept in the text 'Herein is my Father glorified that ye bear much fruit and be my disciples' (15⁸; cf. 17¹⁰, 21¹⁸). The 'end of man' is 'to glorify God'. Christians do this through 'the riches of the glory' of God given through Christ (Eph 1¹⁸⁻²⁰; cf. Ro 9²³; Col 1¹¹, ²⁷; He 3⁶) by 'the Spirit of glory' (1 P 4¹⁴). As so often John has the recapitulatory text—'the glory which thou hast given me, I have given them' (17²²). In this passage John seems to mean Christians' derivative 'glory' while on earth. So Paul speaks both of the Gospel and of his converts as 'our glory' (1 Co 2⁷; 1 Th 2¹⁹ᶠ·; cf. Col 1²⁷; Eph 3¹³). Usually, however, when *doxa* is ascribed to Christians it refers to the future—for instance, Christians 'seek for glory and honour and incorruption' (Ro 2⁷; cf. v. 10, 9²³); God 'calls' them 'into his own kingdom and glory' (1 Th 2¹²; cf. Eph 1¹⁸); they are to be 'manifested' with Christ 'in glory' (Col 3⁴); God is 'bringing many sons into glory' (He 2¹⁰; cf. 2 Ti 2¹⁰); Christ 'in you' is 'the hope of glory' (Col 1²⁷; cf. Ro 5²); Peter says that he already 'partakes of the glory that shall be revealed' (1 P 5[1]; cf. 1[7], 5[4, 10]). The full 'glory' of a Christian is postponed to the future because it cannot be consummate until he shares 'the body of the glory' of Christ (Ph 3[21]). Only then will the 'liberty' of his 'glory' be complete, having its proper scope in a new universe (Ro 8[18-25]). There can be no doubt that the future 'body' of a Christian is to be the medium of the manifestation both of 'spiritual' holiness and what we call 'physical' light (1 Co 15[40-4]). The distinctive New Testament doctrine of 'glory' is that through Christ God 'glorifies' the whole man (Ro 8[30]). The genealogy of ideas can be put in four texts—'God is light', '*I* am the light of the world', '*Ye* are the light of the world', 'Then shall the righteous shine forth as the sun in the kingdom of their Father' (1 Jn 1[5]; Jn 8[13]; Mt 5[14], 13[43]). Throughout all the gamut of the uses of *doxa* there runs the idea of the *manifestation* of God. Under this word too Christians through Christ become like God, for, seeing 'the light of the knowledge of the glory of God in the face of Christ', they 'mirror the glory of the Lord' and are 'transformed into the same image' as their Master (2 Co 3[18], 4[4, 6]). Here the 'face (*prosōpon*) of Christ' means His manifested presence, like *panim* when used of God in Hebrew.

As in LXX the use of *timē*, 'honour', goes with the use of *doxa*. In ten of the forty instances the word means 'price' (e.g. Mt 27[6]; Ac 4[34]; 1 Co 6[20]), and in three passages there is mention of 'honour' paid to *things* (Ro 9[21]; 1 Co 12[23f.]; 2 Ti 2[20f.]). Everywhere else *time* means 'honour where honour is due', the 'honour' that is the proper complement of character. The phrase 'glory and honour' (*12*) is used in doxologies to God (1 Ti 1[17]; Rev 4[9, 11]), and to God and the Lamb (Rev 5[12f.], 7[12]). The phrase also links Jesus and man as God made him (He 2[7, 9]), and denotes the proper complement of salvation at the end (Ro 2[7, 10]; 1 P 1[7]; Rev 21[6]). In the last instance, at least, the phrase includes 'wealth', as the realm of full life. *Time* occurs alone to denote the proper 'honour' due to rulers and masters and benefactors (Ro 13[7]; 1 Ti 6[1]; Ac 28[10]). Within the life of the Church 'honour' is to be rendered to 'wives' (1 Th 4[4]; 1 P 3[7]), to 'elders' (1 Ti 5[17]), and to all fellow-believers (Ro 12[10]). There is only one passage where *time* possibly means 'intrinsic worth', as in such modern phrases as 'a man's honour' (Col 2[23]). *Time* is not 'worth', but like *doxa*, the proper accompaniment of 'worth'.

The last quotations given under *doxa* include two of the words by which LXX renders the Hebrew terms for the 'image' of God. They come from the passage (2 Co 3^{12}–5^{10}) that best illustrates the complex of New Testament ideas relating to the doctrine, not of what man was in the beginning, but is to be at 'the end'. Before turning to this passage, however, it will be helpful to consider the Synoptic account of the Transfiguration, or, better, Transformation. Under this, as already noted, Luke speaks of Christ's 'glory' (9^{32}). He also says 'The form (*eidos*) of his face (*prosopon*) (became) different' (9^{29}). Something shone out from within Him, transforming even His 'raiment'. In the new Testament *eidos* (*5*) always means something inward that expresses itself outwardly (e.g. Jn 5^{37}; 1 Th 5^{22}). Christ's inherent 'glory' shone out through His body and garments. Mark (9^{2}) and Matthew (17^{2}) use the term *metamorphousthai* ('transform'), which means 'to be changed from one form (*morphē*) into another'. In face of the evidence of LXX the presupposition is that in the New Testament *morphe* (*3*) and its cognates (*10*) refer to the outward expression of inward nature, *morphe* being a synonym for *eidos*. Only the idea that God's 'form' (Ph 2^{6}) is not outward forbids this, and the present writer does not think that this is a Biblical idea. At Christ's Ascension, he would infer, the 'form of God' shone out once more, as at the Transfiguration, in 'glory' (cf. 2 Ti 3^{16}). This means that when the Son 'emptied himself' of 'the things' in which he had been 'equal with God', the 'form of God' remained, as it were, beneath 'the form of a servant' (Ph 2$^{6f.}$). As Hebrews puts it, Jesus' 'flesh' was a 'veil' (10^{20}), or, as John says, His 'body' was a 'tabernacle' or 'temple' within which His 'glory' or *shekinah* was hidden (1^{14}, 2^{21}). But at the Ascension the 'body of humiliation' was transformed into the 'body of glory' (Ph 3^{21}), 'this corruptible put on incorruption' and 'this mortal put on immortality' (1 Co 15$^{49f., 53}$). On the way to Damascus Paul saw the *eidos* of the glory of the Ascended Christ (cf. 2 Co 5^{7}). The metaphor of 'putting on' is, of course, derived from the 'putting on' of clothes, but it does not always mean 'put on from outside'. Paul can speak both of '*putting on* the Lord Jesus Christ' and of 'Christ *in* you, the hope of glory' (Ro 13^{14}; Col 1^{27}). Similarly it is those who are 'renewed in the *spirit* of (their) mind' who 'put on the new man' (Eph 4$^{23f.}$), and 'to put on the new man which is being renewed unto knowledge after the image of him that created him' (Col 3^{10}) is to manifest outwardly an inward change. The Hebrew word for 'clothe' or

Q BM

'put on' (*lābēsh*), when it is used of 'strength' (Is 51[8]) or 'righteous-ness' (e.g. Job 29[14]; Ps 132[9]; Is 59[17]) or 'cursing' (Ps 109[18]), denotes the outward expression of inward character, and in these texts LXX renders by Paul's word (*enduein*). To return to the Transfiguration, one must say reverently that 'in the days of (Christ's) flesh' He had two 'forms', one 'veiled' by the other. The former was only 'invisible' in the sense that, except at the Transfiguration, it was out of sight, not in the sense that, as it is spiritual, no one can ever see it. The doctrines of the veiled 'form' and of 'glory' go very closely together.

With the Transfiguration in mind, we may turn to 2 Co 3[12]–5[10]. It is necessary to look at Paul's general argument in the whole passage. In it the 'new life in Christ Jesus' shows itself in four ways or stages—working, so to say, from within outward. First there is the 'earnest (*arrabon*) of the Spirit' (5[5]), or alternatively, since 'the Lord is the Spirit' (3[17f.]), 'Christ in you the hope of glory' (Col 1[27]). Second, by 'the Lord, the Spirit' the Christian is 'transformed' (*metamorphousthai*) into 'the same image' as His Lord (cf. 4[4]), and so into an ever-mounting 'glory' (3[18]). Third, the Spirit brings to the Christian 'freedom' (3[17]; cf. Ro 8[21]) to be what he ought to be and longs to be, and so he is able, like Paul, to fulfil his 'ministry' (4[1ff.])—a ministry that involves the 'renouncing' of the 'works of the flesh' and the bringing forth of 'the fruits of the Spirit' (cf. Gal 5[13-25]). Fourth, while this 'ministry' must needs now be fulfilled in the 'earthly house of the tabernacle' of the 'mortal body', in the end the body itself will be so 'clothed upon with a habitation from heaven' that 'what is mortal'—i.e. 'flesh and blood'—will be 'swallowed up' by im-mortal 'life' (5[1-4]). It will be seen that here there is both a parallel and a contrast with what has been said about Jesus. On the one hand, when any man is 'in Christ Jesus' there is a 'new creation' (2 Co 5[17]), as there had no need to be in his Lord, and, since the Christian 'mirrors' the light of God's 'glory', this is *changing* his 'form' into the unchanging 'image' of his Lord (3[18]). On the other hand, this 'form', as in 'the days of (Jesus') flesh', is at present hidden by the 'tabernacle' of the body (5[1]), and so the Christian is called to 'bear about in the body the dying of Jesus' so that the 'life of Jesus is manifested in (the) body' (4[10]). In the end, however, 'the earthly house of (this) tabernacle will be destroyed' (*kataluein*—cf. 14[58]) and 'what is mortal will be swallowed up of life' (5[1, 4]).

For the present purpose the most relevant point here is the suggestion that, according to Paul, the Christian has, or is beginning to have, a hidden *morphe* which, in our sense of the words, is neither 'spiritual' nor material, though it is related to both. He 'has put on the new man', which is 'being renewed unto knowledge after the *eikon* of him that created him' (Col 3¹⁰). In the present writer's opinion there is nowhere in the Bible any suggestion that God 'created' anything that is *merely* spiritual, and he holds that the New Testament use of 'create' (*ktizein*) and its cognates bears this out. If this be so, the 'new creation', of a man who is 'in Christ Jesus' (2 Co 5¹⁷) is more than a restoration of 'moral and spiritual qualities'. It is a 'new creating' of the whole man—spirit and 'form' and body.

The New Testament use of *morphe* (with its cognates) and *eikon* may now be examined in greater detail. In the LXX, as has been seen, the two terms always stand for something that can be seen (though it may, of course, be covered). Apart from Ph 2⁶ᶠ·, *morphe* itself only occurs once in the New Testament (Mk 16¹²) and there it denotes something visible. The derivative noun *morphōsis* (2) once describes 'the law' as the *outward* expression of 'knowledge and the truth' (Ro 2²⁰) and once a hypocritical *appearance* of 'godliness' (2 Ti 3⁵). The verb *summorphizesthai* (*1*— Ph 3¹⁰) denotes a stage in the process by which Paul came to 'know' Christ. First, on the way to Damascus he had begun to know 'the power of his resurrection'; now, through 'the fellowship of his sufferings', the Apostle's life in the present body is being '*conformed* to his *death*'. Here *morphe* means, not the 'form' of the 'inward man', but of the 'outward'. It corresponds to the 'form of a servant' that was Christ's 'in the days of his flesh' (2⁷). As the Apostle says elsewhere, he 'bears branded on his body the marks of Jesus' (Gal 6¹⁷). This 'form' can be seen now—but the 'form' of the 'inward man', which is like the Risen Christ's, will only be seen hereafter. When Paul 'attains to the resurrection of the dead' the outward 'body', visible now in its 'humiliation', will be 'transfigured outwardly' (*metaschematizein*) so as to be of 'the same form' (*summorphos*—2) as Christ's in His 'glory' (v. 21). For an hour at the Transfiguration Jesus' hidden 'form' shone through and 'transfigured' the outward; at His Resurrection it did so for ever. It will be the same for Paul at *his* resurrection. In another passage *summorphos* is used, by implication, of the 'conformation' of 'the *inward* man' to 'the image of (God's) Son', through which the Christian is 'glorified' (Ro 8²⁹ᶠ·). *The 'inward man' has a 'form' that is hidden now but will be seen hereafter.* There remain the verbs *morphousthai* (*1*) and *metamorphousthai* (*4*). The first is used in the phrase 'until Christ is formed in you' (Gal 4¹⁹), which is another way of saying 'until ye are conformed (in the 'inward man') to the image of his Son'. *Metamorphousthai*, used as we have seen, in the story of the Transfiguration, occurs also in the phrase 'transformed into the same *image*' (2 Co 3¹⁸). It also occurs in the phrase 'Be ye transformed by the renewing of your mind' (Ro 12²). Here Paul is exhorting the Romans to 'present their *bodies* a living sacrifice'. The passage at least admits an exposition parallel to the above—first, there is 'the renewing of the mind' through the Spirit; with this there goes a transformation of a man's hidden, inward 'form'; this two-fold change shows itself in the present life through the 'outward man' of the body. Most of the passages where *morphe* or a cognate occurs demand, and the rest admit, the interpretation that, as in LXX, it describes the visible expression of inward character—with the addition, however, that for the Christian there is a new 'form' which, while it is visible and can be seen, cannot be seen *now*, for it is hidden.

In Ro 12² Paul, by way of contrast with *metamorphousthai*, says to his readers 'Be not *fashioned* according to this Age'. Here the verb is *sunschematizein* (*2*), a derivative of *schēma* (*2*), which, unlike *morphe* and *eidos*, denotes the *merely* outward (1 Co 7³¹; Ph 2⁸). The Roman Christian is not to be one thing inwardly and another outwardly (cf. 1 P 1¹³⁻¹⁶). This is just what Satan and other hypocrites are, as a text says that uses *metaschematizein* (*5*) three times (2 Co 11¹³⁻¹⁵). This verb occurs along with *summorphos* in Ph 3²¹, which declares that at the Resurrection even the 'body' of the Christian shall at last be glorious, for the inward *morphe* will 'trans-figure' the outward *skema*. These verbs are not found in LXX (and the noun only once—Is 3¹⁷). The New Testament passages under *skema* and its cognates serve to bring out the fact that *morphe*, unlike *schema*, does not denote anything *merely* outward. It is the outward expression of inward life.

In discussing *morphe* the term 'image' (*eikōn*—*22*) has several times emerged. There is no doubt that outside Paul it always means something visible. In the Synoptics it is used of the 'image' on a coin (e.g. Mk 12¹⁶); in the Apocalypse, under the phrase 'the image of the wild beast' (e.g. 13¹⁴ᶠ·), it ten times describes an *idol* that comes to life; and in Hebrews it is set alongside a 'shadow', which is, of course, visible (10¹), both words probably being used in a literal-*cum*-symbolical sense—i.e. after the manner known best in Philo. Paul uses *eikon* of idols (Ro 1²³), and of a Christian's present and future 'body' (1 Co 15⁴⁹). These, of course, are all visible. The last passage speaks of the 'image' of 'the second man', Christ, in His ascended glory. The presumption is that in Paul's five remaining passages *eikon* also means something visible. In two of these the exposition of its meaning is involved with that of *morphe* (Ro 8²⁹; 2 Co 3¹⁸). As has been seen, this is visible, even when hidden. In one passage in Colossians (1¹⁵) Christ, 'the first-born of all creation', is related to 'the *unseen* God' as His 'image' (that can be seen); in two others (2 Co 4⁴; Col 3¹⁰) it presumably also means something visible. In the remaining text, discussed in the last chapter, a man is 'the image and glory of God' (1 Co 11⁷). Here the LXX parallels suggest that it refers to a visible image in man *now*. In the other passages the *morphe* of the Christ is 'the *eikon* of God'. The writer of the Epistle to the Hebrews (1³) calls it *character*, 'impress' (as on a coin). *Eikon* denotes, not the 'spiritual and moral' unity of the Son with the Father, but its manifestation. The Christian, whose new 'form' the body hides, is 'being transformed into the same image', and therefore already begins to manifest outwardly a 'spiritual and moral' likeness to God through his body, even though that 'earthly tabernacle' is mortal, for already through 'the indwelling Spirit' he is 'the holy shrine (*naos*)' of the glory or *shekinah* 'of God' (1 Co 3¹⁶ᶠ·). Both *morphe* and *eikon* denote the visible expression of an inward 'mind' (Ph 2⁵). The Christian's mind and his *morphe* (or *eikon*) are indissoluble. This account of the meaning of the phrase 'the image of God' implies that, while in the Old Testament it denotes something visible in which *every* man is like God *now*, in its Christian sense it denotes, first, something visible in which *Christ* is like God (though it was hidden during His life on earth), and second, something visible, which is already taking 'form' within every Christian, and which will *fully* manifest itself only in *the future*. Throughout the passages *eikon* and *morphe* denote a visible manifestation of inward character. As has been seen, this is anticipated in one passage in the Book of Wisdom, where the writer declares that, when God created man, He 'made him an *eikon* of his own *idiotes*' (2²³), but there the reference is to the old creation, not the new. In the New Testament the basis

of the doctrine of man's likeness to God is the doctrine that man
is meant to be like Him, and that the believer begins to be like
Him, in *character*. The *outward* manifestation of this spiritual likeness begins, but is not consummated, in a holy life here. *Eikon* and
morphe go with *doxa* and denote the *visible* complement of character
which will be perfected in the 'body of glory'. In Paul, as in his
Master while on earth, the 'tabernacle' or 'temple' (Jn 2²¹) of
the present body had its own 'form', but within Paul another
'form', like that of Jesus' hidden 'glory' in the days of His flesh,
was beginning to be; at death Christ would 'transfigure' the 'form'
of the body that suits the *psyche* into the 'form' of the body that
suits the *pneuma* (Ph 3²¹; 1 Co 15⁴⁴).

It is important to notice the exact *differentia* of the Apostle's
doctrine. All men have believed that every visible thing—i.e.
everything that *can* be seen, whether it *is* seen or not—has a 'form',
or, to use the commoner English word, a 'shape'. This was so
among both Hebrews and Greeks, as among other peoples. But
the ordinary man does not examine this belief. If it is analysed
for him and he is asked, 'Do you believe that "form" is *physical* but
not *material*?', his usual answer would be 'Yes'. Both Plato and
Aristotle analysed the concept, and, each in his own way, found
it a large place in his philosophy. Both taught that it is not
'material', for it is of ultimate value and for both 'matter' (*hule*)
is just the one thing that *per se* has no value. It is not in Paul's
belief in 'form' that his teaching is distinctive, but in his doctrine
that the Christian man has *two* 'forms'—one that is seen now and
one, hidden now, but that will be seen hereafter. It is more than
probable that he based this doctrine on the story of the Transfiguration of Christ, when, for once, *His* hidden 'form' showed
itself. As already suggested, the doctrine of the Two Forms
seems strange today, but an approximation to it might be reached
if a bud were said to have two forms—the one *now* seen in the
shape of the calyx and the other *to be* seen when the flower bursts
forth. There are other partial analogies, of course, in the egg
and the chrysalis. It might be said that a chicken within the shell
has two forms—the form of the shell and the hidden form of a
bird—and similarly with the butterfly in the chrysalis. At one
point, however, all these parallels fail. The flower, the chicken,
and the butterfly *discard* one form in order to 'manifest' the other.
Paul's teaching is that some day the 'hidden' form of the Christian
will, not discard, but *transfigure* the form that is visible now, and

the 'mortal' will be 'swallowed up of life' (2 Co 5⁴). 'Transformed' and 'swallowed up' are synonyms.

Paul's doctrine of 'the man within' (*esō* or *esōthen*) and 'the man without' (*exō*) fits in with this account. The 'man without is being destroyed' but 'the man within is being renewed' (2 Co 4¹⁶). There are Synoptic hints that a *sinner's* 'man within' is evil (Lk 11³⁹; Mt 7¹⁵). A text in Romans (7²²ᶠ·) requires that 'the man within' includes the 'mind', and a passage in Ephesians (3¹⁶) that in the Christian it is the realm of 'the Spirit' and of 'power'. Peter has a parallel phrase 'the hidden man of the heart' (1 P 3⁴) which appears to consist of 'a meek and quiet spirit' *and* 'the incorruptible' apparel of its *morphe*. It is tempting to suppose that 'the man within' is altogether 'spiritual', but to use the term *anthrōpos* (man) to mean this has no warrant in the Bible. It is probable that when Paul says that 'this corruptible must *put on* incorruption, and this mortal must *put on* immortality' (1 Co 15⁵³ᶠ·), he is using *enduein*, as in LXX, to denote the outward expression of an inward gift (e.g. Job 29¹⁴; Is 51⁹; cf. Lk 24⁴⁹). There is a similar use of 'endue' in English. It originally meant 'clothe', but in the phrase 'Until ye be endued with power' (Lk 24⁴⁹, A.V.) and in the prayer 'Endue thy ministers with righteousness' the verb refers to an inward gift even though it comes from outside. Paul means that at last the 'man without' will match the 'man within'. But this belongs to the book on the Hereafter.

Paul uses the word for 'put on' or 'clothe' both of the 'putting on' of the transforming 'body of glory' and of the 'putting on' of 'the new man' (1 Co 15⁵³; Eph 4²⁴). These, however, are not to be confused, for the first relates to the future and the second to the present. Christians 'put on the *new man*' now. The phrase 'the new (*neos*) man' has its opposite in 'the old (*palaios*) man' (e.g. Eph 4²²). Here the question arises: 'Are the two phrases "the old man" and "the new man" synonymous with the two phrases "the man without" and "the man within"?' It seems clear that 'the new man' may be equated with 'the man within', for both are said to be 'being renewed' (2 Co 4¹⁶; Col 3¹⁰). They are both the outcome of Christ's inward work through the Spirit. If there is any difference between them, it is that under the phrase 'the new man' the *change* through 'renewal' is emphasized and under 'the man within' the *result* of the change. But, on the other hand, 'the old man' is *not* to be identified with 'the man without'.

Though 'the man without' is perishing, it is not sinful *per se*, for it is the body and this is a 'temple of God' (e.g. 1 Co 3¹⁶ᶠ·). The 'old man', on the other hand, is sinful, for whenever Paul speaks of 'the old' and 'new man' he is discussing sin and righteousness (Ro 6¹⁻¹¹; Eph 2¹¹⁻²², 4¹⁷⁻²⁴; Col 3⁵⁻¹⁴). The metaphor in 'put off the old man' and 'put on the new' is probably derived from the symbolism of baptism, where old garments were put off before the rite and new ones put on after it. The old garments typify sin and the new ones righteousness 'in Christ'. In a passage where Paul expounds baptism without this metaphor, he says that the believer's 'old man was crucified with Christ'. Another of the passages (Col 3¹⁰) brings us back to the word '*eikon*'. It runs: 'Seeing that ye have put off the old man with his practices, and have put on the new man, which is being renewed unto knowledge (*epignosis*) after the *image* of him that created him.' In this one text the 'image' of God seems to be related to 'knowledge' and this does not suit *eikon* if it means 'form'. But, on the exposition here given, 'the new man', or 'the man within', includes *both* 'mind' *and* 'form'. If so, then in this text the word 'knowledge' implies the idea of the 'renewal' of the 'mind' (cf. Ro 12²), and the phrase 'the image of him that created him' the 'renewal' of the 'form'. The last phrase in the text will then mean that 'the new man' is 'renewed in knowledge as suits the form of Christ'. This interpretation of *eikon* explains the relevance of the next verse. When man was created at the first 'in the image' of God, outward differences, such as those between 'Greek and Jew', 'barbarian' and civilized, 'bond and free', did not exist.⁴ Similarly, wherever there is a Christian, whatever his race or culture or class, there, beneath the body, is the 'form' (as well as the 'mind') of 'the new man'. It may be added that this need not mean that the old 'image' or 'form' *altogether* perished at the Fall. Paul has a text which refers, as already seen, to this 'image', and which clearly implies that it still exists (1 Co 11⁷; cf. Ja 3⁹). Even if 'renew' is taken to mean 're-create', Paul knows of a 'new creating' through which 'old things pass away' by 'becoming new' (2 Co 5¹⁷). The old 'form' disappears by transfiguration. If the interpretation of 'form' or 'image' given here is accepted, the answer to the question 'Was the image of God *altogether* lost at the Fall?' is 'No'.

This account of *morphe* and *eikon* means that the early Christians,

⁴ In this reference to *creation* Paul does not include 'male and female', as in Gal 3²⁸.

like the Hebrews, believed that God has a 'form', which, though men do not see it (Col 1¹⁵; Jn 1¹⁸), yet can be seen. This involves, of course, a doctrine about God that most Christians do not hold. To discuss this subject does not belong to the present theme, but the writer has made a note about it at the end of the book.

Under the term *homoios* and its cognates (*101*) the New Testament parts company with LXX. These terms do not now always denote a *visible* likeness. They have the same wide range as 'like' in English. Often—as when 'the kingdom of heaven' is said to be 'like' this or that—one of the two things compared is visible and the other invisible. The texts relevant to the present subject are few. As already seen, James (3⁹) says that men are 'made after the likeness of God'. Here there may be a reference to visible likeness. This is more certain in a passage where John refers, not to what *all* men now are, but to what *Christians* are to be. He says that 'the world' does not 'recognize' Christians because, though they are already 'the children of God', 'it is not yet *made manifest* (*phaneroun*)' what they shall be, but they themselves know that, when they 'see (Christ) as he is' at His manifestation, they will be 'like him' (1 Jn 3²). The term *homoioma* (*6*) occurs five times in Paul—once of men who had not sinned like Adam (Ro 5¹⁴); once of the 'likeness' of some idols to 'the image of corruptible man' (Ro 1²³); twice of Jesus' 'likeness' to men (Ro 8³; Ph 2⁷); and once of Christians' 'likeness' to Christ in His death and resurrection (Ro 6⁵; cf. 2 Co 4¹⁰ᶠ·). The last passages bring us once more to Paul's doctrine of the 'old' and 'new man'. The others illustrate the wide variety in the use of words of this group. They may denote likeness of *any* kind. The Greek term *idiotes*, used once in Wisdom, does not occur in the New Testament. Under *tupos* (*15*), the remaining rendering of *tzelem*, only the text where Adam is called 'a *figure* of him that is to come' is at all relevant (Ro 5¹⁴). Elsewhere this word is usually rendered 'pattern' and, while it may denote something literally visible (He 8⁵; cf. Ex 25⁴⁰ LXX), it more often means 'example' (e.g. Ph 3¹⁷; 1 P 3⁵), and refers to the true man's likeness to Christ, not in 'form' but in behaviour—'in love, in faith, in purity' (1 Ti 4¹²). To denote the whole New Testament doctrine of what man ought to be, the 'Likeness of God' is a better phrase than the 'Image of God', for the former, unlike the latter, denotes a spiritual likeness as well as its manifestation.

D

The last subject in Chapters Two and Four is *perfection*. Before considering the New Testament teaching on this subject some truths may be named that Christianity, like other higher religions, takes for granted. First, it is always assumed, though rarely asserted, that God Himself is perfect. While each religion conceives His perfection in its own way, in the Bible God is conceived as the one perfect Person who shows His perfection primarily in perfect *character*. Second, it is assumed that it is His will that His worshippers shall be perfect. In the higher religions their perfection, however finite, tends to be defined in the same terms as God's. In the New Testament it is always assumed, though rarely asserted, that believers are to be 'perfect (after the same type) as their Father in heaven is perfect' (Mt 5⁴⁸). Third, it is assumed that God can and will make His worshippers perfect *in the end*. To believe anything else would be blasphemy. Under these three truths the subject of perfection is approached from the side of God. When it is approached from the side of man a contradictory phenomenon appears. There is an intense feeling, which is often most intense in the best of the worshippers, that, at any rate in this life, a man cannot be perfect—or, at the least, that there are no contemporaries who *are* perfect. Yet, in spite of this conviction, certain men are sometimes called 'perfect' or 'blameless' or 'innocent'. For instance, Chaucer speaks of a 'parfite knight'. This means that these men are thought to be as good as is 'humanly possible'—that is, the adjectives are used in a way that is 'relative' to the 'universe of discourse', human nature. Behind these two uses there lies, at least for men of keen moral insight, the conviction that no *man* is 'perfect' in the *absolute* sense of the word. This does not merely mean that no man can be as perfect as God because of the difference between the infinite and the finite. It means also that no man now attains the perfection that is *proper to man*. In the Bible the hindrance is sin. From all this it follows that in the higher religions there tends to be a kind of antinomy under the doctrine of perfection—*God* can and will make a man perfect; but *man* cannot be perfect.

In considering the New Testament use of the terms found in LXX a beginning may be made with the negative words. These are *amōmos* (*8*—'unblemished'), *amemptos* with its adverb (*7*— 'blameless' and 'blamelessly'), *akakos* (*2*—'viceless'), *anamartētos*

(*1*—'sinless'), *athōos* (*2*—'innocent'). Of these *athoos* is only used in relation to Jesus (Mt 27[4, 24]), and *anamartetos* only occurs in the *Pericope Adulterae*, with the implication that none of the woman's accusers is 'sinless' (Jn 8[7]). Of the other terms *amomos* is used twice, and *akakos* once, to describe Christ (He 9[14]; 1 P 1[19]; He 7[26]). *Amemptos* is used of Zechariah and Elisabeth (Lk 1[9]) and of Paul before his conversion (Ph 3[6]), while *akakos* occurs in the plural to describe a class, 'the innocent' (Ro 16[18]). The last three passages give clear examples of the relative use of the terms; they do not imply absolute perfection. There is a passage where 'blameless' is used of a 'covenant' (He 8[7]). This leaves six instances where *amomos* is used of Christians, and four where *amemptos* occurs similarly. They may be divided into three classes. First, there are two texts where *amomos* describes what Christians are to be when 'the end' comes (Jude [24]; Rev 14[5]). Second, there is one passage which calls God to witness that at Thessalonica Paul and his fellow-preachers had behaved 'holily and righteously and blamelessly' before the believers (1 Th 2[10]). It does not seem likely that here Paul claims more than a relative perfection. 'Blameless' is used in the way in which we speak today of 'a man of blameless life', a use which has anticipations in LXX. In the remaining seven passages the third and commonest use appears. The texts all describe the Christian *aim*. In all of them there are illuminating parallel adjectives. In Ephesians Paul uses 'unblemished' with 'holy' twice—once in praying for Christians (1[4]), and once in describing Christ's purpose for the Church (5[27]). One text in Philippians unites *amemptos* and *amomos*—'That ye may be blameless and harmless, children of God unblemished' (2[15]). In Colossians (1[22]) Christ's purpose is to 'present' believers 'holy and unblemished and unreprovable before (God); if so be that (they) continue in the faith, grounded and stedfast'. Similarly in First Thessalonians Paul prays that 'the Lord' may 'stablish (his readers') hearts blameless in holiness before our God and Father at the coming of the Lord Jesus' (3[13]), and that 'the God of peace himself' will 'sanctify (them) wholly' and that (their) 'spirit and soul and body' may be 'preserved entire in the coming of our Lord Jesus Christ' (5[23]). Certain characteristics of this group of passages, significant also for the rest of the discussion, may be noted. First, *Christ's* perfection is the type of Christians' perfection. Then, the accompanying adjectives and phrases, some of them echoing Old Testament terminology, give a kind of definition of what Paul meant by Christian perfection. The recurrent term is *hagios*, and, as already shown, Christians are both 'holy' and to become 'holy'. Third, the passages, as already implied, describe what Christians *are to be*, not what they *are*. Fourth, some texts describe what they are to be *at the Parousia*, but some seem rather to denote Paul's hope for Christians *now*. It was not in him to believe that God either could not or would not answer his prayers for perfection *in the present life*. He, no doubt, often offered the Christians' inevitable prayer: 'Keep us this day without sin'. Did he add a mental reservation: 'But I know that Thou hast never answered, and never wilt answer, this prayer for so much as one man during so short a time as one day'? It is true that there is the Colossian phrase, 'if so be that ye continue in the faith', but surely Paul does not here mean 'a thing that I know to be impossible'. He did not mock either God or Christians by offering impossible petitions. On the other side, however—apart, possibly, from 1 Th 2^{10}—there is no text that declares that any Christian *is* already absolutely 'unblemished' or 'blameless'. Finally, in all the passages except one the context explicitly states that it is God's purpose to make Christians 'blameless' through Christ, and in the one exception this is implied (Ph 2^5). Christ died to make 'blamelessness' practicable.

Of the positive words *haplous* (2) may be taken first, with its adverb *haplōs* (1) and its noun *haplotes* (7). The literal meaning of *haplous* is 'single' and all three words denote 'single-mindedness'. Jesus uses the first in the phrase 'If thine eye be single' (Lk 11^{34}). James has the adverb in a description of the single-minded way in which God *gives* (1^5). Paul, who alone has the noun, uses it four times of the pure motive with which Christians too should *give* (Ro 12^8; 2 Co 8^2, 9$^{11, 13}$), and twice of the temper in which Christian slaves should serve heathen masters (Eph 6^5; Col 3^{22}). It is clear that here he is describing what ought to be—but also what may be. It is clear too that he emphasizes inward motive more than outward act. It was one thing, for instance, to give grudgingly to the collection for the poor saints at Jerusalem and another to give the same amount 'single-mindedly'. The remaining passage has no such limited 'universe of discourse'. It runs: 'For I espoused you to one husband, that I might present you a pure virgin to Christ. But I fear, lest by any means, as the serpent beguiled Eve in his craftiness, your thoughts should be corrupted from the *single-mindedness* and the purity which is unto

Christ' (2 Co 11³). Precise logic would require the exegesis that
at the first the Corinthian Church had been as 'pure' and 'single-
minded' as Eve before the Fall. The whole series of passages
teaches that 'single-mindedness' is an element in a practicable,
rather than a practised, perfection.

The next word is *katartizein* (*12*), with its two nouns, *katartisis* (*1*)
and *katartismos* (*1*). In their secular use these words refer to
handicraft. Men may 'finish' building a wall, like the returned
Jews (Ezr 4¹²), or 'mend' a broken net, like the Sons of Zebedee
(Mk 1¹⁹). The root idea is 'to complete in all its parts', to 'inte-
grate'. God is said to 'complete' praise and 'ages' (Mt 21⁶; He
11³); Paul speaks of vessels of wrath, 'completed unto destruction'
(Ro 9²²); and Hebrews of a 'completed body' (10⁵). In all the
other passages the reference is to the *process* by which Christians
are being 'completed', not to a 'completion' that they have
already attained. Jesus promises that when a disciple is 'completed', he shall be 'as his master' (Lk 6⁴⁰). One Christian may
'mend' another as men may mend a net (Gal 6¹; 1 Th 3¹⁰; cf.
Mk 1¹⁹). Paul has four passages that speak in various ways of the
'completing' of the saints (1 Co 1¹⁰; 2 Co 13⁹, ¹¹; Eph 4¹²). Both
Hebrews and First Peter testify that it is God's purpose to make
Christians 'complete' (He 13²¹, 1 P 5¹⁰). The words describe a
process that is going on now and may be finished now. When
Paul bids the Corinthians 'Be completed' (2 Co 13¹¹), he is not
adding *sotto voce* 'but you can't be till the end comes'.

Another word *holoklēros* (*2*), as in LXX, contrasts with *katartizein*
for it always denotes *present* completeness. The noun, *holoclēria* (*1*),
is used of the 'wholeness' of a healed body (Ac 3¹⁶; cf. 4¹⁰). James,
speaking of the 'perfect' (*teleios*) outcome of 'patience', interprets
this by *holokleros*, 'lacking in nothing' (1⁴), and Paul, using a
synonym *holotelēs* (*1*, not in LXX), prays first that 'the God of
peace will himself entirely sanctify' the Thessalonians, and then
that they 'may be *kept* complete' till the Parousia (1 Th 5¹³).
Under these words the possibility of 'completeness' before the
End is clearly implied.

The last word under the subject is *teleios* (*19*). With it there go
an adverb, *teleiōs* (*1*); a verb, *teleioun* (*23*); two abstract nouns,
teleiŏtēs (*2*) and *teleiōsis* (*2*); and a noun, also *teleiotes* (*1*), denoting
'one who makes (anything) *teleios*'. Three passages that are not
relevant to the immediate subject will give an idea both of the
variety and unity of the meanings of these terms. Joseph and Mary

are said to have '*fulfilled* the days' appointed for the Passover (Lk 2⁴³); Paul speaks of '*accomplishing*' his 'course and ministry' (Ac 20²⁴); and the writer to the Hebrews says 'the law *made* nothing *perfect*' (7¹⁹). In all these passages, though in different ways, there is the idea of the fulfilment of something *appointed by God*. This is explicit in 'there shall be a *fulfilment* of the things spoken unto her *from the Lord*' (Lk 1⁴⁵). A further and important idea appears in the contrast 'milk for babes, solid food for the full-grown (*teleios*)' (He 5¹³ᶠ·). This shows that this group of words, unlike the *katartizein* group, can be used in reference to *growth*. Here it is important to note that with anything that grows—a plant, for instance—there is a perfection appropriate to each *stage* in a process, which leads on to a further perfection appropriate to further stages—that is, there may be progress through a series of 'perfections' until at last consummate and final perfection is reached. In other words, there is a *progressive* perfection. A child might be called 'perfect' at a year old; again, at five years old, and so on. In other words, there is a sense in which the *immature*, which is *ipso facto* imperfect in one sense, may be called 'perfect' in another. 'Eternal life' hereafter no doubt involves both constant growth and the perfection appropriate to every stage in growth. Paul relates the concept of 'growth' to Christians *in this life* in a passage where he speaks both of 'a *full-grown man*', of 'children', and of 'growing up' (Eph 4¹³⁻¹⁵; cf. 2²¹, 4¹⁵; 1 P 2²). At the same time, of course, a child, through his own fault, may at any stage be less nearly 'mature' in mind than he ought to be at that stage (1 Co 3¹, 14²⁰). This means that 'imperfect' sometimes means 'sinful', though at others it may denote an unsinful immaturity. The concept that Christians ought to 'grow' is, of course, common (e.g. 1 Co 3⁶⁻⁹; 2 Co 9⁸, ¹⁰, 10¹⁵; Col 1⁶, ¹⁰, 2¹⁹; 2 P 3¹⁸).

In the Synoptic Gospels *teleios* and its cognates are rare. While it is everywhere assumed that God is perfect, His perfection is only explicitly named once (Mt 5⁴⁸). In one text, 'On the third day I am perfected' (Lk 12³²), there is, as will appear below, an idea that is worked out in the Epistle to the Hebrews. The adjective *teleios* is twice used about discipleship. To the Young Ruler Jesus says 'If thou wouldst be perfect' put away your stumbling-block of wealth and 'come, follow me' (Mt 19²¹)—which implies that Jesus' way of life is the way of perfection. The only other text is 'Ye therefore shall be perfect (after the same manner) as your heavenly Father is perfect' (Mt 5⁴⁸)—as a candle is like Orion. Here Luke has 'pitiful' (*oiktirmōn*—6³⁶), which brings out the fact that in this text love is 'the universe of discourse' (Mt 5⁴³⁻⁸). To the old command 'Thou shalt love thy neighbour' current thought had long added 'and hate thine enemy' (e.g. the Gentiles). This was signally to fail to 'complete (*plēroun*) the law and the prophets' (v. 17). Jesus 'completes' the exposition of Old Testament principles with 'Love your enemies', for God loves His. While, however, the *word* only occurs once in the Sermon on the Mount, and then in the exposition of one thing, forgiveness (cf. 6¹², Eph 4³¹⁻5²), the *idea* permeates the whole Sermon. It is agreed—not least by those who, unlike Jesus (7²⁴⁻⁷), think that He teaches an 'impracticable ideal'—that the Sermon is a 'counsel of perfection'. Like all the rest of the New Testament passages that speak of the Christian way of life, it is an exposition of the two Great Commandments. These teach that the way to be perfect is to love God utterly and therefore to love men in the way in which He loves them. Both commandments are *God's* commandments—that is, in the New Testament as in the Old, the definition of perfection is 'to do the will of God'. As in the Old, too, the primary realm of perfection is the ethical (as derivative from the spiritual). But there is also a point of contrast—found in Jesus' recurrently regnant '*I* say unto you'. This means that already Christian perfection is defined both as 'to do the will of God' and 'to do the will of Christ'—or, as Christ's prayer in John puts it 'to keep *thy* word' and 'to keep *my* word' (14²³, 17⁶). The Son is the medium of perfection.

James uses the words rather often (6). He writes, like all New Testament writers, in order that his readers may be 'perfect and complete, lacking in nothing' (1⁴). God is the origin of 'every perfect boon' and therefore the begetter of believers (1¹⁷ᶠ·). Their 'faith' 'works itself out' in 'patience', and persistent patience will 'perfect' this 'work' (1³ᶠ·). They have 'the perfect law', the 'law of liberty', and are called to 'continue' in it (1²⁵). This one phrase is enough to show that James is a Christian writing to Christians. Again, 'faith' is 'made perfect' by 'works' (2²²). The remaining passage is about the tongue, and runs, 'If any stumbleth not in word, the same is a perfect man' (3²); but this need not mean that any Christian is already perfect. James, indeed, had just said 'In many things we all stumble'. The context shows that he means that if any man unerringly 'bridles' his tongue, this is as clear evidence of perfection as if a rider were unerringly to guide his horse or a helmsman his ship. But is either rider or helmsman quite unerring? All James' uses of the term exhibit one idea—that if a Christian practises his faith in his 'only begetter' and goes on doing so, this will issue in his perfection. He does indeed suggest that Paul's paradigm of faith, Abraham, did in fact perfectly practise his faith (2^{22}), but for a Christian Abraham's could only be a relative perfection. This practical writer teaches an ideal, but it is a practicable ideal, and a practicable ideal *now*. Peter, in his one instance of the terms, speaks of a 'hope' that is itself attainable now though its fulfilment is future. He exhorts the children of God to 'gird up the loins of (their) mind', 'hoping perfectly' for the fulfilment of 'grace' in the Parousia (1 P $1^{13, 23}$). This connexion of hope with the Parousia is implicit in James ($5^{7f.}$). Once more the same conclusion is reached. James and Peter are speaking of a practicable perfection, but neither mentions any man who altogether practises it.

These terms are frequent in the Epistle to the Hebrews (*14*). Their use may readily be integrated under its dominant idea. The writer teaches that 'the true tabernacle, which *the Lord* pitched, not man' (8^2) is 'in the heavens', and that this is 'the greater and *more perfect* tabernacle' (9^{11}). This implies that while the Mosaic tabernacle, being a 'shadow' of the heavenly tabernacle, had 'of old time' (1^1) its relative perfection, the heavenly tabernacle itself is absolutely perfect because its Priest is perfect. This leads to the writer's most noteworthy idea. In order to be man's perfect Saviour, the Son must 'partake of flesh and blood' and Himself be 'made perfect through sufferings' (2^{10}, $5^{8f.}$, 7^{28}). Even for the 'sinless' Jesus (4^{15}) there was a *process* of perfecting in a particular realm. In the life of 'the pioneer of (men's) salvation' there was a developing perfection (2^{10}). It was not until the Resurrection that Jesus was a perfect *saviour*. In the LXX the word 'perfected' had been used of the High Priest to interpret the word 'anointed' (*christos*, Lv 21^{10}), but there was no 'perfecting through the Levitical priesthood', for, as 'the law made nothing perfect', the ancient priests could not make worshippers 'perfect' ($7^{11, 19}$, 10^1), especially at the architectonic point, 'as touching the conscience' (9^9). It is Jesus who 'cleanses the conscience' for, being Himself 'without blemish', He is the 'pioneer and perfecter of faith' (11^{14}, 12^2). With this writer this means faith *in God* ($11^{1ff.}$). It is probable that the phrase 'By *one* offering he hath perfected *for ever* them that are being sanctified' (10¹⁴) should be taken to refer to the eternal issues of the Crucifixion, for the parallel phrase is 'By (God's) will we have been sanctified through the offering of the body of Jesus Christ *once for all*' (10¹⁰). Jesus' work is already complete, even though its out-working in men takes time. The alternative rendering, 'By one offering he hath perfected *continually* them that are being sanctified', would mean that the 'saints' are called to a progressive perfection. They may be perfect, stage by stage, like healthy children. This inter-pretation is unlikely, however, for it would imply that *only* the faultless (though immature) are 'being sanctified', and, as already seen, in the New Testament the words 'saint' and 'sanctified' are used of very faulty Christians (cf. 12¹⁴ᶠᶠ·). The readers of the Epistle were at least faultily ignorant, for the writer complains that they are still 'babes' in Christian knowledge when they ought to have been ready for 'solid food', like 'mature men' (*teleios*), and he goes on to say, in effect, 'Let us leave the ABC and press on to perfection' (5¹²–6¹). 'Mature' here denotes a relative perfection in the realm of knowledge. The writer has another idea under these terms. He says that 'without us' all the faithful men of the past cannot be 'made perfect' for they did not 'receive (the fulfilment of) the promise' of God (11³⁹ᶠ·). Here there is the concept of the perfection *of a society*, wherein each member perfects the others. There is a picture of this society in the passage where the writer, having described 'Mount Zion, the city of the living God, the heavenly Jerusalem'—the site of 'the true tabernacle' where Jesus, 'the mediator of a new covenant' offers 'the blood of sprinkling'—names amid the throng 'the spirits of righteous men made perfect' (12²²⁻⁴). This writer's teaching about per-fection is organic—God, being, of course, determined on perfec-tion, not only sends His Son to save, but makes Him perfect Saviour through suffering; through Jesus all believers are being made perfect; they themselves need 'to press on to perfection', for only in the free and eager can the grace of Christ find full scale and scope; every believer, though imperfect, already belongs to the community of saints (12²²); in it God will at last fulfil His enterprise of perfection. On one exposition of one text (10¹⁴) the writer gives the answer 'Yes' to the question 'Is it possible for even one Christian to attain now a perfection appropriate to the present stage in his growth?', but probably he leaves it unasked and unanswered. Like the other New Testament writers, this one sets his readers'

RBM

minds, not on what they already are, but on what they are to be.

Considering the bulk of his letters Paul uses these words sparingly (*10*). The 'universes of discourse' of the texts are various—seven have an immediate, though not exclusive, reference to 'knowledge' or 'mind' or 'wisdom' (Ro 12[2]; 1 Co 2[6], 13[10], 14[20]; Eph 4[13]; Ph 3[15]; Col 1[28]); one refers immediately to 'love' (Col 3[14]); only the remaining two passages refer directly to the whole range of the Christian life (Ph 3[10-14]; Col 4[12]). Of the passages about perfection of *mind* five present it as a *goal*, two of them using the contrast between the 'babe' and the 'mature' or adult (1 Co 13[10f.], 14[20]). The first of these, which in its wider context describes the 'love' that is the 'bond of perfectness' (Col 3[14]), teaches that 'knowledge' *must* be imperfect until we see God 'face to face'. None the less Paul is urgent that his readers may and should *grow* in knowledge *now*. The idea that there is a perfection appropriate to each stage of growth is readily applicable to the mind.[5] There are only two passages where Paul's texts can be taken to teach that there are Christians who already have a 'perfect' mind. One of these runs: 'Howbeit we speak wisdom among the perfect: yet a wisdom not of this age . . . but we speak God's wisdom in a mystery, the wisdom that hath been hidden' (1 Co 2[6f.]). Here the Apostle is expounding his claim that 'Christ crucified' is 'the wisdom of God' (1[23]). He has three contrasts in mind—a contrast with Greek philosophy (1[22]; Ac 17[23, 30]); a contrast with the Mystery Religions (1 Co 2[7], 13[2], 14[2]; Col 1[26f.]); and, though less obtrusively, a contrast with the teaching of the Wisdom Literature about 'the wisdom of God' (cf. 1 Co 1[19f.]). It is therefore likely that the sentence 'I speak wisdom among the perfect' means 'men of mature (or adult) mind will understand that Christianity is true wisdom and that Christians need not allow such of their neighbours as are more or less acquainted with Greek philosophy or are initiates in Mystery cults, to call them "fools"' (1 Co 2[0], 2[7]). It is Christians who have the perfect wisdom because in 'Christ crucified' they have, or ought to have, learnt the 'wisdom *of God*'. This also suits the other text, 'Let us therefore, as many as be mature, be thus minded' (Ph 3[15]), for the Apostle is thinking of 'the excellency of the *knowledge* of Christ Jesus' (v. 8, 10), and by the word 'thus' he urges his readers to

---

[5] A small boy was once given 'full marks' in an arithmetic examination. This, of course, did not mean that he was a perfect mathematician, but that his paper had a perfection relative to an early stage in development.

the passionate 'pressing on' that he has just described (v. 12).
Indeed, when he adds 'If in anything ye are otherwise minded,
even this shall God reveal unto you: only, whereunto we have
already attained, by the same rule let us walk', he implies that he
is not speaking of a Christian's final perfection. While this
passage refers to the mind, it treats of the whole of the Christian
life. The parable of the racer, which Paul had just used, of course
suits the idea of a relative perfection, for at a given moment a
racer may have reached the point that he ought to have reached
at that moment—but he does not think about that. Paul's one tense
message is that there is a 'goal' and a 'prize' still far ahead, and
that the more 'mature' a Christian is, the more he urges his course
toward it. Of himself he says 'not that I am already made perfect,
but I press on' (v. 12). Unlike the Wisdom writers, he is fully
aware that for this he needs 'the power of God' as well as 'the
wisdom of God', but is not Christ both? (1 Co 1^{24}). He can
'apprehend' because he 'is apprehended'—'lay hold' because
Christ has 'laid hold' (Ph 3^{12})—'do all things in him that strength-
eneth' him (4^{13}). In Colossians Epaphras 'agonizes in prayer'
that his fellow-believers may 'stand perfect' and Paul bids them
'put on love, which is the bond of perfectness' (Col 3^{14}, 4^{12}).
Paul's emphasis throughout is on a perfection that is not yet
reached but is practicable 'in Christ'. In the two passages (1 Co
2^6; Ph 3^{15}) where he speaks of Christians as though they were
already perfect, he is referring to those who are no longer babes but
are of 'adult mind'—and an adult mind should not cease to grow.

In the Gospel and First Epistle of John *teleios* occurs once, and
teleioun nine times. In the Gospel the verb is used once of the
'fulfilment' of Scripture (19^{28}), once of the future but practicable
'perfecting' of the disciples (17^{23}), and three times of Jesus' own
'accomplishing' or 'perfecting' the 'work' that God had given
Him to do (4^{34}, 5^{36}, 17^4). These three texts, in effect, repeat the
teaching of the Epistle to the Hebrews. As the latter teaches that
God 'perfected' the Saviour 'through suffering', so John teaches
that the Son 'perfected' His 'work' on the Cross. The word 'It is
finished' (*tetelestai*) is twice used to denote the completion of the
terrible task (19$^{28, 30}$). In John's Epistle the terms are always used
of the 'perfecting' of Christians. They belong to two passages
(2$^{3-6}$, 4$^{7-21}$). In the first there is a cluster of phrases which give
the writer's account of Christian perfection—'Whoso keepeth
(Christ's) word, in him verily hath the *love* of God (i.e. love for

God) been *perfected*. Hereby know we that we are *in him*: he that saith he *abideth* in him ought himself also to *walk* even as he walked' (1 Jn 2⁵ᶠ·). To expound these phrases would be to expound a large part both of the Gospel and Epistle. The sentence belongs to the paragraph in which the writer states the purpose of his letter (2¹⁻⁶). Apparently some of his readers claimed to be sinless. While he rebukes their self-deceit and reminds his readers that the Christian Gospel tells of God's way of saving *sinners*, he begins by saying 'My little children, these things write I unto you *that ye may not sin*'. The particular purpose of the second passage (4⁷⁻²¹) appears in the words 'If *we love one another*, God *abideth* in us, and his love is *perfected* in us' (v. 12). The whole paragraph is an exposition of 'love'—from its source in God who 'is love', through its 'manifestation' in the Incarnation and Atonement, to its issue in Christians' love for God and therefore in their love for one another. The central verses of the passage spend themselves upon the word 'abide' (v. 12–18). The verses where *teleios* and *teleioun* occur (v. 16–19) speak of the fearlessness at the very judgement of those whose 'love' is 'perfected' through 'abiding in him' and who therefore love one another. 'We love (both God and man) because he first loved us.' In both passages the writer is urging Christians who have begun to love that they should be 'perfected' in love. He holds up Christ as the perfect example of believers' 'walk' or way of life (2⁸). They are 'children of God' (3¹) who, like children in earthly homes, sometimes disobey, and so do not 'abide' in love.

The phrase 'children of God' occurs at the beginning of a passage where the writer, though he does not use *teleios* and *teleioun*, speaks of sinlessness (3¹⁻¹²; cf. 5¹⁸). He says 'Whosoever abideth in him sinneth not', 'Everyone who-has-been-begotten of God sinneth not', 'Everyone who-has-been-begotten of God doeth no sin, because his seed abideth in him; and he cannot sin because he hath-been-begotten of God' (v. 6, 9), and, on the positive side, 'He that doeth righteousness is righteous, according as (*God*) is righteous' (v. 7). Are not children like their father, whether he be God or devil (v. 10)? Here the word 'cannot' means, 'cannot because of what they *are*', and illustrates the final New Testament doctrine of freedom. This meaning of 'cannot' and 'can' is fairly frequent, especially in the Fourth Gospel (e.g. Mk 2¹⁹; Ro 8⁷ᶠ·; 1 Co 2¹⁴; He 3¹⁹; Jn 3²⁻⁵, 5⁴⁴, 7⁷, 9¹⁶, 14¹⁷). Since 'child of God' is a synonym for 'he that-is-begotten of God' (e.g. 5¹ᶠ·), these texts *could* mean that *every* Christian is sinless, for the passage opens with the wondering claim 'we are called, *and are*, children of God' (3¹). This is the basis of the whole paragraph. But it is plain that the writer does not mean that *all* Christians are sinless, as this exposition would require (cf. 1⁸). Again, it is at least hazardous to take 'begotten of God' in this passage in a peculiar sense and to deduce that here and here only it denotes *some* Christians—namely, those that have been *fully* 'begotten' and so are sinless. On the other hand, it is equally hazardous to assume that no Christian can be sinless until he dies and that the writer of the Epistle, speaking of *all* Christians, means that only at death are they fully 'begotten of God', for he does not say that 'Everyone that is begotten of God will *at last* be sinless' but that he 'does not sin', 'doeth no sin', and 'is not able to sin'. It is true that at the beginning of the passage he does speak of a future perfection—'It is not yet made manifest what we shall be. We know that when he is made manifest, we shall be like him, for we shall see him as he is'—but, as the words 'manifest' and 'see' suggest, the writer seems here to be speaking of the *'glory'* of the transfigured body of a Christian when the Age ends in the Parousia (cf. Ph 3²). Again, it is an almost desperate exegesis to insist that in this passage the use of the present tense implies that the meaning is 'does not *habitually* sin', even if this were true of *all* Christians. To the present writer it seems that, for the most likely interpretation of this difficult passage, one must begin by remembering that the writer is an experienced *teacher* who is teaching his 'little children'. In teaching he is fond of using phrases beginning 'Every one that is (or 'does') so-and-so' (*pas* with a present or perfect participle). There are eleven examples in the Gospel (e.g. Jn 3⁸, ¹⁵ᶠ·, 6⁴⁰, 8³⁴, 11²⁶) and fifteen in the Epistles (e.g. 1 Jn 2²³, 3¹⁵, 5¹; 2 Jn ⁹). When the writer uses such a phrase, the sentence that follows expounds it. The meaning is 'If a man is (or does) so-and-so this or that follows *from the meaning of the word itself*'. For instance, 'Every one that believeth that Jesus is the Christ is begotten of God' means 'to believe in Christ is, by its very nature, to be begotten of God—as you will see if you think for a moment'. Similarly, the phrase 'Every one that abideth in him sinneth not' means 'If you will consider what the phrase "abiding *in* God" *ipso facto* requires, you will see that it is incompatible with sin'. In 3⁹ the writer adds the clause, 'because his seed abideth in him', to draw out the truth that if a man is a 'child *of* God' he will not sin. It is an exegesis of the undeniable connotation of the phrase. But how then can the writer call people who are not sinless 'children of God', adding the emphatic phrase 'such we are' (v. 1f.)? It is bad logic but good psychology—and good teaching. Arnold of Rugby set out to train his boys to be 'Christian gentlemen', and *therefore* from the first *addressed* them as 'Gentlemen'. It would be quite easy to imagine his saying, if some boys were found lying: '*Gentlemen*, some of you have lied. Every gentleman tells the truth. No *gentleman can* lie.' He would hold up to them an ideal that they had already *begun* to realize in their way of life. A true teacher knows how and when to assume that his scholars are what he wants them to be. In effect he says, to use a current phrase, 'Be what you are'. It is the same with the great Johannine teacher. He says '*Children of God*, some of you *sin*. Every child of God doeth righteousness and nothing else. No child of God *can* sin.' He adds the conclusion from this—'Every child of God since he expects final perfection at the Parousia, "purifieth himself even as *he* is pure" ' (v. 3). In education, logic is sometimes a good servant but it is always a bad master. The question 'Is there any such thing as a perfect Christian, even in a sense relative to his stage of growth, *now*?' does not fall within the purview of John's paragraph. None the less this writer, like the others, is presenting a *practicable* ideal.

The New Testament teaching about perfection may be gathered in a few sentences—God is perfect; it is His will that men should be like Him in the realm of righteousness and love; He sent His Son, who Himself was perfect man, that this may be; Christ is able to make a believer perfect now with the perfection relative to the stage of his growth in the Christian life; there are other stages ahead of him, wherein his perfection will have grown farther; there is a consummate and final perfection that awaits eternity. The New Testament writers never refer to Christians who *are* perfect in any *final* sense. Still less does any Christian in that book himself claim any such perfection. How could he when he thought of Jesus? None, indeed, claims even a relative perfection if the exegesis offered above is correct. Would it be possible for a man to do so and remain humble? Again, what man knows the whole truth about his own subconsciousness? May not sin lurk unawares there? The Apostolic writers show no interest in the question: 'Are there any perfect men?' Their uniform message is 'By the grace of Christ go forward!' None the less they never suggest that Christ *cannot* make a man all that he ought to be *now*. To them this would have been apostasy. Under this doctrine, as under all others, the Christian answer to the question 'What ought a man to be?' is 'Every man *ought* to be—and therefore every true believer *will* be—perfect like Christ, and thereby like God.'

If a comparison were attempted between the New Testament account of perfection and that of the Old Testament and the later Jews, there would be need of a full discussion of the doctrines of Sin and Grace. These are to be examined in other volumes. Only a very brief summary can be given here. There were two differences. The first roots in the Christian account of sin. Here there is no traffic with the idea that a man does not sin, whatever his motive, until he acts. This means that even if a man be 'according to the righteousness which is in the Law blameless', he is still a sinner if he ever *chooses* to do wrong—and apart from Christ he cannot help choosing to do wrong. Apart from Grace every man has evil in his 'heart' and so will inevitably sin. The idea 'I can do right if I like' has gone. 'All have sinned and come short of the glory of God.' If the New Testament account of sin be taken alone it is utterly pessimistic. But here the second *differentia* in its account of sin—and therefore, by inference, of perfection—starts forward. 'Where sin abounded, grace did much more abound.' Through Christ perfection is possible. Here as everywhere else, the distinctive New Testament doctrine roots in Christ. As noted more than once earlier, there are a few Old Testament passages that imply a deeper account of sin than what may be called the current or representative account. It is just these passages—Jeremiah's prophecy of a 'covenant written on the heart', Ezekiel's promise of the gift of a 'new spirit', and the Psalmist's plea for a 'new creation' (51^{10})—that the Christians claimed for Christ.

Finally, it will be seen that in many parts of this chapter it is maintained that, in the New Testament as in the Old, the passages where 'the image of God' is mentioned play a quite subordinate part in the doctrine of man's likeness to God, and that this really bases on the use of such terms as 'holy', 'righteous', 'wise', and even 'perfect', both of God and man. It may be debated whether in *unredeemed* men there are any relics of this kind of likeness, but there can be no doubt that the New Testament teaches that Christ has set Himself to make *believers* like God and that He is doing this. In the Christian doctrine of man the final word is 'Through Christ man is to be like God'.

THE VISIBLE FORM OF GOD

As HAS been suggested earlier, there seems to be no text in the Bible that unmistakably teaches that the Unseen God cannot be seen. This opens a subject that does not belong to the present book, but, in order to prevent misunderstanding, the writer may add a few notes about it.

With the belief in a God who cannot be seen there usually goes the belief that 'God is everywhere'. The texts most commonly quoted are Ps 139 in the Old Testament and Jn 4²⁴ ('God is spirit' —i.e. a 'spiritual being') in the New. But the Psalmist's meaning seems rather to be that wherever he goes God speeds thither before him. Even if he flees to Sheol, or, what for him is farther away, to 'the uttermost parts of the earth', God has forestalled him. This concept—that God can be anywhere He wants to be 'in a flash'—suits other Old Testament passages, both early and late (e.g. Jg 5⁴; Ps 18¹⁰; Ezk 1¹⁴, ²⁸). The Johannine text is not incompatible with this, for under both *pneuma* and *ruach*, 'spirit' is like a moving wind rather than the omnipresent air (e.g. Ezk 1⁴, ²⁰; Ac 2², ⁴; Jn 3⁸). The text in John means that, wherever men 'worship God in spirit and (therefore) in truth', God is there.

Perhaps this account of the unlimited mobility of God is a better approximation to what is meant by His transcendence of space than the idea that He is omnipresent. The term 'transcendence', of course, suggests something that the human mind may guess at, but can never compass. It may be suggested, however, that the same kind of statement may be made about the transcendence of space as is often made about the transcendence of time. Under the latter phrase the term 'eternity' is used, and it is often maintained that, because God works in history and still more because in Christ He entered into history, there must be something of ultimate value even in time and history, however unable men are to define it. This means that there is something of ultimate value in change—for history is the process of change. The antinomy emerges that God is 'changeless' so far as changelessness is of value, and that He 'changes' so far as change has value. (Of course, we ascribe both 'change' and 'changelessness' in some degree also to man because of his 'personality'. A man is both 'the same man' as he was ten years ago, and 'a different man'.) May it not be that under 'space', the other category in history, similar claims may be made? Unfortunately there are no words current under space that correspond to 'eternal' and 'eternity'. Perhaps 'supernal' and 'supernity' would serve. Under this claim it would be suggested that there is something of ultimate value in space as well as in time, for the doctrine of the Incarnation means that God entered into *both*. This would mean that there is something of value in 'form' as well as in 'change', for, just as time is known in change, so space is known in 'form' or 'shape'. A second antinomy would follow—that God has no 'form', so far as there is value in formlessness, but that He has 'form' so far as there is value in form. It hardly seems reasonable to hold a doctrine about 'time' and refuse to apply it to 'space'.

INDEX OF HEBREW, GREEK, AND ENGLISH TERMS

References to cognates are included under those to principal terms

prothumos: 90, 150, 172
prophets: 13ff., 34, 42ff., 48, 143, 147, 189, 190, 249
psyche: 68, 71ff., 74f., 79, 80f., 86, 96, 133, 138ff., 141f., 148, 159, 161, 165, 185
psychology, Hebrew: 4f.
ptoma: 161
purity: 50, 248; see also *hagnos, katharos, tahor*
put on: 227f.; see also *enduien*

qadosh: 39ff., 111ff., 115, 127

rachamim: 23f., 78
radah: 28f.
ratzah: 28, 91, 92
reins: see *kelayoth, nephros*
righteousness: 205, 222; see also *tzaddiq, dikaios*
ro'sh: 20, 151
ruach: 9ff., 68, 73ff., 83, 142, 250

saint: see *hagios, qadosh*
sanctification: 205; see also holiness
sarx: 81f., 142, 153ff., 161, 185
schema: 229, 230
scribe: 101
semnos: 113f., 194f.
separation: 114
shagag: 90
shalem: 60ff., 124, 126, 127
shemen: 23
soma: 71, 80f., 96, 153, 161ff., 185
sonship: x, 121ff., 177f., 207ff., 246ff.
sophia: 68, 98ff., 204ff.
sophron: 204, 206
soul: 162, 184f.; see also *nephesh, psyche*
spirit: 160, 162, 179f., 184f., 190ff., 204, 205, 206, 212, 213, 214, 215, 216f., 222, 227, 228, 230, 231, 233; see also *ruach, pneuma*

splangchna: 78, 152
stear: 78, 152
suneidesis: 86f., 167ff.
sunesis: 98, 108f., 166, 204, 206

tahor: 50, 114f.
tamam: 61ff., 125f.
tapeinos: 164
teknon: 123f., 208
temunah: 30, 94
teleios: 124, 126ff., 239ff.
temptation and trial: 155, 156
thelein: 89ff., 172ff., 177, 185
time: 120f., 224, 226
tob: 38f., 110
tongue: 18f., 76f., 150
transcendence: 250f.
transfiguration: 224, 227, 228, 229f., 232
tupos: 94f., 235
tzaddiq: 38, 109
tzelem: 29f., 37, 94, 235

vagar: 120

weakness: see *basar, sarx*
will: 22, 31ff., 77, 96, 104, 106f., 150, 151, 204, 207, 221, 241; see also *'abah, boulesthai,* freedom, *ma'en, thelein*
wind: see *ruach*
wisdom: 147, 160, 244f.; see also *chokmah, sophia*

ya'ats: 91f.
yashar: 88, 110
yeled: 124
yetzer hara: 129, 160

zamam: 83
zoe: 68, 69ff., 71f., 73, 133ff., 140, 142

INDEX OF SCRIPTURE REFERENCES

THE OLD TESTAMENT

THE NEW TESTAMENT

*When a passage occurs in more than one of the Synoptic Gospels, it is usually quoted under Mark if it occurs in the Second Gospel; in other instances, usually under Luke.